CASE STUDIES IN ABNORMAL BEHAVIOR

SECOND EDITION

CASE STUDIES IN ABNORMAL BEHAVIOR

Robert G. Meyer
University of Louisville

Yvonne Hardaway Osborne
Louisiana State University

ALLYN AND BACON, INC.

Boston   London   Sydney   Toronto

Library of Congress Cataloging-in-Publication Data

Meyer, Robert G.
    Case studies in abnormal behavior.

    Includes index.
    1. Mental illness—Case studies.   I. Osborne,
Yvonne Hardaway, 1950–   . II. Title.
RC465.M44   1987   616.89′09   86-26487
ISBN: 0-205-10472-X

Printed in the United States of America

10 9 8 7 6 5 4 3 2   92 91 90 89 88 87

Series Editor: John-Paul Lenney
Editorial-Production Service: Harkavy Publishing Service
Text Designer: Denise Hoffman
Cover Administrator /Designer: Linda K. Dickinson

To Monika Meyer: Still quite a case and still delightful.

CONTENTS

PREFACE

Research articles in abnormal psychology necessarily focus on specific theories and experiments: texts in this area integrate a vast array of literature on historical, descriptive, research, diagnostic, and treatment issues. Some texts do a good job of bringing in "chunks" of case material to demonstrate particular points. However, texts cannot do justice to their other goals if they provide any significant number of in-depth cases. *Case Studies in Abnormal Behavior, Second Edition* helps the reader regain a sense of how the whole person experiences and reacts to the diverse factors studied in abnormal psychology. The abstract and conflicting concepts of this field can thus be seen in the context that eventually counts—the totality of an actual person who has the disorder.

The cases presented in *Case Studies in Abnormal Behavior, Second Edition* are based on actual recent cases, though identifying details have, of course, been changed to protect people from even the small chance that they would be recognized. Most cases have been the experience of the authors; a few were donated by other clinicians who have substantial experience or special expertise with a particular disorder. For example, Dr. Paul Salmon, a clinical neuropsychologist at the University of Louisville who also works with children, was kind enough to provide several of the organic mental disorder and childhood disorder cases. We have also included a couple of cases published in journals. These cases either make an original point or demonstrate a particular point of view, as in Chapter 2.

Readers will note that cases provided by the authors and not reprinted from other journals are assigned names with a logical or mnemonic relationship to the syndrome being studied; for example, Agnes–agoraphobia, and Perry–paranoid schizophrenia. Though this may at times sound corny, we have found it to be a helpful technique for most readers. Students have found this to be a useful device, since it adds clarity to classroom discussion and enhances recall of the cases if needed during a test.

The reader may note the high number of case studies in this book. Feedback from our students and from other professors and their students indicated that case studies in most other books were generally too long and included irrelevant detail. The cases in this book contain the full details of background material that are relevant to etiologic, diagnostic, and therapeutic considerations; yet, hopefully, they are not overly long. Thus, a full spectrum of case studies is provided, perhaps more than in any previous case study book. Also, cases from all categories of the Diagnostic and Statistical Manual (DSM) of the American Psychiatric Association are detailed, contrast cases within the major categories are given, and some other cases that deal with other important patterns are presented.

Relevant and detailed family and social history data are presented in almost all of these case studies, since such data give the reader clearer ideas about how specific behavior patterns were generated and maintained. A few case studies have little background data, such as in the case of Harry, in which an abrupt organic trauma is the focus of disorder, or else if it seems highly probable that genetic factors dominated the development of the disorder. In cases such as Harry's, we present more detailed information regarding present behavior and the responses in psychological evaluations. All cases go through to a natural, although not always successful, conclusion. As in most experiences, much can be learned from failure.

The authors wish to thank the many teachers, colleagues, and students who contributed so much to the knowledge and experience that led to this book. There are far too many to thank individually, though primary mentors, such as Albert Rabin, Bertram Karon, Norman Abeles, Mary Clarke, and Will Edgerton, deserve a special thank you. We are very grateful to Professors David Bolocofsky, Ernest Dahl, Jane Ellen Smith, and Geoffrey Thorpe for their review of the text. Much appreciation is extended to John-Paul Lenney, our Allyn and Bacon editor, for his support and advice. We would also like to acknowledge the helpful input in writing these cases from Rhett Landis, Ken McNiel, Phil Johnson, Curt Barrett, Donna Cundiff, and Michael Moll, as well as the extensive help in organizing and typing the manuscript provided by Sharon Mills, Sandy Hartz, Suzanne Paris, and Juanita Chatman.

INTRODUCTION

The field of abnormal psychology has evolved through many theoretical orientations. In the first half of this century, the Freudian psychoanalytic model, already developing a more broad spectrum psychodynamic orientation (Gedo, 1986), clearly dominated the study of abnormal psychology in North America. At the same time, the seminal behavioral studies of John Watson and Mary Cover Jones established behaviorism as an important influence in the study of abnormal behavior. While behaviorism, and more specifically, behavior therapy, was coming into bloom in the 1950s and 1960s (Wolpe, 1958; Ayllon and Azrin, 1968), a "third force" was emerging, marked by diverse theories, many new psychotherapies (Garfield, 1981), and a varying and differing interest in diagnosis and etiology. At the same time, psychodynamic theory was further diversifying (Kohut, 1977; Gedo, 1986) and showing a renewed concern for experimental verification (Silverman, 1976; Silverman & Weinberger, 1985; Cann and Donderi, 1986). Meanwhile, behavior therapy was (1) becoming less wedded to theory (Lazarus, 1971), (2) expanding its concern back to at least some aspects of the mind under the influence of the cognitive behavior modifiers (Meichenbaum, 1977, 1986), (3) developing a broader perspective on environmental variables under the social learning theorists (Bandura and Walters, 1963; Mischel, 1969), and (4) in general helping facilitate the overall trend in the mental health field toward greater emphasis on the experimental verification of assessment and intervention techniques (Bausell, 1986; Kerlinger, 1985).

Teachers and practitioners alike have reflected the increasing sophistication inherent in this maturing and diversification process. Very few would now argue that any one technique or theoretical approach answers all or even most of the diagnostic, etiologic, and treatment questions that arise (Saccuzzo and Kaplan, 1984). Certain theories and techniques have more relevance to certain disorders. In this vein, it is interesting that the "sphere of relevance" of an approach is most closely centered on the original group that was studied or treated when the approach came into being.

Freud's specific theories became less relevant as society lost some of the repressions of the Victorian era (possibly only to take on other repressions). Carl Jung's treatment techniques, which focus on uncovering "spiritual" yearnings and on creating a sense of meaning, arose primarily in the therapy of middle-aged males who had "made it big" in their careers, but who lived the feelings expressed in Peggy Lee's classic refrain, "Is that all there is to that?" Just as the client-centered therapy techniques of Carl Rogers seem most appropriate to bright and introspective clients (similar to the graduate ministerial and psychology students he first worked with), the behavior therapist's "token economy" is most effective when dealing with clients who are institutionalized and show marked deficits in basic social and interpersonal skills.

Concomitant with this growing awareness that no one theory or technique holds all the answers is the concept that a number of techniques may be necessary to handle any one case. This "multimodal" approach is an underlying assumption in this book; it is dramatically emphasized in the case of Roger, discussed in the section on theories and techniques.

The eclecticism inherent in the ideas stated above is another assumption in this book. The authors also confess to a slight leaning toward a social learning formulation in most instances. There are several reasons for this. First, social learning theory's broad-based acceptance of many cause-paths to disorder allows a more comfortable melding with most specific theories. For example, biological causes of behavior are neither contrary to nor contradictory of a social learning approach. Also, the absence of an "in-group" language and theory structure in social learning theory allows easier communication with specific theorists and facilitates an emphasis on empirical verification.

The terminology used to designate the disorder patterns in this book is that of the *Diagnostic and Statistical Manual*, published by the American Psychiatric Association. The use of this terminology does not indicate a belief that it is a perfect, or even excellent system. There have been telling criticisms from various quarters (Schacht, 1985; Kaplan, 1983; Garmezy, 1978; Zubin, 1978). However, it is clear that (1) no other system is even close to the level of acceptance accorded the DSM; (2) there are increasing demands from third-party payers (the insurance companies and the government) for specific DSM diagnoses in even routine or minor client contacts; and (3) the DSM system has attempted to operationalize the criteria for diagnoses, has responded to feedback from researchers and practitioners in its revisions from DSM-I (1952) to DSM-II (1968) to DSM-III (1980) DSM-III-R, and now to DSM-IV, and thus is open to change in future editions based on accumulated data (Millon and Klerman, 1986). The authors feel it would be a major disservice to ignore substantially the DSM system, and deemphasizing it would particularly hurt those people (such as psychology, pre-med, nursing, social work, criminal justice, and education students) who are likely to have to deal with this system in their careers.

Outline of the Case Studies

The first chapter in this book, that of General Grigorenko, clearly highlights the social and political issues inherent in defining abnormality and subsequently applying that label to an individual. The second chapter, on theories and techniques, first presents the case of Danielle, who manifests a most common problem, a persistent though not constant moderate level of anxiety, several simple phobias, and some allied mild depression. After Danielle's case is detailed, there is an analysis of the etiology and treatment that could be expected from the five major theoretical viewpoints: psychoanalytic-psychodynamic, behavioral, cognitive, humanistic-existential, and biological. The chapter closes with a multi-modal treatment approach, wherein techniques from a variety of theoretical perspectives are blended together to treat a case of exhibitionism.

The third chapter is the first to focus on a specific syndrome: anxiety disorders. In contrast to the simple phobias (which are also a subgroup of the anxiety disorders, and which were discussed in Chapter 2), more severe cases are presented here, specifically agoraphobia and the obsessive-compulsive disorder. This chapter closes with a relatively recent addition to the DSM, the posttraumatic stress disorder, which is considered as an anxiety disorder.

Chapter 4 combines the dissociative disorders and sleep disorders, since the altered state of consciousness in each provides some interesting contrasts. The dissociative disorders are exemplified by a case of multiple personality, the sleep disorders first by a sleepwalking case and then by a case that combines a disturbance of the sleep-wake cycle with insomnia. Chapter 5 looks at the psychogenic pain disorder, a commonly observed subtype of the somatoform disorders.

Chapter 6 is concerned with severely disruptive syndromes: the schizophrenic and paranoid disorders, as seen in cases of undifferentiated schizophrenia, paranoid schizophrenia, and the paranoid personality disorder. Schizophrenia is a subgroup within the overall conceptual category of "psychosis," which essentially designates a loss of reality contact. The two schizophrenia cases allow a contrast between paranoid schizophrenia, the most well-integrated form, and undifferentiated schizophrenia, in which functioning has especially deteriorated. These two forms are then compared with the nonpsychotic paranoid personality disorder pattern. The other category of very severe disorders, the affective disorders, are detailed in Chapter 7 in cases of major depressive disorder and bipolar disorder; again, both of these are psychotic disorders.

In combination with the case of exhibitionism from Chapter 2, the spectrum of the psychosexual disorders are seen in Chapter 8. Cases of both male and female sexual dysfunction are noted, as well as a case of transvestism. Chapter 9 (addictive disorders) discusses three of the most common disorder patterns in our society: alcohol dependence, prescription drug abuse, and cocaine abuse.

Complementing the discussion of the personality disorder pattern (paranoid) found in Chapter 6, Chapter 10 has two of the more important personality disorders—the histrionic and antisocial patterns. Somewhat related issues are then found in the disorders of impulse control, seen in cases of a borderline personality disorder associated with rape, pathological gambling, kleptomania, and child abuse. The last case offers a transition to Chapter 12 on childhood disorders. In this chapter, cases of developmental language disorder, attention deficit disorder with hyperactivity, and early infantile autism point to three of the most critical disorders that emerge in childhood. The oppositional disorder and separation anxiety disorder (associated with school phobia) cases then document two common maladaptive channels for the strivings of identity and independence that are often a concern in middle childhood and adolescence. Classic disorders of adolescence and early adulthood, anorexia nervosa and bulimia, end this chapter.

Chapter 13 offers three cases in which a clearly defined organic factor has caused psychological symptomatology. The first case documents a person's disorder and virtually complete recovery of psychological functioning subsequent to having an entire half of the brain removed. The second case shows how depression can result from organic trauma, and the last case focuses on Alzheimer's Disease.

Chapter 14 is concerned with the interaction of psychological disorder and legal issues. Providing a transition from the prior chapter, the first case discusses legal "incompetence" in handling personal affairs as a result of brain dysfunction from aging and alcohol. In the second case, the focus is on the all-important issue of how to discriminate true disorder from malingering, and from the unique and related factitious disorder. The last case, of John Hinckley, who attempted to assassinate President Reagan, examines the legal concepts of insanity, incompetency to stand trial, and involuntary civil commitment as it relates to predicting dangerousness.

The full spectrum of cases provided by this book should develop an awareness of the diversity inherent in the modern study of abnormal psychology.

REFERENCES

Ayllon, T. and Azrin, N. (1968) *The Token Economy: A Motivational System for Therapy and Rehabilitation*. New York: Appleton-Century-Crofts.

Bandura, A. and Walters, R. (1963) *Social Learning and Personality Development*. New York: Holt, Rinehart.

Bausell, R. (1986) *Experimental Methods*. New York: Harper & Row.

Cann, D. and Donderi, D. (1986) Jungian personality typology and the recall of everyday and archetypal dreams. *Journal of Personality and Social Psychology, 50,* 1021–1030.

Garfield, S. (1981) Psychotherapy: A 40-year appraisal. *American Psychologist, 36,* 174–183.

Garmezy, N. (1978) Never mind the psychologists: It is good for the children. *The Clinical Psychologist, 31,* 1, 4–6.

Gedo, J. (1986) *Conceptual Issues in Psychoanalysis.* Hillsdale, N.J.: The Analytic Press.

Kaplan, M. (1983) A woman's view of DSM-III. *American Psychologist, 38,* 786–792.

Kerlinger, F. (1985) *Foundations of Behavioral Research.* New York: Holt, Rinehart and Winston.

Kohut, H. (1977) *The Restoration of the Self.* New York: International Universities Press.

Lazarus, A. (1971) *Behavior Therapy and Beyond.* New York: McGraw-Hill.

Meichenbaum, D. (1977) *Cognitive Behavior Modification.* New York: Plenum.

Meichenbaum, D. (1986) *Stress Inoculation Training.* New York: Pergamon.

Millon, T. (1986) On the past and future of the DSM-III. In T. Millon and G. Klerman (Eds.) *Contemporary Directions in Psychopathology: Toward the DSM-IV.* New York: Guilford.

Mischel, W. (1969) Continuity and change in personality. *American Psychologist, 24,* 1012–1018.

Saccuzzo, D. and Kaplan, R. (1984) *Clinical Psychology.* Boston: Allyn and Bacon.

Schacht, T. (1985) DSM-III and the politics of experience. *American Psychologist, 40,* 513–521.

Silverman, L. (1976) Psychoanalytic theory: The reports of my death are greatly exaggerated. *American Psychologist, 31,* 621–637.

Silverman, L. and Weinberger, J. (1985). Mommy and I are one: Implications for psychotherapy. *American Psychologist, 40,* 1296–1308.

Wolpe, J. (1958) *Psychotherapy by Reciprocal Inhibition.* Stanford, Calif.: Stanford University Press.

Zubin, J. (1978) But is it good for science? *The Clinical Psychologist, 31,* 1, 5–7.

1

Concepts of Abnormality

The first case in this book, the true story of General Grigorenko, an exiled Soviet general, dramatically highlights some of the problems in simply defining abnormal behavior. A traditional method of defining abnormal behavior has been to use statistical norms. However, this only establishes extremes, and does not per se discriminate between positive and negative patterns or characteristics. Also, because of the commonness of a pattern—for example, drunk driving and anxiety—it may be labeled as normal.

Defining abnormal as the absence of optimal or ideal characteristics is another possibility. The problem of definition is then shifted to what is "optimal" and who decides; plus, most normal individuals are not that close to the ideal.

In any case, most will generally agree that abnormal behavior is behavior that significantly differs from some consensually agreed upon norm, and which in some way is harmful to the affected person or to others. More specifically, components of a judgment of abnormality often include the following four concepts.

Deviant refers to behavior that differs markedly from socially accepted standards of conduct. In many cases, the word has negative connotations.

Different also suggests behavior that varies significantly, at least statistically, from the accepted norm, but does not usually have negative connotations.

Disordered implies a lack of integration in behaviors; the result may be impairment of a person's ability to cope in various situations.

Bizarre suggests behavior that differs extremely from socially accepted norms. In addition, it connotes inadequate coping patterns and disintegration of behavioral patterns.

Additionally, several general guidelines that are consistently relevant to a judgment of abnormality have evolved throughout history, modern research studies, and across most cultures. These criteria can be summarized as follows:

1. Some recurring behaviors that seem indicative of potential, developing, or existing mental disorders are (a) inability to inhibit self-destructive behaviors, (b) seeing or hearing things that others in the culture agree are not there, (c) sporadic and/or random outbursts of violence, (d) consistent inability to relate interpersonally in an effective manner, (e) persistent academic and/or vocational failure, (f) anxiety and/or depression, and (g) inability to conform to codes of behavior whether or not one verbalizes a desire to do so.

2. The most consistent criteria for deciding whether or not any specific individual is abnormal are (a) the deviance (or bizarreness) of behavior from the norms of society, (b) the continuity and/or persistence of disordered behavior over time, and (c) the resulting degree of disruption in intrapersonal and/or interpersonal functioning.

3. The continuum of behavior ranges from clearly normal adjustment to definitely abnormal adjustment. Many people's behavior belongs in that middle area where decisions regarding abnormality are difficult.

4. A specific abnormal behavior pattern is seldom inherited, but genetic factors help predispose a person to abnormality of one sort or another.

5. The causes of any one abnormal behavior pattern are usually multiple.

6. Indicators of abnormality are not necessarily obvious or flagrant. In many cases, the signs are uncommon and/or subtle.

7. Both long-term and transient social value systems affect judgments of whether or not a person is abnormal.

8. A psychological handicap often has a more negative effect on interpersonal relationships than does a physical handicap.

9. The label of psychological abnormality often continues to be applied by others to a person even after the disorder no longer exists. Such a label, resulting from people's expectations and responses, may even prolong some aspects of the psychological disorder.

10. In most societies there is a substantial overlap between judgments of mental abnormality and criminal behavior; the same specific behavior may receive either label, depending on who is doing the labeling.

Rates of Mental Disorders

There have been numerous efforts over the last several decades to apply effectively such criteria as the above to determine the overall rates of mental disorder. Earlier endeavors in this area provided some useful data, but all prior efforts pale in comparison to the landmark study developed by the National Institute of Mental Health which was initially reported in a series of six articles in the October 1984 issue of the *Archives of General Psychiatry*, from which the following material is abstracted.

The sheer scope of this study is unprecedented. Over 17,000 representative community residents (virtually a fivefold increase over the most exhaustive prior studies of this research quality) were sampled at five sites (Baltimore, New Haven, North Carolina, St. Louis, and Los Angeles). These residents were administered a thorough and standardized structured interview, using the Diagnostic Interview Schedule, and were then interviewed a year later. Unlike many earlier studies, this research was not restricted to reporting on hospitalized mentally disordered persons, or on prevalence of treatment, or on current symptoms or level of impairment. Instead, all of the thirteen major disorder categories of DSM-III were considered.

From the perspective of six-month prevalence rates (how many people show a particular disorder at some time in the six months during which the population is assessed), these findings indicate that about 19 percent of adults over age 18 suffer from at least one mental disorder during a given six-month period.

The types of problems reported include the following:

1. Anxiety disorders, such as phobias, panic disorders, and obsessive-compulsive disorders. (See Chapter 3.) Afflicting about 8 percent of those surveyed, this appears to be the most common group of psychological problems. It includes specific intense fears, such as fear of heights or animals, as well as "agoraphobia," a fear of leaving the familiar setting of home.

2. Abuse or dependence on drugs, afflicting an estimated 6 to 7 percent of the population. (See Chapter 9.) About four-fifths of the cases are linked to alcohol.

3. Affective or mood disorders, such as major depression and manic-depression, which affect about 6 percent of adults studied. (See Chapter 7.) Depression, a feeling of hopelessness that can sometimes lead to suicide, is often accompanied by eating and sleeping problems and reduced activity. It may alternate with mania, involving increased activity and delusions of grandeur.

4. Schizophrenia, the most severely disabling of mental illnesses. (See Chapter 6.) Found in about 1 percent of the population, it can involve psychotic disturbances in thought, accompanied by withdrawn or bizarre behavior and hallucinations. Another 1 percent are affected by antisocial personality disorders—deeply ingrained behavior patterns, such as a low frustration level and an inability to feel guilt, that bring a person into conflict with others.

Somewhat different results are obtained from the perspective of lifetime prevalence rates (measuring how often disorders occur in the lifetime of the persons who are sampled). From this viewpoint, it would appear that the most common disorder pattern is substance abuse, at close to 20 percent (alcoholism, 13 percent; other drug abuse, 5.5 percent). (See Chapter 9.) The 5.5 percent rate, for example, means that between 5 and 6 of every 100 persons sampled showed enough problems in this area to warrant an initial clinical diagnosis of substance abuse disorder.

There was also a high rate for the anxiety disorders (Chapter 3) of 12–20 percent and for the affective disorders (Chapter 7) of 8–9 percent. The variable estimates for the anxiety disorders reflects the fact that there was a much higher assessed rate of anxiety disorders in Baltimore than in the other sites (our hypothesis is that this was around the year the football Colts left for Indianapolis and the baseball Orioles didn't do all that well either). The overall rate in these studies for schizophrenia (Chapter 6) was 1.0–1.5 percent, and 2.5 percent for the antisocial personality disorder (Chapter 10).

Breaking down the anxiety disorder category, phobias are observed at about 10 percent, the panic disorders at 1.5 percent, and the obsessive-compulsive disorder at 2.5 percent. Breaking down the affective disorders, bipolar was found at close to 1.0 percent, major depressions at about 5.5 percent, and dysthymic disorder (a milder form of depression) at 3 percent.

This project also looked at differences in rates of mental disorder among those who lived in central city areas, in suburbs, and in small towns or rural areas. For schizophrenia, organic brain disorder, alcoholism, drug abuse, and antisocial personality, the rates were highest in the central city, at a middle level for suburban areas, and lowest in the rural/small town populations. Rates in all areas were relatively even for major depressions and phobias, though somatization disorders, panic disorders, and some affective disorders were a bit higher in rural and small town areas than in the others. The only disorder that was found to be higher in the suburbs was the obsessive-compulsive disorder, not surprising in light of the dynamics of that disorder. (See Chapter 3.)

Issues relevant to the prior points, issues, and statistics will occur throughout this book, and several are especially evident in the following case of General Grigorenko.

/ A Normal Person Viewed as Pathological

**The Case of
General
Grigorenko**

"Is Adolf Hitler crazy?" Bohner asked eventually—the sort of damn-fool question too many people ask as soon as they hear a man is a psychologist. (p. 136)

— Len Deighton
Goodbye Mickey Mouse

This book opens with a case of an apparently normal individual who has been viewed as psychopathological, specifically paranoid, within the political system in which he was raised. We provide some context data on General Grigorenko and then present the actual interviews with him, as well as some of the conclusions gathered by the author of the article.

Background

Pyotr Grigorievich Grigorenko rose from meager circumstances to obtain the rank of Major General in the Soviet Army. He was considered an important military theoretician and received many honors and accolades. However, during the early 1960s, in the midst of these honors, he turned dissident. He was given a psychiatric examination at the time and was declared mentally ill, with specific reference made to paranoid thinking thought to be generated by atherosclerotic brain disease. He was placed in a hospital for the criminally insane. Two years later, in 1978, he was able to reach the West, whereupon he requested a psychiatric examination. He had hoped to use the results of that examination on his return to the Soviet Union. However, the Supreme Soviet published a special decree, signed by Leonid Brezhnev, taking away Grigorenko's citizenship and in effect making his return to his homeland impossible. He had not yet taken the examination, yet still decided to go through with it. It was initiated in December 1978.

The following selection is the part of Reich's (1980) article that provides the Grigorenko interview material. After the interview, Reich concludes that Grigorenko shows no signs of mental disorder or of any impairment of thought processes. Even though there is some evidence of atherosclerotic disease, the conclusion of all concerned is that this does not detract in any significant way from his ability to process information adequately and to perceive events accurately. Psychological examination found Grigorenko to be of superior intellectual ability, particularly in the areas of verbal learning and retention. This exam also found him able to shift his point of view easily, which would be contrary to a paranoid diagnosis, and then described him as having "a highly developed sense of truth, one who characteristically seeks to understand and validate his experiences" (p. 321).

To be objective, it should be noted that this examination took place several years after the Soviet psychiatrists found him to be paranoid, and his thought processes and emotional patterns may have changed in that time. In any case, here is the dialogue with General Grigorenko, which should help readers make their own judgments in regard to his normalcy.

The Case of General Grigorenko: A Psychiatric Reexamination of a Soviet Dissident

Walter Reich

Grigorenko acknowledged that his speech at the Party congress in 1961 was his first public act of dissent. But upon further questioning it became clear that the

From: Reich, W. The case of General Grigorenko: A psychiatric reexamination of a Soviet dissident. *Psychiatry*, 1980, *43*, 303–323. Copyright © 1980 by The William Alanson White Psychiatric Foundation, Inc. Reprinted by special permission of The William Alanson White Psychiatric Foundation, Inc.

moral convictions represented by that act were evident before. He recalled that the first time he had any difficulty was in 1941, on the day of the Nazi invasion of his country, when in a private conversation that was later revealed to his superiors he criticized Stalin's lack of planning for the war.

> *Grigorenko:* I was saved from death by a firing squad because Stalin fled and chaos overcame the leadership. What also helped me was that I had a very good relationship with, and was respected by, the military commander of that front, and they did their best to hush it up. If not for the confusion at the top, no one in that area would have dared defend me. But there was no reaction from above, so that the commanders (at the front) took the initiative in defending me. But of course I had to recant publicly. I had to denounce what I had done and swear I was faithful to Stalin.
>
> *Reich:* Did you know what you did was dangerous?
>
> *Grigorenko:* Of course I knew; I didn't expect to be caught, since what I said was part of a private conversation between two people.

Grigorenko's second difficulty with authorities occurred in 1949, during his defense of his Master's dissertation. In its first chapter, the dissertation contained implied criticisms of the military theories of unnamed high-ranking officers. Grigorenko was advised to excise that chapter from the dissertation.

> *Grigorenko:* (Smiles) Finally they convinced me to change it. . . . The man who helped me (to the decision to compromise) asked me, "Do you want to make a scientific discovery or do you want a degree?" I told him that I thought that was the same thing. And he said, "No, it's not the same thing; first you get your degree and then you should make scientific discoveries." Once he explained that in that way, I followed his advice. You have to carry out a task in a stepwise fashion.
>
> *Reich:* Aren't you interested in truth? Are you willing to compromise truth?
>
> *Grigorenko:* (Calmly) Well, I think that when something concerns a matter of principle, no compromise is possible. A dissertation on such a subject, though, doesn't involve matters of principle. Truth did not vanish, it wasn't betrayed. After all, everyone read that dissertation (in the process of its consideration), and what had to be said was said. And when it was finally voted upon (at the ceremony of the defense of the dissertation), it was approved unanimously (for the first time in the history of the academy), and (the vote) was greeted with applause.
>
> *Reich:* So you distinguish between important things and unimportant things—between things that are worth fighting about and things that are not worth fighting about?
>
> *Grigorenko:* Of course.
>
> *Reich:* So why did the Soviet psychiatrists consider you unwilling to change your views, unwilling to change?
>
> *Grigorenko:* I'm prepared to change if I can be convinced, by discussion, that I'm wrong. That man, my thesis advisor, convinced me, so I changed.

I engaged Grigorenko in a further discussion of specific political views. In fact, my first challenge to him in the interview had to do with the content of his views during the mid-sixties, and that challenge provoked him to some spirited reflection on his former ideas regarding Leninism and on the revisions of those ideas that he developed during his confinement in a psychiatric hospital in 1965. It appeared that the depth of his feelings in response to this subject had to do, at least in part, with the past insistence by Soviet psychiatrists that his political ideas were somehow inadequate or that he was characterologically unable to change or moderate them. When I reminded him of his Leninist position and of his change in that position in 1965, a change he had recorded in a memoir, he acknowledged that he had decided then that it was a fundamental error to rely on the dogma of Leninism. He said that in thinking about the matter during his hospitalization, he had decided that he had been naive. He saw that it was necessary to take the present into account and that it would be impossible to go back 50 years. That revision, he said, represented a drastic change in his views. At that time, he explained, "I started to consider Leninism as a delusion. . . . I left the hospital with the idea that one had to fight in the open and appeal to the laws. I gave up on the conspiratorial, underground way to achieve change." As Grigorenko spoke about that change in his views, he grew increasingly animated. Although I attempted to ask him about other matters, he continued to return to the topic. Clearly, it had affected him and he felt the need for continued elaboration and clarification. However, there was no evidence of an inability to leave the subject of the discussion, or of an obsessional, perseverative quality to his answer.

Much of the interview was taken up with an exploration of the motivations for Grigorenko's dissent and risk-taking acts, the clarity of his purpose, and the sense he has and has had of himself—the sense, that is, of his personal power and capacities.

> **Reich:** Why (did you persist in your struggle)?
>
> **Grigorenko:** The Soviet psychiatrists asked me the same question. It's not a personal cause. It's a social, communal cause. Someone always has to start. I always liked to repeat the verse by Yevtushenko written when he was still a real poet. He wrote, "When lack of talent summons itself to fight for truth, then talent, I am ashamed of you." . . . This (Soviet) system of government should not be tolerated by people, but it never happens that everyone rises against it. There always have to be people who start—then others will follow. And those who start regardless of whether or not they are talented, or have special abilities—they become a slogan, a banner, for those who follow. This places a particular responsibility on them and they should not abandon the cause. You are responsible not just for yourself, but also for the cause in the eyes of those who follow. During my life, in my faithful service to communism, I caused a lot of damage to my people, and I wanted, at least in my remaining days, to repair it. . . . What's the sense of living one extra year if you continue in the fraud of not facing things? It's better to live the rest of your life creatively so that you will not be ashamed in the eyes of your grandchildren. (At this point Grigorenko appeared sad, but continued to speak carefully and deliberately.) I have always considered the inner impulses to serve as a vocation inspired—instilled in my soul—by God.
>
> **Reich:** Why in your soul? After all, only a few people did what you did.
>
> **Grigorenko:** No, this is not true. It's just that I became known. It was just luck

that I became known, mostly as a result of the campaign in my defense (organized by my wife). There are many who did more than I did, but no one knows about them.

Reich: Did God put it in their souls, too?

Grigorenko: I think so. I think that Providence plays a greater role in the lives of people than we think.

Reich: Do you think that you have some kind of special relationship with God?

Grigorenko: No. Even though I firmly believe that God exists in the world, and that there is some Supreme Reason, I unfortunately cannot absorb myself fully in prayer. . . . Some people can detach themselves and allow themselves to be fully absorbed in prayer, but I can't. For example, I feel that I can't proselytize using the name of God – I can mention it in a private conversation, but I think that there are people chosen by God for that. We have such a man in the Soviet Union. This is Father Dudko, who one can say, really contains God within him.

I further questioned Grigorenko in order to see if I could find any grandiose trends – any sense of himself as somehow superhuman, divine, possessed of extraordinary powers or knowledge, or of being centerstage, or being more important than he could possibly be. I was alerted to one possible area of grandiosity by his mention of a conversation about him that he attributed to members of the Politburo. He said that one dissident leaflet he had written, "Why We Don't Have Bread," had been discussed by them. When I explored the matter further to see whether he thought he was somehow constantly and centrally on the minds of the Soviet leadership, he explained, matter-of-factly, that a month after he had distributed that leaflet, Brezhnev had made a speech listing some of the same circumstances that were cited in his leaflet, and that he was then told about a conversation that had taken place at a high level shortly after that speech in which someone made the comment, "Well that almost sounded as if it had been written by Grigorenko."

Reich: Who said that?

Grigorenko: It was a member of the Central Committee – it was a small group that discussed it.

Reich: The Central Committee was aware of General Grigorenko?

Grigorenko: (Laughs) Of course, I was sent to the hospital by the Central Committee – not by the psychiatrists. And it was said, "Don't allow him to get to trial."

Reich: You mean you were talked about (in high places) – Brezhnev had a discussion about you back then in 1965 or perhaps in 1969?

Grigorenko: Well, Brezhnev knows me very well . . . Khrushchev talked about me (too).

In this interchange, as well as in other parts of the interview, Grigorenko's theories of how others, including those in high places, related to and thought of him were based on reasonable evidence or conservative inference. There was no suggestion of an inflated belief in his own importance to the world as a whole or to the Soviet leadership in particular; rather, he related what he believed to have been small but significant decisions made by persons at high levels regarding his acts and his fate, as fitting responses, under Soviet political conditions, to the dissenting behavior of a Soviet Major General. Earlier, he had pointed out to me that he had personally known Brezhnev during World War II; and he later explained that it should not be inconceivable that Brezhnev would now be aware of and talk about him in his private conversations, or that he could be the focus of the conversations of other high-ranking Soviet leaders. The series of answers, in addition to previous answers regarding his relationship with God and his personal mission, suggested that his sense of himself was a modest one, that he viewed himself as relatively unimportant in the cosmic scheme of things, and that he felt that irony and chance rather than some special destiny had fashioned his prominence and his fate.

Finally, I attempted to gauge Grigorenko's capacity to assess reality, both now and in the past—his capacity to assess the nature of the historical moment and to respond to it, as well as his capacity to appreciate danger from without and to moderate his behavior in response to that danger. I brought up, again, the event that had precipitated his political troubles in 1961, the speech he made as a Party delegate criticizing certain official Party policies.

> *Reich:* In 1961, when you made that speech, it was, after all, after the era of Stalin. The period of repression had eased; and while, obviously, it was dangerous to speak out, it was not a capital offense. Would you have said the same thing ten years earlier, during Stalin's terror—during the late forties or early fifties? Or, to put it another way, what stopped you (from speaking out then)?
>
> *Grigorenko:* At that time I couldn't have made such a statement because I didn't measure up to it. I was a faithful communist. The difference between 1951 and 1961 is not just a difference of ten years, but in the fact that the Twentieth Party Congress took place in 1956, from which I learned that what I had considered to be local mistakes were really widespread perversions of the Party line. And after 1956, I had (time for) another five years for observation and reflection. This is the way I was able to become worthy of making the statement that I made (in 1961). And as for what you said, Dr. Reich (that I organized my underground group in 1963 knowing then it was not then a capital crime), let me tell you that I was convinced then that if I would be found out I'd be killed.
>
> *Reich:* So if your understanding had been the same in 1951 as it had been in 1961, you would have done (then) what you did later: you would have done that under Stalin, too?
>
> *Grigorenko:* (Smiles) As an old historian, a military historian, I have to object to that question. One cannot say what would have happened if the past was other than the way it was. I was no different then. I was the way I was. And whether I could have been different under different circumstances is just a matter of speculation.

Comment

In these excerpts from the extensive interviews with General Grigorenko, Reich explores the major areas through which paranoid ideation is usually manifest.

First, General Grigorenko recounts the events that led to his hospitalization. Reich's questions are quite pointed and could be expected to elicit inflammatory and elaborate defenses from a paranoid individual (Heilbrun, Blum, and Goldreyer, 1985). Instead, General Grigorenko appears to respond with the reasoned and measured thinking that is characteristic of his responses throughout the interviews. The impression is one of an intelligent and sensitive man who evaluates the validity of his conclusions. This cognitive strategy is contrary to the description of paranoid thinking proposed by Shapiro:

> . . . a suspicious person is a person who has something on his mind. He looks at the world with fixed and occupying expectation and he searches repetitively and only for confirmation of it. He will not be persuaded to abandon his suspicion or some plan of action based on it. On the contrary, he will pay no attention to rational arguments except to find in them some aspect or feature that actually confirms his original view. (Shapiro, 1965, p. 56.)

Further, Reich searches for indices of obsessional concerns, grandiose self-perceptions, and impaired judgment. General Grigorenko evidenced an understandable concern and emotional involvement in discussing the evolution of his political ideas. However, as Reich points out, the inflexible perseverative quality of paranoid ideation was not evident. Nor did Grigorenko present his difficulties as more important than those of others. Finally, Grigorenko's ability to process reality and to consider consequences before his actions is apparent in his comparisons of political climates and his understanding of them in 1951 and 1961; Reich's thorough examination would suggest that Grigorenko was never really mentally disordered, and that the actions taken against him by the Soviets were politically motivated. However, from a scientific point of view it is true that the data are either not clear or not available to completely rule out several other possible explanations as to why Soviet and American diagnosticians differed in their assessment of the general. For example;

1. Both were seeing the same behavior, but one group simply made a mistake.
2. Within the Russian cultural tradition, deviance of any sort is more likely to be seen as a valid indicator of abnormality.
3. Within the traditions of Russian medicine, even evidence of a minor atherosclerotic process is more compellingly suggestive of disorder.
4. Both groups were using essentially the same diagnostic criteria in their judgment, and both were accurate. General Grigorenko was, in fact, disordered at the time of the first exam, but had, for some unknown reason, sufficiently recovered by the time he was examined in the U.S.

The extent to which behavior that deviates from the usual is labeled in accordance with social context variables and the bias of observers has received considerable attention (Rosenhan, 1973; Szasz, 1967; Scheff, 1975; May, 1981; Eaton, 1985; Garfield, 1986). Suffice it to say that the expectations of observers, the relative social status of the individual in question, and the anticipated consequences of the unusual behavior may result in such diverse labels as emotionally disturbed, heroic, martyred, independent, egocentric, genius, and rebel, all with major implications for clinical diagnosis and treatment. As in the case of General Grigorenko, unusual behavior may result in ostracism, forced treatment, and/or incarceration. In this vein, all societies on occasion lean toward prejudicial labeling of nonpathological behaviors (Eaton, 1985; Rosenhan, 1973); that is, the disorder may be in the eye of the beholder. Hence, expertise, consensual validation, as well as wisdom and compassion are needed to avoid problems such as those found in General Grigorenko's case.

REFERENCES

Eaton, W. (1985) *Sociology of Mental Disorders*. New York: Praeger.

Garfield, S. (1986) Problems in diagnostic classification. In T. Millon and G. Klerman (Eds.) *Contemporary Directions in Psychopathology: Toward the DSM-IV.* New York, Guilford.

Heilbrun, A., Blum, N., and Goldreyer, N. (1985) Defensive projection: An investigation of its role in paranoid conditions. *Journal of Nervous and Mental Disease, 173*, 17–25.

May, R. (1981) *Existential Psychology*. New York: Random House.

Rosenhan, D. (1973) On being sane in insane places. *Science, 179*, 250–258.

Scheff, T. (Ed.). (1975) *Labeling Madness*. Englewood Cliffs, NJ: Prentice-Hall.

Shapiro, D. (1965) *Neurotic Styles*. New York: Basic Books.

Szasz, T. (1967) *The Myth of Mental Illness*. New York: Dell.

2

Theories and Techniques

There are today diverse approaches to the assessment and treatment of mental disorders. As will be evident in the second case in this section (Roger, the exhibitionist), many of these treatment techniques can be blended into a multi-modal individualized intervention program. In the first case (Danielle), we will first discuss the particulars of the case history, and then examine how the major theories would explain how these problem patterns came about, and what would be the primary treatment plan based on each particular theory.

Multiple Theoretical Views on a Case of Moderate Anxiety, Depression, and Simple Phobias

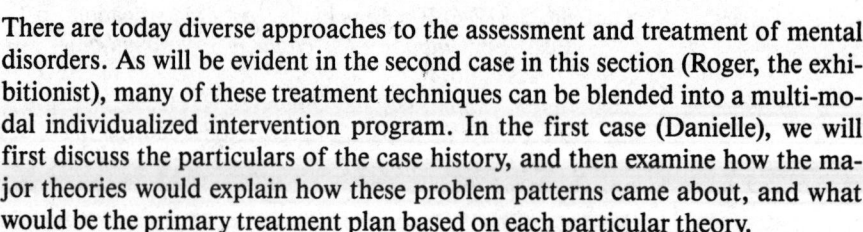

The Case of Danielle

Complaining that he suffered from acrophobia, which is the abnormal fear of heights, the athlete said, "I went to Paris and visited the Eiffel Tower last year. I started going up and then I quit. I couldn't stand the height."

The athlete was Billy Olson, who had just set a world indoor pole vault record of 19 feet 5½ inches.

— Sarasota Herald Tribune 2/11/86

The case of Danielle concerns a most common pattern: some simple phobias as well as persistent, though not constant, moderate anxiety and depression. Numerous individuals at one time or another suffer from similar disorders. However, many do not seek professional treatment, for a variety of reasons ("It costs too much"; "I don't think they could help me"; "That kind of stuff is only for people who are really crazy"; "Nobody in my family has ever gone to a psychologist, so I just couldn't go to one"; etc.). However, such attitudes are especially unfortunate here, as the prognosis for controlling problems such as Danielle's is good.

We will now discuss Danielle's case history, and then present how the major theories (psychoanalytical-psychodynamic, behavioral, cognitive, humanistic-existential, biological) would approach the etiology and treatment of her disorder.

The Case of Danielle

Danielle, who has just turned twenty-six, presented herself to a university-based psychology clinic complaining of problems with her work and marriage as well as being generally unhappy.

A structured interview and several psychological tests were administered. What emerged was a picture of a young woman who had suffered from a variety of phobias as well as varying degrees of depression and anxiety throughout most of her life. Yet, from most perspectives, she had usually functioned within the normal range on most dimensions. She had a normal childhood, and both Danielle and her parents would have characterized her as reasonably well adjusted and happy. Her grades were above average throughout grade school and high school, and although Danielle struggled academically in college, she did manage to graduate with a business degree, with a major in marketing. She started to work on her MBA, but reports feeling "just burnt out" with school. She quit to take a low-echelon job in the marketing department of a large firm in a major city about 300 miles from the area where she grew up and went to college.

She was introduced to her future husband shortly after moving to that city and they were married after a rather brief but intense courtship of four months. The intensity waned almost immediately after the wedding, and they settled into a routine marked neither by contentment nor by obvious problems. They seldom fought openly, but developed increasingly "parallel lives," wherein interactions (including sexual ones) were pleasant but minimal.

Embedded in this overall life structure were the difficulties that had moved Danielle to come to the clinic. Ever since she had been young, Danielle had been afraid of snakes and insects, especially spiders, and from her high school years onward she became anxious if closed in for any length of time in a small room (claustrophobia). She also reported that she occasionally experienced periods where she would feel anxious for no apparent reason ("free-floating anxiety"), and then more rarely would become depressed. Once, when in college, the depression became severe enough that she considered suicide. Fortunately, her roommate was sensitive to the crisis and made sure Danielle went over to the campus counseling center. Danielle's upset diminished quickly enough for her to end therapy after three sessions.

More recently, Danielle had experienced the episodes of anxiety and depression more consistently, and her husband really didn't have much interest in hearing about it. Also, she still had the phobias. She could live with the fears of the snakes and spiders, although her ability to enjoy outdoor activities was substantially reduced. But the claustrophobia had worsened and made some of the meetings required by her job very difficult for her.

Danielle's history was not grossly abnormal in any dimension, but there were aspects that could be related to her developing problems. Though Danielle's birth was normal, she was noted to be a "fussy" child and seemed to startle more easily than did her two younger brothers. Also, her mother was a rather anxious person and on a few occasions had taken to her bed, obviously somewhat depressed and blaming it on "female problems." Though both parents obviously loved and cared for all the children, Danielle's father did not show affection very often. He was demanding of good performance, both in the academic and social areas, and lack of performance usually meant some form of direct punishment from him as well as emotional distance.

Case Analysis

We'll now turn to an analysis of this case from the perspective of each of the major theories, and some other more specific details that emerged in Danielle's case will be discussed in the context of the appropriate theories. The discussion of each of these theoretical perspectives on etiology and treatment will not be presented in great detail. Also, the most commonly accepted theories and treatments for anxiety and depression will be discussed again in the sections of this book that focus on those problems.

Psychoanalytic-Psychodynamic Perspective. Psychoanalysis is the approach originally devised by Sigmund Freud and then elaborated by his early and more orthodox followers. As changes in theory or technique were introduced by persons who still followed the essential points of Freudian theory, these splinter schools (developed first by individuals such as Adler and Jung, later by Klein, Horney, and Sullivan, and more recently by Kernberg, Gill, Bion, Ricoeur, Arieti, Silverman, Shafer, Kohut, and others) were usually termed "psychodynamic" (Reppen, 1985; Gedo, 1986).

However, virtually all of these theorists would see Danielle's problems as arising from an inadequate resolution of conflicts that could have developed in one of the hypothesized stages of development through which each person, as represented by "ego," must proceed to reach maturity: oral, anal, phallic, latency, and genital stages. Conflicts in the Oedipal phase (a prelude to the genital stage), interpreted as the male child's desire to sexually possess the mother and get rid of the father (the Electra phase is analogous in the female) are seen as crucial to a number of patterns (Fenichel, 1945). In Sigmund Freud's classic phobia case, Little Hans first shows his phobia by crying out to his nursemaid that he wants to return home to caress his mother upon seeing a horse-drawn cart overturn. Freud saw this fear as being generated by Hans's Oedipal desires to possess his mother sexually and emotionally. In the Oedipal conflict, because the id's biological demand has to be met by the counterforce of the repressive superego, the net result is expected to be a continuing underlying tension that leaves the person anxious without any explanation, the "free-floating" anxiety experienced by Danielle (Fenichel, 1945).

As regards depression, Karl Abraham's early classic papers (Abraham,

1916) provided the basis for the orthodox psychoanalytic view. He theorized that depressed individuals, unable to love, project their frustrated hostility on to others and believe themselves to be hated and rejected by other people. Abraham related depression to orality and explained loss of appetite and related symptoms in terms of an unconscious desire to devour the introjected love-object. Thus, introjection (rather than the projection that psychoanalysts see as central to the paranoid process) is the psychopathological process, and the depressive's self-reproach can therefore be seen as an attempt to punish those newly incorporated components of the self.

Silvano Arieti and Jules Bemporad (1978) present an updated version of the traditional psychodynamic position. They view the depressed person as one who somehow suffered great loss in childhood; for example, a first child who experienced "paradise lost" when a new sibling near in age grabbed the previously undivided attention of the mother (a situation that did occur with Danielle). The loss could come in other ways, including early parental death (though this does not always produce depression; Ragan and McGlashan, 1986), abandonment, or an abrupt parental decision to prohibit any type of childish behavior and to insist that the child act "grown-up."

Arieti and Bemporad believe that the depressive persistently strives to regain this "paradise lost" by trying to please others, particularly "dominant others." Not surprisingly, these self-generated expectancies often exceed capabilities; failure follows, while self-blame increases and self-esteem decreases.

Psychoanalytic treatment, through techniques like (1) "free association" (having the person say whatever comes to mind, without censoring it—a more difficult task than may initially appear), (2) dream analysis, and (3) analysis of the feelings the client develops toward the therapist (transference), attempts to develop insight into the sources of the anxiety and depression (Berger, 1985). Orthodox analytic treatment, which in reality is today practiced by very few therapists, would have the analyst sitting behind the client who is on a couch, seldom either confronting or responding to the client at any length. To the degree the therapy is less orthodox, and thus more likely to be termed psychodynamic, the therapist is likely to face the client, confront issues more directly, and generally interact more. The insights that are attained, along with the accompanying release of emotion (catharsis), theoretically act to decrease the anxiety and depression, and thus allow the development of more mature and effective coping patterns (Berger, 1985; Gedo, 1986).

A unique psychodynamic therapy has been proposed by Lloyd Silverman and Joel Weinberger (1985). Based on the psychoanalytic thesis that there are powerful unconscious wishes for a state of symbiotic oneness with the "good mother of early childhood," the concept is that gratification of such desires enhances positive psychological functioning. Those who are anxious and depressed are seen as especially needy in this regard.

The major support for this thesis comes from experiments in various laboratories employing the subliminal psychodynamic activation method (Weinberger and Silverman, 1980) with over 40 groups of subjects from varied populations. These studies have reported that a subliminal, 4-millisecond exposure (a speed which does not allow conscious visual recognition of the stimulus) to stimuli intended to activate these unconscious symbiotic-like fantasies (usually the phrase "Mommy and I are one") does produce a positive effect on psychological functioning. Some variation of this technique could have been used as one part of a treatment plan for Danielle.

Behavioral Perspective. Early efforts by behaviorists to explain the development of anxiety and phobias were essentially efforts to translate psychoanalytic thought into learning theory language. However, beginning with John Watson and Mary Cover Jones and later theorists such as Clark Hull and B. F. Skinner and practitioners such as Joseph Wolpe and Arnold Lazarus, the development of anxiety and phobias was explained in terms of conditioning principles (Yates, 1975; O'Donnell, 1985). Thus, anxiety is a learned response that is unpleasant in itself, but which was appropriate at the time of learning. However, the avoidance inherent in the response prevents the corrective learning of newer, more adaptive responses.

The two major ways in which the anxiety responses and phobic patterns are learned are *modeling* and *direct experience learning.* An examination of Danielle's history reveals that modeling played a significant role in the development of her anxiety and phobic responses in response to snakes and insects. As is the case with most people who have such fears, there was no actual, naive traumatic encounter with one of these organisms. Rather, Danielle's mother, as well as her aunt, who often baby-sat for her, would shriek with horror at the sight of a spider, or even the suggestion that a snake might be in the vicinity. Danielle, at some level of consciousness, assumed that if these gigantic and all-powerful adults (from the perspective of a small child) were so afraid of these beings, so ought she. Her modeled responses were accepted and reinforced by those around her. (Note that the different stereotypical reaction to such response in boys may explain why such patterns are not so evident in boys. Also, boys are more likely to be encouraged to have actual encounters with these potential phobia sources.) While modeling can often be an efficient way of learning, as it does save the time and possible pain of trial-and-error learning, sometimes, as with Danielle, these modeled patterns may promote maladaptive behavior (Mineka, et al., 1984).

The simple phobias, of which Danielle's fears of snakes and spiders are good examples, often have simple and specific targets. Since some of these fears—for example, fears of snakes, eating rotten foods, and so on—likely had evolutionary value for humans, some theorists believe this is evidence that there is a greater preparedness to associate anxiety responses to these stimuli (Hugdahl and Ohman, 1977), and this and the modeling contributes to the overall learning process here.

On the other hand, direct experience learning (a potent factor in the development of many phobias) was critical to the origin of Danielle's claustrophobic pattern. When she was young, she was usually punished by spanking, being made to stand in the corner, or withdrawal of reinforcers (staying up late, TV, and so on). However, if she really upset her mother, Danielle would be forced to stay in a small, dark closet until she was quiet and her mother felt calmer. On a couple of occasions, this took several hours. The anxiety and discomfort of the situation were compounded by Danielle's fear of the dark and sense of uncertainty about what was going to happen to her, and produced a panic response. Panic includes a sense of loss of control, the most anxiety-generating experience of all.

As regards depression, the general theories of the early behaviorists were first refined into an overall theory by Ferster in the mid-1960s, and the general concept is that depression can result from either of two processes (Ferster and Culbertson, 1982; Lyons, et al., 1985) that are not necessarily excluding parallel biological issues (Marks and Tobena, 1986). In the first, an environmental change (loss of job, death in the family) sharply lessens incoming reinforcement, and no new methods of obtaining reinforcement have developed. Danielle's depression in college immediately followed the break-up with her boyfriend. They had always spent a great deal of time together, so this abrupt loss of reinforcement precipitated the depression.

Second, behaviorists note that depression can occur from a pattern of avoidance behavior. This is when a person's attempts to avoid aversive situations have become so strong that they preclude behaviors that bring reinforcement; in other words, these behaviors are used to avoid anxiety.

From a treatment perspective, behavior therapists have pioneered some of the most successful treatments for phobias and anxiety, even using such approaches as group therapy (Emmelkamp and Kupers, 1985). The most commonly used technique, however, has been Systematic Desensitization Therapy (SDT), which first develops a relaxation response, sometimes through drugs, but more commonly and controllably through some form of relaxation training. A hierarchy of anxiety-producing stimuli is then produced; with Danielle, for example, for closed spaces, snakes, and spiders (Wolpe, 1973).

In each case, Danielle would be asked to describe the most anxiety-arousing situation she could in each category ("snakes crawling over my body"), and that scene would receive a score of 100. A scene that brings on little or no anxiety ("hearing my professor mention snakes") would receive a 0. While remaining relaxed, the client is gradually moved through each hierarchy in imagination, or "in vitro," and then some live tasks ("in vivo") may be introduced (asking Danielle to handle a snake or sit for a period of time in a small closed room).

An alternative behavioral technique for phobias or anxiety is flooding, or implosion therapy, wherein the attempt is to maximize rather than minimize anxiety. Often carried out in a few longer-than-usual sessions, the person is asked to image more and more anxiety-producing scenes (snakes crawling in and out of various body orifices). The theory is that the anxiety will eventually peak and then extinguish, with the consequence that the phobia gradually lessens.

Regarding Danielle's depression, behavior therapists would emphasize getting her in touch with more interpersonal contacts and sources of positive reinforcement (Turkat, 1985). For her this could mean a return to active sports and learning social skills so that she could have more rewarding interpersonal interactions. Since depressives tend to be overwhelmed by tasks, breaking a goal down into sub-tasks and short-term goals, the "graded-task" approach, is useful.

Also, behavior therapists would help Danielle survey her present range of activities. Since depression tends to simultaneously lessen activity in general and increase the percentage of nonpleasurable activities, contracting, modeling, and stimulus-control techniques could help reverse this process.

Morita therapy, developed by a Japanese professor named Morita, is an approach that combines both behavioral and cognitive elements, as shown in these two quotes from David Reynolds (1984), one of the foremost interpreters of Eastern psychotherapy techniques to Western cultures.

> Behavior wags the tail of feelings. Behavior can be used sensibly to produce an indirect influence on feelings. Sitting in your bathrobe doesn't often stimulate the desire to play tennis. Putting on tennis shoes and going to the courts, racket in hand, might. (p. 100).

> Awareness, awareness, awareness. That is where we live. That is all we know. That is life for each of us. (p. 4).

A Morita therapist would attempt to bring a regular routine into Danielle's life, would de-emphasize talking about the historical antecedents to her problem, would emphasize the growth possibilities in all experiences, including pain and failure, would try to get her to begin to function as if she were psychologically healthy and competent, and would emphasize bringing both attention and awareness into all facets of day-to-day functioning.

Cognitive Perspective. Since cognition refers to a person's thinking pattern, any theorists who talk about disordered thinking patterns as critical to the development of psychopathology can be considered cognitive theorists (Mahoney and Freeman, 1985). In that general sense, psychoanalytic and psychodynamic theorists also have a cognitive perspective.

However, a more specific and focused emphasis on cognition as central to the development of anxiety is found in the works of people like Albert Ellis and George Kelly and such later therapists as Donald Meichenbaum. Kelly's (1955, 1977) theory of "personal constructs" notes that people develop certain beliefs, of which they may be consciously unaware, which cause them anxiety. Albert Ellis (1983) similarly comments on how we adopt such belief-rules as "I must reach a high point of success in whatever I undertake"; "If I ever show aggression or upset to those people close to me, they won't love me." Not surprisingly, no one can ever fully live up to such standards, and anxiety and depression naturally ensue.

Aaron Beck has focused on the development of depression from cognitive beliefs, and the theory evolved from an initial study (Beck and Valin, 1953) which indicated that self-punishment themes occurred with great frequency in the delusions of psychotically depressed clients. Beck would not disagree with the psychodynamic theorists that an early traumatizing event (death of a parent) could predispose an individual to depression. However, his major focus is on distorted thought patterns, and many different paths can lead to such thoughts. Beck and others note that depressives simultaneously (1) *minimize* any positive achievements, (2) *magnify* problems with "catastrophic expectations" ("making a mountain out of a molehill"), (3) tend to polarize their ideas (view issues in extremes, seeing only in black or white and no grays), and (4) *overgeneralize* to a conclusion based on little data (one or two events). These tendencies are often compounded by a sense of "learned helplessness," a view that one cannot do anything to really control or change their world. Low self-esteem, lessened activity, negative mood, and self-punitiveness follow (Beck, et al., 1979; Vestre, 1984).

Regarding intervention, Albert Ellis would directly challenge his client's irrational beliefs (Ellis, 1983). For example, Danielle believed that she could never again be happy, and that if she were to leave her marriage, no one would ever find her attractive again. Ellis would directly confront these beliefs, exploring what the implications and consequences would be if these irrational beliefs were true. This is then followed by challenges to act in accord with the more rational beliefs that the client has labeled as more reasonable.

Beck also tries to help clients bring their beliefs and expectations into consciousness and/or clearer focus, though he is a bit less confrontive than Ellis. He then helps them explore new beliefs. Donald Meichenbaum (1986) goes a step further by first helping clients to eliminate negative subvocal verbalizations such as "I'll always feel bad" or "I can't do it." He then helps the client develop an alternative set of positive self-statements, and to periodically repeat them. Such therapists readily agree with the client's protests that he or she won't believe what they are saying, but try to persuade them that if they persist, they will see an effect. Helping the client to engage in positive images of successful and competent behaviors, possibly introduced through hypnosis, can help here as well.

Humanistic-Existential Perspective. From a humanistic viewpoint, anxiety and depression result from cultural and social structures that impede the full expression of the personality (Maslow, 1954; Rogers, 1961, 1969). The psychodynamicist sees these emotions as determined early in development and maintained by defense mechanisms. The behavior therapist argues that they are a function of experience with a variety of conditions that result in patterns being learned, unlearned, and relearned throughout life. However, the humanist sees anxiety and depression as inevitable as long as societies thwart a person's goodness and inborn drive for self-actualization. Anxiety and depression are therefore a function of the society and will continue until the right kind of social atmosphere is made available.

Two conditions often implicated by the humanists are a repressive society and/or poverty. Poverty obviously limits a person's options, not only in developing the self, but also in remedying disorder and deficit. Within a repressive society, fear of self-expression forces the person to adopt constricted or disordered response patterns, with anxiety or depression as a common response.

Because of this belief, the pure humanist does not focus very much on the concerns of an individual client. The humanist would contend that because the individual is forced to sacrifice to social demands that are inconsistent and arbitrary, the defense strategies that he or she adopts reflect the irrational nature of the society. Anxiety and depression may therefore be a prerequisite for existence in a chaotic world (May, 1981).

Thus, they feel their energy is better directed to righting the original causes. Indeed, Carl Rogers, the founder of nondirective, or client-centered, therapy, virtually ceased doing individual therapy in favor of working with whole subgroups from the perspective of a humanistic educator and social engineer (Rogers, 1969). Directly attacking conditions generated by poverty would not be relevant to Danielle, though it might be with some other cases in this book. (See the case of Abby in the chapter on family violence and child abuse.) It is true that some aspects of Danielle's problem might be open to change by humanistic social engineering, but it's unlikely there would be enough benefit to directly help her in any immediate sense.

Some parts of the community psychology movement are quite consistent with the humanistic approach. The idea here is that a change in social conditions—for instance, through educational efforts or a redirection of social variables—will change the level of disorder (or more likely, act to prevent future emergence of that disorder in persons vulnerable to it).

Existential psychotherapists are more concerned about the individual client. Like the cognitive therapists, they would directly confront the distorted beliefs of the client, probably placing more emphasis on the absurdity or paradoxes inherent in the individual's conditions in the world (Frankl, 1975). At the same time, they might well change the focus of the problem from the original causal conditions—be they social forces, biological disorder, early environment, or whatever—toward the choices the individual has to make in the here-and-now (Boss, 1963). This focus on the here-and-now is also a constant theme in Gestalt therapy, which has strong existential and cognitive components (Van De Riet, Korb, and Gorrell, 1980).

With Danielle, an existential therapist would likely point out that preoccupation with her anxiety and depression allow her to escape the responsibility of making choices in her world. The "parallel life" of her marriage could go on indefinitely, as do many so-called "conflict-habituated" marriages. Making authentic choices can change these and similar patterns, but those choices leave the chooser open to the burden of responsibility for the effects of those choices. An existential therapist would try to get the individual to evade no longer any important choices and their consequences (Frankl, 1975).

Existentialists are also likely to have their clients face squarely the responsibility for past choices, or as is often the case, the results of avoiding a choice

(Boss, 1963). This commonly entails "guilt," and existentialists emphasize the difference between neurotic guilt and true guilt. Neurotic guilt is the experience of anxiety and depression from situations that the person had no part in bringing about, for example, the effects of restrictive early parenting practices. True guilt entails the acceptance of the responsibility for conscious past choices, or lack of choice, and the willingness to accept and be aware of the consequences that cannot be changed, with efforts being made to right as many negative effects as possible. Here, anxiety and depression, especially the "free-floating anxiety" that Danielle occasionally experienced, are seen as possible symptoms of the avoidance of authentic choices and true guilt.

Biological Perspective.   Anxiety and depression, from this perspective, are seen as conditioned by a person's physiology (Kleinknecht, 1986; Marks and Tobena, 1986). Also, some of these physiological conditions may be genetically determined. In Danielle's case, there are some indicators that she may have had some genetic disposition to developing anxiety responses (she was a "fussy" child, was easily startled, and her mother had typically been an anxious person).

The fact that Danielle's mother had apparently been depressed would lead to the suggestion that Danielle's occasional depression had a strong genetic component (though of course this would have allowed Danielle to model the behavior as well). The major biological theories of depression are typically a variation on the theme that depression reflects an alteration in the level of brain transmitters (chemicals that facilitate nerve transmission to the brain). They are generally known as the *catecholamine* theories. Most followers of these theories attribute major depression to a deficiency in the neurotransmitter norepinephrine, though others think serotonin and even histamine are critical. However, it should be remembered that a variety of external or psychological conditions (situationally-generated stress or anxiety, prolonged inactivity, prolonged low-sunlight conditions, or various substances such as caffeine and the "beta-blockers" used to treat high blood pressure and heart pain) can produce physiological changes that in turn generate depression (Lobel, 1984; Bandura, et al., 1985). Evidence does show that genetic variables play a part in significant endogenous (internally generated) depression (Winokur, 1979; Klein, et al., 1985). However, all indications are that the major components of Danielle's depression were exogenous, or reactive to the situational problems in her world.

The biological treatment for anxiety emphasizes chemotherapy with the drugs usually referred to as the minor tranquilizers—the propanadiols such as meprobamate (Equanil) or the benzodiazepenes such as diazepam (Valium) (Hersen, 1986). However, psychological techniques, such as relaxation training, can also be effective in reducing the physiological components of anxiety.

The biological theorist has traditionally used one of two major chemotherapies for any significant depression, the MAO inhibitors and the tricyclics. Both have significant side effects (MAO inhibitors: toxic cardiovascular and liver reactions, problematic interactions with certain foods; tricyclics: dizziness and heart and gastrointestinal disorders). Both require trial-and-error adjustments (titration) on dosages, and both take from several days to several weeks to show an effect. Some believe that these drugs deal with differentially generated depressions—the tricyclics for norepinephrine-based depression, MAO inhibitors for serotonin-based (Lobel, 1984). Also, tricyclics seem to work better with depressives who show some delusional characteristics (Howarth and Grace, 1985). Other, newer drugs—indalpine, mianserin—do not appear to have such severe side effects (Nayler and Martin, 1985), but this really won't be proved until they are used generally for a longer time. In any case, research does indicate that all of these drugs, when they are effective, act almost exclusively to increase the frequency of activity-related behaviors, and they only indirectly and unpredictably change interpersonal and cognitive components (Lyons, Rosen, and Dysken, 1985).

Because not all severe depressions react positively to chemotherapy, and because there is a delayed reaction even when they do, electroconvulsive therapy (ECT), or less commonly, psychosurgery are sometimes used for depression. They do seem to be useful with severe, acute depressions, especially where there is a suicidal component, since the delay in the effects of chemotherapy become even more problematical. Drugs such as carbamezapine, typically used as an anticonvulsant, may negate the need for ECT in some of these cases since it does show a rapid effect (Post, et al., 1986). Even in this relatively small proportion of cases where ECT and psychosurgery are effective, one needs to balance any gain with the irrevocable nature of this type of intervention and the several potentially severe side effects.

REFERENCES

Abraham, K. (1916) The first pregenital stage of the libido. In *Selected Papers on Psychoanalysis*. New York: Basic Books.

Arieti, S. and Bemporad, J. (1978) *Severe and Mild Depression*. New York: Basic Books.

Bandura, A., Taylor, C., Williams, S., Mefford I., and Barchas, J. (1985) Catecholamine secretion as a function of perceived coping self-efficacy. *Journal of Consulting and Clinical Psychology, 53*, 406–414.

Beck, A. and Valin, S. (1953) Psychotic depressive reaction in soldiers who accidentally killed their buddies. *American Journal of Psychiatry, 110*, 347–353.

Beck, A., Rush, A., Shaw, B., and Emery, G. (1979) *Cognitive Therapy of Depression*. New York: Guilford.

Berger, L. (1985) *Psychoanalytic Theory and Clinical Relevance*. Hillsdale, N.J.: Analytic Press.

Boss, M. (1963) *Psychoanalysis and Dasein Analysis*. New York: Plenum.

Ellis, A. (1983) *Rational-Emotive Therapy and Cognitive Behavior Therapy*. New York: Springer.

Emmelkemp, P. and Kupers, A. (1985) Behavioral group therapy for anxiety disorders.

In D. Upper and S. Ross (Eds.) *Handbook of Behavioral Group Therapy*. New York: Plenum.

Fenichel, O. (1945) *The Psychoanalytic Theory of Neurosis*. New York: John Wiley.

Ferster, C. and Culbertson, S. (1982) *Behavior Principles* (3rd ed.). Englewood Cliffs, N.J.: Prentice-Hall.

Frankl, V. (1975) *The Unconscious God: Psychotherapy and Theology*. New York: Simon & Schuster.

Gedo, J. (1986) *Conceptual Issues in Psychoanalysis*. Hillsdale, N.J.: Analytic Press.

Hersen, S. (Ed.) (1986) *Pharmacological and Behavioral Treatment*. New York: John Wiley.

Howarth, B. and Grace, M. (1985) Depression, drugs, and delusions. *Archives of General Psychiatry*, *42*, 1145–1147.

Hugdahl, K. and Ohman, A. (1977) Effects of instruction on acquisition and extinction of electrothermal response to fear-relevant stimuli. *Journal of Experimental Psychology: Human Learning and Memory*, *3*, 608–618.

Kelly, G. (1955) *The Psychology of Personal Constructs*. 2 vols. New York: Norton.

———. (1977) Personal construct theory and the psychotherapeutic interview. *Cognitive Therapy and Research*, *1*, 355–362.

Klein, D., Depue, R., and Slater, J. (1985) Cyclothymia in the adolescent offspring of parents with bipolar affective disorder. *Journal of Abnormal Psychology*, *94*, 115–127.

Kleinknecht, R. (1986) *The Anxious Self*. New York: Human Sciences Press.

Lobel, B. (1984) *Depression*. Rockville, Md.: Dept. of Health and Human Services (DHHS publication # (ADM)) 84–1318.

Lyons, J., Rosen, A., and Dysken, M. (1985) Behavioral effects of tricyclic drugs in depressed inpatients. *Journal of Consulting and Clinical Psychology*, *53*, 17–24.

Mahoney, M. and Freeman, A. (Eds.) (1985) *Cognition and Psychotherapy*. New York: Plenum.

Marks, I. and Tobena, A. (1986) What do the neurosciences tell us about anxiety disorders? *Psychological Medicine*, *16*, 9–12.

Maslow, A. (1954) *Motivation and Personality*. New York: Harper & Row.

May, R. (1981) *Existential Psychology*. New York: Random House.

Meichenbaum, D. (1986) *Stress Inoculation Training*. New York: Pergamon.

Mineka, S., Davidson, M., Cook, M., and Keir, R. (1984) Observational conditioning of snake fear in rhesus monkeys. *Journal of Abnormal Psychology*, *93*, 355–372.

Nayler, G. and Martin, B. (1985) A double-blind outpatient trial of indalpine vs. mianserin. *The British Journal of Psychiatry*, *147*, 306–309.

O'Donnell, J. (1985) *The Origins of Behaviorism*. New York: New York University Press.

Post, R. Uhde, T., Roy-Byrne, P., and Joffe, R. (1986) Antidepressant effects of carbamezapine. *The American Journal of Psychiatry*, *143*, 29–34.

Ragan, P. and McGlashan, T. (1986) Childhood parental death and adult psychopathology. *The American Journal of Psychiatry*, *143*, 153–157.

Reppen, J. (Ed.) (1985) *Beyond Freud: A Study of Modern Psychoanalytic Theorists*. Hillsdale, N.J.: Analytic Press.

Reynolds, D. (1984) *Constructive Living*. Honolulu: University of Hawaii Press.

Rogers, C. (1961) *On Becoming a Person*. Boston: Houghton Mifflin.

———. (1969) *Freedom to Learn*. Columbus, Ohio: Charles E. Merrill.

Silverman, L. and Weinberger, J. (1985) Mommy and I are one: Implications for psychotherapy. *American Psychologist*, *40*, 1296–1308.

Turkat, I. (Ed.) (1985) *Behavioral Case Formulation*. New York: Plenum.

Van de Riet, V., Korb, M., and Gorrell, J. (1980) *Gestalt Therapy*. New York: Pergamon.

Vestre, N. (1984) Irrational beliefs and self-reported depressed mood. *Journal of Abnormal Psychology*, *93*, 239–241.

Weinberger, J. and Silverman, L. (1980) Subliminal psychodynamic activation: An approach to testing psychoanalytic propositions. In R. Hogan and W. Jones (Eds.) *Perspectives in Personality: Theory, Measurement and Interpersonal Dynamics* (Vol. 2). Greenwich, Conn.: JAI Press.

Winokur, G. (1979) Unipolar depression. *Archives of General Psychiatry*, *36*, 47–52.

Wolpe, J. (1973) *The Practice of Behavior Therapy*. New York: Pergamon.

Yates, A. (1975) *Theory and Practice in Behavior Therapy*. New York: John Wiley.

/ A Multi-Modal Treatment Program

The Case of Roger

"That's nice," she said. But seeing him struggle she wanted to laugh. What a misshapen and ridiculous thing the penis was! Half of them didn't even work properly and all of them looked pathetic and detachable, like some wrinkled sea creature — like something you'd find goggling at you and swaying in an aquarium. (p. 140)

— Paul Theroux
Doctor Slaughter

We present below an article published in 1976 in which Dr. Mitch Hendrix and the senior author of this book outlined a multi-modal treatment approach for exhibitionism. The article shows how a variety of different treatment techniques can be blended into a treatment package designed for a specific problem. Additionally, it is important because exhibitionism is one of the most common sexual deviations in our society. Since the article does not go into the DSM considerations and does not give many details of Roger's background, we provide some introductory material before presenting the article.

Diagnostic Considerations

Exhibitionism is the exposing of one's genitals to a stranger in order to obtain sexual arousal. The arousal occurs immediately or shortly after the exposure, and ordinarily the exposure is the only sexual encounter that the individual seeks at the time. It is listed in DSM as a paraphilia, and it is said to occur only in males, though in fact there are female cases (Grob, 1985). Exhibitionists show a particularly high rate of recidivism; more than 20 percent get rearrested for the same offense (Cox, 1980).

Smith and Meyer (1987) have detailed four different personality types that are usually found in exhibitionism. In the Unaware type, the act is simply a secondary result of such disorders as extreme alcohol intoxication or mental retardation. The Characterological type is similar to the rapist in that there is a strong element of hostility in the behavior. The shock expressed by the victim is one of the primary reinforcements. Few exhibitionists are dangerous (estimates range from about 1 to 10 percent), and those who are almost always come from this personality type. The Impulsive exhibitionist is tense and sexually confused, and the behavior is an impulsive response to upset and anxiety.

The last pattern, the Inadequate type, which is the pattern that best fits Roger, is also somewhat obsessional in nature. In addition, this type is relatively shy and introverted and does not have good social relations, particularly with the opposite sex. Though there often is some anger toward women in this type, the exhibitionistic behavior is at the same time a pathetic attempt at ego affirmation, such that there is even hope for later social and/or sexual contact with the victim.

Background

The important features of this particular selection are the treatment issues. Yet, certain aspects of Roger's earlier development should be mentioned because they are consistent with the observations noted in other exhibitionists.

Like many exhibitionists, Roger did not have a consistent and positive relationship with a father or father-substitute. His father abandoned the family when Roger was about seven years old. He has only vague memories of his father, none of which are positive. Roger is an only child. Following the abandonment, Roger's mother reacted to the demands of the single parent role by becoming overprotective and dominating. Though she did not directly reinforce any effeminate behavior in Roger, she always emphasized "dangers" in the world and generally made conservative decisions about any potential risks that Roger might encounter. As a result, Roger feared risk, not only in physical activities, but in interpersonal areas as well.

He did have friends as he grew up, some of whom were close to him, though he never effectively interacted with women. He was seduced when he was twelve years old by a sixteen-year-old cousin. She made Roger disrobe in front of her, played with him until he had an erection, and then masturbated him to orgasm while she also fondled herself. On later occasions she had Roger attempt penetration, though this never led to a satisfying sexual experience for either of them.

Roger began to date with regularity when he entered his senior year in high school. He had intercourse on two occasions during that year, but neither was particularly satisfying to either himself or his partner. He reported that he got more enjoyment out of masturbating in front of his partner than he did actually having intercourse with her, though he always insisted that he wished he enjoyed intercourse more.

The first occasion when he exhibited himself occurred in his junior year in high school when he encountered two younger girls in a field near his school. He had been urinating and did not see the girls until they were very close. He turned and the girls looked, screamed, and ran away. Roger reports he became terribly aroused, and when he came home that evening, he masturbated several times with the images of exhibiting himself. He tried to repeat the pattern regularly, often using the ploy of pretending to be urinating into bushes at spots where he knew women would pass by. He would now masturbate as soon as the woman had passed by him, and this of course further served to reinforce the pattern. In one sense, this was a wise choice. The victim was always in the bind of deciding whether or not the exhibitionism had been intentional or accidental, and for that reason there was seldom a report to the police. But Roger is a bright individual, and knew the risks he was taking. When he came very close to being caught, he referred himself to the psychological training clinic where he went to school.

Now we will present the material from the article, as it details an extensive multi-modal therapy approach.

REFERENCES

Cox, D. Exhibitionism: An overview. In D. Cox and R. Daitzman (Eds.) *Exhibitionism*. Garland STPM, 1980.

Grob, C. (1985) Single case study: Female exhibitionism. *The Journal of Nervous and Mental Disease, 173*, 253–256.

Smith, S. and Meyer, R. (1987) *Law, Behavior, and Mental Health Practice*. New York: New York University Press.

Toward More Comprehensive and Durable Client Changes: A Case Report

E. Mitchell Hendrix and Robert G. Meyer

Roger, a self-referred undergraduate in his mid-twenties, had been sexually exposing himself to females five to seven times weekly for several weeks, and this was the most intense the problem behavior had been in its seven-year history. He estimated his total number of exposures to be between six and seven hundred. Incredibly, he was not criminally apprehended. Roger's exhibitionism occurred in his military service, where he received brief inpatient treatment and was said to have paranoid schizophrenic tendencies. Most recently, on these occasions when the threat of being caught or the likelihood that he would be seen by persons other than the target individual was too high, he would yell obscenities or show female

From: Hendrix, E., and Meyer, R. (1976) Toward more comprehensive and durable client changes: A case report. *Psychotherapy: Theory, Research and Practice, 13*(3), 263–266. Reprinted by permission of *Psychotherapy: Theory, Research and Practice*.

pornographic materials. On occasion, he aggressively grabbed his victim as he exposed himself and spoke obscenely to her. At referral, Roger was doing quite well academically and seemed at least reasonably stable, yet the deviant and schizoid quality of his interpersonal behavior warranted intervention.

Although aversive conditioning techniques might have been considered apropos, the current authors* felt that a more comprehensive approach was warranted. Further exploratory sessions with the client revealed a history of adequate heterosexual functioning apart from his exhibitionism. Very active sexually since puberty, Roger had had a brief marriage and a series of interpersonally superficial sexual partnerships.

Roger was seen for thirty-two sessions within a six-month period. The problem was first reconceptualized as an inappropriate response to heterosexual stimuli rather than sexual deviancy. A very goal-directed and hard-driving individual, Roger could trace sources of tension to his busy schedule, his relationship with his current girlfriend, and to his work. He felt that exposing himself and later masturbating provided him momentary release of frustration and "time out" from tension, although guilt feelings typically followed. Hence, the next step involved progressive relaxation training in the office as a self-control technique and a means of interrupting tension-building response sequences.

He was then given cassette tapes of the relaxation instructions and asked to practice frequently on his own, at the same time recording the time of relaxation and degree of experienced calmness. Autogenic training was later used as an adjunct. Roger was asked immediately to keep a daily log of his sexual behavior, describing in appropriate detail the precipitating conditions and results of both desirable and undesirable sexual responses. Consonant with Goldfried and Trier (1974), self-control was emphasized as the rationale for use of relaxation approaches, the home practice, and the record keeping.

Another aspect of treatment involved desensitization to several hierarchies of interactions with females. Key dimensions were imagined females' attractiveness, dress, ages, and interpersonal styles, as well as the extent of imagined interaction. Cognitive restructuring was employed in an attempt to have the client broaden his range of expected positive outcomes.

In-session work was complemented by in vivo desensitization and practice in interpersonal interactions in a manner similar to that described by Arkowitz (1974). On several occasions the therapist accompanied Roger to interaction settings such as the campus snack shop. There they jointly analyzed situations and discussed interactions as the client conversed with other students, particularly females. His perceptions of other persons' styles were examined and alternative perceptions were proposed by both client and therapist. An additional homework assignment asked Roger to monitor the frequency, nature, and degree of satisfaction of his interactions with others. Behavioral contracts were then negotiated which called for him to interact with others with increasing frequency, and progress was monitored.

A technical matter to be dealt with was that Roger had typically only felt the urge to expose himself if he was further than ten feet from the target female. If he found himself within that radius, he did not lose sexual interest, but he was disinclined to act inappropriately. With close monitoring, a technique which combined

*The first author served as therapist in consultation with the second author.

general relaxation and self-instructions to be calm and behave cordially was designed and implemented. In vivo use of this technique, coupled with desensitization to approaching attractive females, eventually enabled Roger to interact much more frequently with women. He reported a corresponding decrease in both his felt hostility and the urge to expose himself. Positive coping imagery was also used during therapy meetings and by Roger when he practiced relaxation on his own. His developing ease in the company of attractive females allowed him to elicit more and more positive responses from them.

Roger's high rate (almost daily) of indecent exposure declined dramatically shortly after the onset of therapy, but he continued to occasionally expose himself. He was trained to analyze situations in which the opportunity for exhibitionism was great and to administer subvocal self-instructions on how to deal with these temptations. Initially, the strategy was to have him masturbate in seclusion (a response already in his repertoire) instead of actually exposing himself. Later, when it was clear that this response had supplanted the indecent exposure, he worked on fixing the sexual image in his mind and removing himself to a more private setting to masturbate. Finally, he was able to either delay responding to sexual stimuli, or to respond in a more socially appropriate manner, e.g., engaging the female in a conversation. This succession of graded steps seemed to be a major facet of the treatment. At each step, associated fears were extinguished as new skills were developed.

Because it was expected that temptations would sometimes override Roger's self-control abilities, a provision was made for him to call the therapist at the Clinic or at his home, or to stop by the office during periods of difficulty. This variant of delay therapy (Meyer, 1973) offered support and served to interrupt the exhibitionistic response chain.

At Roger's request, an attempt was made to enhance his sexual attraction to his current girlfriend. The therapist suggested that Roger substitute an enticing sexual image of his girlfriend for whatever fantasies he might be imagining during masturbation. At first the substitution was made just before ejaculation. Gradually the substitution was made earlier and earlier. Correspondingly, some suggestions from the work of Masters and Johnson were offered to enhance actual sexual relations with his girlfriend. Assertive training at this point also proved helpful. Feedback from Roger indicated success.

Interspersed among Roger's periods of tension were feelings of pessimism and depression, and he would speak in the bitter tones of a cynic. Experiential focusing (Gendlin, 1969) invariably related these feelings to the avoidance of practical decisions which he needed to make. Later in therapy, Roger was well aware of this trap and worked to confront issues in his life more squarely. Another technique involved replaying sections of earlier therapy tapes. For instance, when he occasionally became discouraged and cynical about the treatment, the therapist played back Roger's earlier comments in which he expressed pride in his progress in himself. Much of the last few sessions was then spent listing alternative courses of career action for Roger's immediate future.

Discussion

The authors attribute much of Roger's success to his self-instructing progressively more acceptable sexual and social responses. Meichenbaum and Cameron (1974) have written that "when the standard behavior therapy procedures (are) augmented with a self-instructional package, greater treatment efficacy, more generalization and greater persistence of treatment effects [are obtainable]" (p. 103). The results of helping Roger talk to himself in more adaptive ways were definitely supportive of this claim and point to the need for clients to experience and enhance perceptions of self-control.

At the time this report was prepared, Roger had not exposed himself for at least three months. Rather, during the last therapy meetings and at follow-ups he continued to present evidence that he was actively seeking heterosexual relationships, was optimistic about his potential, and was experiencing enhanced self-esteem and self-control.

Active follow-up of Roger's posttreatment maintenance is underway. For the present, informal monthly checks will be made of his adjustment. While trying to avoid building in failure expectancies or enhancing dependency, the therapist assured Roger that additional treatment sessions would be available in the unlikely event the problem recurred.

In summation, a presenting problem which might have been dealt with primarily (if not exclusively) via aversive conditioning, was handled here with a melange of techniques. Over the course of a six-month active interaction between client and therapist the following techniques were selectively applied: extensive historical interviewing and client expression of feeling; progressive relaxation (with home practice); autogenic training; self-monitoring and record-keeping; environmental manipulation; assertive training; self-instruction; operant and respondent shaping procedures; desensitization (with in vivo exercises); cognitive restructuring; client-therapist meetings in real world settings; behavioral rehearsal; imagery; delay therapy; Masters and Johnson techniques; experiential focusing; joint review of transcripts of previous therapy sessions; active follow-up agreements. These techniques were not applied mechanistically, but rather in the context of a helping relationship marked by mutual respect and commitment to honesty and responsibility. Roger's complex of new skills and behaviors continues to appear more adaptive and durable.

References

Arkowitz, H. Desensitization as a self-control procedure: A case report. *Psychotherapy: Theory, Research and Practice*, 1974, *11*, 172–174.

Gendlin, E. T. Focusing. *Psychotherapy: Theory, Research and Practice*, 1969, *6*, 4–15.

Goldfried, M. R., and Trier, C. S. Effectiveness of relaxation as an active coping skill. *Journal of Abnormal Psychology*, 1974, *83*, 348–355.

Meichenbaum, D. and Cameron, R. The clinical potential of modifying what clients say to themselves. *Psychotherapy: Theory, Research and Practice*, 1974, *11*, 103–117.

Meyer, R. G. Delay therapy: Two case reports. *Behavior Therapy*, 1973, *4*, 703–711.

Comment

Roger was followed for another year after the article was prepared, and showed no return to the exhibitionistic pattern. However, the very high rate of recidivism in exhibitionists indicates that there should always be a very long follow-up. For those exhibitionists who do return to the pattern, a somewhat more radical technique, aversive behavior rehearsal (Wickramasekera, 1976; Simon, 1986) can be helpful. Aversive behavior rehearsal requires the exhibitionist to perform his usual exhibitionistic pattern in front of an audience and/or mirror, and it can additionally be videotaped for later review. It is best if the audience can respond authentically (for example, laughing and comments such as "It isn't really all that shocking when it's only that big, is it?") while at the same time continually questioning and talking to the exhibitionist so that he does not slip into the reinforcing fantasies that usually accompany his behavior (Simon, 1986). Most, though not all, exhibitionists experience marked anxiety during such sessions, and anxiety facilitates the therapeutic effect. In persons who do not experience much anxiety, it could theoretically be increased by bringing people close to exhibitionist (wife, mother, sister) in as the audience, or by chemically increasing anxiety by injections of sodium lactate prior to the sessions (Liebowitz, et al., 1985).

Speaking of anxiety, we now turn to those patterns of disorder in which the central issue is too much anxiety, i.e., the Anxiety Disorders, the first of the sections on specific disorder patterns which comprise the rest of this book.

REFERENCES

Liebowitz, M., Gorman, J., Fryer, A., Levitt, M., Dillon, D., Levy, G., Appleby, H., Anderson, S., Palij, M., Davies, S., and Klein, D. (1985). Lactate provocation of panic attacks. *Archives of General Psychiatry, 42,* 709–714.

Simon, S. (1986) Personal communication.

Wickramasekera, I. (1976) Aversive behavior rehearsal for sexual exhibitionism. In I. Wickramasekera (Ed.) *Biofeedback, Behavior Therapy and Hypnosis*. Chicago: Nelson-Hall.

3

The Anxiety Disorders

Anxiety is a phenomenon that at one time or another is experienced by virtually all individuals in our culture. In the anxiety disorders, anxiety is experienced either consistently or at least when the person attempts to master the symptoms. In 1980, this category first replaced the former neuroses category, which included disorders in which anxiety was presumed to be "controlled unconsciously and automatically by conversion, displacement and various other psychological mechanisms" (DSM-III, p. 39). The reason for the change was the lack of empirical support for this traditional conceptualization. Disorders in which anxiety is not a manifest feature have now been classified otherwise (for example, as somatoform, dissociative, and affective disorders). Further, some disorders formerly referred to as transient situational disturbances are now included among the anxiety disorders in the posttraumatic stress disorder category. Thus, three categories are within the general class of anxiety disorders: phobic disorders, anxiety states, and posttraumatic stress disorders.

The essential feature of the phobic disorders is a consistent and irrational fear of a specific object or situation that results in a strong desire to avoid the phobic stimulus. The individual recognizes that the fear is an overreaction to the actual danger. The three types of phobia are agoraphobia, social phobia, and simple phobia. Agoraphobia, as seen in the case of Agnes in this section, is a fear of being left alone or finding oneself in public places from which escape might be difficult and/or help unavailable in case of sudden incapacitation. In a social phobia, people fear and avoid situations in which they might be open to scrutiny by others. They are afraid of being embarrassed and often avoid such situations as public speaking or answering in class. The simple phobia diagnosis is a residual category of the DSM and is often referred to as a specific phobia. The phobic stimulus is an object or situation other than being alone or of public humiliation or embarrassment (for example, snakes or spiders as in the case of Danielle presented in Chapter 2.) The simple phobia is the most common phobic disorder; agoraphobics are likely to be more severely disturbed.

There are three anxiety states: panic disorder, generalized anxiety disorder, and obsessive-compulsive disorder. In a panic disorder, the person experiences at least three unpredictable panic attacks within a three-week period (not resulting from heavy physical exertion or true actual threats to life). The sudden panic attacks involve anxiety or even terror and are accompanied by four physical manifestations such as palpitations, chest discomfort, unsteady feelings, trembling, and so forth. The generalized anxiety disorder is characterized by consistent physiologically experienced anxiety of at least one month's duration in an adult who does not present a primary syndrome manifesting phobias, panic attacks, obsessions, or compulsions. The diagnostic emphasis is on muscle tension, apprehension, and autonomic overreactivity. The obsessive-compulsive disorder, discussed in detail in the upcoming case history of Bess, is a relatively common and debilitating disorder that is often difficult to treat. This disorder probably fits least well in the overall category of the anxiety disorders since actual anxiety is often not observed. However, most observers agree that anxiety was at least at some point generic to the obsessions and/or compulsions (Foa and Kozak, 1986).

The posttraumatic stress disorders are reactions to psychologically traumatic events that are generally beyond the range of normal human experience and that would elicit symptoms in most people (for example, rape or assault, kidnapping, military combat, and disasters). The characteristic response involves reexperiencing the traumatic event, depressive and/or withdrawal responses, and a variety of autonomic symptoms. Simple bereavement or upset about marital or business problems are considered to be normal experiences and unlikely to precipitate posttraumatic stress disorders. The two subtypes of posttraumatic stress disorders are (1) acute and (2) chronic or delayed. In the acute subtype, the onset of symptoms occurs within six months of the upsetting event and duration of symptoms is less than six months. In the chronic or delayed subtype, symptoms persist for at least six months (chronic) and/or the onset of symptoms is at least six months after the trauma (delayed). These latter patterns have been commonly noted in veterans of combat in Vietnam and are described in the case of the "Postman" in this section.

The first case in this section is the case of Agnes, an agoraphobic.

REFERENCES

American Psychiatric Association. (1980) *Diagnostic and Statistical Manual of Mental Disorders* (DSM-III), 3rd ed. Washington, D.C.

Foa, E. and Kozak, M. (1986) Emotional processing of fear: Exposure to corrective information. *Psychological Bulletin, 99,* 20–35.

/ *Agoraphobia*

The Case of Agnes

He was city-bred and city-oriented, an urbanite in every respect; the so-called great outdoors had always given him an unsettled feeling of inefficacy, as though these sharp open spaces somehow abrogated both his worth and his ability to maintain complete control. A mild form of agoraphobia, he supposed; but there was nothing to be done about it. (p. 170)

— B. Pronzini and B. Malzberg
Acts of Mercy

Agoraphobia is especially marked by an irrational fear of leaving one's home and its immediate surroundings. It is often preceded by various panic attacks (Liebowitz et al., 1985; Chambless, 1985) and accompanied by depression (Breier, Charney, and Henninger, 1984). Agoraphobics often insist that friends or family members accompany them when they leave their "safe" area. As a result, they eventually become tiresome and thus aversive to those around them, which compounds the disorder. Agoraphobia is quite common and is considered to be the most severe of the phobic disorders (Chambless et al., 1984; Telch et al., 1985).

Phobic disorders generally consist of knowingly irrational and unreasonable fears of an object or situation along with accompanying secondary avoidance behaviors. In agoraphobia, these avoidance behaviors focus on situations in which one might be left alone or be unable to attain help from others if some catastrophe were to occur (Sinnott et al., 1981). Agoraphobia is more frequently diagnosed in women, especially those who are in their late teens and early twenties. Sometimes the age of onset is much later, as is the case when a woman who has been an active housewife all her life becomes agoraphobic in response to the "empty nest" syndrome; that is, her children leave home and she needs to develop a new life style.

In the DSM, agoraphobia is defined as the persistent avoidance of any situation, particularly being alone, where people fear they could not be helped or reach help in the event of an "emergency."

The Case of Agnes

Agnes is a thin, reasonably attractive forty-three-year-old Caucasian female who was brought to the community mental health center in the eastern seaboard city in which she lived. Her twenty-two-year-old daughter brought her to the clinic, stating that Agnes was driving her crazy with requests that she accompany her everywhere. Agnes reports that she has experienced agoraphobic symptoms off and on during the last seven years, but the intensity has increased substantially in the last six months. Even when not experiencing agoraphobia, she shows at least a moderate level of tension and anxiety.

For the past four years, Agnes has also suffered with what she refers to as "heart disease." She has often taken herself to a cardiologist, complaining of rapid or irregular heartbeats. The physician always reassured her that he saw no pathology and stated he felt that it was probably a result of anxiety and tension. He advised her to exercise regularly and prescribed tranquilizers for any severe episodes of anxiety. Agnes occasionally uses the tranquilizers, but not to any significant extent. It is interesting that she has never experienced any of the symptoms at home, even though she does heavy housework without any assistance.

The agoraphobic pattern took a severe turn for the worse six months ago during the middle of winter, while Agnes was visiting her daughter. Her daughter had taken her own child to a movie, leaving Agnes alone in their home. There had been a severe snowstorm the day before, it was difficult for cars to get about, and Agnes became fearful that she was isolated. She tried to call her sister who lives in a nearby city, only to find that the phone was dead. At this point, she began to panic, noticed her heart beating rapidly, and thought she was going to have a heart attack. When Agnes's daughter eventually came home after the movie and some shopping, Agnes was distraught. She was lying on the couch crying and moaning and had started to drink to try to lose consciousness. After her daughter had returned, Agnes continued to drink, and with the added reassurance of her daughter, she managed to fall asleep. When she awakened, she felt better and refused to seek help for her fears. In the last six months, she has had other similar experiences of near panic at the thought of being alone.

Agnes's husband, who is a sales representative for a national manufacturing company, spends a lot of time on the road. When he is home, he refuses to listen to Agnes's complaints. But the problem is not as apparent then, since Agnes relaxes considerably when her husband accompanies her on outings. Even though she can acknowledge that her behaviors are absurd and unwarranted by demands in her environment, Agnes is still compelled to perform within this pattern. As is often the case with agoraphobia (Breier et al., 1984), Agnes showed an accompanying level of depression, since she has a sense of helplessness about controlling the events of her world. In that sense, she reflects the phenomenon referred to as "learned helplessness."

Agnes did not have a difficult or unhappy childhood. Her father was authoritarian and discouraged rebellion in his children, though he was otherwise warm and affectionate with them. Her mother was passive and submissive and manifested mild agoraphobia herself though she would never have been allowed to seek professional help for her condition.

Agnes's father had a moderate drinking problem and was prone to whip Agnes's older brother when he was intoxicated. This older brother was the one family member who was overtly rebellious and independent.

Throughout her school years, Agnes was described as a "good student" and as "teacher's pet." She did have one or two girlfriends with whom she could talk to about her worries, but she was not active socially. She did not participate in school activities and was not very outgoing with other students. Because Agnes was somewhat plain in appearance, she was not "pulled out" of her withdrawal by any males who might have shown some interest. When free of school and schoolwork, she assisted her mother in domestic duties.

Following high school graduation, Agnes took a job as a secretary with hopes of saving money for college. She did not make enough at first, and had to remain at home. When she was twenty years of age, she met her husband at a church gathering, and they were married within the year. She continued her work as a secretary in order to help him finish his last year of college. Her husband was stable and undemonstrative and, like her father, was a bit authoritarian. Agnes thus found it easy to become passive and dependent in response to him. She continued to long for a college degree, but never really made any efforts to pursue it. After the birth of her daughter, she had another pregnancy which ended in a miscarriage. This upset her so much that she refused to think of becoming pregnant again. Throughout the early years of her marriage, Agnes was stable in her functioning and only occasionally showed nervousness or anxiety. Yet, as noted above, in recent years she has shown increased problems.

Etiology

A number of factors in Agnes's background make it understandable that she would eventually develop an agoraphobic response. First, she had always been timid and shy; it is probable that genetic temperament factors at least partially influenced her development in this pattern (Kendler, Heath, Martin, and Eaves, 1986). However, the pattern was also greatly facilitated by her parents. Her father was clear in what types of behaviors he expected—he did not want any rebellious behaviors, particularly from his daughter, and was quick to suppress any such behavior. On the other hand, he was affectionate, and his affection was clearly reserved for times when deference to his authority was apparent. Agnes's mother was a classical model for agoraphobic behavior. She was deferent and passive, and at the same time showed anxiety coping patterns that had an agoraphobic quality to them. She also kept Agnes involved in domestic activities through late adolescence, which did not encourage her to experiment with new, independent roles.

Agnes's lack of physical attractiveness precluded being drawn out of her developing withdrawal patterns by attention from males, and her lack of social or athletic interests reinforced her lack of attention from peers. When Agnes eventually married, her husband's similarity to her father's authoritarianism facilitated the promotion of passive and dependent behaviors. Even though she hoped someday to return to college and develop a career, she never made any efforts to bring this to fruition. It is probable that her husband would have quashed this desire.

Agnes's miscarriage caused her first panic-like response, but it was controlled by the structure of the hospital and the sedative medication she received. The miscarriage was a tremendous threat, since it was in the area of child caring that she had found her primary source of self-definition. She carried a fear of reexperiencing this panic, and as a result avoided future pregnancies while throwing herself into the care of her home and daughter. It is interesting that while Agnes's husband demanded passivity in his wife, he allowed and reinforced independent and even masculine behaviors in his daughter. Thus, he was provided with a companion in fishing and golf, which his wife had never considered. This allowed the daughter to escape the cycle that had been passed to Agnes from her mother and probably from other women in the family before her. Her daughter's independence, however, distressed Agnes because it threatened her own sense of being needed. As her daughter became more independent, Agnes became more liable to anxiety, which then channeled into agoraphobic responses. The heart palpitations and slight arrythmias that naturally accompany anxiety in many individuals provided her with another focus for her anxiety. However, she was not classically hypochondriacal (Meister, 1980): she did not seek out a variety of physicians to look at her symptoms, she did not present a wide variety of symptoms, and in general she attended to the comments and advice of her physician.

Once she had experienced a true panic reaction, she was sensitized to anticipate a fear of helplessness, a very frightening feeling. As a result, she engineered a wide variety of behaviors to keep her from reexperiencing a panic. The patterns she developed were initially successful, since remaining at home kept her calm. Yet such a pattern requires giving up much in the world, including the support of her husband and daughter, who increasingly found her behaviors tedious and irritating. As this occurred, she became more isolated, thus coming closer in actuality to the feeling of being alone emotionally and to the consequent panic she feared so much (Fisher and Wilson, 1985; Foa and Kozak, 1986).

Treatment

A number of treatments are potentially useful in dealing with agoraphobia. The specific diagnosis that Agnes received was agoraphobia with panic attacks. Incidentally, it should be noted that some of her behaviors might also have suggested the diagnosis of avoidant personality disorder. But there is very little concern about symptoms in the avoidant personality—the person may be socially isolated and passive, yet seems unconcerned about this behavior and evidences little desire to change it.

Systematic desensitization (SDT) is commonly used with a wide variety of phobias. SDT can be adapted to group treatment and does not require a substantial number of sessions. It is particularly effective for simple, discrete phobias (Wolpe, 1981).

If SDT is done in a group, the experience has the added advantage of providing real-life modeling from the other members of the group. As agoraphobics move through SDT, they may often need assertive training, for the passivity and timidity common to agoraphobia make assertive training a helpful adjunct. Certain of the tranquilizing drugs, such as propranolol and phenelzine, can help control the panic attacks associated with agoraphobia. These drugs are most helpful for individuals who do not initially respond to SDT intervention (Kahn et al., 1986). The use of drugs, however, causes problems with side effects and presents an implicit message that these persons cannot do much to help themselves.

Occasionally, other symptomatology surfaces after the behavioral treatments have dealt with the specific referral symptom. This is not an indication of symptom substitution, because in most instances, the other pathology has always been there. When the more debilitating primary symptoms are relieved, the person can turn his or her attention to other problems. Marital problems and secondary gain patterns especially occur with agoraphobia (Sinnott et al., 1981). For example, Agnes's controlling response toward her daughter is this kind of side effect. Insight-oriented psychotherapy can be helpful in breaking the dependence roles that so often interfere with the agoraphobic's development of new responses.

One of the most effective techniques for agoraphobia is implosion therapy, or flooding (Chambless, 1985; Chambless et al., 1984), in which the goal is to maximize one's anxiety, whereas SDT attempts to keep it at a minimal state while the person gradually confronts the feared stimuli. Implosion therapy is thus ideal for agoraphobics such as Agnes since she already shows a moderate ongoing level of anxiety. Implosion therapists attempt to maximize anxiety and yet keep the person in continued confrontation with the feared stimuli so that the anxiety peaks, or in the language of the behaviorist, "extinguishes." (Boudewyns and Shipley, 1983). A cognitive explanation for the extinction phenomenon asserts that the person has simply discovered that the expected catastrophic events do not occur, even under maximal stimulus conditions. As a result, they become aware that nothing warrants their extreme fear, and they gain an increased sense of control.

Agnes's Treatment.   Agnes was scheduled for an open-ended (no built-in time limit) implosion session. This type of session is standard since it is difficult to predict how long it will take the anxiety to peak. Agnes was asked to imagine different variations of her greatest fears, such as being left alone, being helpless, and going into a panic. The therapist then continually used graphic and vivid language throughout the session to maximize the images in Agnes's imagination. Agnes had been told ahead of time that this technique would bring on anxiety, but she had to commit herself to stay with it, with the assurance that the therapist would be there with her. She did so, and even when the scenes produced intense anxiety, she continued to hold the scenes in her imagination. If she had not done so, the result would have been counterproductive rather than simply neutral. The following excerpt is from the dialogue used in her first treatment session:

> ***Therapist:*** Agnes, keep imagining the scenes just like you have been doing—you're doing very well. I want you to imagine yourself at your daughter's house. It is a cold bleak day. The wind is howling and all of a sudden the electricity goes out. Imagine that intensely. You rush to the phone and pick it up only to realize the phone is also dead. Now you realize that with the electricity off, the furnace will not turn on and it is gradually getting much colder.
> ***Agnes:*** I'm scared, I don't want to see that. Can't we stop?

Therapist: No, remember you must go on and keep these images in your mind. You're feeling colder. It's getting darker and now your heart starts to beat wildly. It's not beating right. You can feel it going wrong. You're really scared now and you know that no one's coming back home.

This type of suggestion, along with suggestions concerning being abandoned as an old person, a lonely death, or having another miscarriage, were suggested throughout the three sessions it took for Agnes to begin to be able to face her fear and make some new and positive steps. Her anxiety peaked and extinguished several times in those three sessions, as more than one peaking and extinction phase is usually required. Once Agnes began to feel more confident, she was included in group therapy and also had a few marital therapy sessions with her husband. She recovered significantly over a period of five months. Though over the years she is likely to have occasional return bouts of at least a mild form of the agoraphobia, her increasing confidence and positive behaviors indicate that she will be able to bounce back and handle those situations.

Comment

Agoraphobia literally means "fear of open spaces." However, the person with agoraphobia may eventually develop an intense fear of any situation outside home—particularly when alone. Agoraphobics often present related fears of dying, fainting, disease, and panic attacks without assistance. Also, more than any other phobic disorder, agoraphobia is associated with other behavior problems, such as exhaustion, tension, obsessive thoughts, headaches, and/or depersonalization. Generally, this disorder has more in common with panic disorders than with the other phobic disorders, which tend to be monosymptomatic and therefore difficult to treat (Chambless, 1985; Fisher and Wilson, 1985).

In Agnes's case, the following factors contributed to her debilitating agoraphobia: (1) a probable temperamental predisposition toward excessive organismic arousal to stress, (2) her mother's modeling of mild agoraphobic symptoms, and (3) her father's contingent affection. Against these historical factors, Agnes's response to the miscarriage in her second pregnancy was her first experience with extreme anxiety. She was frightened by the magnitude of her experienced distress and immediately decided to avoid (with certainty) another experience of overwhelming helplessness by refusing to become pregnant again. The typical mild anxiety that pervades the agoraphobic's life between panic episodes was exacerbated in Agnes's case by her own daughter's independence, which threatened Agnes's sense of being needed. These variables combined with Agnes's limited social development had caused her inability to cope with loneliness and anxiety except through increased withdrawal and fearfulness. Her family's impatience with Agnes's symptoms increased her isolation and encouraged her manipulation of her daughter's affection.

The immediate focus of treatment was Agnes's excessive anxiety, which was successfully treated with implosion therapy. Agnes's anxiety level was allowed to escalate beyond her previous tolerance level so that it would "extinguish" and she could see that her fearfulness was unwarranted. Tricyclic antidepressants were helpful in reducing Agnes's accompanying depression (Breier et al., 1984). Afterwards, Agnes's social skills deficits and dependence were treated through group and marital therapy. The prognosis for Agnes is favorable, although mild agoraphobic episodes are predicted if unusual psychosocial stress occurs. To the extent that she acquires more adaptive coping responses to stress and effective strategies for decreasing anxiety-provoking events, she can be expected to maintain adequate social functioning and independence. However, she is not so likely to attain fully normal and positive functioning as are persons with a simple or social phobia.

REFERENCES

Boudewyns, P. and Shipley, R. (1983) *Flooding and Implosion Therapy*. New York: Plenum.

Breier, A., Charney, D., and Henninger, G. (1984) Major depression in patients with agoraphobia and panic disorder. *Archives of General Psychiatry, 41*, 1129–1135.

Chambless, D., Caputo, G., Bright, P., and Gallagher, R. (1984). Assessment of fear in agoraphobics. *Journal of Consulting and Clinical Psychology, 52*, 1090–1097.

Chambless, D. (1985) The relationship of severity of agoraphobia to associated psychopathology. *Behavior Research and Therapy, 23*, 305–310.

Fisher, L. and Wilson, T. (1985) A study of the psychology of agoraphobia. *Behavior Research and Therapy, 23*, 97–108.

Foa, E. and Kozak, M. (1986) Emotional processing of fear: Exposure to corrective information. *Psychological Bulletin, 99*, 20–35.

Kahn, R., McNair, D., Lipman, R., Covi, L., et al. (1986) Imipramine and chlordiazepoxide in depressive and anxiety disorders. II. *Archives of General Psychiatry, 43*, 79–85.

Kendler, K., Heath, A., Martin, N., and Eaves, L. (1986) Symptoms of anxiety and depression in a volunteer twin population. *Archives of General Psychiatry, 43*, 213–221.

Liebowitz, M., Goreman, J., Fryer, A., Levitt, M., Dillon, D., Levy, G., Appleby, H., Anderson, S., Palij, M., Davies, S., and Klein, D. (1985) Lactate provocation of panic attacks. *Archives of General Psychiatry, 42*, 709–714.

Meister, R. *Hypochrondria*. (1980) New York: Taplinger.

Sinnott, A., Jones, B., and Fordham, A. (1981) Agoraphobia: A situational analysis. *Journal of Clinical Psychology, 37*, 123–127.

Telch, M., Agras, W., Taylor, C., Roth, W., and Gallen, C. (1985) Combined pharmacological and behavioral treatment for agoraphobia. *Behavior Research and Therapy, 23*, 325–336.

Wolpe, J. (1981) Behavior therapy versus psychoanalysis: Therapeutic and social implications. *American Psychologist, 36*, 159–164.

/ The Obsessive-Compulsive Disorder

The Case of Bess

"Eccentricities? What pops to mind immediately were those weird routines—compulsions, I guess you'd call them. Used to drive me nuts watching them."

"Many of them?"

"Oh, yeah, let me count the ways. Shoelaces had to lie flat against his shoes. Going on or off the field he would run by the right side of the goalpost only. First step up the stairs had to be with the left foot. Before going into a game the first time he'd have somebody slap his shoulder pads exactly three times. The long white sleeve of the sweatshirt we wear under our jerseys always had to be visible. He always sat in the last row of the plane—claimed it was safer . . . shall I go on?" (p. 112)

— William Kienzle
Sudden Death

The essential component in the obsessive-compulsive disorder is the presence of persistent and repeated obsessions (images, thoughts, or impulses that are experienced by the individual as a product of external source apart from personal volition) and/or compulsions (commonly defined as ritual behaviors, such as counting behaviors, repetitive checking of the body, or hand washing, again characterized by a lack of volition). Although the obsessive-compulsive disorder is listed as one of the anxiety disorders in the DSM, the direct experience of anxiety is not so evident as in the other anxiety disorders, where simple observation reveals that the person is suffering anxiety (Rasmussen and Tsuang, 1986). Rather, in this disorder, the person avoids anxiety by cooperating with obsessions and compulsions, and anxiety is experienced when the person attempts to resist these behaviors. Even though obsessive-compulsive patterns are at least initially recognized as irrational by the person performing them, the individual seldom goes into a panic experience or becomes blatantly upset in the face of bothersome stimuli (Persons and Foa, 1984).

These obsessive-compulsive behaviors are seen as ego-alien, or foreign to one's personality disorder. In the latter category, the behaviors are ego-syntonic; that is, they are not viewed by such persons as conflicting with the essential aspects of their personality.

The obsessive-compulsive disorder has traditionally been thought to be relatively rare, at least compared to other anxiety disorders. It does not seem to be a clear and consistent pattern in more than 1 percent of the population (Turner, Beidel, and Nathan, 1985). However, this could be because of a lower rate of reporting; people with this disorder control their anxiety better than do people with other anxiety disorders, such as agoraphobics, so they would feel less pressure to seek treatment (Robins and Helzer, 1986). Obsessive compulsives tend to be more intelligent and from a higher social economic class than do other neurotics. This characteristic makes sense, since the minor variants of this disorder, such as meticulousness and persistence, are efficient and productive, particularly in a society that is so taken by the idea of external achievement (Rachman, 1980).

The diagnostic criteria also include the individual's recognition of the senselessness of the behavior, stress when attempting to change the behavior, and difficulty functioning within a normal given role and in various social situations. Although ritualistic behavior often occurs in schizophrenia, the behavior is delusional rather than ego-alien.

The Case of Bess

Bess is an attractive twenty-seven-year-old upper middle class woman. She lives by herself in a well-kept apartment in one of the best sections in town. Yet, she has few friends, and social activities play a small role in her life. Most evenings, she works rather late and then comes home, fixes her own dinner, and reads or watches television until she gets ready to fall asleep. Frequently, she needs alcohol and a sleeping pill to get to sleep. She is an only child; her parents were divorced when she was ten years old. She was raised primarily by her demanding mother, and had sporadic contact with her father. Bess is a successful accountant for a large manufacturing firm and spends a lot of time with her work. She is a perfectionist, but this is generally functional in accounting.

Bess's mother often expressed her love for her and spent a great deal of time with her. At times, it was as if she had no other activities in her world that could give her a sense of meaning. Yet, Bess does not recall the time with her mother as filled with warmth or fun. Rather, her mother focused on activities in which Bess could "improve herself." She was constantly setting up lessons for Bess to take, and they would usually fight over whether or not Bess was really trying hard enough at these lessons. When home, her mother consistently emphasized the virtues of cleanliness and neatness. There was a lot of struggle between them over these issues. Her mother would constantly nag her for not having the things in her room "in order." Bess would work at this task when she was ordered to do so, but the minute her mother turned her attention away, Bess would allow things to get disorderly. Her mother continually emphasized to her that this attitude would hurt her "when she got older," yet she never made it clear how it would hurt her.

Her mother showed an inordinate concern about cleanliness. She would make sure that Bess washed her hands thoroughly each time Bess went to the bathroom or for any reason touched herself in the genital area. Her mother was especially repulsed by the smell of the bathroom and had a variety of deodorants and incense candles available to counteract these odors. Anything rotten or dirty was lumped into this category and was immediately cleaned and deodorized.

Like most children, Bess had times when she felt unhappy. When she expressed these feelings, her mother would immediately try to talk Bess out of them. Her major point seemed to be "I love you so much, and spend so much time with you, how can you be unhappy?" If Bess further expressed her unhappiness, it would quite clearly upset her mother.

Bess enjoyed visiting her father, who lived in a nearby city. He was more relaxed about the world, though he had not been very successful and had moved through a series of jobs. He was generally a happy person and attended to Bess when she was there, though he seldom kept in contact when she was absent. Her mother was never happy when Bess went to see her father and subverted this contact whenever possible. She never failed to take the chance to point out to Bess how her father's "laziness" had brought him nothing from the world and implied that he did not support them the way he should.

Though Bess in various ways resisted her mother at home, she lived out her mother's value system in school. She worked very hard and was meticulous in preparing assignments, and because her intellect was higher than average, she consistently succeeded. At the same time, she was seen as a "do-gooder" and was not popular with her peers. She did not get involved in class activities and spent most of her time preparing her lessons and then doing chores around the house.

She also was quite active in the Methodist religion, in which her mother raised her. This was generally a positive experience for her, though there were occasions when she became very upset about whether she "had been saved" or whether she was a "sinner." The upset usually passed quickly as Bess pushed herself further into her school work or into any activity prescribed by her church for dealing with these concerns. As Bess moved into late adolescence, she became more and more beset by erotic fantasies. She was never totally sure whether this was against her church's rules, but she supposed it was. Bess would try to control these fantasies by doing repetitive tasks or other kinds of activities that distracted her attention. She particularly became a fan of crossword puzzles and jigsaw puzzles. These would occupy her for hours, and her mother was happy to buy her the most complex puzzles available. But occasionally the erotic fantasies arose when Bess had few defenses available, and she would then engage in orgiastic bouts of masturbation.

Bess had surprisingly little difficulty interacting with males as friends, yet she never seemed to know how to deal with romantic and sexual issues. As a result, she seldom dated anyone for any length of time. She did become enamored of a boy at a nearby college when she was a senior in high school. He constantly pressed her for sex, and she would refuse. However, one night she gave in when they had been drinking too much at a party. They then had sex virtually every day for a couple of weeks, at which time Bess began to fear pregnancy. It turned out her fears were well founded, to the horror of her mother when she was told. She immediately arranged an abortion and never really allowed Bess to think out whether this was what she wanted. After the abortion, she took Bess on a trip to Europe, during which time she strictly chaperoned her. When they returned, the boyfriend had found another lover, as Bess's mother had hoped.

Bess slipped into the role of "top student," received many honors, and then easily moved into the consequent role of "up-and-coming young career woman." Her involvement in her job absorbed most of her time, and it was clear that she was a rising star in the firm. Bess continued to have vague anxieties about dating, marriage, having a family, and other related issues. She handled these anxieties by throwing herself even harder into her work. At the same time, however, she began to experience symptoms that focused around the issue of cleanliness, a pattern not dissimilar from her mother's.

This concern with cleanliness gradually evolved into a thoroughgoing cleansing ritual, which was usually set off by her touching her genital or anal area. In this ritual, Bess would first remove all of her clothing in a preestablished sequence. She would lay out each article of clothing at specific spots on her bed, and examine each one for any indications of "contamination." She would then thoroughly scrub her body, starting at her feet and working meticulously up to the top of her head, using certain washcloths for certain areas of her body. Any articles of clothing that appeared to have been "contaminated" were thrown into the laundry. Clean clothing was put in the spots that were vacant. She would then dress herself in the opposite order from which she took the clothes off. If there were any deviations from this order, or if Bess began to wonder if she might have missed some contamination, she would go through the entire sequence again. It was not rare for her to do this four or five times in a row on certain evenings.

As time passed, she began developing a variety of other rituals and obsessive thoughts, usually related to using the toilet, sexual issues, or the encountering of possible "contamination in public places." As her circle of rituals widened, her functioning became more impaired. She was aware of the absurdity of these behaviors, but at the same time felt compelled to go through with them and did not constantly question them. Finally, the behaviors began to intrude on her ability to work, the one remaining source of meaning and satisfaction in her world. It was then that she referred herself for help.

Etiology

One of Freud's primary views of obsessive-compulsive individuals was that these persons were still functioning at the anal-sadistic stage of development and that conflicts over toilet training were critical in their development (Adams, 1985). This theory has some "face validity," or apparent truth, in many cases, including Bess's. However, these common concerns about dirt related to toilet training could occur simply because this is one of the first arenas in which parent and child struggle for control of the relationship. It is also usually the first period in which whole sequences of parental behavior are integrated and modeled by the developing child. Hence, it is easy for these types of concerns to become the content of obsessive-compulsive features. It is also clear that these issues are not relevant to a substantial number of obsessive-compulsives (Rasmussen and Tsuang, 1986).

Obsessive-compulsives usually model much of their behavior from parents, who are typically "repressors." Repressors are sensitive to the "discomfort of anxiety" (Ellis, 1979), and as a result develop numerous coping patterns to avoid that discomfort. Even though obsessive-compulsives do not often report much present anxiety, they usually first manifest it on physiological measures and physiological tests (Rachman, 1980). A common defense against anxiety for the obsessive-compulsive is the use of "intellectualization" (talking around the core issue of a conflict in order to avoid its true impact). This pattern is effective in many areas, such as school and work. But when it is used to deal with anxiety, it is not effective in the long run, as it does not actually serve to gain corrective information (Foa and Kozak, 1986).

Bess's development shows most of these factors. Her mother was a thoroughgoing model for obsessive-compulsive behavior, and Bess had no significant access to other models. Her mother was also adept at inculcating guilt, and voided any of Bess's attempts to dissipate her conflicts by voicing and sharing her concerns and upsets. Bess's pattern of religious involvement furthered the development of guilt, and, as is common with most adolescents, sexual concerns provided a ready focus for the conflicts.

The rituals that the obsessive-compulsive develops serve to keep the individual from fully confronting the experience of anxiety or the feeling of loss of control (Reed, 1985). Bess had long ago learned that involvement in academic subjects not only brought her inherent rewards, but at the same time served to distract her from her conflicts and impulses. She feared that if she gave in to the unacceptable impulses, she would not be able to control her behavior. As a result, she often vacillated between overcontrol of impulses and indulgence, as was evident in her masturbatory patterns. Like many obsessive-compulsives, Bess feared that if she let down her guard and followed her impulses, that she might never again regain control, and "control" is important to obsessive-compulsives. Hence, any activities that distracted her were welcomed. Her obsessive interest in puzzles is an instance of her trying to distract herself in activities that are often pleasant accompaniments to a full life. Her ritual cleansing was another way of distracting herself from the void of meaning in her world and from the anxiety that was always at the edge of her awareness. Yet, as she most feared, she gradually lost control of these patterns and they began to dominate her world to the point of interfering with the area that had always provided meaning and satisfaction—her work.

Treatment

A wide variety of treatments have traditionally been applied to the obsessive-compulsive personality, yet none has achieved spectacular success, since this is one of the most difficult neurotic disorders to treat. This difficulty is probably because the conflicts and anxiety have already been covered over by the obsessive-compulsive patterns (Rasmussen and Tsuang, 1986). Also, such individuals seem to fear the passivity (that is, loss of control) implied by the "patient role."

Psychoanalysis has had some success with the obsessive-compulsive personality. However, the danger with this technique is that the obsessive-compulsive individual has had a long history of using intellectualization as a defense mechanism (Rabin, 1968), and the technique of free association in psychoanalysis easily lends itself to the abuse of intellectualization. Psychoanalysis can be helpful only if the therapist can skillfully keep the client away from this pattern.

Psychosurgery has traditionally had a reputation of success in some cases of obsessive-compulsive disorder, but in actuality it is seldom effective. Medication has occasionally been useful in allaying some of the underlying anxiety or depression while the therapist tries to break through the defense patterns, but in and of itself has not really been significantly helpful (Mavissakalian and Michelson, 1983).

Several behavioral techniques have been helpful. Implosion therapy, or flooding, a technique described in detail in the case history on agoraphobia (Boudewyns and Shipley, 1983) has been used occasionally. The difficulty with this technique is that obsessive-compulsives are usually so well defended that it is hard to get them to maximize their anxiety and experience the peak of the conflict, which is theoretically required. For that reason, most therapists do not choose to use implosion therapy with obsessive-compulsives.

A second technique that has been of help is "thought stopping." In this technique, presented in more detail in the case history of Randy, the transvestite, the therapist teaches the client to use a verbal command (such as "Stop!") to interrupt thoughts or compulsive behaviors as soon as they emerge into awareness. A third technique, not unlike thought stopping, is referred to as "covert assertion." Here, the client is taught to make a strong positive statement declaring that he or she refuses to proceed with the compelling dictates of the obsessions or compulsions. This statement, often in the form of a declarative sentence, is first asserted out loud with the therapist and is eventually used subvocally any time an obsessive-compulsive impulse emerges (Cautela and Wall, 1980).

The fourth technique is "covert modeling." The client and the therapist together construct an imaginary scene in which the client encounters the obsessive or compulsive condition. The client and therapist then also construct an appropriate nonpathological way of countering and dissipating the strength of the obsessive-compulsive mechanism (Cautela and Wall, 1980).

Lastly, "paradoxical techniques" may be used (Seltzer, 1986). For example, the client is asked to go ahead and purposefully proceed with the unwanted thoughts and behaviors, only to exaggerate them. Doing these behaviors on purpose, in varying patterns, seems to give the client a greater sense of control over the behaviors, and therapy can proceed to build upon this developing sense of control.

In various combinations, these behavioral techniques, particularly those that act to prevent the response early in the sequence (Rachman, 1980; Mavissakalian et al., 1985), have proven to be as effective as any approach for this most difficult syndrome.

Bess's Treatment. Bess's therapist chose to start the treatment with thought stopping. She first asked Bess to let the obsessions just flow freely, and to raise her hand to let the therapist know when she was doing so. Some time after Bess had raised her hand, the therapist shouted "Stop" and then asked Bess to examine her consciousness. Naturally, the train of obsessions had been disrupted. They did this several times, and then the therapist asked Bess herself to shout "Stop" whenever she felt herself in the midst of these obsessions. She was then asked to practice this in her natural world as well and was given a small portable shock unit to amplify the effect. Whenever Bess shouted "Stop" to herself, she also gave herself a moderately painful electric shock from the unit that she had strapped inconspicuously under her dress. This thought stopping demonstrated to Bess that her obsessions could actually be controlled. In that sense, it was the basis on which her therapist could train her in new, positive behaviors (Ost et al., 1981).

Bess and her therapist then used covert modeling. They developed an imaginary scene during which, as the feelings of contamination arose, Bess visualized herself first laughing at the concerns. She then visualized herself handling some of the contaminated garments, or even touching herself in the genital or anal area while laughing and seeing herself as confident in the situation. These images were practiced in the therapy hour. She was then instructed always to follow up any thought stopping with covert modeling.

Bess also contracted with her therapist that if she did not respond as instructed, she was to penalize herself by performing one task from a list of odious (to her) chores that she had composed with her therapist. This list included such things as eating some undesirable foods for supper or unplugging her television set for the entire night. Likewise, each time she had successfully carried out her therapy practices for an entire day, she was allowed to reinforce this by choosing from a list of pleasant activities that they had also constructed, such as attending a favorite ballet or getting "the works" at her beauty salon.

Together, these techniques helped Bess substantially diminish the obsessive-compulsive patterns within four months. She and the therapist also continued to work on the void of positive activities in Bess's life. She was in therapy for approximately two years before she achieved what she considers to be an adequate success. Even so, at various points in the ensuing years Bess occasionally experienced a reemergence of the concerns that she had experienced. On one occasion, she did return for several therapy sessions in order to work these through, though she was usually able to deal with any residual patterns by the skills she had learned in the original therapy sessions plus training in new skills to cope with these impulses (Foa et al., 1983; Mavissakalian et al., 1985).

Comment

The obsessive-compulsive disorder is at least initially experienced as a distressing loss of control over one's thoughts and actions and is usually somewhat incapacitating because it interferes with other behaviors and patterns (Rachman, 1980). As in Bess's case, the primary goal of treatment is to get such persons to suspend these actions long enough to find out that the dreaded, usually vaguely conceptualized outcomes will not occur—for example, by the thought-stopping technique that was successful with Bess's compulsions. Another technique that has been successful with compulsive behavior is "response prevention." Response prevention involves temporarily blocking the compulsive response so that extinction can occur; for example, dismantling the faucets in order to prevent compulsive hand washing.

Bess was able to diminish her obsessive-compulsive patterns to a substantial degree within four months. Unfortunately, she had developed obsessive-compulsive behaviors over an extended period of time and in response to numerous situations before they became troublesome enough for her to seek professional help. The resulting deficits in social skills and emotional responsiveness required considerable therapeutic attention; thus, her therapy lasted for two years. Even then, obsessive thoughts and compulsive actions are fairly probable responses for her under stress, and minor patterns still occasionally reappear. They will decrease in frequency and intensity as Bess's emotional adjustment and social skills improve.

REFERENCES

Adams, P. (1985) The obsessive child: A theory update. *American Journal of Psychotherapy*, *39*, 301–313.

Boudewyns, P. and Shipley, R. (1983) *Flooding and Implosion Therapy.* New York: Plenum.

Cautela, J., and Wall., C. (1980) Covert conditioning in clinical practice. In A. Goldstein and E. Foz (Eds.), *Handbook of Behavioral Interventions.* New York: John Wiley.

Ellis, A. (1979) A note on the treatment of agoraphobics with cognitive modification versus prolonged exposure "in vivo." *Behavior Research and Therapy*, *17*, 162–164.

Foa, E., Grayson, J., Steketee, G., Doppelt, H., Turner, R., and Latimer, P. (1983) Success and failure in the behavioral treatment of obsessive-compulsives, *Journal of Consulting and Clinical Psychology*, *51*, 287–297.

Foa, E. and Kozak, M. (1986) Emotional processing of fear: Exposure to corrective information, *Psychological Bulletin*, *99*, 20–35.

Mavissakalian, M. and Michelson, L. (1983) Tricyclic antidepressants in obsessive-compulsive disorder. *Journal of Nervous and Mental Disease*, *171*, 301–311.

Mavissakalian, M., Turner, S., and Michelson, L. (Eds.) (1985) *Obsessive-Compulsive Disorder.* New York: Plenum.

Ost, L., Verremalm, A., and Johnson, J. (1981) Individual response patterns and the effects of different behavioral methods in the treatment of social phobia. *Behavior Research and Therapy*, *19*, 1–16.

Persons, J. and Foa, E. (1984) Processing of fearful and neutral information by obsessive-compulsives. *Behavior Research and Therapy*, *22*, 259–265.

Rabin, A. (Ed.) (1968) *Projective Techniques in Personality Assessment.* New York: Springer.

Rachman, S. (1980) *Obsessions and Compulsions.* Englewood Cliffs, N.J. Prentice-Hall.

Rasmussen, S. and Tsuang, M. (1986) Clinical characteristics and family history in DSM-III obsessive-compulsive disorder. *The American Journal of Psychiatry*, *143*, 317–322.

Reed, G. (1985) *Obsessional Experience and Compulsive Behavior.* Orlando, Fla.: Academic Press.

Robins, L. and Helzer, J. (1986) Diagnosis and clinical assessment: The current state of psychiatric diagnosis. In M. Rosenzweig and L. Porter (Eds.) *Annual Review of Psychology, 37,* Palo Alto, Calif.: Annual Reviews.

Seltzer, L. (1986) *Paradoxical Strategies in Psychotherapy.* New York: John Wiley.

Turner, S., Beidel, D., and Nathan, S. (1985) Biological factors in obsessive-compulsive disorders, *Psychological Bulletin, 97,* 430–450.

/ Posttraumatic Stress Disorder

The Case of Ryan, the "Postman"

I hoped there would be no more surprises. I had survived enough ambushes and doubted my capacity to endure many more physical or emotional shocks. I had all the symptoms of Combat Veteranitis: an inability to concentrate, a child-like fear of darkness, a tendency to tire easily, chronic nightmares, and intolerance of loud noises—especially doors slamming and cars backfiring—and alternating moods of depression and rage that came over me for no apparent reason. Recovery had been less than total! (p. 4)

— Phillip Caputo
A Rumor of War

The posttraumatic stress disorder is a maladaptive reaction to a psychologically traumatic event that is usually considered to be outside the range of average human experience, and as such would seriously distress most people (Pearce et al., 1985). Its characteristic symptomatology involves: (1) the reexperiencing of the traumatic event, (2) a reduction of involvement with the external world (a kind of "psychic numbing"), and (3) various related autonomic, cognitive, and/or emotional symptoms. The traumatic event, such as military combat or a natural disaster, is usually reexperienced in recurring dreams (often nightmares), persistent memories, and/or dissociative states. The distancing from the external world is commonly seen in lessened affect, decreased interest in formerly interesting activities, and/or detachment from others. Additional symptoms include sleep disruption, hyperalertness, guilt over survival, memory or attention disturbance, and avoidance of stimuli that might arouse memories of the traumatic event.

The disorder is sublabeled *acute* if symptomatology occurs within six months after the stressor and lasts only six months. It is considered *delayed* if symptoms develop more than six months after the event, and *chronic* if they last longer than six months. The severity of impairment suffered as a result of the disorder ranges widely, with preexisting personality characteristics apparently influencing both etiology and severity of reaction.

This disorder should not be confused with the adjustment disorder, which also involves a maladaptive reaction to a stressor. In the adjustment disorder, the stressor is usually less severe, more common, and not vividly reexperienced. The posttraumatic stress disorder category was a late addition to DSM-III. However, it has proven to be a useful and valid psychodiagnostic category (Pearce et al., 1985), recognizing the consistent maladaptive reaction processes that follow exposure to atypical and severe stress (Davidson and Baum, 1986). The conflict in Vietnam, and its subsequent effects on the participants, particularly played a major role in the recognition of this syndrome (Boulanger and Kadushin, 1986).

The Case of Ryan, the "Postman"

Ryan, known by his friends in the army as the "Postman," was a twenty-one-year-old Caucasian, first seen by staff psychologists at the Veterans Administration hospital in the fall of 1970. At that time, he quietly stated that he was seeking help at the "request" of his fiancée, who had threatened to break off their engagement unless he did so.

A check into his background revealed that he had been honorably discharged from the army the previous summer following a tour of duty in Vietnam. He had been reserved and aloof on his return home, and his family and friends had simply assumed this was a natural reaction to readjustment to civilian life, noting that he was obviously happy to be home.

About a month after his return, to no one's surprise, he announced his engagement to his high school sweetheart. However, he did raise a few eyebrows by taking a job at a local factory instead of returning to college to obtain his degree in forestry, which had been his lifelong dream. He seemed dissatisfied with the job from the beginning. He worked lethargically, grew irritable at the slightest frustration, and remained detached from his fellow workers. It was also about this time that he experienced his first panic-filled dissociative state.

His roommate, an old friend with whom he shared an apartment, recalled that one night, after a particularly rough day at work, Ryan had fallen into a light sleep in a chair while watching television. After turning off the television, his roommate walked across the room to lock the front door. Just as he shoved home the bolt of the dead lock, Ryan awakened and hit the ground yelling something unintelligible. His eyes were wide open, as he rapidly scanned the room. He appeared to be having difficulty breathing, was trembling, and was sweating profusely. After calming down somewhat, he complained of dizziness and "feeling odd," and swore his roommate to secrecy concerning the incident.

Ryan recalled that in the days following that first incident, his irritability and anger grew even worse and he began to have nightmares. The only people with whom he retained even a semblance of closeness were his family and fiancée, and even those relationships lacked their characteristic warmth and spontaneity. In an attempt to break him out of an ever-increasing depression, his fiancée finally convinced him to join her and his grandfather in a quiet stroll through some of the woods on his parents' property. This was a formerly enjoyable activity, but on his return home, he had up to that point declined to go along.

Ryan remembered that during the walk, after some initial apprehension, he had actually felt relaxed for the first time in a long while. However, when a helicopter suddenly flew over, he dropped to a crouched position, frantically scanning the woods and shouting orders. After getting him back to the house, his grandfather and fiancée watched helplessly as he broke down crying, admitting that this had been the second such occurrence. It was at this point that his fiancée responded to his objections to seeking help with the threat of terminating their engagement.

Ryan's History

Ryan was the oldest of two boys and a girl raised in a small town, fifteen miles outside a large northwestern city. His father was a physician who was already forty when Ryan was born. His mother, eight years younger than his father, dedicated all of her time to her firm though protective upbringing of the children. The family was of "good stock," and serious illness and death were unfamiliar to Ryan as he grew up.

He was polite, bright, and happy as a young boy, and while he enjoyed the company of other people, he also loved being by himself on occasion, particularly outdoors. The family owned several hundred acres, and he spent many weekend afternoons in the woods with his favorite grandfather, who taught him how to hunt and appreciate nature. Ryan also proved to be quite athletic; he lettered in high school basketball and baseball, but never developed an interest in football, somewhat out of respect for his mother's worry that it was "too violent."

By the summer of 1968, Ryan was nineteen years old, stood 6 feet tall and weighed 175 pounds. He had grown into a rather independent yet surprisingly sensitive young man, with an easygoing laugh and a sparkle in his eyes. Though friendly to everyone, he considered himself to have only two or three close friends, along with his steady girlfriend, whom he had dated since his sophomore year in high school. A good student, he had just finished his first year at a state university working toward a degree in forestry when he received his draft notice. Though at the time of his draft lottery he felt that his number was in the "safe" range, he had not anticipated the sharp escalation of United States involvement in Vietnam in 1968. Although understandably unhappy about the two-year interruption in his life plans, he nonetheless accepted the notice as a responsibility he had to fulfill.

Following a tearful farewell and what seemed to him to be a whirlwind training period, Ryan found himself in an Army Ranger unit operating in the Central Highlands of Vietnam. He was a member of a six-man squad that would spend anywhere from four to twelve weeks at a time in the field. Their mission was to make contact with enemy forces, at which point they would engage the enemy or else radio their position for an air strike and fall back. His initial job, as was that of most men newly rotated into such a squad, was radio operator. This position was "inherited" by most newcomers due to the weight and cumbersomeness of the radio, and the danger involved in carrying it, since the enemy would naturally try to knock out the radio to prevent notification of their position.

Two other positions usually "inherited" were those of the "point" and "slack" men. These two men would walk approximately 15 yards ahead of the other four, with the point man in the lead checking the ground for booby traps, while the slack man followed close behind scanning the cover immediately ahead for any hint of "Charlie." It was the position of "point" for which Ryan was being groomed, due in part to the recognition of his skills in the field previously developed by his grandfather. It was also around this time that he was no longer known as Ryan, but rather as the "Postman," a nickname resulting from the quantity of mail he would receive from home, most of which he would carry into the field in his helmet.

In writing home, the Postman found it extremely difficult to find the words to express his experiences, though words such as *scared, cold, hot, wet,* and *lonely* certainly applied. However, one word seemed to sum up the totality of the whole experience: *waiting.* The very nature of the job dictated that something was going to happen, yet there was absolutely no way of knowing when it would occur. Compound this with the knowledge that if the "point" man missed as much as one small clue his next step could be his last, and one can begin to understand the Postman's experience. However, as the Postman tried to explain in his letters, and as did probably thousands of others like him, one had to live through it to understand the nature of combat in Vietnam (Boulanger and Kadushin, 1986).

The only bright spot in his ordeal, if there was such a thing, was a friendship that developed with Winston, a fellow draftee who had been rotated into the squad shortly after the Postman's own arrival. Even though the friendship was based on their mutual respect for nature, it was the rather unusual way in which their respective interests in nature proved complementary that made the relationship special. For while the Postman had all the instincts and knowledge of a pathfinder, Winston's specialty was in the area of botany, his college major. They seemed to enter into almost a mutual information exchange when time allowed, each teaching the other their knowledge.

Unfortunately, this ad hoc nature seminar had an unhappy ending about two weeks after Winston succeeded the Postman at "point." Possibly some aspect of the Southeast Asian flora caught Winston's eye when he should have been concentrating on the ground ahead. The Postman never had a chance to find out; both Winston and the "slack" man were blown apart by a grenade booby trap.

The Postman's withdrawal from reality following the death of his friend proved extensive enough to warrant his temporary removal from his squad for treatment of combat fatigue. The application of the crisis intervention principles of immediacy, proximity, and expectancy (discussed later in this case) had drastically improved the success rate of the treatment of combat fatigue in Vietnam. In fact, the Postman was back with his squad within a week, though his sparkle and spontaneity were gone.

Following his return, the Postman kept himself rather distanced from other squad members. In addition, he strongly objected to anyone other than himself taking the position of "point" for the remaining five months of his tour of duty, even as it approached its end, a time when most men understandably became very protective of themselves. As a tribute to his skill, however, his squad experienced no death or injury related to booby traps during this period.

Etiology

Several key factors were involved in the Postman's development of a posttraumatic stress disorder, the most obvious of which was the nature and severity of the stressor (Davidson and Baum, 1986). Military combat has long been recognized as an extremely stressful experience, and combat in Vietnam proved to be even more so due to the guerrilla-style, hit-and-run fighting. There were no front lines behind which one was safe. Death could come from an unseen sniper, a booby-trapped trail, and even from "innocent" women and children. This was particularly true of action in the field, with survival literally depending on hyperalertness. Such an attitude had to be maintained virtually twenty-four hours a day, for anywhere from thirty to ninety days at a time, particularly in such positions as "point" and "slack."

There was also a certain trade-off in the Vietnam conflict regarding the rotation system that was used. The policy of rotation after twelve months of duty was a factor in the decrease in cases of combat exhaustion during that conflict, apparently as a result of the establishment of a date of expected return from overseas (DEROS), recognized by the service as a clear point at which the stress would cease. However, at the same time, the system usually had men returning home within forty-eight to seventy-two hours at the end of their tour of duty, offering them little in the way of "decompression" from their traumatic experience (Kelly, 1985).

Experience with posttraumatic stress suggests that "decompression" is a natural and necessary process for many individuals following such an extreme stressor (Figley, 1981). Decompression involves a gradual "coming to grips" with the traumatic event and the eventual acceptance and integration of the experience into the self. As with civilian disasters, this process often necessitates a rehashing of the experience, a process which many returning servicemen find almost impossible to go through for several reasons. First, the system of rotation was highly individualized in the sense that a soldier rarely returned home with his buddies, a situation in which common experiences could at lesat be shared and discussed. Second, the swiftness of the return allowed little time for adjustment to the inevitable culture shock generated by moving from the pressures of jungle warfare back into the alternative pressures of a highly technological society. Third, far from the respect and gratitude expected, many returning veterans found themselves bearing the hostility generated by the nation's growing dissatisfaction with the war effort. Rather than offering the necessary supportive environment and listening to the horrors these veterans had experienced, people rejected or at best chose to ignore them. With no outlet for their pent-up frustrations, anxieties, problems of conscience, and emotional confusion, it is small wonder that many such veterans (both men and women) developed, and continue to develop, problems in adjusting to civilian life (Figley, 1981).

As acknowledged in the DSM, predisposing characteristics of the person may play a role in the development of a posttraumatic stress disorder. This often refers to the existence of prior psychopathology. However, in the Postman's case, any predisposing "weakness" probably came from the absence of any emotional or stress "inoculation" in his life history; for example, no threatening illness, his rather protected upbringing by somewhat older parents, and the small size of his home town. Thus, when confronted with the extreme stress of warfare in Vietnam, he lacked a substantial arsenal of adaptive coping methods that might have been learned from lesser stressors and that would have served to prepare him for response to later stress (Kelly, 1985).

Lacking this psychological toughness, the Postman's already pressed defenses had been overwhelmed by the horror of seeing a close friend blown to bits. This shock to his unprotected system was so severe that it forced a temporary "shutdown" of reality processing, with consequent development of an extremely "thick" emotional insulation. Such a defense was probably furthered by his already introspective nature (Feshbach and Weiner, 1986). The cost of such protection was the suppression of all feelings and emotions arising from the incident, particularly guilt. For not only did he experience the common "survivor's guilt ("Why him and not me?"), but he also felt that his own skills should not have let something like that happen. This feeling was reinforced when his guilt-induced claim to the "point" resulted in no further casualties for the remainder of his tour. Thus, he agonized, if he had never originally relinquished that position, the deaths would never have occurred.

Even though such feelings were initially kept out of consciousness, the Postman's return to the intimate relationships with his family and fiancée created problems. The emotional base and depth of those relationships slowly wore through his tough insulation. The return of feelings also meant the return of painful memories. As they slipped closer to consciousness, such strong cues as the sound of a helicopter or a metallic sound similar to the click of a rifle bolt elicited the hidden emotions, much as occurs in posthypnotic suggestions (Brown and Fromm, 1986).

Treatment

The principles of crisis intervention noted earlier that have been employed in cases of "combat exhaustion" in the field also provide an excellent framework within which to treat posttraumatic stress syndromes. In this case, *immediacy* refers to the early detection and treatment of the disorder, with an emphasis on returning individuals to their typical life situations as quickly as possible. *Proximity* emphasizes the need to treat them in their ongoing world by avoiding hospitalization. Lastly, *expectancy* is the communication from the therapist that while the client's reaction is quite normal, it is not an excuse for functioning inadequately—the "sick role" is not reinforced (Meyer, 1983).

Within this framework, the particular symptomatology of a specific case can be treated by a variety of methods. For example, an individual may be taught a controlled relaxation response through progressive relaxation, autogenic training, or any other form of systematized relaxation training, to treat acute panic attacks and chronic autonomic arousal (Foy et al., 1984). In the case of the latter, the concomitant use of biofeedback has also proven helpful. In some cases, tranquilizing medication to be taken "as needed" serves to give the individual a feeling of control while learning other techniques, though any indications of potential for substance abuse place limitations on this practice. Hypnotic techniques may be used in a similar fashion (Brown and Fromm, 1986).

If such clients can be convinced to work on the relaxation training in a group setting, they become aware that others share the problem and they may also begin to discuss the problems in a quasi-group-therapy fashion. This discussion facilitates entry into actual group therapy, where clients may come into greater contact with the sources of anxiety. Specific fears or phobias that then surface can be treated by such methods as systematic desensitization (SDT) (Wolpe, 1958).

An overall supportive atmosphere of warmth, understanding, and whatever empathy is possible is also important. Since the environment to which these individuals return should be similarly supportive, sessions with family and friends can help them understand the nature of the problem and the role they can play in successful readjustment (Figley, 1981). Such a resource was valuable to the development of Ryan's treatment plan (he refused to be called by his nickname after returning home).

Ryan's Treatment.   An alert staff member at the VA hospital to which Ryan originally inquired about help noted his strong attachment to both his father and grandfather, so he referred Ryan to a rather "fatherly" therapist. True to the hunch, rapport was easily established despite the somewhat coercive nature of the referral. After some trust was developed, Ryan was induced to attend weekly "rap sessions" held for veterans at the hospital, which, although painful, did help him to face the memories that he had for so long attempted to suppress.

Both processes emphasized the recognition that the disorder was an understandable reaction and that the resulting anxieties had to be approached and dealt with if a desired level of adjustment was ever to be attained (Greist et al., 1980). Ryan's specific focus eventually turned to his guilt over the circumstances of his friend's death, a guilt that permeated the memory of everything associated with his Vietnam experience. The therapies allowed him to realize that despite the injustice of the deaths, he himself had not failed in any responsibility to the two men killed. The effectiveness of his relaxation training also played an important role in dealing with the generalized anxiety that had resulted from the guilt. Such anxiety is problematic in many cases of a posttraumatic stress disorder, as it often remains despite the recognition of its irrationality.

Another focus of attention at this point were the cues that had apparently triggered his dissociative states. Discovering these to be the sounds of a helicopter or a metallic click, was employed (Wolpe, 1958). Ryan was urged to use a controlled relaxation response in handling his fears and anxieties associated with the particular sound through the progressive stages of (1) imagining the sound in different situations, (2) listening to a recording of the sound, and (3) eventually having in vivo experiences with the source of the sound. This last stage consisted of an actual ride in an army helicopter and several sessions of having a rifle randomly bolt loaded and fired near him. Therapy could not entirely eliminate a fear response to these cues (Mineka et al., 1984), but it did extinguish their ability to elicit a dissociative state. Just as importantly, it showed Ryan a method by which he could adaptively handle such anxiety when it occurred.

Another resource that played a vital role throughout his treatment and subsequent recovery was the supportive, caring atmosphere provided by his family and fiancée. Involved from the beginning, they attended several sessions, both with and without Ryan, to gain an understanding of the problems he faced and to learn what role they could play in his recovery. This served to revive the former intimacy of their relationships with Ryan and also taught them how to be supportive without reinforcing the "sick role."

Comment

The tremendous amount of change inherent in modern society has furthered the possibility of experiencing an event sufficient to generate a posttraumatic stress disorder. As with the adjustment disorder, the use of the intervention principles of immediacy, proximity, and expectancy is helpful, but these need to be bolstered by techniques that allow a catharsis, such as the rap sessions in which Ryan participated. It is also important that the victim be helped back into a network of support systems (such as family) and begin to orient toward the future with new plans and hopes.

For example, at the point of formal therapy termination, Ryan was making plans for marriage and a return to school to finish his degree in forestry. However, he did realize that the traumas he had experienced would likely haunt him to a degree, possibly for the rest of his life. Thus, he was going to continue to make the rap sessions as needed. Yet, he now felt he had faced and conquered the worst times and sensed that he had the family support and coping skills to maintain and further his positive adjustment.

REFERENCES

Boulanger, G. and Kadushin, C. (Eds.) (1986) *The Vietnam Veteran Redefined: Fact and Fiction*. Hillsdale, N.J.: Lawrence Erlbaum.

Brown, D. and Fromm, E. (1986) *Hypnotherapy and Hypnoanalysis*. Hillsdale, N.J.: Lawrence Erlbaum.

Davidson, L. and Baum, A. (1986) Chronic stress and the posttraumatic stress disorders. *Journal of Consulting and Clinical Psychology, 54*, 303–308.

Feshbach, S. and Weiner, B. (1986) *Personality*. Lexington, Mass.: D. C. Heath.

Figley, C. (1981) Working on a theory of what it takes to survive. *APA Monitor, 12(3)*, 9.

Foy, D., Sipprelle, R., Rueger, R., and Carroll, E. (1984) Etiology of post-traumatic stress disorder in Vietnam veterans. *Journal of Consulting and Clinical Psychology, 52*, 79–87.

Greist, J., Marks, I., Berlin, F., Gournay, K., and Noshirvani, H. (1980) Avoidance versus confrontation of fear. *Behavior Therapy, 11*, 1–14.

Kelly, W. (Ed.) (1985) *Post-traumatic stress disorder and the war veteran patient*. New York: Brunner/Mazel.

Mineka, S., Davidson, M., Cook, M., and Keir, R. (1984) Observational conditioning of snake fear in rhesus monkeys. *Journal of Abnormal Psychology*, *93*, 355–372.

Meyer, R. (1983) *The Clinician's Handbook*. Boston: Allyn and Bacon.

Pearce, K., Schauer, A., Garfield, N., Olde, C., and Patterson, T. (1985) A study of post-traumatic stress disorder in Vietnam veterans. *Journal of Clinical Psychology*, *41*, 9–14.

Wolpe, J. (1958) *Psychotherapy by Reciprocal Inhibition*. Stanford, Calif.: Stanford University Press.

4

Dissociative and Sleep Disorders

The dissociative disorders, traditionally referred to as the hysterical neuroses, dissociative type, are characterized by a sudden disruption or alteration of the normally integrated functions of consciousness. This disturbance is almost always temporary, though it may wax and wane, particularly in amnesia and fugue. With the exception of the depersonalization disorder, the dissociative disorders occur rarely, and consideration must be given to the faking of this type of disorder in order to avoid some social or moral responsibility (Schachter, 1986). (See also the case of Frank in Chapter 14).

The various subcategories are: psychogenic amnesia, an acute disturbance of memory function; psychogenic fugue, a sudden disruption of one's sense of identity, usually accompanied by travel away from home; multiple personality, the domination of the person's consciousness by two or more separate personalities (the classic, and in many ways the most severe of the dissociative disorders as demonstrated in the following case of Molly); and depersonalization disorder, a disturbance in the experience of the self in which the sense of reality is temporarily distorted.

There is also a category called other dissociative disorders, which is simply a residual category. The patterns commonly included in this diagnosis are those of persons who experience a sense of unrealness not accompanied by depersonalization and who also show some trance-like states.

It can be argued that the depersonalization disorder, also referred to as the depersonalization neurosis, is not appropriately included in this general category, as there is no substantial memory disturbance. Yet there is a significant, albeit temporary, disturbance of the sense of reality, and thus the identity is certainly affected.

The sleep disorders are included in this chapter since they are analogous to the dissociative in that they also involve an altered state of consciousness. Yet, sleep, though an altered state, is a normal process, and in parallel fashion, the disruptions are usually not as severe as they are in the dissociative processes. There are a wide variety of possible disturbance patterns, and the cases herein deal with the most common and important patterns: Sam—sleepwalking; Ilse—insomnia.

REFERENCE

Schachter, D. (1986) Amnesia and crime: How much do we really know? *American Psychologist, 41*, 286-295.

/ The Multiple Personality Disorder

The Case of Molly	*You want to go where everybody knows your name.*
	— from the theme song of *Cheers* (NBC television series)

No disorder has proven more fascinating to the public than multiple personality, and on many dimensions it is the classic and usually most severe dissociative disorder. Several books dealing with the topic, such as *The Three Faces of Eve* and *Sybil*, have become popular best sellers and were subsequently made into movies. Despite the attention that these popularizations have received, multiple personality remains one of the least understood psychological disorders, in part because reliable reports in the professional literature are quite rare.

The DSM defines multiple personality disorder (MPD) as the presence of two or more distinct personalities within one person, each of which is relatively complete and integrated and maintains its own pattern of behavior, thinking, and social relationships. Each of these entities may be dominant and control behavior at different times or in different situations. MPD is the most extreme of the dissociative disorders. While persons exhibiting psychogenic fugue typically experience only one "switch" to another personality, "multiples" experience many personality alternations over an extended period of time. The alternate personalities generally serve important functions which the core personality cannot manage for itself (Spanos, Weekes, and Bertrand, 1985). Unfortunately, many people believe that MPD is closely related to schizophrenia, possibly because this latter term literally means "split mind."

It is difficult to judge the incidence of MPD. After the celebrated case of Mary Reynolds, described by S. L. Mitchell in 1817, only 76 cases were reported in the ensuing 127 years (Taylor and Martin, 1944). Since 1944, the number of reported cases has increased somewhat, with Winer (1978) finding over 200 documented cases. More recently, Bliss and Jeppsen (1985) have suggested that perhaps 10 percent of all psychiatric patients are multiples, though few clinicians would find this figure believable. Thigpen and Cleckly (1984), as well as Gruenewald (1984), have suggested that much of the apparent increase here may be due to the glamour accruing to both patients and therapists claiming the disorder, as well as attempts by clients to escape legal difficulties by presenting themselves as "split personalities." Of the cases documented to date approximately 90 percent are women (O'Regan, 1984).

An additional complicating factor stems from the very nature of MPD. In most cases the core personality is completely unaware of the alternates, though the reverse need not be true (Osgood et al., 1976). Since the alternates usually have specific roles, they are unlikely to seek treatment on their own. The core personality is often aware of "blackouts" or lost time, but is unlikely to discuss these problems with anyone. When multiples do enter treatment it is often for reasons other than the primary disorder, such as suicide attempts or criminal behavior: the most common diagnoses initially given are major depression and schizophrenia. Most multiples are only identified as such after some extended contact with mental health specialists who eventually observe one or more of the alternatives in vivo (Bliss and Jeppsen, 1985; O'Regan, 1984).

The Case of Molly

Molly was initially seen through a university-based outpatient clinic for a variety of complaints. She presented herself as a very depressed and withdrawn woman of 34, despite being extremely intelligent and artistically gifted. In addition to her depressed mood she reported frequent panic attacks and a host of specific phobias, leading her therapist to initially entertain a diagnosis of agoraphobia (See the case of Alice, the agoraphobic). Molly also complained of many somatic disturbances including frequent and severe headaches, insomnia, conversion symptoms, and anorexia. She also reported a history of two suicide attempts, but was quite vague in describing the circumstances that led up to these episodes.

A number of immediate difficulties confronted Molly. She was in danger of losing her job as a graphic artist, partly because she had missed work on several occasions and could offer no explanation for her absence. In a number of cases, bizarre sketches and drawings had been turned in for the projects to which she was assigned, but Molly denied any knowledge of these and claimed that someone else must have been trying to sabotage her. She was deeply in debt as a result of impulsive buying sprees, though often her purchases seemed out of character. Finally, she was in danger of being evicted from her apartment, allegedly because she entertained too frequently and loudly. When asked about the inconsistency of these behaviors with the retiring, frugal, and conservative front presented to the therapist, Molly became very uncomfortable and offered a vague explanation for her difficulties.

An attempt was made to gather a complete history, but met with a number of problems. Despite Molly's intelligence she seemed to have remarkable difficulty recalling major portions of her life. In some cases she seemed not to be recalling her own experiences, but recounting them secondhand, as if she had merely heard stories about herself from others and was repeating them to satisfy the therapist's requests. A vague history was pieced together at some length.

Molly was raised in a small midwestern town a few hundred miles away. Her parents were in their forties when she was born, and had no other children, apparently because they were rarely intimate. She recalls that her mother was somewhat aloof and uninvolved with the family, often taking weekend trips out of town to visit her own mother and father who lived in the same state. On these occasions she generally left Molly with her husband. Molly's father worked sporadically as a salesman, and the family relied heavily on income from the mother's real estate and stock holdings. Molly remembered little about her father, other than his violent temper and provocative behavior, which attracted considerable negative attention from others in the community.

In public the family were devout Baptists, as was everyone else in this rural community, and thus they attended many church-related activities. Molly's mother remained stoic throughout these assemblies, while the father took part energetically, proclaiming himself a champion of virtue. The church's strictures set a tone of restrictive and punitive child-rearing and allowed few outlets for someone of Molly's developing intellect and artistic gifts. Despite these experiences, Molly presented herself as a devout Baptist.

Aside from church-related activities, the family had little contact with others in the community, the father's strange behavior having alienated nearly everyone. It was this social isolation that seemed to weigh on Molly's mother, for she had been popular and outgoing as a young woman. A promising musician, she gave up her career hopes upon marrying. Trips to her home town took on the character of pilgrimages back to happier times, times which did not include her husband or child. The family was visited on occasion by a succession of the father's relatives, and Molly often observed heated arguments over the presence of these interlopers.

For all of his orthodox claims in public, the father's behavior at home was quite strange. He drank heavily on a daily basis and was often loud and derisive to both Molly and her mother. By watching her mother, the child learned to withdraw from his tirades. He was also sexually provocative toward his wife while Molly was present, often fondling her breasts and genitals while trying to convince her to have sex with him. The mother was quite unresponsive to these demands and seemed totally unmoved by his advances. On several occasions Molly's mother was physically abused, though she would deny that any abuse occurred.

Molly's school performance was erratic and inconsistent with her abilities, even given the anxiety she must have experienced as a result of her home life. She reported that she "must have missed a lot of school due to illness," thus leading to her poor performance, though she did not specifically remember any protracted illnesses. She also noted that her headaches began when she was a small child and often kept her from remembering the lessons at school. She did not get along well, claiming that the teacher and the other children had often accused her of strange behaviors which she did not remember. She felt that they were being unfair to her.

Molly's social development was greatly impaired. She had difficulty making friends, as noted above, and her father often thwarted any attempts she made in this direction. When he felt that she was spending too much time with another child, he would begin to develop new chores and restrictions calculated to make these interactions impossible. He was often critical of the other children and families in the town and would tell Molly that persons outside the family were only out to hurt her. His fears that she would discuss family matters with others often assumed paranoid proportions. Molly eventually gave up any attempts to interact with her peers or to discuss her situation with anyone else. Through high school, her life consisted of school, chores, and hours of solitude spent on drawing and sketching. She did not date at all, though she was a reasonably attractive young woman.

As she neared the end of high school, her father became increasingly ill and eventually became bedridden. Her mother continued to absent herself from the home whenever possible, requiring that Molly look after her father, an ironic reversal of their earlier roles. He became obsessed with the notion that Molly was involved in sexual relationships, though she asserted that she was a virgin in the fullest sense of the word. While the father's illness progressed he became increasingly confused, forgetful, and bizarre. As her graduation from high school approached, the father's control over the family had slipped considerably, and she began to make plans for higher education. While her grades were lacking, her artistic gifts were impressive, and she had little difficulty gaining acceptance into a college art program. Her father died shortly after she enrolled.

Molly's collegiate career proceeded in fits and starts. She did well initially, but was suddenly beset with guilt when she realized that she had felt relieved by her father's death. The resulting depression and self-recriminations apparently led to her first suicide attempt. Thus, after completing only one semester, she missed a full academic year. A pattern developed wherein she would do well for a time, only to find herself slipping, and she would then return home. In all, Molly took seven years to earn her bachelor's degree. She was unable to make friends and still had no age-appropriate contacts with men.

Following college, Molly lived with her mother and tried to earn a small income by giving private art lessons. Her health degenerated and she experienced a number of "female problems." The town physician subsequently identified and treated the root of these problems—a previously undiagnosed case of syphilis. The physician allowed word of her illness to spread, and she was now completely ostracized by the town, despite her vigorous denial that she could have contracted a venereal disease. She subsequently moved away to escape this condemnation, but only after making her second suicide attempt.

At the age of twenty-seven Molly arrived in the city where she sought treatment. Despite her uninteresting job, she found a number of intellectual outlets, including night classes at the university, museums, concerts, and libraries. The less restrictive and intrusive atmosphere agreed with her, and she reported an unremarkable first few years in the city. Eventually, however, she began to experience more frequent headaches, memory disturbances, a number of phobic fixations, and the like. Her difficulties continued and she eventually felt that she might be losing her mind. She occasionally found strange drawings in her portfolio in a style not her own. Likewise, her closet contained clothes she did not remember purchasing and people she did not know approached her and called her by other names. As her difficulties continued to mount she became increasingly distraught and, fearing further suicidal impulses, she sought treatment through the university.

A Changing Clinical Picture
Molly's therapist spent a number of sessions attempting to establish a working rapport with her, but she remained very anxious in the therapy sessions and seemed to be withholding something. While significant personality problems

were clearly present, Molly appeared so resistant at the outset that the therapist chose to pursue some simple relaxation exercises aimed at reducing her anxiety-related symptoms. He expected that this strategy would allow Molly to develop greater trust in the therapist so that they could subsequently address more personal, emotionally-charged issues. Attempts at conventional deep muscle relaxation procedures were ineffective. Eventually her therapist attempted to employ some focused-imagery techniques similar to hypnosis. These exercises required that Molly imagine very vividly a different time and place which the therapist described as soothing and tranquil. It was at this point that their work together changed dramatically.

During the first attempt at guided imagery, Molly was somewhat reluctant, but she persevered and eventually seemed to respond quite well. She reported being able to visualize the scenes suggested by the therapist and appeared very relaxed and comfortable. After half an hour or so the therapist suggested that she try to recall some real images from her past, images she associated with contentment and relaxation. After a few moments the therapist asked her to describe what she was imagining. Molly spoke in a soft, childlike voice and described a quiet summer afternoon playing with a childhood friend. Because this information did not fit with the history the client had given, the therapist asked for more information about this friend, named Ruth. Molly reported that they had been close friends for a few years in childhood beginning when they were each about five years old. Whenever Molly's father had "upset" her, Ruth would comfort her by drawing pictures and reading children's storybooks. When asked why her father did not interfere in this relationship as he did with others, Molly responded that "he didn't know about us." Upon terminating the imagery exercise, the therapist noted that Molly's speech and mannerisms seemed to revert to her usual tense and constricted mode of interacting with him, and when he asked why she had not mentioned this close friend earlier in the therapy, Molly reacted with stunned silence. She knew no one named Ruth, and asserted that she had never said otherwise. She became extremely upset with the therapist and only agreed to return after considerable reassurance.

Recognizing that some type of dissociative process had been involved in Molly's strange behavior, the therapist chose to employ more formal hypnotic techniques in the ensuing sessions. Over the course of several weeks a variety of bizarre behaviors were observed, and on each occasion the client was able to report more details of her history, including extensive physical and sexual abuse. On some occasions Molly seemed calm and detached, sometimes guilt-ridden and depressed, and at others seductive. As her mood varied so did her behavior, including gestures, posture, speaking style, and tone of voice. Molly never appeared psychotic in the usual sense of the word, though she did evidence "trance logic," a failure to think completely rationally that is often seen in hypnotic subjects. After consultation with a regional authority on dissociative disorders, the therapist pursued treatment under the tentative assumption that Molly was, or at least resembled, a multiple personality.

The initial stages of this renewed treatment effort required that Molly be made aware of some of the historical material she had revealed during hypnosis. As on the first occasion that she dissociated, she reacted with intense denial to some of the more distressing aspects of her past. Only after several months of supportive therapy did she agree to continue with exploration of her dissociative personas.

Ultimately seven alternate personalities or personality fragments were identified through extensive hypnotic interviews. Ruth, the childhood friend, was the first to appear. Initially an imaginary friend similar to those many children claim for a time, she served as a distraction from a variety of physical tortures imposed by Molly's father while her mother was away. As the level of abuse and concomitant anxiety increased, so did Ruth's autonomy as a separate psychic entity. While Molly was amnesic for many of the most distressful episodes of her early years, Ruth had knowledge of all of Molly's experiences up to about age nineteen.

Ruth identified Deliah and Deidre, who subsequently made themselves known in the therapy. They appeared when Molly was 9, in response to new abuses, primarily sexual, imposed by the father. Initially Molly resisted his advances, but was beaten and threatened into submission. She eventually tried to minimize her torment by submitting to the father if he would agree not to hurt her. The phrase "I'll make a deal with ya" took on a pathetic tone in their relationship. Deliah and Deidre appeared suddenly on a Sunday morning at church after the father had sodomized Molly the night before. As the minister railed against sexual perversion Molly was overcome by guilt and collapsed, and Deliah, a temptress-child able to forestall this guilt, was born. Her name was derived from Delilah, a figure in the minister's sermon, but modified to fit with Molly's experience and was thus logically dubbed "deal ya." Deidre would then assume control immediately after Deliah had appeared and served primarily as a repository of guilt and remorse. While these alternates all had some knowledge of Molly's experiences and of one another, by this period Molly's dissociative barriers were so rigid that she was completely amnesic for the alternates. She was only aware that she seemed to lose long periods of time. Suddenly "waking up" in situations she could not remember became a common experience. When she first tried to discuss this with adults they suggested that she might be crazy or possessed, and she quickly learned to keep these experiences to herself.

When Molly reached puberty an uncle visiting with the family became sexually attracted to her. One of the unsavory relatives to which her mother had objected, he eventually raped Molly with her father's assistance. (See the case of Charles, concerning child sexual abuse, later in this book.) While Deliah and Deidre had successfully managed the emotional crises arising from the prior incestual contacts with the father, this new insult subverted the naturally developing sexual instincts associated with puberty and provoked a primal rage which transcended their existence and ultimately led to the splitting off of two new alternates, Stacey and Billy. Stacey (short for Anastasia, Greek for "one who will rise again") controlled the body intermittently during Molly's adolescent years. Stacey's primary function was to preserve the intense romantic and sexual yearnings of this developmental stage. A gifted artist, it was Stacey's work which most impressed others, and unlike Molly she learned to paint in oil and to sculpt. Billy, a professed homosexual, served as a protector and took control only when physical defense of the body was called for. This male personality arose as a result of Molly's need to be as strong as a man to defend herself against her father and uncle, but he was symbolically emasculated as a result of her understandable loathing for men in general. Molly remained oblivious to these alternates. When Stacey and Billy interacted with the therapist they seemed characteristically adolescent.

After her father's death, Molly experienced a number of day-to-day problems getting along at college. She was quite isolated and began to fantasize about having a wiser friend and confidant who could help her through these difficulties. In much the same way that Ruth had been formed, Monica soon took shape. In fact, Monica served many of the same roles that had previously fallen to Ruth, and by the time Molly herself reached twenty, Monica had become the repository for collective memory. She was cooperative in treatment since it was her job to handle problems in the most expeditious manner.

The final dissociative split took place following Molly's extended illness at age twenty-seven. Her father had, in fact, died as a result of tertiary syphilis, and he had given the disease to Molly. Because she was amnesic for the episodes of incest, she could not account for her illness. Barbara (which traditionally means "mysterious stranger") arose to handle the condemnation of others in the backward town of Molly's youth, and to manage her transition into life in a larger city. After the stifling intrusiveness of Molly's past, Barbara was careful to ensure anonymity in their new residence. Barbara seemed to be a more worldly version of Stacey, a mature incarnation of female sexuality who was somewhat promiscuous. She preferred one-night stands to ongoing involvements, for obvious reasons. She was stylish, educated, and cultured, and had a large number of friends, none of whom were known to Molly. Her clothes, expensive and chic, filled Molly's closet and depleted her bank account. Barbara eventually obtained a part-time job at a museum and established a checking account in her own name. Unfortunately, Barbara also liked to travel and did so unpredictably. On one occasion she went to another city only to relinquish the body to Molly, who was understandably upset and became suicidal.

Etiology

Dissociative processes are a part of normal functioning, though the propensity for their use varies among individuals. Many kinds of stressful events can produce extreme dissociative phenomena, such as natural disasters and combat fatigue. The extreme manifestations seen in MPD quite often stem from long-term stress associated with severe physical and sexual abuse. A recent study even estimates that 97 percent of the reported cases of MPD involved such abuse, while the remaining 3 percent stemmed from shocking disasters (O'Regan, 1984). In Molly's case there was a pattern of escalating abuse by the father that evidently contributed to the initial personality split. As part of his early tortures, he would burn the soles of his daughter's feet and then lock her in the attic. Punitive deprivation of this sort seems to potentiate a child's need for companionship, often leading the child to invest a great deal of energy and emotion in fantasizing a comforting protector. The mother's repeated absence from the home and inability to protect her child contributed to Molly's need for solace from an imaginary friend. This entity typically becomes the first alternate personality or fragment, as was the case with Molly's production of Ruth.

MPD can also be seen as a learned response within the family. Research suggests that in most instances at least one parent is severely disturbed (Stern, 1984). Molly's father was clearly disordered, though it is not clear what diag-

Molly's Dissociation and Reintegration

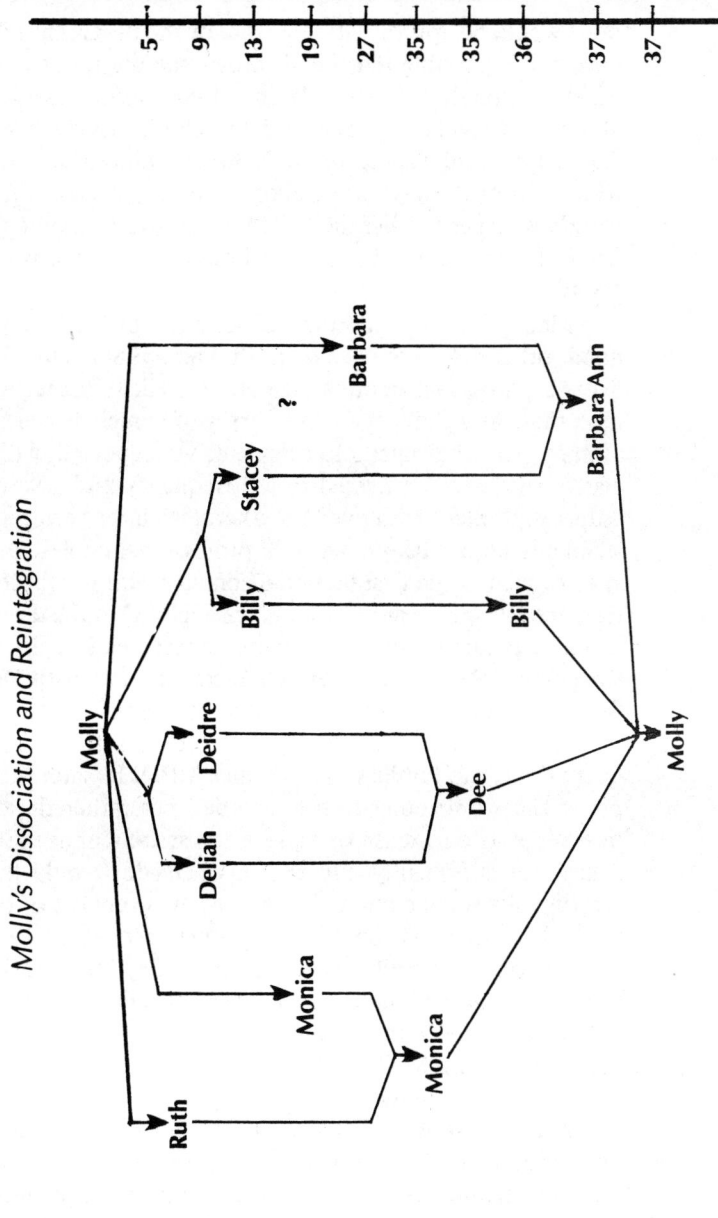

The diagram shows the relationships among Molly's alternates and the order in which they appeared. Chronological order of dissociation and reunification proceeds from top to bottom of the diagram. Numeric values reflect Molly's age in years at the time of each event.

nosis would be appropriate. Because of the progressive degeneration of his behavior it is possible that his disorder was the result of syphilis of the brain,
which eventually led to his death. Molly's mother served as a "facilitator" of
abuse. She regularly abandoned her child, leaving her to a man she herself
feared and avoided. The mother's own withdrawal served as a model for Molly,
who had to withdraw into elaborate fantasy because she could not physically
withdraw as her mother did. The father's overt pathology and the mother's inability to confront it both contributed to the genesis of Molly's dissociative
disorder.

Many multiples report the dissociation of the first alternate in early childhood, often before the age of 6 (Putnam, 1984). This first dissociation establishes a pattern wherein sudden stresses elicit further alternates that arise to
meet these new challenges. In a survey of clinicians working with multiples, an
average of 13 alternates and fragments was reported, with the number of dissociated entities being related to the frequency and severity of abuse. Cases of
"super-multiples" with over 100 alternates have been reported, but are understandably given little credence in professional circles. In Molly's case, sudden
stresses such as the first incestual contacts with her father, rape by a male relative, and the moves away from home each led to the development of new alternates. It is not uncommon for two alternates to split off at the same time,
sometimes with very different characteristics, as with Deliah and Deidre, and
Stacey and Billy. Many multiples also have cross-gender alternates.

Molly's family was deeply involved in a fundamentalist religion, a frequent finding in families that produce MPD. It is not the religious involvement
per se that contributes to the disorder, but rather the perversion of it which
may serve as an excuse or vehicle for serious abuse (Schoen, 1985). Molly's
father was sufficiently odd that his behavior would have come under close
scrutiny in a small community, but his avid support of the local church served
to reduce suspicions about him. In other cases abusive parents seize upon religious dogma as a rationale for the pain they inflict. Molly also received conflicting messages about her identity as a result of the father's religious zeal. In
public he and his family were vocally pious, in private they were secretive and
perverse, leading Molly to have intense identity confusion that may also have
contributed to her dissociations.

Many persons find it difficult to imagine the underlying mechanism of
dissociation. It seems implausible that truly distinct personalities could share
the same neural patterns. The most promising explanation for this phenomenon appears to be a state dependent learning (SDL) model. An organism's
state at any given time is a function of conditions in the environment as well as
physical and psychological conditions. Information learned under certain conditions is best recalled in the exact same state, and may be inaccessible under a
different state. It is hypothesized (Braun, 1985) that dissociation is an extreme
form of SDL. Multiples may acquire memories and behaviors while in a state
of extreme stress, and are later amnesic for this information while in a more

normal state. Once the stressful state is reinstituted, the memories and behavior return, and may appear to belong to a different person. This model would help explain why alternate personalities tend to be very emotionally responsive, while the core personality seems affectively blunted or drained. It would also explain why alternates seem to have specific functions and tend to appear only in situations which call for that function.

Treatment

The classical treatment approach with MPD makes extensive use of hypnotic techniques (Edmonston, 1986; Gruenewald, 1984). Because hypnosis is often viewed as a structured or purposeful form of dissociation, it can help to make the transition from one alternate or ego state to another more predictable and manageable. An alternative explanation holds that hypnosis merely produces a placebo effect, giving the client a rationale to give up dissociative symptoms. The usual strategy is to elicit each of the alternates and discover their peculiar memories and characteristics to gain a working knowledge of the elaborately divided self-system of the client. Next, the therapist negotiates with each alternate for some kind of therapy contract. This process often meets with considerable resistance, because some alternates may be very hostile, destructive, or negativistic, while others may be immature, egocentric, or seductive toward the therapist. Eventually, each must be convinced that they stand to gain from being integrated into a whole person.

The process of "fusion," or joining of two or more alternates, is often dramatized in popular accounts of MPD. It can be seen as a more elaborate effort to help the client reconcile conflicting motives and ideas, as is common in many types of therapy. Hypnosis may be used to contact the alternates and encourage them to become active at the same time. Some clinicians make videotapes of the alternates and show them to one another during a waking state. The order of fusion generally follows two patterns. Alternates that dissociated at the same time or serve similar roles are brought together first. The therapist then attempts to reconcile remaining personality fragments with the core personality in roughly the order in which they split off. This process may involve hypnotic age regression of the core personality to the appropriate time period.

While some therapists have attempted to use antipsychotic drugs in treating multiples, these efforts have had limited success (Putnam, 1984). Antianxiety medications may be useful during periods of extreme stress as the process of fusion is underway.

Molly's Treatment. As noted above, the therapist began to use hypnotic methods to seek out and meet each of the alternates. Like many multiples, Molly was completely unaware of their existence and initially resisted this explanation for her strange experiences. Fortunately, Ruth and Monica served as "memory trace" alternates who together had memories for Molly's entire life, as well as the relationships among all of the other alternates. Ruth and Monica readily agreed to participate in a treatment aimed at merging all of the personalities into one. As a first step, a journal or diary was instituted, with each personality agreeing to make brief notations in it when in control of the body. This information served to reassure Molly that she was not a raving lunatic during her amnesic periods, and convinced her that the alternates were legitimate parts of herself. It also allowed the therapist to anticipate problems and negotiate solutions. For example, Stacey spent her time with a rowdy group of teenagers and liked to host parties at Molly's apartment, hence her difficulties with the landlord. When she made entries about these parties, it became possible to negotiate for behavior that wouldn't create problems for Molly.

Ruth and Monica seemed to merge spontaneously over a number of months, in part due to hypnotic exercises, and in part as a result of increasing knowledge of one another through the journal and discussions with the therapist. This combined entity continued to use Monica's name.

Deliah and Deidre seemed logical targets for fusion, but were quite resistive. Deliah felt no need to experience the painful affect that Deidre carried with her, and found it difficult to relate to the therapist without being seductive. Likewise, Deidre could not accept Deliah's immorality. They were eventually convinced that each could benefit from the other, and would be better able to effect their wishes in the real world if they cooperated. They were henceforth known as Dee.

In a sense, Stacey, Billy, and Barbara formed a triangle with Stacey connecting the other two. Though Stacey and Billy dissociated at the same time, the therapist chose to work toward merging Stacey with Barbara first. Barbara was the eldest alternate and had the most pleasing life style when dominant. She was thus likely to be most resistant to merging with Molly. She had more in common with Stacey than with any other alternate, and it was thought that this merger would lessen her resistance, an expectation that was borne out through the therapy. This hybrid alternate announced herself as Barbara Ann (from Barbara and Anastasia).

Through the journal, videotapes, and therapist's reports, Molly heard details of her history of abuse and neglect, but seemed strangely unaffected by them. This lack of affect continued when Monica and Molly were in the process of merging. The new Monica knew the details of Molly's life, but seemed emotionally detached from the traumatic episodes. When attempts to merge Dee with Molly were undertaken, the situation changed dramatically. The reacquisition of the memories themselves was extremely traumatic, and Molly required daily therapy sessions for several weeks to manage the anguish she felt. Similar problems were encountered in working with Billy and the new Molly. Integrating this much more complete Molly with Barbara Ann was anticlimactic. The new Molly was a much stronger, more assertive, and more respectable person than before, and Barbara Ann, for all her alluring mystery, felt a need for a full history and identity. Molly perceived Barbara Ann as beautiful, educated, and talented and was clearly in favor of acquiring these traits for herself. They merged gradually with little difficulty.

Of course, none of this integrative process was as simple as it sounds. The client's experience was of a gradual weakening of the dissociative barriers that had divided her previously. Ultimately, Molly came to realize that the very disparate motifs represented by the alternates were not foregone at all but natural parts of her own psyche. She was clearly one person with all the thoughts, feelings, and competencies of the alternates expressed through her simultaneously. Therapy continued for several months longer and focused on dealing with the collected trauma of Molly's life. Eventually, she came to recognize that her multiplicity was, in a sense, an achievement, since it allowed her to preserve the best parts of herself in the face of a life that could have destroyed her.

Molly completed a master's degree in fine arts at the university and eventually left her job at the graphics company. She now is a freelance artist, working in oils as Stacey had. She enjoys traveling and she goes to exotic places to find new subjects. Molly now identifies herself as an agnostic. She has had several brief but emotionally satisfying lesbian affairs and reports that she is still unable to form close attachments to men. She has had no major dissociative experiences for over two years.

Comment

The reader will note that the above account does not address the issue of the "reality" of MPD as a clinical entity. Many clinicians have noted that MPD can often be an iatrogenic disorder, one that is superimposed on a variety of amorphous complaints by the therapist's suggestions that multiplicity would explain the client's condition (Gruenewald, 1984). Since many of these persons are frightened by their experiences, they might be particularly vulnerable to such suggestions.

A second reason for skepticism stems from the occasional attempts of malingerers to escape criminal responsibility by presenting themselves as "split personalities." In this regard it is important to note that such a deception is extremely difficult to perpetrate. Kenneth Bianchi, one of the "Hillside stranglers," was eventually identified as a gifted faker attemping to present himself as a multiple to establish an insanity defense. For more information on malingering and psychological methods of detecting deception, see the case of Frank in this volume.

When malingerers fake MPD, they do so to mislead others, but in Molly's case there were no identifiable motives for her to present herself as a multiple. Some clinicians have suggested that hysterical clients might mislead themselves into believing that they are multiples. From a practical standpoint, Molly's therapist felt that the distinction between a "real" multiple, and someone who merely believed herself to be one was unimportant, if not meaningless. Because the MPD conceptualization led to successful treatment, it was deemed useful and appropriate in this case. Obviously, therapists should use caution to guard against saddling their clients with a diagnosis of MPD if at all possible (Spanos et al., 1985).

Most clinicians accept the notion of MPD in principle, but would argue that this disorder is very rare and difficult to diagnose (Osgood et al., 1976; Thigpen and Cleckley, 1984). Recent interest in MPD and the tremendous rise in reports have stemmed primarily from the work of a dozen clinicians and researchers who have a great deal of their professional identity invested in the concept. Our knowledge of this puzzling disorder would be greatly enhanced by increased involvement of mainstream psychologists and psychiatrists who could bring more diverse perspectives to bear on the problem.

Finally, it is important to note the recent attention which has accrued to the problem of child abuse. Given the likely etiological link between abuse and MPD, it is appropriate for clinicians to pay more attention to dissociative phenomena in childhood (Kluft, 1984).

REFERENCES

Bliss, E. and Jeppsen, E. (1985) Prevalence of multiple personality among inpatients and outpatients. *American Journal of Psychiatry, 142* (2), 250.

Braun, B. (1984) Towards a theory of multiple personality and other dissociative phenomena. *Psychiatric Clinics of North America, 7* (1), 171.

Edmonston, W. (1986) *The Induction of Hypnosis.* New York: John Wiley.

Gruenewald, D. (1984) On the nature of multiple personality: Comparison with hypnosis. *The International Journal of Clinical and Experimental Hypnosis, 32,* 170-190.

Kluft, R. (1984) Treatment of multiple personality disorder. *Psychiatric Clinics of North America, 7* (1), 9.

Mitchell, S. (1817) Mary Reynolds: a case of double consciousness. *Transactions of the College of Physicians of Philadelphia.* Third Series, 10, 1888.

O'Regan, B. (1984) Multiple personality—Mirrors of a new model or mind? *Institute of Noetic Sciences Investigations, 1* (3, 4), 1.

Osgood, C., Luria, Z., Jeans, R., and Smith, A. (1976) The three faces of Evelyn: A case report. *Journal of Abnormal Psychology, 85,* 247-286.

Putnam, G. (1984) The psychophysiologic investigation of multiple personality disorder: A review. *Psychiatric Clinics of North America, 7,* 31-39.

Schoen, E. (1985) *Religious Explanations: A Model From the Sciences,* Durham, N.C.: Duke University Press.

Spanos, N., Weekes, J. and Bertrand, L. (1985) Multiple personality: A social psychological perspective. *Journal of Abnormal Psychology, 94,* 362-376.

Stern, C. (1984) The etiology of multiple personalities. *Psychiatric Clinics of North America, 7* (1), 149.

Taylor, W. S., and Martin, M. (1944) Multiple personality. *Journal of Abnormal Psychology, 39,* 281.

Thigpen, C. and Cleckley, H. (1984) On the incidence of multiple personality. *The International Journal of Clinical and Experimental Hypnosis, 32,* 63.

Winer, D. (1978) Anger and dissociation: A case study of multiple personality. *Journal of Abnormal Psychology, 87,* 368.

/ *Sleep Disorders*

The Cases of Sam and Ilse

The little girl did not want to go to sleep in a neighbor's house unless the bedroom door was left open. "Why, you're not afraid of the dark — a big girl like you?" the neighbor teased.

"Yes, I am," the little girl cried.

"But you're not afraid of the dark at your house."

"I know," answered the little girl, "but that's my dark."

— Anonymous story

Sleep is a most important event. An altered state of consciousness, and in that sense analogous to the dissociative disorders, sleep restores us physiologically and psychologically. Indeed, studies indicate that those who sleep less than four hours a night are 180 percent more likely than average to die at an early age, and paradoxically, those who sleep ten hours or more are 80 percent more likely to die early. Those who do sleep regularly spend approximately 3,000 hours a year in bed.

Yet, we all differ in our sleep patterns. People of the same age may sleep for varying lengths of time, at various times, while still falling within the normal range. People sleep for different lengths of times at different ages. Newborns need from thirteen to sixteen hours of sleep, and after that the need, on the average, starts to decrease so that those who are past 50 years of age need about seven hours. Also, we require more sleep when we are sick, stressed, or have been involved in strenuous activities, and women need more during menstruation and pregnancy (Gackenbach, 1985; Guilleminault, 1981).

There is great variety in sleep disorders, just as there is in normal sleep patterns. There had been little recognition of sleep disorders in the DSMs until DSM-III-R, which included a number of patterns including sleepwalking, several types of insomnia, narcolepsy, sleep and dream terror disorders, and disorders of the sleep-wake cycle.

We will now present two cases that detail three of the most important and common patterns: the sleepwalking disorder in the first case and chronic insomnia and disruption of the sleep/wake cycle in the second. The first case, of Sam, focuses on sleepwalking.

Little or no research has been done on the control of sleepwalking, though as early as 1968, Silverman and Geer eliminated one patient's nightmares by systematic desensitization (SDT). Most people do not view sleepwalking as more than an unavoidable nuisance. Even in the case presented, it was not the sleepwalking per se that was the problem, since the patient had walked in his sleep at a regular and high rate for nine years.

The Case of Sam

It is no small art to sleep: to achieve it one must keep awake all day.

— Friedrich Nietzsche
Thus Spake Zarathustra

Sam, a 24-four-year-old white male, came in at the instigation of his wife. During a recent act of sleepwalking he took down a shotgun, loaded it, and prepared to fire at imaginary burglars. His wife awakened to find herself looking into the end of the gun. Luckily, her screaming did not stimulate him to fire, but rather woke him up. She insisted that he see someone the very next day. He had previously walked in his sleep four to five times per week without incident ever since he was 15 years old. His wife had tolerated this, and only occasionally complained of being awakened by his fumbling about.

All indications from talking to Sam and his wife were that Sam had a very normal and happy childhood. He had no more than the usual childhood diseases, was obviously loved and well cared for by his parents, and never showed any childhood maladjustment.

Sam did casually mention that since his first year of college he had always suffered anxiety before taking tests and had resorted to tranquilizers with little success. He said he was now becoming more anxious as time loomed for his bar examination.

Etiology

There is no indication that psychological disorder is common in the background of persons with a sleepwalking disorder (Guilleminault, 1981; Webb, 1968). However, as with Sam, episodes become more frequent when the person is under stress or is fatigued. Though it was the dangerous incident with the shotgun that brought Sam to treatment, other aggressive or destructive incidents were never observed in Sam's history. Such incidents seldom happen with sleepwalkers.

Similar to Sam's, most sleepwalking episodes usually last anywhere from a couple of minutes to forty minutes. Episodes usually occur in the nonrapid eye movement (NREM) period, that component of sleep that typically contains the EEG delta activity (sleep stages 3 and 4).

Sleepwalkers often just sit up, make a few movements, and then go back to sleep—only on certain occasions do they proceed to actual walking. When they do walk, they show a blank stare (which can appear eerie or frightening), are poorly coordinated, can see and maneuver around objects, and usually are amnesic for the experience, which is the dissociative component.

Sleepwalking usually begins and is most common in childhood, and approximately 15–20 percent of the population have sleepwalked at least once. There may be a genetic component, since the disorder does tend to run in families, and it is more common in males (Guilleminault, 1981; Gackenbach, 1985).

Treatment

Relaxation techniques were first employed (Kazdin, 1984), especially as there seemed to be a possible relationship of the gun incident to the test anxiety. A seven-item hierarchy of anxiety-arousing situations was agreed upon, ranging from "hearing about a friend who has a test" through "trying to study several days before the tests," up to the most anxiety-including item—"receiving the test paper and looking it over."

Sam said his wife was a light sleeper and often awakened during the sleepwalking because her bed was close to his, and the only exit from his bed was along a narrow aisle between the beds. He agreed to have her bed moved into contact with his so that he would have to wake her by crawling over her. His wife purchased a loud whistle, which she was instructed to keep by the bed and to blow anytime she was awakened by his sleepwalking. She was to chart each act of sleepwalking and how long it took him to react to the whistle.

Since Sam's bar exam was one month away, he was seen twice a week for SDT. (Kazdin, 1984; see also the case of Danielle in Chapter 2.) He was seen for a total of ten sessions (five weeks). In the meantime, he had dismantled the firing pin of his shotgun.

Sam sleepwalked four times during the first week. His wife immediately blew the whistle and woke him. He sleepwalked five times the second week, twice the third, and no more from the fourth week on. He had no negative reaction to the whistle.

During the first week, he was still unable to study effectively. However, in the second week he accomplished the amount of studying he felt necessary. This change persisted, and there was a minimum of felt anxiety. He passed his bar exam with a mark somewhat higher than he expected even under optimal conditions.

At a three-month follow-up he reported he had walked in his sleep twice more, but each time when his wife had blown the whistle he had awakened immediately. At a one-year follow-up, he reported only two more such incidents. He had had no problem studying or concentrating in his law work.

We now turn to an even more common problem, insomnia and the disruption of the sleep cycle.

The Case of Ilse

*Mr. Answer Man, what is the existential equiva-
lent of infinity? Why, insomnia, Sandy, good old
insomnia.*

— Norman Mailer
Of a Fire on the Moon

Ilse is 42 years old, and has two well-adjusted children, ages 21 and 19. The older
is married and lives across town from her and the younger is a sophomore at the
state university some ninety miles from the medium-sized eastern seaboard city
where Ilse lives.

Ilse had married while in college, and almost immediately became pregnant
with the first child. She finished her B.S. and R.N. degrees. The marriage had its
problems but had been generally satisfying to her and lasted until Ilse was 34. At
that time her husband rather abruptly announced that he had become involved
with another woman and did not want to continue the marriage.

Ilse was shattered by this, but within a year had recovered. She had been
working part-time as a nurse, but immediately took a full-time job. As the children
grew older, she added some occasional part-time jobs, and with the aid of child
support and judicious investing, has become financially stable. She has developed
a wide range of outside interests, and a number of good, close friends, and would
generally be considered happy by both herself and her friends.

However, since adolescence Ilse has been troubled by occasional bouts of
disturbed sleep, and they have bothered her increasingly over the last several
years. Most often, she will go to sleep without much trouble, awakening after
ninety minutes or so. She then is unable to get back to sleep very easily, sometimes
going the rest of the night without any decent sleep. On certain other occasions,
she was unable to get to sleep in the first place, and spent the night moving about,
getting only snatches of sleep. Also, during especially stressful periods in her life
(change of work hours, problems with her boyfriend or one of her children), she
would have a nightmare, often awakening with a scream from a vivid and frightening nightmare, usually shaking and in a cold sweat.

She consulted with her physician, an internist. She gave her an array of physical tests, told her she was fine, and gave her a prescription for some sleeping pills
that she advised her to take only if she needed them. They were useful when she
took one on a particularly stressful night before leaving town on a long trip. But Ilse
would occasionally take them for a number of nights in a row. They would knock
her out the first night or two, then would do little more than make her sleep deeply
for three or four hours, after which she had even more consistent difficulty returning to sleep than she had experienced before using the pills.

She returned to her internist, who told her there was really nothing more that
she could do, and she referred Ilse to a neurologist. The neurologist gave her several other tests, told her she was fine, and prescribed another brand of sleeping
pill, with much the same result as before.

Ilse was disappointed and upset, and she tried several techniques which she
had read about in nursing journals. Unfortunately, she was also siphoning off a few
sleeping pills at a time for her own use from the patients on the general medicine
ward where she was a supervisor, and occasionally she took these for a few nights

in a row. Almost nothing helped here, probably because she was constantly mixing pills and techniques with no rhyme or reason.

The sparse follow-up data available suggests that Ilse's problems continued. From her own perspective, she is likely to see her problems as worsening, since she will need somewhat less sleep anyway as the years go by. It's regrettable that Ilse's case occurred before clinics specifically designed to treat sleep disorders became more common. It's very likely that if she could have been referred to one, the outcome would have been more positive. Such clinics would have given Ilse advice and counseling much like the following.

Treatment

Though Ilse has occasionally experienced nightmares, the primary issues are her delayed- or advanced-phase sleep cycle disorder (awakening after three to four hours of sound sleep and having problems going back to sleep) and her insomnia (the inability to get to sleep in the first place). Though such sleep disorders can be secondary to other psychopathology, or caused at least in part by external issues such as allergies, aging, alcohol, types of food eaten, or side-effects of medications (Gackenbach, 1985; Grant and Reed, 1985; Bootzin, Engle-Friedman, and Hazlewood, 1983), none of this appears to apply to Ilse.

The humorist and old-time movie star W. C. Fields once said that the best way to get a good night's sleep was to go to bed. He should have added "at a regular time every night, and within a regular routine." He should have also advised that if you do not fall asleep within fifteen to thirty minutes to get up, and only come back to bed when you actually feel sleepy. The important point is to consistently associate the bed with falling asleep. People with problems like Ilse's should not work in bed or read or watch TV for long periods of time. They should establish a set routine and stay with it.

A sleep clinic would then have looked at other issues with Ilse. After an initial interview and review of medical records, a physical exam and a battery of questionnaires and psychological tests are given, along with a polysomnogram. A polysomnogram, through electrodes attached to the face and head during an actual sleep period, records brain waves, muscle movements, and eye movements, the data from which helps pinpoint any abnormalities. If no great abnormality is located, then eating, exercise, and napping patterns are considered, and suggestions for other potentially useful techniques are made.

As noted above, the first goal would be to help somone like Ilse establish a regular bedtime routine. Regarding eating patterns, Ilse would be advised that a late heavy meal often has a negative effect, but a small portion of certain types of food at bedtime is positive for most people. Specifically, foods that are high in the amino acid 2-tryptophan (such as milk products, poultry, tofu, and eggs) have been found to aid sleep. Sweet, starchy foods high in natural carbohydrates, such as bread, bananas, and figs help liberate the 2-tryptophan. The process is even further facilitated by a small portion of foods high in both fat and carbohydrates, e.g., peanuts, Brazil nuts, and avocados.

Napping and exercise patterns also need to be assessed. Napping has been defined as an unconscious twenty-five-minute rest without pajamas, and it does seem to be an aspect of the body's natural biorhythms (Webb, 1986). It does help those who need it to catch up on their sleep, but naps late in the day can facilitate an insomniac pattern.

People who get little or no vigorous exercise are more prone to insomnia and sleep cycle disorders. Good vigorous exercise three or four times a week helps develop more restful sleep patterns, and it is even better if it is carried out in the late afternoon or early evening.

Other techniques have been found useful with certain people: (1) a warm bath before bed; (2) yoga or other slow stretching exercises; (3) slow, repetitively melodic music; (4) repetitive sound, such as white noise; (5) a distracting, repetitive internal dialogue ("counting sheep"); (6) certain herb teas—catnip, scullcap; kava-kava, periwinkle; (7) use of certain vitamins, especially the B vitamins and calcium and potassium. Relaxation training and/or biofeedback training may also be instituted by a therapist, and possibly psychotherapy can reduce the stress and conflicts that lead to sleep disruptions similar to those that Ilse experienced (Patterson, 1986).

REFERENCES

Bootzin, R., Engle-Friedman, M., and Hazlewood, L. (1983) Sleep disorders and the elderly. In P. Lewinsohn and L. Teri (Eds.) *Clinical Geropsychology*. New York: Pergamon.

Grant, I. and Reed, R. (1985) Neuropsychology of alcohol and drug abuse. In A. Alterman (Ed.) *Substance Abuse and Psychopathology*. New York: Plenum.

Gackenbach, J. (Ed.) (1985) *Sleep and Dreams: A Sourcebook*. New York: Garland Press.

Guilleminault, C. (1981) *Disorders of Sleep and Waking*. Reading, Mass.: Addison-Wesley.

Kazdin, A. (1984) *Behavior Modification in Applied Settings*. Homewood, Ill.: Dorsey.

Patterson, C. (1986) *Theories of Counseling and Psychotherapy*. New York: Harper & Row.

Silverman, I., and Geer, J. (1968) The elimination of a recurrent nightmare by desensitization of a related phobia. *Behavior Research and Therapy*, *6*, 109–111.

Webb, W. (1986) Personal communication.

5

The Somatoform Disorders

Persons with somatoform disorders, like those with the factitious disorder (see Chapter 14), manifest complaints and symptoms of apparent physical illness for which there are no demonstrable organic findings to support a physical diagnosis. Thus, an accurate diagnosis in this group of disorders can be difficult (Robins and Helzer, 1986). However, the symptoms of the somatoform disorders are not under voluntary control, as are those of the factitious disorders. Thus, the diagnosis of somatoform disorder is made when there is good reason to believe that the person has little or no control over the production of symptoms. While factitious disorders are more common in men, somatoform disorders occur more frequently in women.

There are four major subcategories of the somatoform disorders: somatization disorder, conversion disorder, psychogenic pain disorder, and hypochondriasis. There is also a catch-all category, atypical somatoform disorder, in which individuals are placed if they fit the general criteria for somatoform disorder but not the specific criteria of the other four major categories.

Somatization Disorder.   The chronic though cyclic multiple somatic complaints that mark this subcategory of the somatoform disorders are not primarily due to any physical illness. Yet they may be mixed with other symptoms derived from an actual disease, so arriving at this diagnosis is initially difficult. It is not uncommon for this disorder to be an exaggeration of symptoms associated with a previously cured physical disease.

The diagnosis of somatization disorder is difficult because a self-report of symptoms combined with apparent prior history is convincing at first to most physicians. When they later discover there is no physical disorder they are inclined to put these clients in the too-commonly used categories of "crank" or "crock," and attempt in various ways to avoid spending any time with them. Since it is the supportive atmosphere of the physician's manner and/or the hospital structure that is at least one of the needs of persons with a somatization disorder (and to a degree the conversion disorders), such evident rejections begin to lay bare the underlying inadequacy of these persons to cope effectively with their world.

The symptoms are often presented in a vague though exaggerated fashion. Incidentally, this dramatic component was the linkage between the traditional diagnostic terms "hysterical neurosis" and "hysterical personality." Fortunately, the DSM-III terminology did away with some of the confusion inherent in these labels. Hysterical personalities are now referred to as having a histrionic personality disorder (see the case of Hilde in Chapter 10). Hysteria is typically subsumed under one of the somatoform disorders, usually as a conversion disorder that is still sublabeled hysterical neurosis, conversion type.

Conversion Disorder. This pattern is similar in many respects to the somatization disorder. The difference is that in the conversion disorder there is a specific symptom or a related set of symptoms, and these symptoms are either used for the attainment of some secondary gain or they express a psychological conflict. Conversion symptoms are not under voluntary control. Psychogenic pain disorder, which is discussed in detail in the upcoming case of Pam, can be considered a subcategory of conversion disorder where the specific symptom is simply pain.

With some of the psychosexual dysfunctions (see Chapter 8), it may be difficult to decide whether the problem directly expresses a psychological issue and is thus technically a conversion disorder or whether it is a physiological response to anxiety. In actuality, it may be a mixture of both. For these reasons, as well as for convenience, all of these cases are included in the psychosexual disorders.

A conversion disorder is still referred to as a "hysterical neurosis, conversion type," and such individuals are said to manifest *la belle indifference*, an attitude in which there is little concern about the apparent serious implications of the disorder. Persons with a conversion disorder appear to be aware at some level that their complaints do not predict the further dire consequences that others might infer from them. Although indifferent to their presenting symptoms, emotional "ups and downs" (lability) in response to other stimuli is commonly noted.

La belle indifference attitude is not found in all conversion disorders. Some people develop their symptoms under extreme stress and manifest that stress quite directly. Yet, even in these individuals, anxiety seems to dissipate over the duration of the disorder in favor of a focus on physical symptoms.

Hypochondriasis. Hypochondriacs unreasonably interpret normal or relatively unimportant bodily and physical changes as indicative of serious physical disorder. They are constantly alert to an upsurge of new symptomatology, and since the body is constantly in physiological flux, they are bound to find signs that they can interpret as suggestive of disorder.

In one sense, hypochondriacs do not fear being sick; they are certain they already are. Hypochondriasis is a relatively common pattern from adolescence to old age. It is seen most frequently in 30- to 40-year-old men, and 40- to 50-year-old women (Meister, 1980). Meister also believes that there are many "closet hypochondriacs"—those who do not constantly go to physicians, but are heavily involved in health fads, checking of body behaviors, and discussion of their concerns with close friends (who may relish this quasi-therapist role). These people would not earn a formal DSM diagnosis, as they do not fit some of the specific requirements, such as seeking out medical reassurance and going through physical examinations. Nonetheless, they manifest the disorder.

A number of common factors have been observed in the development of hypochondriasis:

1. In most hypochondriacs, there has been a background marked by substantial experience in an atmosphere of illness. This could include identification with a significant other who was hypochondriacal or early exposure to a family member who was an invalid.

2. Hypochondriacs have often had a strong dependency relationship with a family member who could express love and affection in a normal or intense fashion during periods when the hypochondriac had been ill, yet was distant or nonexpressive at other times.

3. Hypochondriacs often channel their psychological conflicts and their needs for existential reassurance into this pattern. As a result, the hypochondriac pattern of behavior may mask a mid-life crisis or some other challenge that is not being met effectively.

4. A certain subgroup of hypochondriacs are postulated as having a predispositional sensitivity to pain and body sensation. This could be stimulated by prior physical disorder in systems in which the hypochondriacal pattern is now manifest.

All of these factors are naturally facilitated by reinforcement of the hypochondriasis in the client's world. Avoidance of tasks or demands because of being sick is often noted here. A most entertaining portrayal of this disorder is presented by Woody Allen in his 1986 movie *Hannah and Her Sisters*.

Psychogenic Pain Disorder. This fourth subcategory, more fully explored in the case study below, is a disorder in which physical pain has no physiological explanation.

REFERENCES

Meister, R. (1980) *Hypochondria*. New York: Taplinger.
Robins, L. and Helzer, J. (1986) Diagnosis and clinical assessment. In M. Rosenweig and L. Porter (Eds.) *Annual Review of Psychology 37*. Palo Alto, Calif.: Annual Reviews.

/ *Psychogenic Pain Disorder*

**The Case of
Pam**

*They breathe truth that breathe their words
in pain.*
— William Shakespeare
Richard II

The psychogenic pain disorder appeared as a new category in the DSM-III, but, as noted earlier, it is in reality a subcategory of a classical diagnostic group, the conversion disorder. Psychogenic pain disorders are conversion symptoms that center on an experience of pain for which there is no plausible physiological explanation. Often, the pain may be initiated by a real traumatic event, such as an accident. In other cases the pain merely asserts itself gradually until it is entrenched in the sufferer's life style. (Katon, Egan, and Miller, 1985).

Conversion disorders differ from the factitious disorders in that the conversion sufferer is not consciously aware that the symptoms they experience are unreal, with no physical basis. The notion that pain, sometimes serious and debilitating, is all in one's head is sometimes difficult to accept. It is important to note that the experience of pain takes place not at the perceived site of discomfort, but in the brain, and a variety of central nervous system operations may influence pain experiences. Techniques such as Lamaze (for childbirth) are based on the assumption that appropriate attitudes and emotions can minimize pain. Psychogenic pain often seems to be the flip side of this process, with conversion-prone persons experiencing intense symptoms with minimal provocation (Bonica, 1983).

Until the last century a variety of florid conversion disorders were relatively common. Some patients would mysteriously lose sensation in all their extremities or suffer sudden seizures. Recent advances in medicine have made it possible to clearly debunk any apparent validity to others in these extreme displays, and they have nearly disappeared. Relative to these sorts of conversion disorders, the incidence of psychogenic pain has increased dramatically, perhaps because vague, diffuse pain symptoms are far more difficult to identify as inaccurate (Srinivasan, Murthy, and Jamakiramaiah, 1986). The psychogenic pain disorder thus presents a special diagnostic challenge that requires the collaboration of psychologists and medical specialists, who are often the first to encounter the psychogenic pain symptoms.

The Case of Pam

The body never lies.
— Martha Graham

Pam was 38 years old when first seen at the pain clinic. She reported that she had suffered with recurrent hip pain since her early teens, and she linked this difficulty to a car accident that occurred when she was 17. Her regular physician, a gynecologist, had referred her to an orthopedic surgeon some time previously, but this evaluation yielded no conclusive explanation for the ongoing pain. Her hip pain was sporadic, sometimes confining her to bed for a day or two. On the other hand, she and her husband had recently taken a skiing vacation with no ill effects.

Pam also reported frequent headaches, which she characterized as "migraines, definitely." Like her hip pain, the headaches were an intermittent problem, sometimes being quite severe while later disappearing altogether for several weeks. The headaches had begun about two years previously, shortly after Pam and her family had moved into the area. Again, Pam was referred to a medical specialist, a neurologist, for evaluation. The neurologist noted that her description of the headaches did not correspond to a typical migraine pattern and was unable to find a plausible explanation for them. He initiated the referral to the pain clinic in cooperation with Pam's gynecologist.

Finally, Pam had recently seen a daytime television show that described premenstrual stress (PMS) and suggested that this would explain both of the above two problems as well as several new infirmities. The gynecologist reported that this possibility had already been considered and did not account for Pam's problems. Hence, "functional" or psychogenic factors would need to be evaluated.

Etiology

At the pain clinic Pam was seen by several health care personnel. Thorough medical, psychological, and social histories were taken, and numerous psychological and medical tests were performed. Finally, a multidisciplinary team reviewed all the available data and found that a variety of psychological factors probably served as the primary sources of both the headaches and the hip pain.

Pam was the second youngest of four children, a position which insured that she received little individual attention from her parents. Her younger sister was pampered as the baby of the family, while her older brother excelled in sports. Because he was several years older, his achievements seemed to overshadow those of the younger children. This effect was heightened by the attitudes of Pam's parents, who felt that males should be competitive and outgoing and who rewarded this behavior in a variety of ways. They also expected their daughters to strive for success, but in more traditional female roles such as music and academics. Pam came to adopt a traditionally feminine view of herself and confined herself to these outlets.

Pam described her parents as cool and aloof. They rarely showed affection toward one another or toward their children. On the whole the family had little social contact with others in the community, except for formal events centering on church and school activities. Pam and her siblings found that emotional displays of any kind made their parents uncomfortable, and so they learned to hide their feelings. Pam recalled that her parents did seem more caring and tender toward her whenever she suffered a childhood illness, such as the measles.

Pam's father spent little time with the family, instead devoting himself to his career. The children were troubled by their father's absence, but Pam's mother quashed any complaints. She shamed the children for complaining while their father was working so hard to be a good provider. While the children suspected that their mother also resented the father's absence, she never expressed this directly. Instead, she behaved with superficial charm toward her husband. Whenever he did wish to spend time with her, she suddenly became tired or ill, thus frustrating his limited attempts toward intimacy. Pam came to adopt her mother's style of suppressing frustrations with others, only to express them in indirect ways. This pattern depended in part on her expectation that she would be made to feel guilty if she voiced her discontent overtly.

Pam reported that her mother suffered a variety of gynecological problems, and that she frequently consulted her physician. On occasion her vague complaints would require that she stay off her feet for several days. During these episodes the father would demand that the children do nothing to upset their mother, thus indicating that he believed the illnesses were stress induced. He behaved solicitously toward his wife until she felt better, then frantically threw himself back into work to "catch up." A predictable cycle was established with the mother becoming ill and dominating the family briefly, only to have things return to normal as soon as she felt better. Pam learned firsthand that ill behaviors could be effective in gaining attention from (and control over) otherwise disinterested family members.

Pam was an attractive girl who reached puberty rather early. She was initially pleased by her resulting popularity and became involved in a variety of school-related activities. Upon entering high school, she hoped to begin dating, viewing this as a logical extension of her social life. Consistent with her parents' reluctance to confront many aspects of human intimacy, they did not discuss sexuality with her, and she was quite naive about the role it might play in dating. Despite her parents' attempts to screen her boyfriends, Pam inevitably dated boys who pressured her to become sexually active. Surprised by these advances, she resisted anything more than light petting at first. Eventually she became involved in a long-standing relationship, and in this context she felt less inhibited. She found the warmth and intimacy of these interludes a welcome change from the emotional coldness of her family. While she began to enjoy more sexual experimentation, she had moral reservations about these activities and experienced considerable emotional conflict as a result. Ultimately, Pam and her boyfriend progressed to having intercourse in the back seat of his car. Following one of their initial encounters, they were involved in a car wreck on the way to her parents' home, when Pam was 17. Each sustained a variety of minor injuries, and Pam complained that her right hip was stiff and sore. Physicians found no sign of injury and suggested that this pain would go away in a few days.

Despite these predictions, Pam's hip pain continued and came to interfere with many of her activities, including dating. After several months the boyfriend began dating someone else, and Pam's pain gradually subsided. This relationship had produced considerable conflict for Pam, but her "injury" provided her with an indirect means of escape. She did not have to break off the relationship herself or insist that the boyfriend stop pressuring her for sex. It is not unusual for conversion symptoms, including psychogenic pain, to symbolically reflect the underlying anxieties they mask; in this case, Pam's pain localized near the genital area.

After high school Pam continued to live at home while attending a local community college. While her grades would have permitted her to attend a more prestigious institution, her parents preferred that she remain within their control. Pam resented the implication that her educational advancement should give way to their wishes, but she protested little. She met her husband through the community college, and they married after a brief romance. In many respects, this liaison served as an escape from her parents' domination, and was particularly effective since they did not approve of her husband-to-be.

Pam reported that her husband, John, is a very conventional, hard-working individual. He has an M.B.A. and works for a local bank in an administrative capacity. Like Pam's father, John puts in considerable overtime and seems to have little involvement with his family. His expectation is that Pam will take care of all the domestic duties while he will be the "breadwinner." The couple has three children ranging in age from 9 to 15. The children participate in athletic and artistic activities in addition to attending a private school. The family is comfortably upper middle class. She perceives the demands placed on her as onerous and would like to escape some of these. Her pain experiences may help her do this.

When asked about the strengths and weaknesses of her marriage, Pam had difficulty in identifying strengths, other than that she believes her husband is "substantial." She feels that their relationship lacks much real emotional commitment. Pam was able to identify one area of conflict. The family had moved every two to three years because John felt it was necessary to advance his career. At present, Pam is very comfortable with her home and social circle. While she finds it difficult to make friends, she has become close to several people in the community and is resistant to another move.

She was uncharacteristically adamant about her position when John once again mentioned "moving on" approximately two years ago. She felt guilty for this outburst and resolved not to act so hotheaded in the future. Her recurrent headaches began shortly thereafter. Pam now has some realization that she can tell when John wants to discuss moving, and it appears that her headaches serve to preempt these overtures. They may also provide an escape from the many demands her children place on her.

Treatment

Because a broad range of factors may contribute to psychogenic pain, many types of interventions have been employed with some success (Aronoff, 1985; Kulich and Gottlieb, 1985). One group of approaches centers on confronting the lack of a plausible physiological explanation for the pain while pointing up the psychological "rewards" for the pain experience. Techniques associated with reality therapy and confrontation-insight therapy may be useful. Such confrontations must be carefully managed, however, to prevent flight from treatment. Since for these persons intense relationships are often anxiety-provoking, they instinctively withdraw from therapists who attempt to cut through their superficial defenses.

Behavioral techniques provide a second major line of attack. Merely changing the client's environment to eliminate secondary gains may serve to reduce the frequency or intensity of psychogenic pain experiences. Also, biofeedback has been found to help alleviate many types of pain, even if no clear pathophysiology exists (Nigl, 1984). Contracting with the client to increase the number of activities they attempt may divert attention and energy away from the pain experience. These efforts are consistent with the finding that many persons experiencing psychogenic pain may be clinically depressed. Depressed persons also tend to benefit from attempting a wider range of activities.

A third general approach entails training the client to relate to others in more positive and explicit ways. Often their pains and illnesses serve to gain attention and caring from others, or to relieve the client of responsibilities they find overwhelming. Assertiveness or social skills training may help the individual to express their needs clearly, thus reducing the need for more manipulative behavior. Work on problem-solving (Haley, 1976) or related issues may help the client manage demands adequately.

Pam's Treatment. Pam's evaluation at the pain clinic took four weeks to complete. During this period she was asked to keep a journal of her pain experiences and a variety of other activities and events. Once the team had determined that her pain was primarily, if not entirely, psychogenic, the journal data were helpful in pointing out many contributing factors. She was gently but firmly confronted with the possibility that her hip pain and headaches served several purposes of which she was unaware.

During the initial phase of therapy, Pam was encouraged to explore several characteristics of her early life which predisposed her to pain disorder. She came to recognize that her passivity and dependency, inability to confront negative emotions, and proneness to guilt stemmed from the family milieu in which she was raised. Subsequently she was encouraged to explore ways in which she might be reenacting the patterns of behavior her mother had used in her own marriage.

Homework assignments for Pam initially focused on increasing positive activities outside her usual domestic drudgery (McCaul and Malott, 1984). Special emphasis was placed on health-related behaviors such as exercise and diet. Subsequently, she felt healthier and more energetic, factors which greatly reduced her expectations that she would be ill or in pain. Biofeedback was useful in giving her more of a reality-based perception of physical sensations and symptoms (Nigl, 1984). She also contracted to increase contacts with her friends. It was far more inconvenient to have a headache or sore hip when it would conflict with a luncheon engagement or some other pleasurable activity.

Pam's skills in relating to others came under scrutiny in the course of therapy. Social skills and assertiveness-training methods were used to enhance her ability to make appropriate requests of others, to express her opinions openly, and to refuse requests politely.

The husband, John, was also brought into the therapy effort. It was noted that he shared a number of his wife's attributes, including difficulty in expressing emotions and passivity in confronting problems. It became apparent that the family's repeated moves had been motivated not so much by career necessity as by John's inability to confront normal difficulties in the workplace. The ongoing but veiled conflict over an impending move was subsequently reduced. A brief, but intensive course of couples therapy helped both Pam and John to become better able to work out potential problems quickly, rather than experience ongoing anxiety over their lack of resolution (Haley, 1976). The couple also found that their relationship became more emotionally passionate and John found that he wanted to spend more time with his wife. Pam's need to gain attention through incapacity was thus negated.

Ultimately, Pam made a very successful recovery from two recurrent and debilitating problems. Her treatment was facilitated by the multidisciplinary nature of the pain clinic (Kulich and Gottlieb, 1985). Many persons experiencing psychogenic pain have been told by an acquaintance or family member that "it's all in your head," and hence refer themselves to a variety of medical specialists in an attempt to validate their pain experience. These persons often receive treatments that they do not need, such as analgesic medications, which are basically ineffective. Side effects and iatrogenic health problems may be the ultimate result. As with the factitious disorder (see the case of Frank in Chapter 13) it is important that these persons be identified rather than left to flounder in the conventional medical system (Aronoff, 1985).

Comment

Persons who suffer with psychogenic pain seem to fall along a continuum ranging from those whose pain is primarily a reflection of some type of psychological conflict to those whose symptom production is dominated by secondary gain (Srinivasan et al., 1986; McCaul and Malott, 1984). Most conversion disorders involve each motif to some degree, as was the case with Pam. Her hip pain initially arose because of intense internal conflict, and was apparently prolonged because it was so effective in eliciting secondary gains. Once the pattern of illness behavior and concessions from the environment is established, it is common for these persons to acquire additional symptoms. New complaints often arise in the face of new demands or if the old symptom is somehow discredited.

It was noted that Pam seized on the notion of premenstrual stress once medical specialists began to question the physiological basis of her head and hip pains. While the medical community now recognizes PMS as a legitimate syndrome that affects a significant number of women, it is also a good candidate for adoption by conversion-prone persons largely because its pathophysiology is still unclear and because it can produce a wide array of nonspecific symptoms. It is thus difficult to differentiate from cases of conversion symptoms. Other complaints, such as "whiplash" injuries, which are difficult to verify empirically, may serve as the *raison d'être* for conversion symptoms.

As noted earlier, the major distinction between conversion and factitious disorders lies in the degree of conscious motivation to present false symptoms. Persons with the factitious disorder know that their illness is false and engage in a variety of strategies to convince others of its reality. Persons with conversion symptoms seem to have deceived themselves. The motives for believing that their symptoms are real may seem obvious to others, but not to the client. Since it is common for these persons to be psychologically naive, psychogenic explanations are often poorly received, and considerable work must sometimes be done before these persons are able to confront their own maladaptive coping strategies.

REFERENCES

Aronoff, G. (Ed.) (1985) *Evaluation and Treatment of Chronic Pain.* Baltimore: Urban & Schwarzenberg.

Bonica, J. (Ed.) (1983) *Proceedings of the Third World Conference on Pain (Advances in Pain Research and Therapy— Vol. 5)* New York: Raven.

Haley, J. (1976) *Problem-Solving Therapy: New Strategies for Effective Family Therapy.* New York: Harper & Row.

Katon, W., Egan, K., and Miller, D. (1985) Chronic pain: Lifetime psychiatric diagnoses and family history. *American Journal of Psychiatry, 142,* 1156–1160.

Kulich, R. and Gottlieb, B. (1985) The management of chronic pain. In D. Upper and S. Ross (Ed.) *Handbook of Behavioral Group Therapy.* New York: Plenum.

McCaul, K. and Malott, J. (1984) Distraction and coping with pain. *Psychological Bulletin, 95,* 516–533.

Nigl, A. (1984) *Biofeedback and Behavioral Strategies in Pain Treatment.* Jamaica, N.Y.: Spectrum.

Srinivasan, K., Murthy, R., and Janakiramaiah, N. (1986) A nosological study of patients presenting with somatic complaints. *Acta Psychiatrica Scandinavica, 73,* 1–5.

6

The Schizophrenic and Paranoid (or Delusional) Disorders

Especially severe forms of psychopathology, characterized by perceptual, cognitive, affective, communicative, motor, and motivational disturbances, and specifically denoted by a loss of contact with reality, are termed "psychoses." Some psychotic reactions are obviously organic; that is, associated with brain disruption due to physical causes such as diseases of the nervous system, brain tumors or injuries, toxic drug or chemical reactions, or circulation disturbances. These reactions are classified among the organic disorders and the addictive disorders in this book.

More prevalent are the functional psychoses that do not stem fully and directly from a known physical defect of the brain. There are three major classifications of functional psychoses: affective, schizophrenic, and paranoid. The affective psychotic disorders, which are discussed in the following section, are characterized by extreme fluctuations of mood, with related disturbances in thought and behavior. The DSM also includes the category "Psychotic Disorder Not Elsewhere Classified," which consists of the schizophreniform disorder (schizophrenic symptoms of less than one month's duration), the brief reactive psychosis (schizophrenic symptoms of less than two weeks' duration), the schizoaffective disorder (where schizophrenic and affective symptoms are both prominent and developed at about the same time), and the atypical psychosis.

The primary focus of this section is on the DSM diagnostic categories of the schizophrenic disorders and the paranoid (or delusional) disorders. The major symptoms of schizophrenia involve withdrawal from reality, with flat or inappropriate emotional reactions and marked disturbances in thought processes. Delusions, hallucinations, and stereotyped mannerisms are common associated features (Endicott et al., 1986).

Schizophrenia has been recognized as a disorder since Mòrel's (1857) description of a 13-year-old whose intellectual, moral, and physical functions gradually and inexplicably deteriorated over time. Mòrel used the term *demence precoce* (mental deterioration at an early age); he thought the deterioration was caused by hereditary factors and was virtually irreversible. Several modern theories of the disorder do not differ very much from Mòrel's views. *Dementia praecox*, the Latin form of Mòrel's term, was used by Kraeplin (1899) to refer to the rather large class of disorders that have features of mental deterioration beginning early in life. Bleuler (1911) introduced the term *schizophrenia* (split mind) to indicate his belief that the chief characteristics involved a lack of integration between thoughts and emotions and a loss of contact with reality.

There are several different types of schizophrenia. Disorganized schizophrenia is marked by grossly inappropriate emotional responses and blatantly disturbed thought and behavior patterns. Catatonic schizophrenia is manifested by extreme withdrawal or excitement patterns. Undifferentiated schizophrenia, as in the case of Sally, involves a variety of symptoms, and is often the eventual diagnosis applied to chronic cases. In paranoid schizophrenia, as in the case of Perry, the least overtly disturbed form of schizophrenia, disorder is not so extreme, there is usually less premorbid symptomatology, and the disorder typically emerges later in life. This pattern is then contrasted with the case of Lloyd, diagnosed as a paranoid personality disorder. Though disturbed, Lloyd does not show the thought disorder, disorganized behavior, or the hallucinations that are seen in Perry.

Paranoia (a paranoid disorder) is characterized by the gradual development of a complex, intricate, and elaborate delusional system. A delusion is a firmly held belief that the individual maintains despite objective evidence to the contrary and lack of support for it from most other people. The delusional systems in paranoid psychotic reactions are usually based on misinterpretations of actual events. Once the inaccurate premise is established, the other delusional aspects that follow seem logical.

There are several types of delusions, but primarily three are seen: delusions of grandeur, delusions of reference, and delusions of persecution. Persons with delusions of grandeur believe they are some exalted being such as Jesus Christ or the President. Persons with delusions of reference misconstrue chance events as having a direct relevance to their life style. For instance, thunderstorms may be perceived as messages from God, or such persons may immediately conclude that they are the topic of other people's conversations. Individuals who have delusions of persecution feel they are targets of various conspiracies against them. These delusions are typically developed in this order: reference, grandeur, persecution. First, the individuals develop the belief that they are special and have been singled out for attention by others. They then gradually come to the conclusion that this special attention is the result of admirable and coveted characteristics that only they possess. It is then a short step to believing that others are so jealous and threatened by these qualities that they are spying on, plotting against, and/or planning to eliminate them.

Generally, persons with a paranoid disorder are more functional than are those with a schizophrenic disorder. Schizophrenia is debilitating in most areas of intellectual, emotional, and psychological functioning, and includes noticeable and pervasive decline from the previous level of functioning. In the paranoid disorder, pathological symptoms are more compartmentalized and other functions are preserved. In fact, an extensive interview with a paranoid patient may reveal no marked abnormalities if the areas of delusional material are not mentioned.

We now present the first case, Sally, in which we see undifferentiated schizophrenia, a particularly severe level of disorder.

REFERENCES

Bleuler, E. (1911) *Dementia Praecox oder die Gruppe der Schizophrenia*. Leipzig: Deuticke.

Endicott, J., Nee, J., Cohen, J., Fliess, J., and Simon, A. (1986) Diagnosis of schizophrenia. *Archives of General Psychology, 43*, 13–19.

Kraeplin, E. (1919) *Dementia praecox and paraphrenia* (8th German ed.). R. Barclay and G. Robertson (trans.). Edinburgh: Livingstone. (Originally published 1899.)

Mòrel, B. (1857) *Traite des Degenerescences Physiques, Intellectuelles et Morales*. Paris: Bailliere.

/ Undifferentiated Schizophrenia

The Case of Sally

"Your secret dreams that grow over the years like apple seeds sown in your belly, grow up through you in leafy wonder and finally sprout through your skin, gentle and soft and wondrous, and they have a life of their own . . ."

"You've done this?"

"A time or two." (p. 99)

— W. P. Kinsella
Shoeless Joe

Schizophrenia exacts a tremendous cost from both society and the person who suffers from it. It is the most severe form of psychosis (lack of reality contact) when seen from an overall perspective including severity of overall disturbance, prognosis, speed of recovery, and emotional and physical costs to the client, the family, and society (Mirsky and Duncan, 1986; Eaton, 1985).

About one out of every hundred people in the United States will be diagnosed as schizophrenic at least once in their lifetime. This 1 percent rate has been consistent across cultures and across the years within our own culture (Marsella, De Vos, and Hsu, 1985; Myers et al., 1984).

Schizophrenia in general is marked by thought disorder, hallucinations, and delusions. A study by the World Health Organization (1981) indicates that, across virtually all cultures, the most prominent symptom of schizophrenia is lack of insight, a symptom that appears to be analogous to the loss of reality contact that is the hallmark of the psychosis. Other common symptoms are auditory and verbal hallucinations (hearing rather than seeing things), ideas of reference, and suspiciousness.

The following case of Sally is an example of undifferentiated schizophrenia. As we see with Sally, a person who eventually shows an undifferentiated pattern often has shown earlier disorganized, catatonic, or even paranoid patterns.

Paranoid schizophrenia, marked by varied delusions of grandeur or persecution, and often without much consistency in the organization of these delusions, is discussed in the next case in this section, that of Perry. Disorganized schizophrenics, previously termed hebephrenic schizophrenics, show very fragmented behavior patterns, often accompanied by silly or inappropriate giggling. Catatonic schizophrenia is subdivided into two groups. Withdrawn catatonics, like Sally at one point, show prolonged periods of stupor and non-responsiveness, and sometimes a "waxy flexibility" wherein they allow themselves to be moved into different postures in which they can stay for surprisingly long periods of time. Excited catatonics, on the other hand, show very hyperactive and agitated behavior, often being destructive to people or objects, apparently inadvertently.

Some people with the above patterns stabilize at one of these diagnoses. However, most long-term schizophrenics show various symptoms at various times and usually show a mixed and/or varying pattern of symptoms eventually, thus earning a diagnosis of undifferentiated schizophrenia (American Psychiatric Association, 1980).

The Case of Sally

Sally did not start life with the best roll of the dice. In spite of her physician's warning, her mother persisted in her two-pack-a-day smoking habit even while she was carrying Sally. Also, Sally's birth was difficult, and for a period of time her breathing was disrupted, causing her to turn blue for a moment or so.

There's also reason to believe Sally may have inherited some vulnerability to schizophrenia. Her maternal grandfather had always been known in the family as an "eccentric," though people less fond of him preferred to call him "crazy" or "nuts." He had developed a number of unique religious beliefs, and also was known in the community for having placed a variety of unusual mechanisms on the roofs of his barns, supposedly to bring in "electromagnetic energy" to help his livestock grow. Since farming in those days did not demand the organizational and financial skills that it does today, while at the same time providing plenty of room for odd and/or person-avoidant behaviors, he was never brought to the attention of any mental health professionals.

Sally was generally slow to develop. She walked and talked late, but at the same time was a most active child. She was never formally diagnosed as "hyperactive," but clearly was above average on this dimension.

Her parents' marriage was filled with conflict, and they even separated for almost ten months when Sally was 2 years old. They reunited, and entered into what would best be termed a long-term conflict-habituated marriage.

They were both devoted to Sally, especially since after two miscarriages subsequent to Sally's birth, they were advised against having any more children. Sally's father traveled quite a bit because of his position as a sales coordinator for a farm machinery company. When he was home he would play with Sally a lot, but he could be quite critical if he thought she was not behaving (and later achieving) at the level he thought she should be at. Her mother, on the other hand, developed an intense, almost symbiotic relationship with Sally.

She was intent on developing Sally's potential especially when it became evident Sally did not always seem to understand information in the way it had been presented to her. She would spend long hours "instructing" Sally, even when Sally was a very young child. It soon became apparent, to even a casual observer, that her mother got more out of these contacts than Sally did, and that she became very psychologically dependent upon Sally. As Sally grew older, her mother often kept Sally home from various activities, to "protect her" from assorted perceived dangers.

Sally was of above-average intelligence. However, in spite of her mother's intense coaching and Sally's withdrawal into studying (and fantasy behavior), she was only average or below in most subjects. It was always as if her thought processes were, as one teacher put it, "just a bit off center."

Sally did have an occasional friend, but her mother's overprotection and Sally's occasional odd behavior and thought processes so kept her out of the flow of activities that she could never really make long-term deep friendships. In fact, when it appeared that Sally had any possibility of having a deep friendship, her mother's intrusions became more pronounced, and the promise of that relationship was destroyed.

Sally was a quiet and mildly shy child. Also, because she did not have the feedback inherent in friendships and an active social life, she developed even more odd interests and mannerisms. These in turn served to distance her further socially.

She graduated from high school and was allowed to board at a nearby college. However, the stress and shock of her new surroundings was too much for her. She started talking to herself, and her assigned roommate quickly managed to get assigned to another room. One afternoon the dorm counselor found Sally in her room, sitting in a chair, staring at the floor. Sally was unresponsive, and indeed, her limbs could be moved about and would then stay in place, almost like a plastic doll.

Sally was in a withdrawn catatonic state, marked in this case by a condition referred to as "waxy flexibility." She was hospitalized and improved rapidly. She tried to return to school, but became more and more reclusive, often skipping classes. Her mother brought her back home "to take care of her," and Sally degenerated even further, at one point showing a pattern of almost totally unresponsive behavior, interrupted occasionally by periods of giggling and rocking behavior, traditionally termed a hebephrenic pattern.

Sally's father finally insisted that Sally return to the hospital. She did, but when she showed some improvement, her mother again brought her home and did not continue the recommended outpatient treatment.

Sally was able to get a part-time job as a clerk in a nearby store that did a low-volume business, so it did not place great demands on her. She spent almost all of her free time at home, doing some jobs around the house and spending the rest of the time in her room.

About this time, her father suffered a fatal heart attack, making Sally's mother even more dependent on her daughter. Sally had now taken to wandering about on her way home from work, possibly as a defense against the intensity of her mother's needs. Her behaviors were also becoming more bizarre. One day the police found her walking in the shallows of a pond in the town park, muttering to herself. They took her to the local hospital, and she was then transferred to a nearby mental hospital.

Etiology

Just as there are a variety of symptoms in schizophrenia, so also may a number of causes contribute to an eventual case of schizophrenia. In one case, certain factors may be primary, whereas in another case other factors may be more critical.

It's also important to remember that there are various types of causes for schizophrenia. The several possible "original" causes for schizophrenia are termed *generic variables*. The most immediate manifestation of the disorder is an *information processing deficit*, evident in problems in attention, perception, and memory (Green and Walker, 1986; Cornblatt and Erlenmeyer-Kimling, 1985; George and Neufeld, 1985). The variables that immediately produce these symptoms are labeled *mediating* variables. It's also important to note that there are *maintenance* variables—variables that do not generate the disorder but serve to maintain and even increase its symptoms (Monroe and Steiner, 1986).

Various generic (original) causes of schizophrenia have been proposed. There is good evidence that there may be a genetic predisposition to schizophrenia, which may operate as a compelling cause in some individual cases and only be a contributing factor in other cases (Gottesman and Shields, 1972; Hartmann et al., 1984). It's very possible that Sally's eccentric grandfather actually suffered from schizophrenia, though this is unclear as there never was a formal diagnosis.

Because of the nature of schizophrenia's symptoms, any potential cause of brain disorder (genetic problems, birth disorder, trauma, viral or infectious disorder) may be an original cause of schizophrenia (Mirsky and Duncan, 1986; Brown et al., 1986; Strauss, 1985). Sally's birth traumas, possibly furthered by her mother's heavy smoking during the pregnancy, could have generated some asphyxiation, possibly a combination of anoxia (loss of oxygen to brain tissue) and increased carbon dioxide tension in the blood and tissues, which leads to an acidic metabolic condition that results in tissue damage. These original causes can in turn lead to neurological disorder or imbalances of brain chemicals such as dopamine, serotonin, or norepinephrine (Mirsky and Duncan, 1986; Hartmann et al., 1984).

Psychological disorders, such as early psychological conflict or family disorder, can also be a critical variable in the development of schizophrenia. While most theories don't see it as an original cause in and of itself, it can certainly be very important in the development, amplification, and maintenance of the disorder. For example, research (Miklowitz et al., 1986; Bateson et al., 1956) indicates that two concepts, intrafamilial expressed emotion (EE) and communication deviance (CD) are especially contributory, and they both appear to be operative in Sally's case. Expressed emotion refers to a family situation in which parents are emotionally overinvolved and overprotective (as was Sally's mother) or are highly critical (as was her father, at least on occasion).

Communication deviance is a measure of the degree to which an individual is unable to establish and maintain a shared focus of attention with someone while carrying on a dialogue. This could result from brain disorder, but could also result from early conflict or familial disorder. This was also evident in Sally's history.

Pre-Morbid Factors in Schizophrenia. Even with the potential multicausal background of schizophrenia, there are pre-morbid factors that predict the emergence of schizophrenia as well as a common sequence of what often takes place in the development of schizophrenia (Mirsky and Duncan, 1986; Monroe and Steiner, 1986; George and Neufeld, 1985; Cornblatt and Erlenmeyer-Kimling, 1985; Hartmann et al., 1984). Pre-morbid factors are those factors associated with, but not necessarily causal to, the later development of schizophrenia. Only a few of the factors listed below may be noted in any one case, but they are common across cases.

1. A schizophrenic parent or parents or—a less potent variable—the presence of other schizophrenic blood relatives. For sons, separation from even a disturbed mother seems to be more damaging than it is for daughters. For daughters, the earlier a mother becomes schizophrenic, the greater the likelihood they will, too.

2. A history of prenatal (pregnancy) disruption or birth problems.

3. Slowed reaction times in perception (such as slowness in becoming aware of a stimulus) or very rapid recovery rate of autonomic nervous system after some stress or novel stimulus.

4. Hyperactivity, signs of central nervous system dysfunction (such as convulsive disorder), or evidence of enlarged cerebral ventricles (the spaces between brain tissue).

5. Low birth weight and/or low IQ relative to siblings.

6. Early role as odd member of family or scapegoat.

7. Parenting marked by inconsistency and by emotionally extreme (both positive and negative) responses and double messages; parental rejection par-

ticularly when one parent's negative effect is not countered by corrective attention and care from the other parent.

8. Rejection by peers in childhood or adolescence; being perceived by both teachers and peers as more irritable and more unstable than other children.

These factors interact with those noted previously to produce the following common developmental sequence in schizophrenia, one that evidently operated in Sally's situation.

A Developmental Sequence in Schizophrenia. Problems in (1) attention, affect, and information processing naturally lead to (2) an increase in odd interpersonal and speech behaviors, a decrease in information helpful to effective coping, and greater interpersonal distancing. As these occur, (3) interpersonal rejection by peers and family members increases. Concomitantly, (4) academic and vocational performance declines.

Operating out of a restricted social and information base, the person experiences (5) feelings of depersonalization. There are also (6) a loss in self-identity, or, in psychodynamic terms, a weakening of ego boundaries.

At this point, (7) hallucinations or delusions are likely, signaling a breakdown in the sense of self and in the standard coping behaviors. Also, (8) formal thought disorder, increased depersonalization, and more disorganized behaviors occur as allied patterns. The person may now be informally labeled as "mentally ill." Any significant continuance usually leads to (9) hospitalization, which in turn may reinforce and amplify any withdrawal or dependency patterns. Society now also formally labels and stigmatizes the person as psychotic and thus out of touch with reality.

This sequence is common, though not inflexible; hospitalization may occur earlier in the sequence, other factors later. One feature, however, is constant: in our culture the label of schizophrenia is difficult to discard even when the person manages to behave normally.

Treatment

Given the multi-symptom nature of schizophrenia, it is not surprising that a variety of treatments are needed even to just stop and/or reverse the course of the disorder. Total cures are not common, but many schizophrenics can be returned to at least adequate functioning in their job and community.

Chemotherapy with the major tranquilizers, usually with the phenothiazines (such as chlorpromazine, [Thorazine]), the butyrophenones, or the thioxanthenes, is often effective in reducing many of the major symptoms of schizophrenia. While extremely helpful in many instances, there are disadvantages to the various chemotherapies: (1) many parts of the schizophrenic process are not helped; (2) they don't work at all with a sizable minority of schizophrenics; (3) achieving the right dosage is difficult, and overmedication often results; and (4) significant side effects are common, especially with long-term use, which is required in most cases (Hersen and Breuning, 1986; Curran, Monti, and Corriveau, 1982).

A variety of other physical treatments are occasionally employed for schizophrenia: electroconvulsive treatment (ECT), dialysis, psychosurgery, and megavitamin therapy. However, there is little data to indicate that these are of any significant help, and there are potentially negative side effects with all of these interventions (Ban, Lehmann, and Deutsch, 1977; World Health Organization, 1981; Hersen and Breuning, 1986).

Supportive individual and group psychotherapies, possibly abetted by family or marital therapies in certain cases, are usually part of any overall treatment program for schizophrenics (Cattell, 1986; Jacobson and Gurman, 1986.) To the degree that the schizophrenic is at a low level of overall functioning, confrontive techniques may also help in getting the client to at least respond. Also, with such severely deteriorated schizophrenics, token economies are useful in modifying a wide range of behaviors, including some of the bizarre mannerisms that distance others, and also in promoting more positive social skills. Milieu therapy (at times just a euphemism for the hospital environment) is also helpful in reorienting the schizophrenic to more appropriate social behaviors. Other adjunct therapies, such as biofeedback, occupational and expressive therapies, and environmental and nutritional planning can also be useful. Training in more appropriate cognitive strategies and in ways to avoid the information processing distortions that occur with schizophrenia are necessary as well (Miklowitz et al., 1986; Curren et al., 1982).

A most critical step is aiding the schizophrenic to make an effective transition back into family and community (Howells and Guirguis, 1985). Indeed, it makes little sense to put forth significant time and effort when the problem first comes to the attention of social agencies or treaters, and then provide only minimum attention when clients return from the hospital to the community (or analogously, when criminals go from prison back into society).

Assuming that some effective treatment is occurring, the following positive prognostic signs predict an adequate remission once schizophrenia is diagnosed (Mirsky and Duncan, 1986; Monroe and Steiner, 1986; Strauss, 1985; Howells and Guirguis, 1985; Hartmann et al., 1984). These variables should be considered as correlated factors rather than explicit causes of such remission.

1. Sexual-marital status: married, or at least a prior history of stable sexual-social adjustment.
2. A family history of affective rather than schizophrenic disorder.
3. Presence of an affective response (elation or depression) in the acute stage of the disorder.
4. Abrupt onset of the disorder: reactive rather than process schizophrenia.
5. Onset later than early childhood.

6. Minor or no paranoid trends in the disorder.
7. Higher socioeconomic status.
8. Adequate pre-morbid vocational adjustment.
9. Pre-morbid competence in interpersonal relationships.
10. Short stay in hospital.
11. No history of ECT treatment.
12. Tendency to be stimulation-receptive rather than stimulation-avoidant.
13. Clear precipitating factors at the onset of disturbance.

Sally's Treatment. Sally's mother subverted any real treatment at the time of Sally's first two hospitalizations. Thus, Sally was not effectively treated until late in the process of her disorder, a not uncommon occurrence with schizophrenics (Mirsky and Duncan, 1986; Eaton, 1985).

In her third hospitalization, Sally was immediately put on chemotherapy, in this case Thorazine, was included in an inpatient therapy group, and talked to her psychiatrist for a half-hour or so about twice a week.

She showed some fairly rapid improvement on some of the more obvious symptoms, such as talking constantly to herself, sometimes in an obvious response to voices she heard. However, some of the deeper, or more "negative" symptoms (Strauss, 1985)—for example, her disturbances in attention and thinking—remained. Eventually, she was released back to her mother's care, which meant that, in spite of attempts to deal with her large overlay of social deficits through outpatient therapy procedures, Sally made no more progress.

Indeed, there were several relapses. Also, these relapses began to be more common. The symptoms were now many and varied, though not always so flamboyant as in some of the earliest episodes, thus now earning her the diagnosis of undifferentiated schizophrenia.

At the last contact with her therapists, Sally was in the hospital. The prognosis for any substantial cure was very poor, and it is probable that she will continue the pattern of going in and out of hospitals, and it is possible she will become so "institutionalized" that she will at some time not be able to return to the community at all.

REFERENCES

American Psychiatric Association (1980) *Diagnostic and Statistical Manual of Mental Disorders* (3rd ed.). Washington, D.C.: American Psychiatric Association.

Ban, T., Lehmann, H., and Deutsch, M. (1977) Negative findings with megavitamins in schizophrenic patients. *Communications in Psychiatry, 1,* 119–122.

Bateson, G., Jackson, D., Haley, J., and Weakland, J. (1956) Toward a theory of schizophrenia. *Behavioral Sciences, 1,* 251–264.

Brown, R., Colter, N., Corsellis, J., Crow, T., et al. (1986) Postmortem evidence of structural brain changes in schizophrenia. *Archives of General Psychiatry, 43,* 36–42.

Cattell, R. (1986) *Psychotherapy by Structured Learning.* New York: Springer.

Cornblatt, B. and Erlenmeyer-Kemling L. (1985) Global attentional deviance as a marker of risk for schizophrenia. *Journal of Abnormal Psychology*, *94*, 470–486.

Curran, J., Monti, P., and Corriveau, D. (1982) Treatment of schizophrenia. In A. Bellack, M. Hersen, and A. Kazdin (Eds.) *International Handbook of Behavior Modification and Therapy*. New York: Plenum.

Eaton, W. (1985) *Sociology of Mental Disorders*. New York: Praeger.

George, L. and Neufeld, R. (1985) Cognition and symptomatology in schizophrenia. *Schizophrenia Bulletin*, *11*, 264–285.

Gottesman, I. and Shields, J. (1972) *Schizophrenia and Genetics: A Twin Study Vantage Point*. New York: Academic Press.

Green, M. and Walker, E. (1986) Symptom correlates of vulnerability to backward masking in schizophrenia. *American Journal of Psychiatry*, *143*, 181–186.

Hartmann, E., Milofsky, E., Vaillant, G., Oldfield, M., Falke, R., and Ducey, C. (1984) Vulnerability to schizophrenia. *Archives of General Psychiatry*, *41*, 1050–1056.

Hersen, M. and Breuning, S. (1986) *Pharmacological and Behavioral Treatment*. New York: John Wiley.

Howells, J. and Guirguis, W. (1985) *The Family and Schizophrenia*. New York: International Universities Press.

Jacobson, N. and Gurman, A. (Eds.) (1986) *Clinical Handbook of Marital Therapy*. New York: Guilford.

Marsella, A., De Vos, G., and Hsu, F. (Eds.) (1985) *Culture and Self: Asian and Western Perspectives*. New York: Tavistock.

Miklowitz, D., Strachan, A., Goldstein, M., Doane, J., Snyder, K., Hogarty, G., and Falloon, I. (1986) Expressed emotion and communication deviance in the families of schizophrenics. *Journal of Abnormal Psychology*, *95*, 60–66.

Mirsky, A. and Duncan, C. (1986) Etiology and expression of schizophrenia: Neurobiological and psychosocial factors. In M. Rosenweig and L. Porter (Eds.) *Annual Review of Psychology 37*, Palo Alto, Calif.: Annual Reviews.

Monroe, S. and Steiner, S. (1986) Social support and psychopathology: Interrelations with preexisting disorder, stress, and personality. *Journal of Abnormal Psychology*, *95*, 29–39.

Myers, J., Weissman, M., Tischler, G., Holzer, C., et al. (1984) Six-month prevalence of psychiatric disorders in three communities. *Archives of General Psychiatry*, *41*, 959–970.

Strauss, J. (1985) Negative symptoms: Future developments of the concept. *Schizophrenia Bulletin*, *11*, 457–460.

World Health Organization. (1981) *Current State of Diagnosis and Classification in the Mental Health Field*. Geneva: World Health Organization.

Paranoid Schizophrenia

The Case of Perry

Ninety-nine percent of the people in the world are fools and the rest of us are in great danger of contagion.

— Thornton Wilder
The Matchmaker

Paranoid schizophrenia is an interesting and a severe disorder. In order to apply a diagnosis of paranoid schizophrenia, the person must first meet the overall criteria for schizophrenia, which can be fulfilled by any of the following: (1) grossly inappropriate or flat affect, (2) catatonic (rigid) or disorganized behavior, (3) loosening of associations (form of thought disorder), (4) significant delusions or hallucinations, excluding auditory hallucinations of only one or two words. An active disorder phase must be present, and the schizophrenia must continue for at least six months and can include prodromal (symptom emergence), active, and residual phases. The disorder is specifically labeled as paranoid schizophrenia when the symptom picture is dominated by preoccupation with grandiose or persecutory delusions, delusions of jealousy, or hallucinations with a delusional content.

Several other characteristics typically distinguish the paranoid schizophrenic from other categories of schizophrenia. Paranoid schizophrenia is likely to occur later in life and has a more stable course over time than do other forms. There is a high level of suspiciousness, and yet a lower likelihood of a severe disorganization of personality in paranoid schizophrenics (Gillis and Blevins, 1978; Bernheim and Lewine, 1979; Lazar and Harrow, 1985; Karson and Bigelow, 1986). Indeed, they show a rigid sense of personal boundaries and beliefs (Johnson and Quinlan, 1985) and different cognitive strategies (Highgate-Maynard and Neufeld, 1986). Yet paranoid schizophrenia is differentiated from other forms of the psychotic paranoid disorders (paranoia, acute paranoid disorder) because it is the most disorganized paranoid disorder (Watt, 1985), and by different cognitive strategies (Highgate-Maynard and Neufeld, 1986). There are usually a wider variety of delusions, and they are less organized than those found in paranoia and acute paranoid disorder. Gillis and Blevins (1978) find paranoid schizophrenics to be less impaired in their cognitive judgments than nonparanoid schizophrenics, and others have noted some differences in body-build and chemistry.

The Case of Perry

Perry was first institutionalized at age 35. He had been picked up by the police, who thought he was drunk. They took him to a detoxification unit associated with one of the local hospitals. It is true that he had been drinking; however, even when his system had obviously been cleared of the alcohol, he still showed very strange behavior patterns. He talked about having been contacted by a variety of alien creatures, who would park their space vehicle in the field behind his apartment building. His discussion was not logical, and he often skipped from one thought to another. He said the aliens talked to him "for a real long time about a lot of things." He told different stories at different times about what these discussions focused on. At other times, he indicated a fear that he would be kidnapped by these creatures and talked about a variety of ways to keep them from capturing him, including certain bizarre incantations and prayers. At times, he would appear to be very frightened and would report he had just seen one of these creatures.

As soon as it became clear that alcohol was not his primary problem, he was transferred to the state mental hospital. When his symptoms persisted, he received a diagnosis of paranoid schizophrenia. His sister, who said he had always been a bit strange, reported that the odd behaviors had definitely increased in recent months. She took out commitment papers on him, and after an initial observation period, he was committed to the hospital for sixty days.

Perry is a Japanese-American, whose father, a Caucasian, met his Japanese wife-to-be when he was stationed in Japan at the end of World War II. They returned to the United States shortly thereafter, and Perry's father took a job as a machinist in a large factory. His mother stayed home until Perry and his sister, two years younger, were old enough to go to school. She then took a job with a power company, first as a clerk, and later in a supervisory position.

Perry's birth was normal and uncomplicated. He did show some problems in social adjustment in the second grade. Several students delighted in picking on him, apparently because of his slightly different physical appearance that reflected his Japanese-American ancestry. He became quite sensitive to this and such teasing easily induced him to fight. The teasing dropped off in the later grades, though Perry always remained sensitive to any comments in this regard.

Perry's parents were devoted to him and his sister, and they seldom used any form of physical punishment. When Perry did something bad, his father and mother both used shaming techniques as their primary mode of discipline. They apparently felt that if they could induce a humiliation experience, it would prove aversive enough to prevent any repetition of the behavior. Overt expressions of shame and humiliation by Perry were often sufficient to diminish their anger and obtain forgiveness.

Perry did above average work in school, though he was never able to spell well. In the first two grades Perry had an ineffective teacher who did not like him though it was never clear why this was so. He was always ashamed of his poor performance in spelling, especially as there was a glaring discrepancy between his ability in this area and in other areas, and it was something he could not explain to himself or to others. By the time he was in sixth grade, he was regularly having his younger sister help him by correcting his spelling in his written assignments.

When Perry was in the eighth grade, his father was crushed and killed by a piece of machinery at work. The damage was so severe that the coffin was closed at the funeral. Perry had always felt close to his father and was very upset for many months after this.

When Perry went to high school, he became interested in radio and electronics and joined a school club that focused on these interests. He socialized regularly with members of the club, yet had few friends outside of it. He dated only sporadically. He had his first experience with intercourse when he was seventeen, when he was basically seduced by the girl.

Perry attended a university for one year but obtained poor grades, largely because he studied very little. He was primarily interested in electronics and did reasonably well when his coursework had even a remote relationship to this area. At the same time, he did poorly in core courses in the humanities, and so he dropped out of college at the end of one year. He obtained a job as an assistant to a television repairman and also enrolled in vocational school at night to study electronics. He did well, graduated in the upper half of his class, and obtained a job as a technician in a company that manufactured electronic instruments.

By this time, his sister had married. Though she cared for Perry, they had little contact. Perry had been living in a boarding house since he dropped out of college. He decided to move back in with his mother, and she was happy that he did so, for she had been quite lonely.

Perry continued to socialize on occasion with other people whom he met through his interests in electronics and his job, but he was not active socially. He dated occasionally, though he never became serious with anyone. He occasionally had intercourse with girls he dated. Once in a while he would get mildly drunk and pick up one of the local prostitutes for an evening. In the hospital interviews, he verbalized a wish that he had married, even though there was little in his history to support this. He seemed content to stay at home with his mother, who took care of his food and laundry and seldom made any demands on him. She was happy to have him around and, like Perry, she did not have much inclination to socialize.

When Perry was 33, the company he worked for closed the plant. He was offered a job in one of their other plants in another city, but he did not wish to move, and declined. After a couple of months of unemployment, he obtained a job in a large shop that serviced various electronic instruments. He was not nearly so happy now, for he was much more strictly supervised, and he could not use his own initiative as much as he had in his previous job. The pay was also less than he had received, and he did not have a number of his old freedoms, such as a lot of say in what hours he worked. He also experienced friction with his immediate supervisor. However, this supervisor realized that Perry was an excellent technician, so he never forced their conflict into a confrontation.

Perry became even more reclusive, in part because a number of his friends had moved to work in the plant in the other city. His mother began to develop physical problems, which also put stress on him. She was not very self-disclosing as to the extent of her illness, so he had no clear information to lessen his apprehension. He started to spend more time in a small laboratory he had built in the attic of their home. He told several people he was working on some "new communication inventions." When asked for details about these devices, Perry would simply say that he did not want to give out any secrets that could be used against him. Most people thought he was kidding.

Three weeks before the episode that eventuated Perry's being hospitalized, his mother was told she had cancer. She told Perry, yet failed to mention any details or the fact that there was some chance it could be cured. Perry showed little distress when she told him about this, which was surprising in light of his devotion, and more importantly his dependence, on her. Perry had typically used alcohol in moderation, but he started drinking more after this. He had drunk heavily the night before he was hospitalized, and this loss of control was the last link in the chain that led to a full-blown psychotic paranoid break.

Etiology

Several factors in Perry's development contributed to his eventual paranoid adjustment (Haynes, 1986). His Japanese-American background made him an oddity in the almost wholly Caucasian world in which he grew up. Though he did not pose a threat to any of his neighbors and peers and, therefore, did not receive consistent hostility, he was quickly aware of the physical differences (and he supposed that this would apply to other areas as well), so it was easy for him to define himself as out of the mainstream.

Another factor in Perry's background that is common in the history of the development of paranoid behavior is the use of shaming techniques by his parents to discipline him. As Kenneth Mark Colby (1977) notes, the paranoid individual learns very early to use "symbol-processing procedures to forestall a threatened unpleasant affect experience of humiliation, detected as shame signals. . . . In preventing humiliation, the procedures use a strategy of blaming others for wronging the self" (p. 56). Shaming techniques particularly predispose an individual to anticipating the possibility of humiliation and thus to engage in numerous mechanisms to protect the ego from this experience.

Paranoids do differ from normals in terms of how they process information (Highgate-Maynard and Neufeld, 1986), and in this vein, one major technique used by the paranoid is projection (Heilbrun, Blum, and Goldreyer, 1985). Projection was initially hypothesized by Freudian theorists, though they were specifically referring to projection of concern about conflict over homosexuality (Nederland, 1984). More recent formulations have pointed out that it is not necessary to hypothesize a homosexual conflict, and indeed some paranoids are overtly homosexual, which directly contradicts this Freudian theory. On the other hand, the Freudian hypothesis of projection has held up well through the years, and it is clear that many of the paranoid's delusions are projections of their own internal ruminations and concerns (Johnson and Quinlan, 1980, 1985; Heilbrun, Blum, and Goldreyer, 1985).

Perry led an essentially isolated existence, and the friends he did have were centered on specific interests. As a result, he had a more restricted information base on how to function in society, so that he was further isolated (Haynes, 1986). He returned to a dependency relationship with his mother, not only for fulfillment of his physical survival needs, but for simple company also. He encountered a potential humiliation experience in the loss of his job, and so he protected himself by becoming even further isolated in his own inner world (Colby, 1977). When the threat of the loss of his mother became more real to him than before, his anxiety was markedly increased. His usual defenses of isolation and projection were not sufficient, and as a result he resorted to alcohol to dilute his upset. This also was not sufficient, so he resorted to creating his own world, the delusional system. He was not so severely disturbed and blatantly bizarre as some paranoid schizophrenics are, yet his delusions were numerous, and they did not have the clearer focus or organization characteristic of those psychotic individuals diagnosed as either acute paranoid disorder or paranoia.

Treatment

Persons with a paranoid disorder of any sort are seldom likely to be involved in treatment unless coerced in some fashion, such as by imprisonment, hospitalization, or pressure from a spouse (Shemberg and Levanthal, 1984). This is not surprising, because paranoids are suspicious of many, and actually trust few people, if any (Karson and Bigelow, 1986). Also, most therapies, particularly for interpersonal problems, eventually require a degree of self-disclosure and the client's willingness to admit vulnerability. These characteristics are the opposite of some of the inherent qualities that make a person paranoid. Paranoids strongly fear allowing others to see their vulnerabilities and other foibles, as they are then open to a much-feared shame experience or even to attack (especially if they have delusions of persecution) (Colby, 1977; Barrett, 1980). Thus, the critical first step is gaining the trust of the client.

Paranoids who are severely disturbed and thus either dangerous or somewhat disorganized are likely to be hospitalized. Some clinicians have administered electroconvulsive treatments (ECT) to paranoids, possibly with the notion that the paranoids will forget their delusions, but this treatment has shown little success. First, the lack of success is not surprising since the paranoid greatly fears any sense of increased vulnerability and/or loss of control over the self, which is a probable effect of ECT. Second, there is not much evidence that ECT is of any therapeutic value, except possibly for acute severe depression, and there is also a high risk of short- and long-term memory loss as well as brain damage from any continued ECT administration (Friedberg, 1975; Lambourn and Gill, 1978; Squire et al., 1981). The same problems and the lack of positive results have generally been found in the application of psychosurgery to paranoid disorders (Trotter, 1976).

In severe paranoids, particularly paranoid schizophrenics, some chemotherapy strategies have been effective in reducing the more bizarre components. No single drug has emerged as consistently or markedly effective, although some positive results have been obtained with the phenothiazines and with a trifluoperazine-amitriptyline combination.

Direct therapy, based on the theories of John Rosen (1953) and amplified and improved by Karon (1976), attempts to "crash through" the defenses erected by the paranoid. The therapist openly interprets the assumed conflicts of the paranoid, rather than waiting for the client to formulate the conflict as a traditional psychodynamic therapist would do. These interpretations, delivered in gut-level language rather than in polite or scientific terminology, usually focus on what are assumed to be the paranoid's major inner conflicts: sexuality, aggression, and inadequacy.

The irony is that in many cases a therapeutic technique, such as those just described, may reduce the severely disordered behavior only to have the person begin to function as a paranoid personality disorder (see the next case, Lloyd, for characteristics of the personality disorders in general). That is, the person is still suspicious and fearful of vulnerability but can marshal interpersonal resources to escape (sometimes literally) the treatment situation. It is at this point that the issue of gaining trust, as discussed below, becomes critical.

Perry's Treatment. As is typical for most individuals who are committed to a state hospital, Perry immediately received chemotherapy. As noted, the phenothiazines, such as Thorazine, have been helpful with some paranoid schizophrenics, particularly when the person is severely disturbed, anxious, and disorganized in behavior. Though the chemotherapy did diminish Perry's activity level and the overt expression of his delusions, it did not provide any significant cure.

The most critical issue in the treatment of any paranoid disorder is gaining the trust of the client (Barrett, 1980). This is true with any client, but it is doubly important for the paranoid, whose disorder is focused on the issues of trust and fear of loss of control.

In line with the theories of Shemberg and Levanthal (1984) and Colby (1977), the social worker who functioned as Perry's therapist at the state hospital tried to understand the meaning of and accept Perry's delusions. Yet, at the same time, Barrett (1986) emphasizes that the therapist must maintain his or her own integrity. This requires that the therapist accept the paranoid's delusional system while not participating in it.

As is typical in this approach, Perry eventually began to question his therapist whether she thought that his ideas were reasonable. She attempted to communicate two critical points: First, that she could not really disprove Perry's ideas, in large part because it is almost impossible to prove a negative theorem. Second, that she understood how distressing and frightening it would be to experience the world as he did. She tried to point out any similarities that she could find between her own actual life situations and social history and Perry's. This was an attempt to provide Perry with a frame of reference to which he could orient himself. This was done so that he might begin to evaluate information with a new perspective, and also begin to rely on his therapist's advice and help (Shemberg and Levanthal, 1984).

Perry's therapist also attempted, through her own manner and through some bibliotherapy (assigned reading designed to stimulate a therapeutic response) to generate the beginnings of a sense of humor in Perry. Paranoids, somewhat like the compulsive personality disorders, are notoriously lacking in a sense of humor. They cannot take the perspective that many things are not always serious. As a result of this lack of sense of humor, they tend to channel all available information into the serious perspective of their delusional system.

These therapy approaches were successful to a degree with Perry. He eventually began to examine some of his delusional systems with the idea that they might not be totally correct. He did develop a bit of a sense of humor that seemed to help. Since he had not shown the very disorganized behavior for a long period of time, his prognosis was better than others with the same disorder. When he began to function at a reasonably normal level in the hospital, he was transferred to a halfway house. Strong efforts were made to ensure that he had a job and to have his sister provide some social support for him. As was seen in the previous case of Sally, at least a minimally supportive family environment is a critical factor in predicting a client's success in staying out of a psychiatric hospital after release.

Comment and Outcome

Paranoid ideation is a psychopathological pattern that emerges most severely in the often scattered and varied delusions of paranoid schizophrenia, the more ordered delusional system of the paranoid disorders, and then in a more muted (nondelusional) form in the paranoid personality disorder. Fears of vulnerability and avoidance of shame and humiliation, often accompanied by projection, characterize these disorders. Treatment is difficult since the very nature of most treatment approaches (increased self-disclosure and confrontation of the self) are the things the paranoid most fears (Shemberg and Levanthal, 1984). Any significant cure depends on the therapist's ability to generate trust in one who is inherently untrusting (Barrett, 1980, 1986).

In Perry's case, he was maintained on medication for one year, which helped reduce his anxiety level. It also helped him sleep, which had been a problem in the weeks before his most severe upset. Perry did return to work, and with the aid of his therapist, he was better able to adjust himself to conditions there. Unfortunately, Perry has never made much progress in the area of socialization. He has stayed out of the hospital for three years, though he has not always functioned adequately. Of course, the longer he remains out of the hospital, the more positive his chances are for staying out permanently. But the prognosis remains a bit guarded because of his inability to muster the social support systems that develop from adequate socialization skills.

REFERENCES

Barrett, C. (1980) Personality (character) disorders. In R. Woody (Ed.), *The Encyclopedia of Clinical Assessment*. San Francisco: Jossey-Bass.

————. (1986) Personal communication.

Bernheim, K. and Lewine, R. (1979) *Schizophrenia*. New York: W. W. Norton.

Colby, K. (1977) Appraisal of four psychological theories of paranoid phenomena. *Journal of Abnormal Psychology, 86*, 54–59.

Friedberg, J. (1975) Let's stop blasting the brain. *Psychology Today*, August, 18–26.

Gillis, J. and Blevins, K. (1978) Sources of judgmental impairment in paranoid and nonparanoid schizophrenics. *Journal of Abnormal Psychology, 87*, 587–596.

Haynes, S. (1986) A behavioral model of paranoid behavior, *Behavior Therapy, 17*, 268–287.

Heilbrun, A., Blum, N., and Goldreyer, N. (1985) Defensive projection: An investigation of its role in paranoid conditions. *Journal of Nervous and Mental Disease, 173*, 17–25.

Highgate-Maynard, S. and Neufeld, R. (1986) Schizophrenic memory search performance involving nonverbal stimulus properties. *Journal of Abnormal Psychology, 95*, 65–73.

Johnson, D. and Quinlan, D. (1980) Fluid and rigid boundaries of paranoid and nonparanoid schizophrenics on a role-playing task. *Journal of Personality Assessment, 44*, 523–531.

————. (1985) Representational boundaries in role portrayals among paranoid and nonparanoid schizophrenic patients. *Journal of Abnormal Psychology, 94*, 498–505.

Karon, B. (1976) The psychoanalysis of schizophrenia. In P. Magero (Ed.) *The Construction of Madness.* New York: Pergamon.

Karson, C. and Bigelow, L. (1986) The paranoid quotient. *Acta Psychiatrica Scandinavica, 73,* 39–41.

Lambourn, J. and Gill, D. (1978) A controlled comparison of simulated and real ECT. *British Journal of Psychiatry, 133,* 514–519.

Lazar, B. and Harrow, M. (1985) Paranoid and nonparanoid schizophrenia. *Journal of Clinical Psychology, 141,* 145–151.

Nederland, W. (1984) *The Schreber Case: Psychoanalytic Profile of a Paranoid Personality.* Hillsdale, N.J.: Analytic Press.

Rosen, J. (1953) *Direct Analysis.* New York: Grune & Stratton.

Shemberg, K. and Levanthal, D. (1984) Conceptualization and treatment of paranoid schizophrenia. *Psychotherapy, 21,* 370–376.

Squire, L., Slater, P., and Miller, P. (1981) Retrograde amnesia and bilateral ECT. *Archives of General Psychiatry, 38,* 89–95.

Trotter, S. (1976) Federal commission ok's psychosurgery. *APA Monitor, 7,* 4–5.

Watt, J. (1985) The relationship of paranoid states to schizophrenia. *The American Journal of Psychiatry, 142,* 1456–1458.

/ Paranoid Personality Disorder

The Case of Lloyd

"Acute Paranoia was the only conceivable judgment. 'How did they go about their diagnosis?' Venice leaned forward, his large black hands folded as he asked the question. 'Infrared Telescopic motion picture cameras were used over a thirty-day period in every possible situation. In restaurants, the Presbyterian church, in arrivals and departures at all formal and private functions. Two lip readers provided texts of everything said; the texts were identical. There are also extensive, I should say exhaustive reports from our own sources within the bureau. There can be no dispute with the judgment. The man is mad'." (p. 25)

— Robert Ludlum
The Chancellor Manuscript

The paranoid personality disorder is marked by chronic suspiciousness, emotional detachment and isolation from others, and a tendency to be litigious or even pugnacious under stress. The personality disorders are discussed at length in Chapter 10, and the reader is referred to the introduction of that section for a discussion of the general characteristics of those patterns. However, even though this is a personality disorder rather than a paranoid disorder, the case is presented here because the etiological concepts and treatments dovetail with those presented in the preceding case of Perry. At the same time, the symptomatology, etiological considerations, and outcome do differ, and these contrasts should help to elaborate an overall understanding of the phenomenon of paranoid thinking (Watt, 1985b).

The case of Lloyd involves a young man for whom being suspicious and projecting this blame onto others became a lifelong defensive strategy (Haynes, 1986; Heilbrun, Blum, and Goldreyer, 1985). Not only was the strategy counterproductive, but it also predisposed the social environment to respond to him in a hostile manner. Met with social isolation throughout his childhood and adolescence, Lloyd found enough evidence to support his belief system of his "superiority" and of his jealousy of others. Eventually, his functioning declined as his paranoid ideation interfered with objective self-evaluation and prohibited personal growth and satisfaction.

The Case of Lloyd

Lloyd was an only child whose natural mother died of birth complications when he was three months old. He was cared for mainly by the family's housekeeper until he went to college. When he was three, his father remarried, but Lloyd's relationship with his stepmother was never better than amiable indifference. She was active in church and civic organizations and left the rearing of Lloyd to his father and the housekeeper.

Lloyd's father was a senior executive with a large and competitive business firm. He often discussed his problems and frustrations with work during dinner. He was demanding and quickly fired his employees if they did not meet his standards. Also, he was critical of himself and often attributed setbacks in the business to his professional weaknesses. Similar demands were made of Lloyd. His father analyzed all of Lloyd's actions and attributed any instance of less-than-perfect achievement to Lloyd's weak efforts. His stepmother usually agreed with his father, though she placed no demands on Lloyd. Lloyd's memory of the housekeeper was that she was affectionate toward him and cared for him responsibly, yet they were not close and Lloyd did not regard her as a parent.

Lloyd did not attend nursery school or kindergarten and became a behavior problem in the first grade. When his teacher corrected his work, he was resentful and angry. On occasion, Lloyd would scream at the teacher, tear his papers, and refuse to work any longer. When his parents were informed of his behavior, they accused the teacher of picking on Lloyd and expecting too much of him. However, they did get Lloyd a tutor, who helped bring him to the level of first graders who had been to kindergarten and/or nursery school. This served to reduce the intensity of Lloyd's response to criticism. Nevertheless, Lloyd's resentment when corrected was noted by each of his elementary and junior high school teachers.

The family, mainly because of their condescending social attitudes, had few close or intimate friends. Lloyd's playmates were carefully screened during his childhood. As he grew older and brought schoolmates home, his father criticized anyone who was not considered "worthwhile." When his parents thought a friend was unacceptable (most of the time), they were rude and later criticized Lloyd for choosing that friend. Aside from compulsory church on Sundays, followed by lunch with the minister and the families of other church leaders, there were few family activities. Lloyd's father and stepmother were socially active with church- and business-related functions, but Lloyd was seldom included in these functions, and he was sent to visit his (natural) maternal grandparents when his parents vacationed each summer.

Since his parents were so selective about his friends, Lloyd felt he had few options among his schoolmates. Apparently taking his father's lead, he was domineering and condescending toward his classmates. They naturally resented Lloyd's constant bragging about his grades and assertions of genius. Also, Lloyd was a self-appointed classroom disciplinarian and could be counted on to report any misbehavior to school authorities. These social problems were brought to his parents' attention, but they criticized the school and assured Lloyd that the other students avoided him because they were jealous of his superior ability. Lloyd internalized these attitudes and used the jealousy explanation to explain his subsequent unsuccessful interactions with his peers. This attitude further generalized to all areas of accomplishment. The fault always lay with unreasonable expectations, unclear instructions, and/or other external circumstances beyond his control.

Needless to say, Lloyd was generally isolated throughout high school and college. Most of his fellow students found him intolerable. Aside from a few superficial lunch and study buddies, Lloyd had almost no contact with his peers by the time he entered high school. He spent most of his time alone in his room — studying or working with his stamp collection. Both activities proved successful for Lloyd. He graduated with honors from high school and college and he developed a regional reputation when he began to exhibit his stamp collections.

After college, Lloyd took a managerial position with the firm for which his father worked. He worked hard and advanced to regional supervisor within three years. At this point, he began dating a young lady of whom his parents approved. They were engaged and married within the year. The marriage was met with more enthusiasm by the parents of the bride and groom than by the newlyweds themselves. Lloyd's wife, Ellen, was quiet and agreeable though plain and "colorless." Apparently her parents had become concerned that Ellen would not attract a suitable (or timely) husband and were relieved when Lloyd proposed. Lloyd, on the other hand, was flattered by Ellen's uncritical acceptance and minimal expectations of him. The marriage evolved into a nearly platonic and amicable partnership. They did not have children, which resulted more from an unenthusiastic sexual relationship than from any definitive decision.

It was not long before Lloyd realized that his rapidly advancing career had come to a halt. The firm for which he worked was merged with a larger conglomerate, and the positions above were assigned to employees who had been with the conglomerate before the merger. Feeling that he was again the undeserving victim of unfortunate circumstances, Lloyd resigned and took a position with a competitive firm. However, his domineering and critical behavior toward his supervisors had only been tolerated at the first firm because of his father's high position. Lloyd had no such protection in the second job, and created so much resentment among his staff members that he was asked to resign.

Lloyd, who had not experienced a significant failure since first grade, brought suit against the firm, claiming that they had yielded to pressure from the competitive conglomerate to fire him. The suit was quickly dismissed. However, the suit identified Lloyd as a troublemaker and other local firms were now reluctant to hire him. His father was retired by this time and thus unable to use his influence to secure a position for Lloyd. In addition, he criticized Lloyd for not playing the game and accused him of ruining the family's good name.

Lloyd decided to start his own consulting firm and borrowed heavily to establish the business. He did well for a few months, then ran into conflicts with employees and customers. He continually complained of substandard performance and verbally berated clerks, staff members, and even customers on occasion. As a result, there were so many resignations and terminations that the firm became unstable, and then folded. Lloyd's usual externalizations were becoming unacceptable, even to Ellen. She pronounced him a failure in life and filed for a separation (with the approval of her parents). Lloyd's parents agreed that he was a failure in life but saw a divorce in the family as an unacceptable social blight. They urged Lloyd to prevent a divorce and criticized him for being unsuccessful. The separation and business failure were financially draining for Lloyd. He declared bankruptcy, moved to another city, and enrolled in dental school. Ellen was keeping in contact with him, and the separation had made both aware of the dependency they had on each other. However, he could not be shaken from the belief that the conglomerate bore him ill will and had ruined his life in his hometown. He hoped he could get a fresh start in another profession and locale over which the conglomerate had no influence.

Lloyd's problems continued in dental school. First, his negative social tendencies did not change, and there were numerous conflicts with instructors, patients, and dental hygienists. Also, Lloyd's manual dexterity was poor. He performed well on written exams, but his practicum evaluations were barely passing. Lloyd, of course, blamed these low evaluations on prejudiced instructors, difficult patients, errors of timekeepers, and so forth. He did graduate from dental school and passed the written licensing exam with honors. However, he could not pass the practical exam in two tries, refused to attempt it again, and so was unable to practice dentistry as an independent professional. Opportunities arose to work under the supervision of a licensed dentist, but Lloyd regarded these positions as inferior and unacceptable. His reaction to this third failure were extreme rage reactions and sullen anger. He even made some threats of recriminations against several of his dental school professors whom he had especially disliked.

Etiology

The dynamics of this case are analogous to those in the case of Perry. Just as in that case, the use of shaming techniques (Colby, 1977) as a disciplinary technique was a factor in Lloyd's pathology. However, of far greater import was the modeling for social isolation and elitism that Lloyd's parents provided, as well as the direct control over friendships that helped to further the isolation (Haynes, 1986). Their own tendency to project failure on to others (again modeled by Lloyd) and their unwillingness to accept any failures or problems in Lloyd similarly made him unwilling to accept these in himself. There is little or no evidence for a genetic component in paranoid personality disorders, nor for the commonly held belief that gradual hearing loss may be implicated (Watt, 1985a, b).

After Lloyd started to fail, the societal labeling of "troublemaker" and "difficult person to get along with" and the increasing alienation from the few supportive interpersonal relationships he had (Ellen, his parents) made him even more vulnerable. He could not tolerate this status, which resulted in anxiety and even more inappropriate projections and expressions of his chronic anger (Heilbrun, Blum, and Goldreyer, 1985).

Treatment

Ellen, who had been visiting Lloyd on the weekends, became increasingly concerned about his condition. She insisted that he accompany her to see a family physician, which Lloyd agreed to do only after much arguing. The physician prescribed some tranquilizing medication and set up a session with a clinical psychologist in their health maintenance organization.

They had several sessions together, but Lloyd would never allow any trust to develop (Barrett, 1980, 1986). After his anxiety subsided a bit, it became clear that he was only continuing in order to placate Ellen and his parents. The one positive change occurred as a result of the psychologist's referral of Lloyd to a physical therapist to work on his poor manual dexterity. The exercises, combined with some remedial practicum work at the dental school, improved Lloyd's dexterity and he was finally able to pass, though barely, the practical portion of the licensing exam.

He went into practice shortly thereafter. He was able to make an adequate living, though he never developed a good practice because of the unattractiveness of his personality. He eventually divorced Ellen and moved to a distant city, possibly in an attempt to distance himself as much as possible from his prior "failures." He became increasingly involved with an extreme right-wing political organization. He was once arrested for having an unregistered machine gun and had to pay a heavy fine. His personality never did change much; he lived out his life in this manner and died of a heart attack at age 49. Since there had been no history of heart disease in his family, its appearance here is probably support for the concept that chronically repressed anger can be a major generic factor in heart disease (Friedman and Rosenman, 1959; McClelland, 1979).

Comment

The cases of Perry and Lloyd demonstrate the different courses paranoid disorders can take (Watt, 1985b). It is ironic that Perry, who presented an apparently much more severe disorder, eventually made more positive changes. This may have been because the severity of his disorder forced him into a status of vulnerability (thus allowing change), whereas Lloyd was more successful in staying away from a position in which others could break through his system. For the most part, the course of Lloyd's disorder is unfortunately the more probable outcome in the paranoid disorders.

REFERENCES

Barrett, C. (1980) Personality (character) disorders. In R. Woody (Ed.), *The Encyclopedia of Clinical Assessment*. San Francisco: Jossey-Bass.

_____. (1986) Personal communication.

Colby, K. (1977) Appraisal of four psychological theories of paranoid phenomenon. *Journal of Abnormal Psychology*, *86*, 54–59.

Friedman, M., and Rosenman, R. (1959) Association of specific overt behavior patterns with blood and cardiovascular findings. *Journal of the American Medical Association*, *169*, 1289–1296.

Haynes, S. (1986) A behavioral model of paranoid behaviors. *Behavior Therapy*, *17*, 268–287.

Heilbrun, A., Blum, N., and Goldreyer, N. (1985) Defensive projection: An investigation of its role in paranoid conditions. *Journal of Nervous and Mental Disease*, *173*, 17–25.

McClelland, D. (1979) Inhibited power motivation and high blood pressure in men. *Journal of Abnormal Psychology*, *88*, 182–190.

Watt, J. (1985a) Hearing and premorbid personality in paranoid states. *The American Journal of Psychiatry*, *142*, 1453–1455.

_____. (1985b) The relationship of paranoid states to schizophrenia. *The American Journal of Psychiatry*, *142*, 1456–1458.

7

The Affective (or Mood) Disorders

Affect refers to the subjective experience of emotion, whereas *mood* designates a consistent and pervasive emotion that influences our view of our world as well as ourselves. The affective disorders are broadly defined in the DSM as primary disturbances of mood and affect; in contrast to disordered thinking, which characterizes the other two severe disturbances previously discussed (schizophrenia and the paranoid disorders). Included among the affective disorders in the DSM are symptom patterns that were formerly labeled as depressive neurosis and even on occasion as cyclothymic personality disorder. Thus, symptom patterns within this category range from mild to moderate depressive episodes to psychotic affective reactions.

The major categories are those of bipolar disorder, major depression, and the specific affective disorders, which include cyclothymic disorder and dysthymic disorder (Klein, Depue, and Slater, 1985). Bipolar disorder, which replaces the traditional term of manic-depressive psychosis, is discussed in the case of Manuel. It should be noted that no DSM category has been available for a disorder that has only a manic component (high activity level, grandiosity, and euphoric and/or driven emotionality). It is felt (with supporting though not conclusive data) that such patterns virtually always occur in a history that shows at least some evidence of depression (Billings and Moos, 1984; Nurnberger et al., 1979); thus, the designation as a bipolar disorder. The major depressive disorder designates severe, though not usually chronic (in a continuous episode) depression; it is discussed in the case of Dolores, the first case in this chapter.

The inclusion of the full range of mood disturbances within one diagnostic classification by DSM is consistent with the current trend among mental health professionals to consider these disorders along a continuum of affective adjustment (Klein, Depue, and Slater, 1985). Consequently, different diagnoses among the subcategories of affective disorders are made in accordance with criteria of intensity and duration, as opposed to traditional conceptualizations that attempted (not always very successfully) to recognize qualitative distinctions (Lorr, 1986).

Normal depression is characterized by a brief period of sadness, grief, or dejection in which disruption of normal functioning is minimal. Mild disturbances of mood and thought are manifest by apathy, impaired concentration, and increased guilt. These reactions are often responses to discrete environmental events, such as the loss of an important (high stimulus value, though not necessarily loved) other, or disappointments in career or finances. This depression may require no treatment and often lifts with time. Moderate episodes (as discussed in the case of Danielle in Chapter 2) are more disruptive to normal functioning and may be associated with distorted cognitions and/or skill deficits that require various psychological therapies. The more severe (and sometimes psychotic) depressive syndrome necessitates a multi-modal therapeutic approach, usually including chemotherapy, psychotherapy, and cognitive behavior modification techniques such as those employed in the treatment of Dolores.

REFERENCES

Billings, A. and Moos, R. (1984) Chronic and nonchronic unipolar depression. *Journal of Nervous and Mental Disease, 172,* 65–75.

Klein, D., Depue, R., and Slater, J. (1985) Cyclothymia in the adolescent offspring of parents with bipolar affective disorder. *Journal of Abnormal Psychology, 94,* 115–117.

Lorr, M. (1986) Classifying psychotics: Dimensional and categorical approaches. In T. Millon and G. Klerman (Eds.) *Contemporary Directions in Psychopathology: Toward the DSM-IV.* New York: Guilford.

Nurnberger, J., Ruth, S., Dunner, D., and Fieve, R. (1979) Unipolar mania: A distinct clinical entity? *American Journal of Psychiatry, 136,* 1420–1423.

/ *Major Depressive Disorder Associated with a Suicide Attempt*

The Case of Dolores

"Well, I think you got anhedonia. It affects maybe one out of a hundred. It means you can't have fun. No kind of fun. Just like you on a golf course. You look like Torquemada's got the hot pliers on your nuts instead a just enjoying the game." (p. 68)

— Joseph Wambaugh
The Secrets of Harry Bright

Depression is a common malady in our society. It is a disorder of mood and affect, with these primary symptoms: (1) dysphoria (feeling bad) and/or apathetic mood, (2) a loss or decrease in the potency of stimuli (a condition referred to as a "stimulus void"), for example, through the death of an important other, and (3) anhedonia, or a chronic inability to experience pleasure. These symptoms were well described by the existential philosopher and theologian Søren Kierkegaard in his 1844 book *The Concept of Anxiety* (Princeton University Press):

> I do not care for anything. I do not care to ride, for the exercise is too violent. . . . I do not care to lie down, for I should either have to remain lying, and I do not care to do that, or I should have to get up again, and I do not care to do that either. . . . I do not care at all (p. 19).

These primary symptoms are then often associated with a various admixture of the following secondary symptoms: (1) withdrawal from contact with others; (2) a sense of hopelessness; (3) rumination about suicide and/or death; (4) sleep disturbance, especially early-morning awakening; (5) psychomotor slowing or agitation; (6) decrease in and/or disruption of eating behaviors; (7) self-blame, a sense of worthlessness, irrational feelings of guilt; (8) lack of concentration; (9) lack of decisiveness; (10) increased alcohol or drug use; (11) crying for no apparent reason.

Virtually everyone has been depressed at one time or another; indeed, it is a normal response to loss or disappointment. But when it persists and/or becomes so severe that it significantly disrupts a person's world, it becomes pathological.

Approximately 20–40 million persons in the United States have experienced a serious depression of some type, an approximate rate of 12–13 percent which has remained stable for several decades (Murphy et al., 1985). At least 200,000 each year are hospitalized for depression, and it is estimated that up to one fourth of the office practice of physicians who focus on physical disorders is actually concerned with depression-based symptomatology. About 85 percent of the psychotropic medication dispensed for depression is prescribed by nonpsychiatrists, primarily internists, gynecologists, and family practitioners.

Whereas manic disorders and depressions with a manic component usually begin before age 30, depressive disorders can begin at any age. Separation anxiety and school phobia (see the case of Julie in Chapter 12) may be manifestations of underlying depression in young children. Adults who have had one major severe depression have about a 50-percent chance of experiencing another episode, and those who have had several episodes are more likely to shift into a chronic bipolar disorder (manic-depressive) than are those who have had only a single episode (Murphy et al., 1985; Lobel, 1984).

Dimensions of Depression

The normal–pathological continuum is one way of typing or conceptualizing depressions. Other continuums on which one can think of different depressions are: acute–chronic, agitated–slow, neurotic–psychotic, primary–secondary, and of course the unipolar–bipolar dimension that differentiates Dolores' depression (unipolar) from Manuel's (bipolar) in the following cases in this chapter. Another, and a particularly important, continuum is the endogenous–exogenous (Andreasen et al., 1986; Tsuang, Farasone, and Fleming, 1985; Dam, Mellerup, and Rafaelson, 1985). This popular classification system attempts to categorize depressions by cause. Endogenous depressions are assumed to originate from internal psychic and physical causes (such as hormonal disruption); exogenous from external ones (such as personal loss). Endogenous depressives show higher rates of nonsuppression (an abnormal response) on the Dexamethasone Suppression Test than do exogenously depressed persons (Dam, Mellerup, and Rafaelson, 1985).

The four traditional behavioral indications of a significant endogenous depression are (1) generally slowed response patterns, (2) early-morning sleep disruption, (3) more severe mood problems, and (4) significant weight loss without dieting.

Lewis and Winokur (1983) combined their own research with a thorough review of other relevant research to develop three subclassifications of unipolar depressive disorder that reflect the endogenous-exogenous dimension.

1. Depressive Spectrum Disease (DSD): marked by first-degree family members with alcoholism and/or antisocial personality problems. There may or may not be a family history of depression.

2. Familial Pure Depression Disease (FPDD): a family history of depression only—the endogenous group.

3. Sporadic Depressive Disease (SDD): no family history of alcoholism, antisocial patterns, or depression.

The important differences between these groups are (1) the mean age for the first depressive episode is much later for the SSD group (41.3 years) than the DSD (34.6) or FPDD (33.4) groups; (2) the FPDD group is more likely to show an abrupt or acute onset of depression and more total episodes; (3) the DSD group shows a much higher rate of interpersonal (sexual and marital) and legal difficulties; and most importantly, (4) the FPDD group shows a much higher incidence of nonsuppression of serum cortisol in the Dexamethasone Suppression Test, much higher rates of insensitivity to insulin in the recovery phase of depression, and a higher rate of EEG abnormalities during sleep. All of this suggests that the FPDD group is a distinct entity whose depression is related more to neurobiological dysfunction (probably genetically—based in the regulation of the hypothalamine-pituitary-adrenal systems) than to situational trauma or cognitive dysfunction.

Suicide

Some severe depressions do not involve suicide, and some suicides do not involve depression. However, very often when there is a significant depression, such as with Dolores, suicide is a concern. About 25,000 suicides are reported each year in the United States, and there is some evidence that the former rate of 10 to 12 per 100,000 people may now be increasing, especially among adolescents. Several European countries, including Switzerland and Sweden, report rates of about 18 to 25 per 100,000. Traditionally, suicide rates in non-Westernized nations have been thought to be lower: rates of 3.5 and 7 per 100,000 have been reported for Thailand and Uganda, respectively. However, rates as high as 43 and 37 per 100,000 have been found in Mandurai, India, and in Tikapia in the western Pacific, respectively (Tseng and Hsu, 1980).

There is a long list of famous suicides, including Samson, Cleopatra, Ernest Hemingway, Adolf Hitler, Jack London, Amadeo Modigliani, Marilyn Monroe, Virginia Woolf, and so on. However, in general, the typical suicide attempter is most often an unmarried white female with a history of past and recent stressful events who had an unstable childhood and who now has few social supports and lacks a close friend to confide in. On the other hand, the typical suicide completer is most often an unmarried, divorced, or widowed white male who is over 45, lives alone, has a history of significant physical or emotional disorder and, often, of alcohol abuse (Lobel, 1984). At the same time, suicide is the second highest cause of death in the United States for white males aged 15 to 19 (88 per 100,000), though it still ranks far behind accidents (627 per 100,000). About three times as many women as men attempt suicide, but three times as many men actually kill themselves (Shneidman, 1985; Lobel, 1984).

Such statistics, however, often underestimate actual rates. Because suicide still has the taint of sin and crime, coroners and police officers are reluctant to cite it as a cause of death. Moreover, many individuals who commit suicide try to make it look like an accident so their survivors are spared any stigma and can collect on life insurance. Most experts believe that actual rates are from twice to ten times as high as official figures.

The Case of Dolores

Dolores, a 32-year-old white divorced mother of two boys, was hospitalized following a suicide attempt that she planned meticulously. After reading materials on certain prescription medications, including hypnotics, Dolores was sure that she knew the lethal dosages for each. Faking symptoms that she thought would lead to prescription of what she wanted, she made appointments with several physicians and accumulated the medications that they prescribed for her. She was careful to have the prescriptions filled at different pharmacies so that she would not arouse suspicion.

As her plan developed, her friends noticed that Dolores's depression seemed to be lifting and they commented on how much better she looked to them. Dolores agreed that she was "better." When the planned time came, Dolores took a cab to an out-of-the-way motel, registered under an assumed name, paid cash in advance for a three-day stay, and explained her need to be undisturbed while she studied for her final examinations. The motel owner accepted her story and assigned her a fairly isolated room so she could work and sleep odd hours. To make it more difficult for anyone who tried to detoxify her, Dolores discarded the bottles containing her medication. She also mailed her purse and all of her identification cards to her home so that information could not be developed on her.

Dolores took all of her pills, a massive overdose, and went to bed to die. To her surprise, she was awakened three days later, very sick but alive. The puzzled motel owner called an emergency medical service, and she was taken to the hospital. There, Dolores admitted what had happened to her and expressed her regret that her suicide attempt was not successful.

Following extensive detoxification, Dolores was assigned to a multidisciplinary inpatient treatment team consisting of a psychiatrist, a psychologist, nurses, expressive therapists, pastoral counselors, social workers, and others. Psychological testing and other assessments showed that Dolores suffered from depression and continued to be suicidal. The psychiatrist prescribed an antidepressant medication for Dolores, and her psychotherapist, a clinical psychologist, began a program of cognitive behavioral therapy.

It was revealed that Dolores had a family history of "depressive-spectrum" disorder. Her father had swings of mood and drank excessively as if to control them. In time his drinking became alcoholic in style although he never received a diagnosis or treatment for the disease. Dolores's maternal grandfather had been hospitalized for mental illness and her mother had been treated with electroconvulsive therapy for depression. Dolores, the oldest of five children, grew up listening to her mother and father argue and, at times, there was violence in the marital relationship. A dominant theme in the arguments was that Dolores's mother had trapped her father by becoming pregnant, and that she was therefore a whore and a slut. There was no mention of the father's role in the pregnancy, or his character, in these arguments, and apparently Dolores's mother agreed that she was "guilty as charged."

Along with developmental history such as this, the assessment sought to determine whether there were significant life events, such as losses, related to the onset of Dolores's depressive episode. (Such events, of course, do not necessarily cause the depressive episode but may help to understand it.) Dolores's depression had worsened after she learned that she had a hereditary kidney disease and that her sons probably would have it also. In reality, the kidney disease was not disabling and probably would have affected her life very little. Dolores's response to the diagnosis was quite another matter. She exhibited extreme helplessness and hopelessness about the matter. In retrospect, her friends noted that she had not only vegetative signs of depression, such as loss of appetite and sleep disturbance, but also the "cognitive triad" of depression (Beck, 1976). That is, she was negative about herself, about her present experiences, and about the future.

Etiology

There are a variety of theoretical perspectives on the etiology of depression, and these are presented, along with their related perspective treatments, in the case of Danielle in Chapter 2. In the case of Dolores, both biological and psychological factors are involved, as they are in most serious cases of depression (Harlow, Newcomb, and Bentler, 1986; Gonzales, Lewinsohn, and Clarke, 1985; Bandura et al., 1985; Lobel, 1984).

These external and internal factors usually combine in varying degrees in an actual case of depression to produce a self-perpetuating sequence like the following:

Negative environmental condition + biological predisposition ——
Social withdrawal + lowered information processing ——
Inadequate social behaviors + guilt and self-blame ——
Further self-devaluation + social withdrawal ——
More biological change that facilitates depression

One interesting question relevant to etiology is the differential rates of depression in adult males and females (Vredenberg, Krames, and Flett, 1986). Prior to adolescence, symptoms of depression are equally common in males and females. From that time on, females are more likely than males to express their depression directly in mood symptoms, and this divergence persists throughout adulthood. Brown and Harris (1979) found that at least two thirds of adults treated for depression are females. The majority of these clients are of lower socioeconomic status, and are more likely to have accepted the stereotypic passive female role. Passivity in turn facilitates depression. Such women also have fewer options for coping with depression than do women of high socioeconomic status. Several researchers assert that there are indications of an actual higher base level of depression in females (Chevron et al., 1978; Brown and Harris, 1979; Vredenberg, Krames, and Flett, 1986); however, traditional sex role demands still exert a critical influence on this disparity (Miller and Turnbull, 1986).

Chevron et al. (1978) studied the content of the depressive experience in females and males. They found that depressions in females were more likely to be anaclitic, or dependency-oriented, reflecting a loss of satisfaction in relationships. The depressive experiences in males, on the other hand, focused on self-criticism, a perceived failure to live up to competency and goal expectations (Harlow et al., 1986).

There are other reasons why females may be diagnosed depressive more often than males (Miller and Turnbull, 1986; Brown and Harris, 1979). First, they are simply more willing to admit to feeling depressed, whereas males are often brought up to deny feelings suggesting vulnerability. Second, the majority of mental health professionals who make diagnoses are male. It is possible that through the bias of sex-role stereotyping they are more likely to view a series of behaviors as "depressed" in women, yet to give the same behavior in males a different label, such as "adjustment reaction."

Treatment

The case of Danielle in Chapter 2 detailed the options available for the treatment of depression. As with many cases of major depression, the primary treatments used were chemotherapy and cognitive behavior modification.

(Steinbrueck, Maxwell, and Howard, 1983; Lyons, Rosen, and Dysken, 1985; Meichenbaum, 1985; Simons et al., 1986).

Cognitive behavioral therapy (Beck, 1976), such as was done with Dolores, aims at determining the rules that govern the life of the depressed person. It makes the assumption that "what we do and how we think about it determines how we feel." Therefore, Dolores's therapist explored the evidence that she listed as warranting her death by suicide. It was determined that Dolores had married in her teens to get away from her parents' constant fighting. Like her mother, she was pregnant before she married, and her young husband blamed her for the pregnancy. Dolores accepted this view, as her mother had before her, and she justified to herself the beatings that her husband gave her even while she was pregnant. Dolores's marriage was, of course, very unhappy, but she felt too unworthy to think that she might do better. A second child was born of the marriage and Dolores hoped that the event would spur her young husband to love her and to act responsibly. It did the opposite. Finally, Dolores decided to divorce, but, just as the decision was made, she discovered that she was pregnant. Terrified about what her husband would say and very confused, Dolores had an abortion. Unfortunately, she did not have counseling prior to the abortion. Dolores and her husband divorced, but her life improved very little. Her ex-husband gave her little financial support, and she was forced to carry the burden of the children alone. She enrolled in college, part-time, and continued as a working single parent under significant stress.

Cognitive behavior therapy regarded Dolores's dominant view of herself as an important schema or organized set of perceptions. Whatever negative things happened in her life, Dolores saw them as deserved, since, in her view, she was not only a whore and a slut like her mother, but had also killed her unborn child. Positive experiences and responses from others were difficult for Dolores to accept and she had "automatic thoughts" when they occurred ("it must be a mistake since there are good people who should have good luck like this"). When it was discovered that she had a kidney disease, Dolores readily integrated that into her controlling schema. To her it was clear that the rule of her life was that bad things did and should happen to her. However, the fact that the disease was hereditary and the discovery that her son probably would have the disease tipped the balance. She concluded that she had no right to go on living—thus her suicide attempt and the continued suicidal intent.

Dolores had a good response to medication and, within about six weeks, the vegetative (physical) symptoms of her depression had abated completely. She had normal energy, slept normally, and had adequate appetite. Dolores also had a good response to cognitive behavior therapy, especially the technique of "guided discovery," and was able to correct her dysfunctional thoughts. Formal cognitive behavior therapy was continued for about six weeks after Dolores was discharged from the hospital, and she then came in only for "booster" sessions to review self-corrective techniques. While it is possible that Dolores will experience depressive episodes in the future, the prophylactic effect of cognitive behavior therapy is likely to reduce the severity of any future instances of depression.

Dolores's experience with antidepressant medication and cognitive behavior therapy illustrates that depression is quite treatable. Further, most cases of depression can be treated in a fairly brief period of time, and further episodes of depression can be prevented or minimized. Nevertheless, depression is a serious mental illness, because the depressed person may not recognize the symptoms and, worse, may commit suicide before treatment can be initiated. There is little advantage in having a successful treatment for a disorder if it can't be offered to the patient in time.

Gonzales, Lewinsohn, and Clarke (1985) found that depressives who were most likely to relapse showed (1) a greater number of previous episodes of depression, (2) a higher depression level at the entry point into the study, (3) a family history of depression, especially in first-degree relatives, (4) poor physical health, (5) a higher level of dissatisfaction with their major life roles, and probably most surprising of all, (6) are younger in age. Most of these factors are consistent with prior studies, though, with the exception of the higher probability of relapse for younger clients, which is a controversial finding.

Dolores responded reasonably well to imipramine, a tricyclic antidepressant, in that her general motor behavior speeded up—the primary effect of chemotherapy for depression (Lyons, Rosen, and Dysken, 1985). Of equal or greater importance was the cognitive behavior modification and social skill treatments directed at the cognitive and interpersonal components of her disorder (Becker, Heimberg, and Bellack, 1986; Meichenbaum, 1985; Beck, 1967, 1976).

Suicide Types and Prediction

Emile Durkheim (1951) pioneered an emphasis on sociological factors contributing to suicide. Certain subgroups lose cohesiveness, and members feel alienated. His typology of suicidals (anomic—under conditions of normlessness; egoistic—lack of group ties; altruistic—suicide for the good of some cause) is still influential (Shneidman, 1985), as is evident in the following list of types of suicides:

1. *Realistic*: These are suicides precipitated by such conditions as the prospect of great pain preceding a sure death.

2. *Altruistic*: The person's behavior is subservient to a group ethic that mandates or at least approves suicidal behavior, like kamikaze pilots in World War II.

3. *Inadvertent*: The person makes a suicide gesture in order to influence or manipulate someone else, but a misjudgment leads to an unexpected fatality.

4. *Spite*: Like the inadvertent suicide, the focus is on someone else, but the intention to kill oneself is genuine, with the idea that the other person will suffer greatly from consequent guilt.

5. *Bizarre*: The person commits suicide as a result of a hallucination (such as

voices ordering the suicide) or delusions (such as a belief the suicide will change the world).

6. *Anomic*: An abrupt instability in economic or social conditions (such as sudden financial loss in the Great Depression) markedly changes a person's life situation. Unable to cope, the person commits suicide.

7. *Negative self*: Chronic depression and a sense of chronic failure or inadequacy combine to produce repetitive suicide attempts eventually leading to a fatality.

In adults, a number of potential primary behavioral clues appear to predispose an individual to successful suicide attempts (Shneidman, 1985; Mehrabian and Weinstein, 1985):

1. Previous suicide attempts. In this context, the first axiom of psychology could well be "behavior predicts behavior." The second axiom would be "behavior without intervention predicts behavior."

2. Statements of a wish to die, especially statements of a wish to commit suicide.

3. Certain *consistent* life patterns of leaving crises rather than facing them: for example, in relationships, "You can't walk out on me; I'm leaving you," or in jobs, "You can't fire me; I quit."

4. Suicide attempts by an important identity figure (a parent or a hero).

5. Feelings of failure, together with a loved spouse who is competitive or self-absorbed.

6. Early family instability and parental rejection of one's identity.

7. A recent severe life stress, or the presence of a chronic debilitating illness.

Several factors can then increase this potential:

1. A cognitive state of "constriction"; in other words, an inability to perceive any options or a way out of a situation that is generating intense psychological suffering.

2. Easy access to a lethal means; for example, drug overdose is the prevailing form of suicide among physicians.

3. Absence of an accessible support system (family and good friends).

4. Life stresses that connote irrevocable loss (whether of status or of persons), such as the relatively recent death of a favored parent. This factor is particularly important if the person at risk is unable to mourn the loss overtly.

5. High physiological responsiveness—high need for stimulation-seeking in spite of suicide thoughts.

6. Serious sleep disruption and abuse of alcohol or drugs.

7. Depression, particularly when combined with a sense of hopelessness or loss of a sense of continuity with the past or present. As noted earlier, depressions marked by low levels of 5-HIAA increase the probability of suicide attempts.

Suicide Prevention

Several things can be done on both a societal and an individual level to lower the incidence of suicide (Harlow et al., 1986; Shneidman, 1985; Phillips, 1974). Educating the public on the myths and facts of suicide is an important first step. There is also evidence that suicide-prevention telephone hotlines and centers can at least slightly decrease the suicide rate. Lastly, suicide prevention at the societal level requires restriction of media publicity about suicides.

Several precautions can also be taken for prevention of suicide at the individual level.

1. Attend seriously to people who voice a desire to kill themselves or "just go to sleep and forget it all." About two thirds of those people who actually kill themselves have talked about it beforehand in some detail with family, friends, or others (Lobel, 1984).

2. Attend especially to depressed individuals who speak of losing hope.

3. To the degree possible, keep lethal means (guns, large prescriptions of sedatives) away from suicidal individuals.

4. Generate a personal concern toward a suicidal person; a suicide attempt is most often a cry for help. Suicidal individuals need a temporary "champion" who can point them toward new resources, suggest new options, and at least in a small way diminish the sense of hopelessness.

5. Try to get the person to perform some of the following behaviors: (a) engage in regular physical exercise, (b) start a diary, (c) follow a normal routine, (d) do something in which he or she has already demonstrated competence, (e) confide inner feelings to someone, (f) cry it out. Try to get the person to avoid self-medication and other people inclined toward depression.

6. Make every effort to guarantee that a suicidal person reaches professional help. Making an appointment is a good first step; getting the person to the appointment is the crucial second step.

REFERENCES

Andreasen, N., Schaftner, W., Reich, T., Hirschfield, R., Endicott, J., and Keller, M. (1986) The validation of the concept of the endogenous depression. *Archives of General Psychiatry, 43*, 246–254.

Bandura, A., Taylor, C., Williams, S., Mefford, I., and Barchas, J. (1985). Catecholamine secretion as a function of perceived coping self-efficacy. *Journal of Consulting and Clinical Psychology, 53*, 406–414.

Beck, A. (1967) *Depression: Causes and Treatment*. Philadelphia: University of Pennsylvania Press.

————. (1976) *Cognitive Therapy and the Emotional Disorders*. New York: International Universities Press.

Becker, R. Heimberg, R., and Bellack, A. (1986) *Social Skills Treatment for Depression*. New York: Pergamon.

Brown, G. and Harris, T. (1979) *Social Origins of Depression*. New York: Free Press.

Chevron, E., Quinlan, P., and Blatt, S. (1978) Sex roles and gender differences in the experience of depression. *Journal of Abnormal Psychology*, *87*, 680–683.

Dam, H., Mellerup, E., and Rafaelson, O. (1985) The dexamethasone suppression test in depression. *Journal of Affective Disorders*, *8*, 95–103.

Durkheim, E. (1951) *Suicide*. New York: Free Press.

Gonzales, L., Lewinsohn, P., and Clarke, G. (1985) Longitudinal follow-up of unipolar depressives. *Journal of Consulting and Clinical Psychology*, *53*, 461–469.

Harlow, L., Newcomb, M., and Bentler, P. (1986) Depression, self-derogation, substance abuse, and suicide ideation. *Journal of Clinical Psychology*, *42*, 5–20.

Lewis, D. and Winokur, G. (1983) The familial classification of primary unipolar depression: Biological validation of distinct subtypes. *Comprehensive Psychiatry*, *24*, 295–501.

Lobel, B. (1984) *Depression*, Rockville, Md.: Dept. of Health and Human Services (DHHS publication (ADM) 84-1318.

Lyons, J., Rosen, A., and Dysken, M. (1985) Behavioral effects of tricyclic drugs in depressed inpatients. *Journal of Consulting and Clinical Psychology*, *53*, 17–24.

Mehrabian, A. and Weinstein, L. (1985) Temperament characteristics of suicide attempters. *Journal of Consulting and Clinical Psychology*, *53*, 544–546.

Meichenbaum, D. (1985) Cognitive behavior modification. In F. Kanfer and A. Goldstein (Eds.) *Helping People Change*. New York: Pergamon.

Miller, D. and Turnbull, W. (1986) Expectancies and interpersonal processes. In M. Rosenweig and L. Porter (Eds.) *Annual Review of Psychology 37*, Palo Alto, Calif.: Annual Reviews.

Murphy, J., Sobol, A., Neff, R., Olivier, D., and Leighton, A. (1985) Stability of presence: Depression and anxiety disorders. *Archives of General Psychiatry*, *41*, 990–1000.

Phillips, D. (1974) The influence of suggestion on suicide. *American Sociological Review*, *39*, 340–354.

Shneidman, E. (1985) *Definition of Suicide*. New York: Wiley.

Simons, A., Murphy, G., Levine, J., and Wetzel, R. (1986) Cognitive therapy and pharmacotherapy for depression. *Archives of General Psychiatry*, *43*, 43–50.

Steinbrueck, S., Maxwell, S., and Howard, G. (1983) A meta-analysis of psychotherapy and drug therapy in the treatment of unipolar depression with adults. *Journal of Consulting and Clinical Psychology*, *51*, 856–863.

Tseng, W. and Hsu, V. (1980) Minor psychological disturbances of everyday life. In H. Triandis and J. Draguns (Eds.) *Handbook of Cross-Cultural Psychology: Psychopathology*. Boston: Allyn and Bacon.

Tsuang, M., Farasone, S., and Fleming, J. (1985) Familial transmission of major affective disorders: Is there evidence supporting the distinction between unipolar and bipolar disorders? *British Journal of Psychiatry*, *146*, 268–271.

Vredenberg, K., Krames, L., and Flett, G. (1986) Sex differences in the clinical expression of depression. *Sex Roles*, *14*, 37–50.

/ *Bipolar Disorder (Manic-Depressive Psychosis)*

**The Case of
Manuel**

*"Then Big Harry said to me, 'You know, Bobby, I
think old Suicides was crazy.' He was right, too,
because when his family sent for him the man
who came explained to Commissioner old
Suicides had suffered from a thing called Mechanic's Depressive. You never had that, did
you, Roger?' "*

— Ernest Hemingway
Islands in the Stream

That manic and depressive symptoms are components of a single disorder was
suspected by Hippocrates (460–377 B.C.) and has remained a consistent assertion. Since that time, unipolar depression has been distinguished from bipolar
disorder and is currently thought to result from different etiologic factors
(Klein, Depue, and Slater, 1985; Lewy et al., 1985; Goodwin and Guze, 1984).

The diagnosis of bipolar disorder, also referred to as the bipolar affective disorder and affective disorder, and formerly termed the manic-depressive psychosis,
is made whenever manic features are observed, regardless of the presence of
depressive features. As noted earlier, the former DSM-II subclassifications of
(1) manic, (2) depressed, or (3) circular types of bipolar disorder have been
abandoned in light of recent evidence that virtually all individuals with primary manic features have evidenced depressive symptoms at some point (Klein
et al., 1985; Nurnberger et al., 1979). Thus, only depression is considered a
unipolar disorder.

The range of behaviors that typify mania are broad and most commonly
include (1) hyperactive motor behavior, (2) variable irritability and/or euphoria, and (3) a speeding-up of thought processes, called "flight of ideas." Manic
speech is typically loud, rapid, and difficult to understand. When the mood is
expansive, manics take on many tasks (seldom completing them), avoid sleep,
and easily ramble into lengthy monologues about their personal plans, worth,
and power. When the mood becomes more irritable, they are quick to complain and engage in hostile tirades.

Psychotic manic reactions involve grandiose delusions, bizarre and impulsive behavior, transient hallucinations and explosiveness. As such, these reactions may be confused with schizophrenic episodes. However, whereas
schizophrenics (and schizoaffectives) are distracted by internal thoughts and
ideas, manics are distracted by external stimuli that often go unnoticed by
others. Also, whereas schizophrenics (and schizoaffectives) tend to avoid any
true relationships with others during an active phase, manics are typically open
to contact with other people (NIMH Staff, 1977).

Though the onset of discrete manic episodes may be sudden, the disorder
has a generally slow onset in many cases, and as with Manuel, the person's life
history evidences preliminary symptoms in childhood or adolescence that at

some point become more intense and debilitating. Lastly, the presence of a bipolar disorder is not always seen as totally negative, as it is with schizophrenia, and indeed it may even be a spur to creativity.

Creativity, Poetry, and the Bipolar Disorder

The concept that creativity may be a result of psychopathology is hardly new, is a persistent theme of certain authors such as Arthur Koestler, and has been noted by researchers (Winokur, 1978) as well. But more recent research, such as that found in the book *Manic-Depressive Illness* (1986) by F. Goodwin and K. Jamison, offers impressive support that this is so in the specific instance of bipolar disorder (manic-depressive disorder) and especially in relation to certain artistic endeavors.

The list of first-rank artists who appear to have also suffered a bipolar disorder is impressive: poet-painter Dante Gabriel Rossetti, playwright Eugene O'Neill; writers F. Scott Fitzgerald, Ernest Hemingway, Virginia Woolf, John Ruskin, and Honoré de Balzac; and composers Robert Schumann, Hector Berlioz, and George Frederic Handel. Handel, for instance, wrote *Messiah* in a frenetic twenty-four days during a manic high.

But it is poets who are most often bipolars. Byron, Coleridge, Shelley, Poe, and Gerard Manley Hopkins were all bipolars, as were many modern American poets, like Hart Crane, Robert Lowell, Anne Sexton, Theodore Roethke, Sylvia Plath, and John Berryman.

Some might argue that poets tend to be bipolars because poetry often emerges from the inner turbulence of the psyche. But even in the eighteenth century, a time in which poetry did not really focus on such inner upset and complexity, a high proportion of accomplished poets appear to have been bipolars. Thus, the relationship of poetry and bipolar disorder may more directly result from the fact that frenetic but sporadic effort is more effectively productive in poetry than in other areas, and because the imagery inherent in poetry is more like the primitive thought found in severe emotional disruption. Also, the depressions of the bipolar mood-swing provide the fuel of emotional depth to the productivity of the manic high.

As a result, some artists so afflicted avoid therapy, out of a fear that successful treatment would curb their creativity. It appears that in some cases they may be correct.

The Case of Manuel

Manuel was hospitalized for a psychotic manic episode when he was 33 years old. Six weeks before the emergency admission, he had begun exhibiting mild hypomanic symptoms: taking up several new hobbies, treating co-workers to expensive lunches, buying drinks for everyone in bars, and challenging his friends to tennis matches with exorbitant wagers. His wife reported being initially pleased with these actions since Manuel had been depressed and withdrawn for several weeks.

Further, Manuel had been described by his friends and relatives as "moody and unpredictable" since childhood. But this time, Manuel's expansive mood escalated, and his behavior became so inappropriate that his wife asked the police to locate him so that he could be hospitalized. She became concerned when she found a letter from him explaining that he was moving to a hotel to write his memoirs. The letter was lengthy, unsigned, and ended abruptly in the middle of a sentence.

The police had some difficulty locating Manuel. He was eventually found in the city park reciting and writing his life's story for a crowd of encouraging teenagers. He could not be persuaded to accompany the officers willingly and was restrained with handcuffs. He became agitated and verbally obscene, so the police bound his feet and gagged his mouth. When Manuel arrived at the emergency room, he was strongly sedated and transferred to the psychiatric unit for observation.

Manuel's wife, Alicia, was interviewed the next day, and his behavior on the unit was closely observed. Alicia reported that Manuel was a high school mathematics teacher who at night was working toward his master's degree in accounting. Alicia was a former keypunch operator who had stopped working three years earlier when their son was born. They had become engaged in junior high school and married as soon as Manuel (who was a year younger) had finished high school.

Throughout elementary and high school, Manuel had received above average grades, lettered in track, and was sports editor for the school newspaper. He was popular with his peers, although he was perceived as moody and quick-tempered. In high school, he and Alicia settled into a social circle with three other couples with whom they continue to socialize almost exclusively. Manuel attended college and found part-time sales jobs until he received his bachelor's degree. After graduating from college, he taught high school and Alicia became pregnant with their first child, a daughter. Alicia was six months' pregnant at the time of Manuel's hospitalization.

Alicia was able to give detailed information about Manuel's life history, since they had been neighbors as children. Manuel was the only child of parents described as loving and hard-working. His father was self-employed as an electrician, and his mother taught high school business courses. Alicia was aware of a maternal aunt who had committed suicide and also thought that a couple of Manuel's cousins (on his mother's side) were "strange."

Although Alicia described her husband as moody, easily provoked to anger, and somewhat impulsive, she thought their marriage was close and successful. Her perception was that although Manuel was difficult to live with at times, he was otherwise loving, responsible, and attentive toward his family. Alicia noted that he had been depressed about his grades, though this was not an unusual event for him, as he was always disappointed with less than superior performance. According to Alicia, Manuel usually "snapped out of it" within a few days and began to plan for the next semester. However, this latest depression had lasted for many weeks and was replaced with the hypomanic behavior.

After the onset of the switch out of the depression, Manuel's activity level rapidly increased and his behavior became less inhibited and more inappropriate. The students reported to the principal Manuel's sudden outbursts and tangential lectures, and he dismissed Manuel for drunkenness. That afternoon, Manuel came home with a new sports car and a diamond necklace for his wife. He announced that the loss of his job was a sign that he should go into business for himself and "make millions." His behavior continued to escalate, and his wife could not persuade him to seek professional help. Instead, he insisted that he had never felt better, and he argued with his wife for not having faith in his ability to succeed. He also invested their savings in an expensive office building and contracted for extensive renovations in preparation for his new business. He began to tell rambling stories of his childhood to his children and friends and then decided to write his memoirs while the office building was being remodeled.

Manuel's behavior on the psychiatric unit was similar to Alicia's descriptions. He continued to recite and write his memoirs for other patients, though he now claimed that these were the "words of God spoken through Manuel." He engaged in several shouting matches with patients who questioned the truth of his stories. Efforts to interview or test Manuel were futile because he would only discuss the "new gospel" and his future wealth, which had been promised him in return for spreading the "gospel according to Manuel."

Treatment

Treatment for severe manic disorders is usually within an inpatient setting, with a focus on chemotherapy. After the intensity of the episode has subsided, supportive psychotherapy, social skills training, and assistance with legal and vocational problems are often necessary to help the person readjust both interpersonally and occupationally (Mester, 1986). Milder hypomanic disorders can often be managed with outpatient chemotherapy and/or psychotherapy, and psychotherapy is considered the treatment of choice for the cyclothymic disorder — a nonpsychotic affective disorder characterized by rapid mood swings.

The evidence in support of biological cause theories of the bipolar disorder suggests that it almost certainly has a genetic base. The genetic concept is based on the observation that the disorder affects more members of some families than others (Klein et al., 1985; Winokur, 1978; Klerman, 1978) and on the fact that there is a single, effective biological method for treating bipolar mood disorders — lithium (Mander, 1986; Goodwin and Guze, 1984; NIMH Staff, 1977). Lithium, an alkaline metal found in mineral rocks and salt water, has been used as a mineral water cure for various problems since the second century A.D. Lithium relieves the symptoms of acute manic episodes at about a 75-percent effectiveness rate (Goodwin and Guze, 1984; NIMH Staff, 1977), and also acts for some as a prophylactic agent against recurrent manic episodes.

Unfortunately, patients with bipolar disorder are notorious for medical noncompliance (Cochran, 1984; Jamison et al., 1979). Between 35 and 50 percent of patients on lithium maintenance (1) complain of side effects, some of which can be quite serious (Davis et al., 1981), (2) object to having their moods controlled by medication, and/or (3) resent the implication of chronic illness symbolized by regular drug use (Jamison et al., 1979). In Manuel's case, noncompliance was a minor problem that his wife successfully influenced. However, as noted, there were consequent residual problems in his employment and financial status.

Manuel's Treatment. Based on Manuel's behavior on the inpatient unit and in the emergency room, and on the interview with Alicia, the diagnosis bipolar disorder-manic with psychotic features was given, and he was started on lithium carbonate (a lithium salt). The effects of lithium usually take several days to manifest fully in the patient's mood and behavior, so sedative medications are often used initially and then gradually decreased until the desired blood level of lithium has been attained. Manuel was responsive to the lithium and was discharged after three weeks with a prescription for lithium, psychotherapy (Mester, 1986), and regular appointments for medication monitoring. A few sessions of marital therapy were also helpful in repairing the damage to the marriage (Bornstein and Bornstein, 1986). Eventually, Manuel was able to return to his teaching position (after a letter from his therapist explained the disorder, which prompted the principal to remove the "drunkenness" episode from Manuel's personnel records). The therapist also referred Manuel and Alicia to an attorney who reestablished Manuel's competency to handle his affairs (Grisso, 1986), and he then was able to sell the office building, car, and diamond necklace and settle the debts that he had incurred during the episode. For the past two years, Manuel was maintained on lithium. Because of the potentially severe side effects of lithium (Davis et al., 1981), he is now trying to manage without medication and has been relatively successful. It is probable, however, that he will manifest similar episodes at some future point, and he and Alicia have been cautioned to return for a resumption of the treatment if he begins to show the preliminary signs.

Comment

The relationship between psychosocial stressors and episodes of mania or depression is often obvious for first episodes; subsequent episodes, however, can occur without apparent precipitants. Also, the predisposing factors, other than family history, for the development of the bipolar disorder have not been clearly identified (Goff, 1985; Lewy et al., 1985). In Manuel's case, there is evidence of an increasingly stressful life style for a person with marginal frustration tolerance. Perhaps the biologic predisposition combines with the more demanding developmental tasks of late adolescence and young adulthood to explain the typically later onset (late twenties to early thirties) of the bipolar disorder, as is seen in Manuel. It is also possible that the moodiness, quick temper, and unpredictable behavior of Manuel's childhood and adolescence were too clearly reinforced by task avoidance and/or maternal attention and affection. Fortunately, the combination of the lithium therapy, psychotherapy, legal and social interventions, and Alicia's overall support allowed a positive outcome in Manuel's case.

REFERENCES

Bornstein, P. and Bornstein, M. (1986) *Marital Therapy*. New York: Pergamon.
Cochran, S. (1984) Preventing medical noncompliance in the outpatient treatment of

bipolar affective disorders. *Journal of Consulting and Clinical Psychology*, *52* 873–878.

Davis, B., Pfefferbaum, A., Krutzik, S., and Davis, K. (1981) Lithium's effect on parathyroid hormone. *American Journal of Psychiatry*, *138*, 489–492.

Goff, D. (1985) Two cases of hypomania following the addition of l-tryptophan to a monoamine oxidase inhibitor. *The American Journal of Psychiatry*, *142*, 1487–1488.

Goodwin, D. and Guze, S. (1984) *Psychiatric diagnosis* (3rd ed.). New York: Oxford University Press.

Grisso, T. (1986) *Evaluating Competencies: Forensic Assessments and Instruments*. New York: Plenum.

Jamison, K., Gerner, R., and Goodwin, F. (1979) Patient and physician attitude toward lithium: Relationships to compliance. *Archives of General Psychiatry*, *36*, 866–869.

Klein, D., Depue, R., and Slater, J. (1985) Cyclothymia in the adolescent offspring of parents with bipolar affective disorder. *Journal of Abnormal Psychology*, *94*, 115–127.

Klerman, G. (1978) Long-term treatment of affective disorders. In M. Lipton, A. Di-Mascio, and K. Killiam (Eds.), *Psychopharmacology*. New York: Raven.

Lewy, A., Nurnberger, J., Wehr, T., Pack, D., Becker, L., Powell R., and Newsome, D. (1985) Supersensitivity to light: Possible trait markers for manic-depressive illness. *The American Journal of Psychiatry*, *146*, 725–727.

Mander, A. (1986) Is lithium justified after one manic episode? *Acta Psychiatrica Scandinavica*, *73*, 60–67.

Mester, R. (1986) The psychotherapy of mania. *The British Journal of Medical Psychology*, *59*, 13–20.

NIMH Staff. (1977) *Lithium in the Treatment of Mood Disorders*. Rockville, Md.: National Institute of Mental Health.

Nurnberger, J., Ruth, S., Dunner, D., and Fieve, R. (1979) Unipolar mania: A distinct clinical entity? *American Journal of Psychiatry*, *136*, 1420–1423.

Winokur, G. (1978) Mania-depression: Family studies, genetics, and relation to treatment. In M. Lipton, A. DiMascio, and K. Killiam (Eds.), *Psychopharmacology*. New York: Raven.

8

The Psychosexual Disorders

The variations in sexual behavior are limited only by an individual's imagination (Stoller, 1985). The psychosexual disorders are likewise varied, and include syndromes in which psychological factors are assumed to be of major etiological significance in the development of disrupted or deviant sexual behaviors. They include the gender disorders, paraphilias, and the psychosexual dysfunctions. If the disorders of sexual functioning are caused solely by organic factors (a fairly rare occurrence), a psychosexual disorder diagnosis is not made even though there may be psychological consequences. The gender disorders are marked by felt incongruence between the actual physical sexual apparatus and gender identity. If these concerns have continuously existed for more than two years in an adult, are not due to schizophrenia or a genetic disorder, and the person strongly desires to alter the genital structure and live as the opposite sex, it is labeled transsexualism. Otherwise, the diagnosis is either gender identity disorder of childhood or atypical gender identity disorder.

In the paraphilias, sexual arousal by unusual objects or situations may interfere with the individual's capacity for reciprocal affectionate sexual activity. The specific diagnoses are made in accordance with the nature of arousing stimuli; for example, transvestism, pedophilia, voyeurism, sexual sadism. The essential feature of the psychosexual dysfunctions is inhibition in the appetitive or psychophysiological changes that accompany the complete sexual response cycle. Inhibitions in the response cycle may occur in one or more of the following phases: appetitive, excitement, orgasm, resolution. Finally, there is the class of other psychosexual disorders that includes ego-dystonic homosexuality and psychosexual disorders not elsewhere classified. Ego-dystonic homosexuality is applicable only when a sustained pattern of overt homosexual arousal has been a persistent source of distress for a person who has an internalized desire to acquire or increase heterosexual arousal.

The expanded DSM category of psychosexual disorders is indicative of the continuing attitude change toward the description and treatment of sexual problems. Before Freud, sexuality was not discussed in polite society and was seen in the context of superstition, sin, or presumed genetic defects in most medical treatises. Freudian theory brought sexual dysfunctions into more open consideration, even though he attributed them to unconscious childhood conflicts that could be resolved only through psychoanalysis.

Current thinking generally regards psychosexual disorders to be the result of faulty psychosexual adjustment and learning and to be affected in certain cases by genetic and temperament variables. Thus, they are considered responsive to a variety of treatment approaches, such as operant and classical conditioning, biofeedback, hypnosis, and/or sexual reassignment surgery. Outcome studies using these techniques have been generally encouraging, especially for the sexual dysfunctions (LoPiccolo and Stock, 1986; LoPiccolo, 1985; Spence, 1985; Coleman, et al., 1985), for the gender disorders (Blanchard, Steiner and Clemmensen, 1985; Rosen, Rekers, and Bentler, 1978), and to a lesser degree for the paraphilias (Hendrix and Meyer, 1976; Cox, 1980; Carnes, 1985).

REFERENCES

Blanchard, R., Steiner, B., and Clemmensen, L. (1985) Gender dysphoria, reorientation and the clinical management of transsexualism. *Journal of Consulting and Clinical Psychology*, *53*, 295–304.

Carnes, P. (1983) *Sexual Addiction*. New York: Compcare.

Coleman, E., Listick, A., Bratz, G., and Lange, P. (1985) Effects of penile implant surgery on ejaculation and orgasm. *Journal of Sex and Marital Therapy*, *11*, 199–205.

Cox, D. (1980) Exhibitionism: An overview. In D. Cox and R. Daitzman (Eds.), *Exhibitionism*. New York: Garland STPM.

Hendrix, M. and Meyer, R. (1976) Toward more comprehensive and durable client changes: A case report. *Psychotherapy: Theory, Research and Practice*, *13*, 263–266.

LoPiccolo, J. (1985) Diagnosis and treatment of male sexual dysfunction. *Journal of Sex and Marital Therapy*, *11*, 215–231.

LoPiccolo, J. and Stock, W. (1986) Treatment of sexual dysfunction. *Journal of Consulting and Clinical Psychology*, *54*, 158–167.

Rosen, A., Rekers, G., and Bentler, P. (1978) Ethical issues in the treatment of children. *Journal of Social Issues*, *34*.

Spence, S. (1985) Group versus individual treatment of primary and secondary female orgasmic dysfunction. *Behavior Research and Therapy*, *23*, 539–548.

Stoller, R. (1985) *Observing the Erotic Imagination*. New Haven, Conn.: Yale University Press.

/ *Transvestism*

The Case of
Randy

Strange diseases, he thought, demand strange
remedies: he, her.

— John Updike
Bech Is Back

Transvestites, especially males who dress up as females, receive much media attention (Wise, 1985). Transvestism is classified in the DSM as one of the paraphilias, which was first introduced into the DSM-III in place of the older term of sexual deviation. The term paraphilia is used because it apparently is felt to have fewer connotations of sinfulness and disorder; the term also is used in order to emphasize that most sexual behaviors are on a continuum with normal behaviors. The concept of deviance is thought to introduce an unnecessary distancing from normal sexual experiences. Transvestism is defined in the DSM as recurrent and persistent cross-dressing that is initiated for the purpose of sexual arousal and that eventually becomes habitual. The transvestite experiences intense frustration when external circumstances interfere with cross-dressing (Carnes, 1983).

The disorder is relatively rare and occurs more often in males than in females. Most individuals who have been involved in transvestism have cross-dressed by the age of 10, and usually much younger (Stoller, 1985; Bleiberg, Jackson, and Ross, 1986). These individuals usually are married, so this status is likely to generate additional anxiety and depression. Most cross-dressing starts out as a partial phenomenon, but it is likely to generalize to the point at which the person feels compelled to dress fully as a woman and occasionally to behave as a female in public.

Transvestism is commonly confused with transsexualism (Carnes, 1983). The major difference is that transsexualism is considered to be a gender identity disorder whereas transvestism is a paraphilia or sexual deviation. Transsexuals truly feel as if they should be the other sex. In fact, most transsexuals feel so strongly that they have been trapped in the wrong body that they actively pursue surgical alterations (Abramowitz, 1986). Transvestites, however, do not have compelling desires to participate in sex-change surgery. Rather, even though they seek sexual arousal through cross-dressing, they maintain identity with their biological gender.

The Case of Randy

Randy, a handsome 38-year-old black, came to his first appointment at the mental health center with his wife. She was obviously more upset than he was at the time of referral, and she clearly had initiated the idea to come to the center. With some prodding, Randy finally said that he was a transvestite and that he wished to change this. His assertion that he wished to change was not completely convincing, for it was evident that his wife had played a major role in his making that statement.

This was a second marriage for Randy. Even though he had been a transvestite throughout the five years of his marriage, only recently had his wife become aware of Randy's unusual sexual interests. Randy admitted that he had been careless in the last several months. As a result, his wife found certain clothes that led her to the initial, standard conclusion that Randy was having an extramarital affair. Randy's first mistake was that he left a small make-up kit in his clothes pocket, which his wife found when she picked up the coat to take to the cleaners. He was able to provide her with a story that she reluctantly accepted. But then she accidentally discovered a suitcase of "change clothes" in the back of his car. She again assumed that this was evidence that he was seeing another woman, and she became irate and confronted him with the evidence.

Randy then felt he had no option but to explain his behavior. When he did so, it was clear that he had upset his wife much more than if he had told her that he had been having an affair. She said she was not only shocked, but also ashamed and embarrassed, and she insisted that he get help as soon as possible. Although Randy had not been as concerned about the behavior, he realized that he did feel committed to his wife, that he loved her, and that this had hurt her intensely. As a result, he stated that he would make an effort to change.

Social History

In many cases of transvestism, it is not clear as to how the cross-dressing first started and became reinforced. Fortunately, in Randy's case, certain known variables make his inclination toward transvestism more understandable.

Until the age of 2, Randy's mother and father raised him in a normal fashion. However, when Randy was two, his mother contracted a rare respiratory disease, which required her to leave the area and go to a special hospital. Randy's father felt that his wife needed him near her, and also that he could not adequately care for Randy at the same time. Randy's father had a sister whom he trusted could raise Randy adequately, so Randy moved to the home of his aunt. She was a 45-year-old woman who had lived alone ever since a short and traumatic marriage when she was 18. Since that time, she had worked as a legal secretary and had lived a quiet, reclusive life. Though she was devoted to her younger brother (Randy's father), in general she was relatively hostile toward men, and seldom dated since her divorce many years before.

As might be expected, she really had little sense of what child-rearing entailed. When Randy inadvertently picked up some of her shoes and put them on, she saw no problem with this, and indeed thought this was humorous and cute. Randy responded to this reinforcement by trying on other articles of her clothing, and she accepted this behavior as long as he did it only in the house.

At times she would let Randy dress up, and they would have tea parties. She even took pictures of Randy in his feminine dress to put in an album. The basic problem was that she really had no idea of how to deal with a little boy and had no interest herself in the activities that are interesting to most young boys.

Randy's mother died when Randy was 4 years old. His father took a job as a traveling salesman and decided to let Randy continue living with his aunt. Randy's father eventually took a more lucrative job as a sales representative and was not required to travel as extensively. When Randy was 9, his father remarried and brought Randy to live with him and his new wife. The cross-dressing naturally ceased for a time as the usual stimuli that elicited it were now absent. However, his new stepmother once allowed Randy to put on one of her dresses, and she also thought it was very cute. Then, some time after this, she discovered Randy going through her lingerie drawer, and on another occasion she discovered him wearing her underwear. When she reported the incidents to Randy's father, he became very upset and whipped Randy. When they discovered him doing it again, Randy's father and stepmother attempted a homemade version of the therapeutic technique called "negative practice." That is, they forced Randy to dress entirely in women's clothing and wear them for the duration of the day. However, they did not realize that he went into a high state of sexual arousal and masturbated several times during that day. Randy did at least get the message that his parents disapproved of this behavior, and as a result he became secretive about it.

On the surface he showed a rather normal adolescence. He participated in many school activities in high school, and in particular became so skilled in tennis that he was elected team captain. He dated occasionally and in all overt respects seemed to be relatively normal. However, in his secret life, he would often steal or buy women's clothes and wear them while by himself in a woods near their house, or he would wear them when he knew his parents would not be around. He now consistently masturbated to orgasm when he wore the clothes.

Randy continued to date fairly regularly throughout high school and college. These were social rather than sexual events for him, and on those few occasions when he did become sexually involved, he would use fantasies of cross-dressing to initiate and maintain his arousal.

He first married when he was 23, and the marriage lasted about two years. He was only able to experience sexual arousal with his wife when he fantasized being in women's clothes. They did not have sex often, though it was reasonably satisfactory to both when they did. He tried on occasion to give his wife some hints about his interests, but she did not respond. Further, he became aware from her cues that unusual or "kinky" sexual behavior would upset her. They had few mutual interests and eventually little affection for each other. The divorce seemed inevitable and was not remarkably distressing for either party.

After the divorce, there was a noticeable increase in Randy's transvestite behavior. Though he had attained a fine job with an insurance firm, he would occasionally go off on vacation and spend most of the time dressing up in women's clothes and masturbating. Also, he found a club in a nearby metropolitan area that catered to transvestites. Individuals would openly share fantasies about their behavior and would go about the club dressed in women's clothes doing a number of things that any member of a normal club would consider typical, such as having dinner and dancing. Randy managed to keep this aspect of his world separate enough so that it did not interfere with his work or other social behaviors. He met his second wife through his work. They had a number of mutual interests and both were somewhat lonely, so after a short courtship they married.

Etiology

Traditional theories have emphasized the denial of masculinity and castration anxiety as critical in the development of transvestism, but the relevant social learning theory is somewhat more applicable to Randy's case. At a very early juncture in Randy's life, cross-dressing received much attention from the significant other in his world, who at that time was his aunt. She was also the major figure from whom Randy could model behaviors. As a result, Randy was involved almost exclusively in a traditionally feminine world with few other real options to consider. Also, the attention and approval he received from his aunt for cross-dressing were particularly reinforcing (Rosen, Rekers, and Bentler, 1978; Stoller, 1985; Bleiberg, Jackson, and Ross, 1986).

This attention continued at least for a short period of time, when he returned to live with his father and new stepmother. Their later attempt to frustrate this behavior by having him dress up totally as a female and keep the clothes on all day backfired. Their idea was not that bad, however, for negative practice is effective in certain conditions, although it needs to be carefully monitored and must be done in such a way that the experience is clearly aversive. Most parents are not adequately sophisticated psychologically to carry this through. A professional consultation at this point could have turned things around (Wise, 1985). Randy went underground with his behavior, and his parents, of course, were relieved not to see any more evidence of it, ending much upset and embarrassment for them. The behavior waxed and waned throughout Randy's life. It was most prominent when he was experiencing frustration in other interpersonal areas of his life, or when he simply had more options to practice the transvestism.

As is seen in Randy's case, transvestism is a variation of fetishism, particularly from a social learning theory view. A specific object or behavior becomes associated with social and/or sexual reinforcement at an early period. Continued pairing of the behavior with sexual reinforcement, often accidental on the first few occasions, or engendered by another person such as a playmate, further reinforces the pattern. The person then begins practicing it habitually, and it becomes crystallized.

Treatment

The clinician asked to treat a transsexual might consider a referral for transsexual surgery, but such an option would be irrelevant for the transvestite who does not really consider himself or herself to be of the other sex. Actually, whether even a transsexual should undergo this surgery remains a controversial issue among professionals. Some argue that it is unnecessary, and that with counseling and the passage of time, the transsexual can lose the compulsion to change sex. On the other hand, there is some evidence that transsexual surgery is effective in making a certain subgroup of individuals happier and more satisfied with their lives. (Pauly, 1968; Money and Wiedeking, 1980; Money, 1985).

The most effective method for changing any pattern of sexual behavior to another one has been that of aversive conditioning (Sandler, 1985). It was initially used for changing the sexual preference of the homosexual individual, then was expanded into dealing with the wide variety of disordered sexual behaviors. In Randy's case, it was decided to employ the technique of "thought stopping" before using the aversive technique, as it was felt this would enhance the total effectiveness of the treatment program.

During the thought-stopping phase, Randy was asked to envision a scene in which he was cross-dressing. When he was able to develop this pattern of thoughts adequately, he was asked to signal to the therapist that he had done so. His therapist then shouted "stop," and asked Randy if the thoughts had been interrupted. Usually, the thoughts would be interrupted by the startle response. Thus, the client learns that these patterns are not as compelling as they seem. Randy was instructed to use thought-stopping when he found himself considering cross-dressing outside the therapy session. For example, if the thoughts came unwittingly, Randy was asked to shout "stop" or to say it to himself. Thought stopping has proven to be effective with this type of behavior, though it was originally developed for the more inclusive concept of obsessive thoughts. In that sense, the fantasies in a paraphilia can be seen as having obsessive components (see the earlier case of Bess).

The second phase of Randy's treatment was aversion therapy (Sandler, 1985). Randy was asked to sit in a chair in front of a standard movie screen and was hooked up with electrodes to a shock unit. Independent of the shock unit, a piece of rubber tubing was placed around his penis to measure the degree of blood flow to his penis. Randy was shown a series of slides, some of which depicted scenes that would be arousing to a transvestite. Others were of normal heterosexual behavior or of a nude person of the other sex, in this case Randy's wife, to whom he wished to increase his sexual attraction. A slide of a transvestite scene, preferably a slide from pornographic material Randy might have already used to gain arousal, was placed on the screen. Randy was told that he could keep the picture on as long as he wished, but that he would receive an increasingly strong electrical shock as he did. When he eventually asked the therapist to take the picture away, this turned the shock off and a scene of either normal heterosexual behavior or a picture of his wife was flashed on the screen. The rationale here is that the cessation of shock is a reinforcing event, so the aim was to pair the reinforcement with the desired sexual behavior.

When Randy began to notice a change in his sexual preference, which occurred after three half-hour sessions of aversive conditioning and thought stopping, he was asked to participate in controlled masturbatory training. He was told that when he masturbated he was to force himself to imagine desired scenes, such as sex with his wife, at the time of orgasm. Also, he was to try to introduce these scenes in his mind as early as possible in the masturbation sequence. At first, he needed the transvestite scenes to obtain arousal, but gradually he was able to replace these scenes earlier and earlier with imagined scenes of sexual behavior with his wife. In that way, the reinforcement from his sexual arousal and orgasm increased the future arousal of these new images. It was hoped that this would generalize to his wife in actuality, and it did.

Naturally enough, there had been some disruption of Randy's marital situation, so he and his wife also participated in marital therapy (Framo, 1979) and had several sessions of sexual instruction along the lines that Masters and Johnson (1970) suggest. These sessions helped to enhance their long-term relationship. All indications are that Randy's change was thorough and without regression to the transvestite pattern. It is true that in other such cases there might well be a regression on occasion to the earlier behaviors, and booster treatments would be necessary (Wise, 1985).

Comment

Because transvestites are secretive about their behavior and usually cross-dress in private, many are never seen by professionals. Although impersonating the opposite sex is sometimes illegal, cross-dressing is not considered a serious offense and arrests are seldom made. When a transvestite is arrested or otherwise discovered (as with Randy's wife), incarceration is seldom recommended. Some wives of transvestites accept the cross-dressing, are willing to accompany their husbands on public outings while they are cross-dressed, and adapt sexually to that pattern. But, as noted in this case, the usual effect of cross-dressing is marital strain, leading to divorce. For cases for which cross-dressing is a focus of treatment, behavioral techniques supplemented by psychotherapy and social skills training have been generally successful.

REFERENCES

Abramowitz, S. (1986) Psychosocial outcomes of sex reassignment surgery. *Journal of Consulting and Clinical Psychology, 54,* 183–189.

Bleiberg, E., Jackson, L., and Ross, J. (1986) Gender identity disorder and object loss. *Journal of Child Psychiatry, 25,* 58–67.

Carnes, P. (1983) *Sexual Addiction,* New York: Compcare.

Framo, J. (1970) Family theory and therapy. *American Psychologist, 34,* 988–992.

Masters, W. and Johnson, V. (1970) *Human Sexual Inadequacy.* Boston: Little, Brown.

Money, J. (1985) Gender: History, theory and usage of the term and its relationship to nature/nurture, *Journal of Sex and Marital Therapy, 11,* 71–79.

Money, J. and Wiedeking, C. (1980) Gender identity/normal role differentiation and its transpositions. In B. Wolman (Ed.), *Handbook of Human Sexuality.* Englewood Cliffs, N.J.: Prentice-Hall.

Pauly, I. (1968) The current status of the change of sex operation. *Journal of Nervous and Mental Disease, 147,* 460–471.

Rosen, A., Rekers, G., and Bentler, P. (1978) Ethical issues in the treatment of children. *Journal of Social Issues, 34.*

Sandler, J. (1985) Aversion methods. In F. Kanfer and A. Goldstein (Eds.) *Helping People Change,* New York: Pergamon.

Stoller, R. (1985) *Presentation of Gender.* New Haven, Conn.: Yale University Press.

Wise, T. (1985) Coping with a transvestite male: Clinical implications. *Journal of Sex and Marital Therapy, 11,* 293–300.

/ Psychosexual Dysfunction (Impotence)

The Case of
Tim

I was Romeo of the Roaches again, eating the
lamb patties of her hands, licking her yellow
hair. I grabbed her thigh ruthlessly, put my
hand around the ankle of the other leg. I need
you, I said. Bored, but having at it as the male of
the species. I'd been trained. (p. 172)
— Barry Hannah
Geronimo Rex

Psychosexual dysfunction with inhibited sexual excitement is the DSM terminology for the syndromes commonly referred to as impotence and frigidity.
Throughout this case history, we will use the term *impotence*, yet note that
there is general pejorative connotation to the term. That is, impotence suggests
general personality inadequacy and a weakness of character. The standard
term for female psychosexual dysfunction, *frigidity*, in turn suggests a lack of
emotional warmth. But there is no evidence that these implied traits occur
more commonly in individuals who experience these problems (Katchadourian, 1985). It is interesting that the weakness in the male and the coldness in
the female suggested by these terms are the exact opposites of the characteristics most clearly prescribed in the sex roles of our society—competence for
males and sensitivity and warmth for females.

The sexual response cycle is typically thought to be composed of four
stages: (1) appetitive, (2) excitement, (3) orgasm, and (4) resolution. Psychosexual dysfunction pertains primarily to the second stage (LoPiccolo and
Stock, 1986; Katchadourian, 1985).

The DSM characterizes impotence as a recurrent and persistent inhibition
of sexual excitement during sexual behavior, manifested by a partial or complete failure to obtain and maintain erection until the sexual act is completed.
This definition assumes that the clinician has already judged that the individual engages in sexual activity that is adequate in duration, intensity, and focus.
The fact that the term is *psychosexual dysfunction* points out that we are not
talking about a disorder caused exclusively by organic factors, such as a spinal
tumor, nor are we talking about sexual disorder that is the direct result of a
more primary and severe psychiatric syndrome, as for example, from severe
and acute anxiety disorder.

In practice, one has to be rather arbitrary in assigning a label of psychosexual dysfunction. Masters and Johnson (1970) arbitrarily defined it as a clinical problem if there are failures in 25 percent of the attempts at intercourse.
Also, total "erectile dysfunction" (the common term in the research literature)
is fairly rare, and typically suggests a biological cause. More often than not,
the dysfunction is partial. An erection occurs, but it does not persist long
enough to provide satisfaction for the partner or for one's own orgasm to occur (LoPiccolo, 1985; Masters and Johnson, 1970).

The Case of Tim

After suffering silently for some time, as is typical in this syndrome, Tim went to his personal physician asking for treatment of impotence. The physician referred him to a specialist, who through careful medical examination ruled out the various physical and endocrinological factors that can affect impotence. Tim's testosterone level was appropriate, and there was no evidence of severe diabetes or of a circulatory disorder, the most common physical causes of impotence. Though Tim's testosterone level was not abnormally low, it was slightly below average, so a urologist first administered testosterone to see if this might have a positive effect, but there was no relief for Tim. The urologist then attempted to use a placebo, on the assumption that the suggestion could increase Tim's hope and effect a cure. This also was not successful. The urologist then referred Tim to a clinical psychologist who specialized in treating sexual dysfunctions.

The clinical psychologist listened at length to Tim's background as a preparation for initiating appropriate psychological treatment.

Tim is 33 years old, college-educated, and makes a very good first impression. He is handsome and in good physical shape, reflecting his prior occupation as a professional baseball player. He also dresses well, keeps himself well groomed, and relates to others with apparent warmth and interest.

Though he recently has been promoted to assistant vice president in the bank in which he works, the general impression he gives is that he is neither strikingly successful nor interested in his work. Also, in spite of his good first impression, it is quickly evident that he is moderately anxious most of the time. On several occasions, he had trouble articulating some of his concerns, and he needed to get up and move about during the interview.

From his description of his parents, his mother seems to be best described as passive and pious, and his father as authoritarian and perfectionistic. Tim describes his upbringing as "standard middle-class Catholicism." Tim still attends church on occasion, but is clearly not committed at any great depth to a religious orientation. The most important focus in his world still seems to be his relationship to sports. One of his most vivid early memories is of playing in a baseball game as a very young boy, possibly at age 3 or 4, and receiving the cheers of his mother and father as he ran from base to base. Yet, his father was extremely demanding in the area of sports, as was his mother in a more subtle fashion.

His positive early images of his participation in sports are clouded by several other memories of his father's role in his early feelings about sports. His father coached the Little League team on which he played, and would often harangue him if he made any errors, particularly mental errors. His father was also demanding of the other children on the team, but certainly hollered more at Tim, possibly to avoid any accusations of favoritism. It was only when Tim performed competently that his father showed any positive response at all, and, of course, in the early years such moments were not common. Tim's father also demanded a great deal of off-the-field discipline and practice from him. Though it may have taken some fun out of growing up, Tim still refers to it as a "necessary evil that allowed me to develop the skills I needed later."

The most disturbing aspect of his parents' attitudes in this area is that they still so highly value his life in sports, even though his professional career is over because of an injury from which Tim did not recover well. Both of his parents have fixated on his role as a professional baseball player and often refer to his achievements in their discussions of him with family and friends, even though he makes his discomfort apparent when they do so. They seem to have stopped seeing him as a developing person and rather wish to retain their image of him as the successful and applauded athlete.

Tim has one sibling, Jack, a brother three years younger. Tim's brother never showed much interest in sports, yet won the respect of his parents, sometimes grudgingly, because of his accomplishments in academic areas. Surprisingly enough, Tim's parents allowed Jack to pursue an interest in music, possibly because they felt their needs in the sports area would be filled by Tim. Jack never really related well to his father, but generally he avoided hassles of any real dimension. He was clearly his mother's child, while Tim received most of the attention from his father.

Tim himself was ambivalent about his inability to function any longer as a professional baseball player. His career was first curtailed when he injured his foot sliding into a base. He returned and played earlier than he probably should have, before the foot was fully healed. He favored it slightly, which caused a subtle change in his pitching motion, eventually leading to a chronically sore arm. The orthopedic surgeon he consulted told him that he had strained the arm such that it would never return to full functioning. His manager made it clear that Tim would have to work back to an effective approach by first performing again in the minor leagues. Since Tim felt he could work in other areas, he quit rather than return to the transient existence of a minor league baseball player.

Several things made his demise as a baseball player particularly painful to him and his parents. First, he had not made it to the big leagues until he was 29 years old, having spent many more years in the minor leagues than is typical. It also appeared that before the injuries he had been on the edge of true stardom. He had started to win consistently, and there was no reason to believe this would not continue. He was also on a team that could have become champions. His injury curtailed this not only for himself but for the team as well.

It was particularly galling to Tim when some sportswriters suggested that he did not have the courage to "stick with it" and make a success of his baseball career after the injury. The implication was that he did not have enough personal courage to make the required sacrifices to generate a comeback.

Tim married his first wife when he was a junior in college, just as he had moved into a star role on the college baseball team. She was a freshman at the university, and obviously enjoyed the moderate degree of glamour that surrounded Tim. They married after a short courtship and had a child almost immediately. Then it began to dawn on them that they had few mutual interests, as well as totally different views on child-rearing. Though he indicated there were no episodes of impotence in the marriage, their sexual life was sporadic at best. She began an affair with an attorney at the office where she worked and eventually left Tim to marry him. When her new husband obtained a job with a prestigious firm in a distant city, she took Tim's child with her. Tim still manages to see his son, now 11 years old, with moderate regularity, but the distance and the early separation prohibited the development of a strong relationship. In recent years, Tim has dated Pam, a woman with whom he had initially enjoyed a satisfying sexual relationship. She moved in with him a year and a half ago, six months before he made the final decision not to continue with his baseball career. It is clear that Pam never saw Tim's career in sports as something she valued highly.

Tim has not been very clear as to whether or not he loves Pam. Sexual attraction was a major part of their early courtship, and they had a very active sex life in the first several months. Though Pam did not seem to respond specifically to his baseball career, Tim's overall athletic appearance was a strong factor in her initial attraction to him. They have talked of marriage on numerous occasions, but neither has come to feel confident about making that type of commitment. In the meantime, Tim's parents have been upset about the fact that Pam and Tim are living together without having been married, and they never mention Pam to any of their friends.

Tim links the first occasions of impotence with worries generated by sportswriters' criticisms of his alleged lack of desire to make a comeback. He remembers the first incident as occurring on a night when he had been drinking heavily, in large part because he had been upset by reading an article noting how his absence had probably cost his former team a shot at the championship. He had also been feeling uncertain at that time about the permanence of his relationship with Pam. These factors together resulted in a distracted and apprehensive mental set. When he became aware that he did not have a full erection, he became even more anxious, thus deflating what erection he had obtained. Though Pam was not overtly critical at the time, she also had not been very supportive, possibly because of her own ambivalence about the relationship. In any case, Tim saw this as a humiliating experience and naturally anticipated, at least unconsciously, future repetition of such a performance. This expectation brought on anxiety, and Tim continued having problems obtaining or maintaining an erection.

Though Tim was raised with prohibitions against virtually all types of sexual behavior, he did not take his religious views seriously at a conscious level. He had been taught to masturbate by an older male friend. In high school, he engaged in much fondling and petting with Barbara, the first girl he really dated with any consistency. But he had his first experience of intercourse with Carolyn, a good friend of Barbara's. It had been enjoyable, though in the early stages it had been very anxiety-provoking. It occurred in the living room of Carolyn's home, and just as they got started, Carolyn's father called down and asked if anyone was there, scaring Tim and temporarily deflating his erection. But his high drive level at that time came to his rescue, and they continued.

Over the years, there have been several revolutions in the thinking about what are the general causes of sexual dysfunction. The following are some of these general cultural influences. While several stages are no longer heavily influential, these stages should generally be seen as cumulative, i.e., in any one individual case, many (as with Tim) or all of the later insights can be relevant. The approximate year(s) when this idea became an influence is also listed.

- *Moral degeneracy (ancient)*: Masturbation, or virtually any sexual play, in one's early years and/or prior to marriage is seen as a degenerate pattern that leads to later sexual dysfunction as well as brain damage and a wide variety of other diseases. A more sophisticated version of this is the "You only have so many bullets in your gun," which is still prevalent in certain cultural subgroups.

- *Physiological dysfunction (traditional)*: Sexual dysfunction is a result of low hormone production, physiological disruption, or anatomic dysfunction.

- *Arrested psychosexual development (early 1900s)*: Primarily reflecting the theories of Freud, it leads to the conception that long-term psychotherapy is necessary to move one from an earlier stage (for example, allegedly the phallic stage in women who only have clitoral orgasms) to greater maturity, a side effect of which will be adequate sexual functioning.

- *Phobic-like anxiety (1950s)*: Masters and Johnson talked of "sensate focus" and "performance anxiety" (which are refinements of the work of the early behaviorists), but more importantly, they also saw good sexuality as involving a set of skills, which if deficient, resulted in sexual problems.

- *Cognitions about sex (1960s)*: Reflecting the work of the cognitive behaviorists, the sets of thoughts around possible sexual failure, sometimes referred to as "catastrophizing," are critical to sexual dysfunction. This is an evolutionary step up from the phobic-like anxiety theory.

- *System maintenance (1970s)*: No matter what the original cause of the dysfunction, it presently has a function in maintaining the couple or family as stable. Reflects sex therapists' experience that as the dysfunctional partner becomes functional, the relationship often comes under great stress, and if this is not attended to, the improvement will disappear or the relationship may collapse.

While these are generally influential, the following specific issues may emerge in an individual case, such as Tim's.

Etiology

As noted, Tim received a complete physical examination; physical causes that can sometimes generate impotence, such as spinal cord tumors and circulatory difficulties, were ruled out. Also, he spent an evening at the university sleep lab. The tests indicated that he did show nocturnal penile tumescence (NPT), often referred to as erections while sleeping. NPTs commonly occur in normal individuals during the REM stage of sleep, the stage usually associated with dreaming. Though not an infallible indicator, it has generally been found that men with physically based impotence seldom show NPTs, whereas those with primarily psychological impotence show normal NPTs (Fisher et al., 1979).

Several factors, which emerged in the psychological evaluation, contributed to the impotence. Like his father, Tim had a strong need to control the environment around him and felt threatened if changes that he did not control occurred. The divorce, the problems with his baseball career, and the ambivalence about his present girlfriend all suggested a loss of control to Tim and in turn generated anxiety. The impotence provided a practical focus point for the more vague anxiety feelings. But his focus on the sexual concerns created what Masters and Johnson (1970) have termed "performance anxiety." Under performance anxiety, persons take on a spectator role in the sexual act rather than letting themselves fully enjoy the pleasures of the response.

As far as the specific instance that set off the impotence, Tim had experienced fatigue that day and had also overindulged in alcohol, a common factor when individuals first experience impotence. Also, it is important to note that even though his early sexual experiences usually had been successful, they were often associated with a significant level of anxiety (Cohen, Rosen, and Goldstein, 1985).

Over and above his obsessive features, which generated a high need to control events, other characteristics would predict the impotence. Tim revealed that he perceived Pam as moving further into the women's liberation movement than he would like. She had begun to discuss her need to "fulfill her own needs." She had begun to do a lot more flirting while in his general vicinity, a behavior he allowed himself but frowned on in Pam. She had also made some innuendos that Tim had not really worked hard to recover fully from his injury. As a result of these developments, Tim began to perceive Pam as threatening to his self-esteem. When he then experienced the impotence with her, these developing beliefs were strongly reinforced.

Residual guilt from his rather strict Catholic upbringing was also a factor with Tim. He had verbalized some concern about being divorced and now living with another woman, since he was still attempting to maintain a standard role in a church that forbade such behavior. Also, as Welch and Kartub (1978) found, the incidence of impotence is highest in societies in which sexual restrictiveness is highest. In particular, a higher rate of impotence is likely if the society has had a restrictive belief system, and also if it is now rapidly moving toward a more liberal value system.

Treatment

There are a number of treatment options here; the choice in large part depends on whether or not a physical cause is present (Tucker, 1981). For example, administration of testosterone is common, but since Tim's testosterone level was only slightly below average to start with, it was unlikely this would provide a cure.

In some individuals, prosthetic devices have been used (usually, but not always with a physical cause) (Coleman et al., 1985). The Smith-Carrion penile prosthesis is simply two silicone sponges that are implanted surgically in the corpora cavernosa, the two parts of the penis that normally engorge with blood during erection. This device has several problems. First, orgasm does not always occur, and second, there is a permanent erection (this may not seem like a problem for some individuals, but at the very least it does cause embarrassment). Third, and most importantly, certain urological diagnostic procedures are rendered virtually impossible because of the perpetual erection.

As an alternative, the Scott prosthesis, a hydraulic system, can be used. A bulb, which has been implanted in the abdomen or scrotum, inflates the sacs of the corpora cavernosa when it is pressed. A second compression of the bulb deflates the erection. This device has the problems of any mechanical instrument that is implanted in the body, such as possible biological rejection. It also is an expensive procedure. Prosthetic devices would not be appropriate for Tim since the probabilities were high that the disorder could be cured with the less radical and intrusive psychological techniques (Coleman et al., 1985).

It should be noted that the idea of a prosthesis is not necessarily a modern scientific invention, as is documented by R. O'Hanlon in his book *Into the Heart of Borneo* (1984).

> "But Leon, when do you have it done? When do you have the hole bored through your dick?"
>
> "When you twenty-five. When you no good any more. When you too old. When your wife she feds up with you. Then you go down to the river very early in the mornings and you sit in it until your spear is smalls. The tattoo man he comes

and pushes a nail through your spear, round and round. And then you put a pin there, a pin from the outboard motor. Sometimes you get a big spots, very pain-fuls, a boil. And then you die."

"Jesus!"

"My best friend—you must be very careful. You must go down to the river and sit in it once a month until your spear so cold you can't feel it; and then you loosen the pin and push it in and out; or it will stick in your spear and you never move it and it makes a pebble with your water and you die."

"But Leon," I said, holding my knees together and holding my shock with my right hand, "do you have one?"

"I far too young!" said Leon, much annoyed; and then, grinning his broad Iban grin as a thought discharged itself: "But you need one Redmon! And Jams— he so old and serious, he need two!" (pp. 82–83).

Tim's Treatment. Tim's actual treatment first involved several sessions with the psychologist to clarify his feelings about the relationship with his girlfriend, the guilt about sex he experienced at a less-than-conscious level, and his perfectionistic needs. Tim gradually felt more confident of his relationship with Pam, and he asked her to participate in the latter part of the treatment program with him.

This phase of treatment proceeded along the lines suggested by Masters and Johnson (1970); they suggest that it is important to have a partner during the treatment. Because this partner is someone to whom the person will return after the treatment, a sexual surrogate is a poor choice for predicting success-ful outcome. Though it was not used with Tim, group therapy specifically fo-cused on this type of problem can be helpful (McGovern and Jensen, 1985).

The therapist emphasized to Tim and Pam that they were to focus on the pleasures of fondling and petting, and they were admonished not to proceed into intercourse for a time. When they were doing well with this and also were becoming strongly aroused, the therapist suggested that they proceed to inter-course, but not attempt to reach orgasm. Eventually, as their arousal contin-ued to be very high, intercourse was allowed and was successful. The therapist obviously attempts to minimize the performance anxiety by restricting the op-tions. Since they had been specifically admonished not to go to orgasm there was no need to be concerned about performance. This phase of the treatment lasted five weeks, at the end of which Tim and Pam were having satisfactory sexual relationships and at a higher rate than before the impotence started. Other areas of their relationship continued to improve as they clarified the meaning and impact of their communications, and a year after the treatment they got married. The marriage helped Tim's relationship with his parents, but he needed to work on clarifying his dependency on their approval. During some follow-up therapy sessions, he was able to distance himself from this need, while retaining a caring relationship for them.

An interesting sidelight was that Pam reported she was much happier now that Tim was accepting his own passivity and could allow himself to let go of the dominant role on occasion; not just sexually, but in their relationship as a whole. Eventually Tim enrolled in some refresher courses related to his work and also took up a painting course. Painting was an interest he had always had but had never really developed, probably because he feared the implications of femininity and passivity associated with it. All of these changes helped his self-esteem, which, in turn, allowed him to initiate new behaviors, thus creating a positive cycle, the antithesis of the negative cycle often seen in psychopathology.

Comment

Not surprisingly, most men are reluctant to report impotence. Thus, actual rates are difficult to determine. Situational anxiety, especially fear of failure, manifest in the spectator attitude mentioned earlier, is often the critical factor (LoPiccolo and Stock, 1986). The person becomes so involved in critically evaluating his performance that he cannot participate in love-making without feeling self-conscious. Typical sources of anxiety that negatively affect sustained erection include worry over penis size, fear of contagious disease, fear of partner's pregnancy, and ambivalence toward the sexual partner (as was the case with Tim) (Barlow, 1986). Also, levels of alcohol consumption are associated with decreased sexual arousal in males (LoPiccolo, 1985).

As with depression and anxiety, psychogenic sexual dysfunction is often time-limited. Isolated episodes of impotence may occur in response to important vocational demands, prolonged abstinence (due to illness or separation), and/or following vasectomies. The majority of these symptoms disappear without intervention as the impact of external stress subsides. On the other hand, chronic and prolonged impotence can cause a marital relationship to deteriorate and generally results in lowered self-esteem. In Tim's case, it was first necessary to clarify his feelings about Pam and his relationship with her. Once the anxiety about the relationship had lessened, Tim could ask Pam to assist him in the program of systematic desensitization and sensate focusing. The effectiveness of this approach and the resulting improvement in the overall relationship are consistently reported findings.

REFERENCES

Barlow, D. (1986) Causes of sexual dysfunction. *Journal of Consulting and Clinical Psychology, 54,* 140–148.

Cohen, A., Rosen, R., and Goldstein, L. (1985) EEG hemispheric asymmetry during sexual arousal. *Journal of Abnormal Psychology, 94,* 580–590.

Coleman, E., Listick, A., Braatz, G., and Lange, P. (1985) Effects of penile implant surgery on ejaculation and orgasm. *Journal of Sex and Marital Therapy, 11,* 199–205.

Fisher, C., Schiavi, R., Edwards, A., Davis, D., Reitman, N., and Fine, V. (1979) Evaluation of nocturnal penile tumescence in the differential diagnosis of sexual impotence: A quantitative study. *Archives of General Psychiatry, 36,* 431–437.

Katchadourian, H. (1985) *Fundamentals of Human Sexuality.* New York: Holt, Rinehart and Winston.

LoPiccolo, J. (1985) Diagnosis and treatment of male sexual dysfunction. *Journal of Sex and Marital Therapy, 11,* 215–232.

LoPiccolo, J. and Stock, W. (1986) Treatment of sexual dysfunction. *Journal of Consulting and Clinical Psychology, 54,* 158–167.

Masters, W., and Johnson, V. (1970) *Human Sexual Inadequacy.* Boston: Little, Brown.

McGovern, K. and Jensen, S. (1985) Behavioral group treatment methods for sexual disorders and dysfunctions. In D. Upper and S. Ross (Eds.), *Handbook of Behavioral Group Therapy.* New York: Plenum.

Tucker, D. (1981) Lateral brain function, emotion, and conceptualization. *Psychological Bulletin, 89,* 19–46.

Welch, M. and Kartub, P. (1978) Socio-cultural correlates of incidence of impotence: A cross-cultural study. *The Journal of Sex Research, 14,* 218–230.

/ *Female Psychosexual Dysfunction*

The Case of Virginia

I have a coded list of 23 names and numbers in my billfold . . . each time is like the first time all over again, a strain. It's a job. I'll have to do well. I liked it better when they thought they were doing us a favor. I'm sorry they ever found out they could have orgasms too. I wonder who told them (p. 422).

— Joseph Heller
Something Happened

As with males, the traditional term for female psychosexual dysfunction in the DSM is psychosexual dysfunction with inhibited sexual excitement. In this case, the symptoms include both frigidity and vaginismus. As the case developed, it became apparent that vaginismus had to be dealt with first. Vaginismus is a condition in which the vaginal musculature goes into intense involuntary spasms, primarily in the bulbocavernosus muscle, and also in the leviator ani muscles. As a result, intercourse is impossible or is accompanied by extreme pain (dyspareunia) (Cox and Meyer, 1978). Vaginismus is not necessarily associated with sexual inhibition or orgastic problems, though it often is, as we see in Virginia's case (LoPiccolo and Stock, 1986; LoPiccolo, 1985).

The Case of Virginia

Virginia had suffered with her problems most of her life, and indeed had seldom had satisfactory sexual experiences. Yet she waited until three years after she had been married to report her difficulties to her gynecologist. This lag in reporting such difficulties is not uncommon in sexual disorders. Virginia's gynecologist gave her a thorough physical examination, which revealed severe vaginismus, but no physical cause was found. This is not uncommon, since vaginismus and frigidity are often unrelated to physical disorder. The gynecologist then referred Virginia to a clinic that specialized in treating sexual disorders. Virginia's husband was also referred to the clinic since it was quite clear that he also had some sexual disturbance.

Virginia, who is 23 years old, is fairly attractive and pleasant interpersonally. She was initially interviewed alone, during which time she talked about her childhood and adolescence as well as her present concerns. Virginia's family had lived a middle-class existence in a small northwestern town, and her early life would best be described as stable and quiet. Her father was a generally quiet and passive individual, but he occasionally indulged in strong outbursts of anger if Virginia or her younger brother upset him for any length of time. Virginia describes her mother as rather saintly and always warm and supportive. At the same time, there was a repressive atmosphere in the home regarding sexuality. Both her father and mother avoided discussing it, and Virginia learned most of what she knew about sexual matters from her friends in school. Her mother did attempt to discuss menstruation with her, but generally communicated the feeling that it was painful and that she ought not discuss it publicly. Virginia naturally assumed that the whole issue was shameful; in part, this attitude contributed to the substantial pain she experienced during her menarche. Virginia would often skip school and stay in bed during the first day of her menstruation, and she was grouchy and irritable throughout her period.

Though Virginia's father was nominally a Roman Catholic, he did not practice his religion. Her mother, however, was devoted to her fundamentalist religion, often working many hours with several Protestant organizations. She made sure that Virginia and her brother were raised in her faith. Virginia rebelled against this in late adolescence by simply refusing to go to church and gradually drifted away from most of the tenets of her religion. But the admonitions that the expression of sexuality outside of marriage was wrong stayed in the back of her mind and caused her to experience guilt and anxiety on occasion. She began to masturbate regularly when she was 16 years old and for quite a while felt very guilty about it. She had little difficulty experiencing orgasm in masturbation.

Virginia had not been allowed to date until she was 15, and only then when she was with a large group of individuals who were chaperoned to and from an event. She was allowed to date individually when she was 17. Yet, because she was rather quiet and unassuming and because she did not run in the more active groups in her school, she had few dates. Her first romantic interest was a boy named Bill, who was also very passive and did not push her toward any sexual experience. After they had dated approximately one year, they were petting rather heavily. On one of these occasions, Bill inserted his finger in Virginia's vagina and she experienced an orgasm. The spontaneity and intensity of the orgasm scared her, and she became very upset with Bill. They soon ceased dating and Virginia was relatively inactive in this area until she met David, her husband-to-be.

After graduating from high school, Virginia enrolled in a dental hygiene training program at the local community college. As she was nearing the end of her program, she met David, who was an assistant librarian at the college. She was primarily attracted to him because he seemed "older and wiser" than most of the other men she knew. David was mild-mannered and passive, and even after they had dated for several months, they were still only giving each other a goodnight kiss. They married after about one year of dating and even at this point had not done much sexually except mild petting.

Three months before they were married, Virginia developed a vaginal infection and experienced a virtual panic, fearing that she may somehow have contracted a venereal disease. She went to a gynecologist who was competent medically, but did not have much of a bedside manner. He was a bit rough in the examination. He was also slightly sarcastic in telling her that she had no venereal disease and that he could not see why she worried about it, given her sexual history. Virginia came away from the situation shaken and upset and vowed never to go back to him.

Virginia and David's wedding went happily except for an uncomfortable moment when her mother attempted to give her a last minute lesson about sexuality. The most positive thing she could say was that although it would probably hurt the first several times, it "wouldn't be that bad."

As is common when both parties have had little sexual experience, the honeymoon was a disaster. Virginia felt that if she just remained quiet and passive, he would know what to do. David's role by default as the wiser and more experienced person propelled him into taking initiatives, even though he knew little about what to do. He attempted penetration after only minimal foreplay and before Virginia had any vaginal lubrication. Virginia's vaginal muscles contracted almost immediately, causing her intense pain. She screamed and David withdrew right away, very confused as to what he did to cause the pain. They were both so distraught by this event that they did not attempt intercourse again until the third night of the honeymoon. Virginia again had intense pain. This time she attempted to endure the pain, but it was clear to David that it was distressing her and he withdrew, soon losing his erection. They were both upset and embarrassed about the situation and avoided any further attempt at intercourse during the honeymoon.

Since that time they have only attempted intercourse approximately once or twice a month, usually with the same accompanying problems. Never have they been able to continue intercourse to the point that either of them experienced orgasm. They eventually began to engage in mutual masturbation, yet both felt this was "not real sex," and they both reported being dissatisfied.

Virginia did not seek help for several reasons. She was too distressed with the idea of returning to the gynecologist who had been sarcastic and rough with her, and she feared repeating that experience with another gynecologist. Also, she was quite embarrassed and hoped that her mother's prophecy that it would gradually be all right would come true. After three years, the couple began to experience other problems in their relationship, in large part because of their inability to communicate. Also, it was very hard for them to find a way to express affection without having to consider the possibility of intercourse, which by this time they avoided at all costs. Virginia went to the phone book and simply sorted through to a name she somehow felt comfortable with, and made an appointment. Fortunately, this random selection led her to a gynecologist who understood and empathized with her situation.

Etiology

Virginia's background is not atypical for a woman with vaginismus (LoPiccolo, 1985). She is not significantly pathological psychologically, though she does have a background that induced a substantial amount of sexual guilt and repression. Not only was she made to feel that sexuality was sinful, but even more importantly, she felt that it was shameful and dirty. In addition, she had little accurate sexual information provided for her as she grew up and had to resort to information she received from her friends, most of whom were equally uninformed. As a result, many of her general beliefs about sexuality crystallized around inaccurate information.

Consequently, Virginia basically rejected her bodily experiences; she saw them as intrusive and as a cue for anxiety (Crenshaw, 1985). Though she was able to masturbate to orgasm, she always experienced much guilt.

The traumatic gynecological examination that she experienced shortly before her marriage also contributed to her problem. Again, this is not uncommon. Many women with vaginismus fear gynecological examinations, and if there is any insensitivity on the part of the gynecologist, the trauma increases the potential for vaginismus (Tollison and Adams, 1979).

The other major contributing factor was her husband's sexual inexperience. Any normal woman would likely experience some pain if penetration was attempted before any real lubrication had begun. Their mutual inexperience led them to attempt this, which exaggerated the pain experience already initiated by her own expectancies and prior experiences. Her mother's admonition that her initial sexual experiences would cause her pain led her to believe that the severe pain she experienced was a normal response. As a result, she did not immediately seek treatment, and she and her husband indulged in the repeated trials that reinforced the vaginal spasm sequence. Spasms became conditioned responses to all of the attempts at intercourse. From this perspective, vaginismus can be seen as a phobic response, an irrational anxiety that occurs in response to anticipated vaginal penetration. Anxiety and muscular spasms then naturally occur. The spasms cause intense pain, which naturally furthers the strength of the phobic response.

Treatment

The specific treatment for vaginismus is fairly straightforward. In addition to psychotherapy, because of the allied distress, and counseling on how to facilitate sexual functioning (LoPiccolo and Stock, 1986), it involves the use of dilators, graduated in size, which are inserted into the vagina until it relaxes. The next larger catheter is inserted in the next session. Masters and Johnson (1970) recommend that the male partner help insert the catheters and also suggest that he witness any pelvic examinations that occur in an effort to help dispel any irrational fears he may have developed. It particularly reassures him that the vaginismus is not a direct response to his efforts at intercourse. Masters and Johnson (1970) report a success rate of 100 percent with simple vaginismus using this technique. However, as in most cases, Virginia's vaginismus is confounded by other sexual problems.

Virginia and her husband participated in some simple education sessions about sexual matters. They were then taught the technique of sensate focusing, in which emphasis is placed on focusing on the sensations from a sexual experience. Sensate focus is commonly used to treat impotence and frigidity, but in this case, its main function may have been to alleviate guilt and the couple's inhibitions about sexual explorations.

After they had shown progress in this regard, they moved on to the dilators (Tollison and Adams, 1979). The use of dilators can be considered analogous to systematic desensitization therapy, such that the phobic anxiety which caused the spasm is confronted with as in vivo stimulus—that is, with something inserted directly into the vagina. The therapeutic effect occurs because the person is kept relaxed and comfortable so that the spasms ultimately subside (Cox and Meyer, 1978).

The first dilator is very small. Her husband handled the dilator during insertion while Virginia guided his hand. Larger dilators are used as the muscle spasms decrease each time, and ultimately the husband guides the dilator himself. The largest dilators, which are about the size of the erect penis, are kept in place for several hours. It may take five to six weeks of treatment with the dilators before actual intercourse is attempted. Virginia and her husband proved very responsive to this technique, and in four weeks they were able to have intercourse.

Concomitant with the use of the dilators, Virginia was taught the use of the "squeeze technique," since her husband had been experiencing occasional premature ejaculation. The squeeze technique has been highly effective in helping the partner delay ejaculation, thus prolonging intercourse.

Virginia was taught first to manipulate her husband's penis to a full erection and then to place her thumb on the frenulum (on the underside of the front of the penis) with her first two fingers on the opposite sides at the top of the penis, one on each side of the ridge which separates the shaft from the glans. By squeezing hard at this point for about three seconds the urge to ejaculate is substantially lessened, and some of the erection is also lost. At first, this procedure may be repeated every half-minute or so, with gradually greater time periods interspersed (Masters and Johnson, 1970; Levine, 1979).

When they were first allowed to have intercourse, Virginia used the largest dilator for a long enough period of time to allow her vagina to relax fully. Before David inserted his penis, she employed the squeeze technique a couple of times and then straddled him in the female superior coital position. This position allowed her more control plus the ability to pull away if she began to have spasms. If the spasms did recur, then they returned to working with the dilators until she again felt comfortable. At first, both remained motionless for a long period of time as they both became used to the penis being in the vagina. Then David was allowed to thrust enough to maintain his erection and obtain some sexual pleasure, but it was emphasized to him to keep his movement very slow. Gradually, the speed of thrusting is increased, the time of insertion is increased, and different sexual positions are attempted. When they show control throughout these variations, progression to orgasm is allowed.

Virginia and David were highly motivated, not only reflecting their desire to enjoy sexual experience, but also because of their deep caring for each other and the desire to make a good marriage. The combination of therapies took approximately three months. Consistent with the work of Masters and Johnson (1970), it was very successful. They are now enjoying sex consistently, and although Virginia first had difficulty reaching orgasm in intercourse, she now does so with increasing regularity. It is highly probable that the success they attained will continue.

Comment

As with Virginia, the person is physiologically capable of adequate sexual performance in most cases of sexual dysfunction. Most sexual dysfunction occurs when psychological factors exert an inhibitory action over what is normally a series of reflexive responses (Crenshaw, 1985). Virginia's inexperience and certain beliefs (possibly distorted) from her religious training resulted in anxiety and inhibited excitement on the occasion of her first attempt at intercourse. The predictably inadequate lubrication resulted in painful muscle spasms, which in turn generalized as a classically conditioned response to subsequent penetration attempts. The unfortunate encounter with the first gynecologist and her husband's sexual inexperience strengthened Virginia's anxiety about intercourse and worsened the problem. The use of a series of vaginal dilators was a successful treatment for her vaginismus, as it has been in most cases (Tollison and Adams, 1979). This usually needs to be supplemented by therapy to repair the damaged interpersonal interactions in the marriage, as well as probable self-esteem problems (Spence, 1985; Parloff, London, and Wolfe, 1986).

REFERENCES

Cox, D. and Meyer, R. (1978) Behavioral treatment parameters with primary dysmenorrhea. *Journal of Behavior Medicine, 1.*

Crenshaw, T. (1985) The sexual aversion syndrome. *Journal of Sex and Marital Therapy, 11*, 285–292.

Levine, S. (1979) Barriers to the attainment of ejaculatory control. *Medical Aspects of Human Sexuality, 13*, 32–56.

LoPiccolo, J. (1985) Advances in the diagnosis and treatment of sexual dysfunction. Convention workshop. Kentucky Psychological Association. Louisville, 1985.

LoPiccolo, J. and Stock, W. (1986) Treatment of sexual dysfunction. *Journal of Consulting and Clinical Psychology, 54*, 158–167.

Masters, W. and Johnson, V. (1970) *Human Sexual Inadequacy.* Boston: Little, Brown.

Parloff, M., London, P., and Wolfe, B. (1986) Individual psychotherapy and behavior change. In M. Rosenweig and L. Porter (Eds.), *Annual Review of Psychology 37*, Palo Alto, Calif.: Annual Reviews.

Spence, S. (1985) Group versus individual treatment of primary and secondary female orgasmic dysfunction. *Behavior Research and Therapy, 23*, 539–548.

Tollison, C. and Adams, H. (1979) *Sexual Disorders.* New York: Gardner.

9

The Addictive Disorders

Our society considers the use of drugs in order to modify mood, behavior, or comfort to be appropriate under many circumstances. However, for many people, in our society as well as in others, drug abuse and dependence have become serious obstacles to adjustment (Heath, 1986). Only recently have public and professional conceptualizations of drug problems (including alcohol) changed from the archaic indictment of demonic influence or sinfulness to a consideration of the individual's maladaptive choices and response patterns (Peele, 1984). Fortunately, the newer approaches have stimulated investigation of causal factors and effective treatments. These research efforts have also broadened the category of potentially abused drugs. Heretofore, attention was primarily limited to alcohol and heroin. However, DSM now lists ten types of substances: alcohol, barbiturate, opioid, cocaine, amphetamine, phencyclidine (PCP), hallucinogen, cannabis, caffeine, and tobacco. Cocaine abuse, an especially problematic pattern in modern society, is the subject of the last case in this chapter. A common pattern in today's society, prescription drug abuse, is not formally included, though that is the subject of the second case in this chapter.

The diagnostic class of substance use disorders includes undesirable behavioral changes caused by regular use of substances that affect the central nervous system. The distinction is made between mental disorders associated with drug use and nonpathological use for recreational or medical purposes. Substance use disorders are of two types: substance abuse and substance dependence. Substance abuse is defined by a pathological pattern of use (such as the need for consistent use) and by impairment of social or occupational functioning due to use that has lasted for at least one month. Substance dependence is defined by tolerance (need for significantly increased amounts in order to achieve this desired effect) or by withdrawal (development of physiological and/or psychological symptomatology contingent on cessation of use), in addition to the requirements for substance abuse.

Paul, the first case described in this chapter, received the diagnoses of alcoholic hallucinosis (because of his alcohol-generated symptom of hearing voices that were not real) and alcohol withdrawal because of the symptoms of vomiting, trembling, and high anxiety generated by the alcohol. Since there was withdrawal plus consistent use and family disruption over a period of time, he would also eventually receive a diagnosis of alcohol dependence (after an adequate history was gathered).

The introduction to this section notes some of the several DSM diagnoses that the various problematic patterns of alcohol use can receive. The variety here reflects the fact that alcohol-related psychopathology is a major cause of placement in mental hospitals (and of related and costly physical illness, family and social disruption, auto accidents, and so on).

In the last two decades, society has moved from seeing alcoholism as a product of sinfulness or the power of alcohol itself ("demon rum") to viewing it as an "illness." The fortunate consequence of this trend has been the increased awareness of the need for treatment. The focus on "illness," however, has led many alcoholics to ignore the critical importance of their own motivation to change. ("You're the doc; I hope you can cure me.") In this vein, various researchers (Lang et al., 1975; Abrams and Wilson, 1979; Lansky and Wilson, 1981; Orford, 1985; Critchlow, 1986) have found that the uncontrolled expression of sexual and aggressive behavior under the actual alleged influence of alcohol is related more to a belief that one has ingested alcohol than to actually having done so.

REFERENCES

Abrams, D. and Wilson, T. (1979) Effects of alcohol on social anxiety in women: Cognitive versus physiological processes. *Journal of Abnormal Psychology*, *88* 161–73.

Critchlow, B. (1986) The powers of John Barleycorn. *American Psychologist*, *41*, 751–764.

Heath, D. (1986) Drinking and drunkenness in transcultural perspective. *Transcultural Psychiatric Research*, *23*, 7–42.

Lang, A., Goechner, D., Adesso, V., and Marlatt, A. (1975) Effects of alcohol on aggression in male social drinkers. *Journal of Abnormal Psychology*, *85*, 508–518.

Lansky, D. and Wilson, T. (1981) Alcohol, expectations, and sexual arousal in males: An information processing analysis. *Journal of Abnormal Psychology*, *90*, 34–45.

Orford, J. (1985) *Excessive Appetites: A Psychological View of Addiction*. New York: John Wiley.

Peele, S. (1984) The cultural context of psychological approaches to alcoholism. *American Psychologist*, *39*, 1337–1351.

/ *Alcohol Dependence*

**The Case of
Paul**

*"I swear, a certain amount of beer can make a
man feel like he could beat cancer." (p. 16)*
— Larry King
*Of Outlaws, Con Men, Whores,
Politicians, and Other Artists*

Many people still accept the fallacy that alcohol is a stimulant. Alcohol acts pharmacologically first to depress higher brain centers, which consequently results in a loss of inhibition in overt behaviors. With continued alcohol intake, the more complex functions of all brain centers are also suppressed, eventually resulting in unconsciousness. Alcohol is not digested, but is directly absorbed through the intestinal walls and stomach and then metabolized in the liver by oxidation. In the average person, the liver can only break down about one ounce of 100 proof whiskey, or its equivalent, in one hour. Excess amounts remain in the bloodstream and begin to affect the brain, as noted above (Donovan, 1986; Blum, 1984).

Alcohol has been used as long as any drug available today and is used and abused in most societies (Heath, 1986). As far back as 8000 B.C., in the Paleolithic Age, mead, an alcoholic beverage derived from honey, was used. Beer and berry wine were imbibed as early as 6400 B.C. Alcohol has almost certainly been abused for as long as it has been used, and the costs to the abuser, physiologically and psychologically, have always been high. Alcoholism is especially costly to society at large in our present era, as it exacts an enormous toll through alcohol-caused accidents (especially auto accidents), disruption of family life, facilitation of violence in certain individuals, and inefficiency and loss in the business realm (Begleiter, Porjesz, and Chou, 1981; Abel and Zeidenberg, 1985; Jacob, 1986). Such costs are evident in the case of Paul.

The Case of Paul

One Wednesday night, Paul came home from work, greeted his family, and took his normal place in his easy chair and read the paper. Then he ate dinner with his wife and two teenage daughters. After dinner, he worked in his shop for a while on some furniture he was refinishing; but he stopped early and went to his bedroom. Wondering why Paul had quit so early, his wife went in and saw him crawling around the bedroom floor. Paul exclaimed that the "voices" kept telling him to crawl because of his "sins." He was trembling and sweating, had vomited on the floor, and refused to let his wife near him. An ambulance was called, and Paul was taken to the hospital emergency room. The attending physician found him highly anxious, suffering from auditory hallucinations (hearing things that are not there), and confused about time and place.

Jane, Paul's wife, was questioned for any possible causes or explanations for his agitated state. She reported that Paul had been somewhat irritable and restless lately; but she was unaware of any unusual behaviors. She said that Paul had seen a clinical psychologist because of alcoholism. At this point, Paul's episode was diagnosed as alcohol withdrawal (because of the trembling, vomiting, and anxiety) and alcohol hallucinosis (because of the hallucinations). He was sedated and admitted to the detoxification unit. The clinical psychologist was consulted, and Paul's wife was interviewed extensively. The staff of the detoxification team was then able to reconstruct the events that led to Paul's emergency admission.

Paul is a 38-year-old air traffic controller who grew up in a small rural Kansas community. At age 18, he left his hometown to attend the state university, returning only for brief visits. After graduating from college with a degree in aeronautical engineering, Paul remained in the city as an airplane designer. During the next ten years, he worked his way up into managerial positions and then trained for the air traffic controller job. He had held his controller position with the metropolitan airport for five years.

Paul's father was a skilled mechanic and owned a small garage. Paul's mother did not work outside the home and was very devoted to Paul, his two older brothers, and his younger sister. Both parents were high school graduates who strongly encouraged their children to attend college. Presently, Paul's brothers are successful real estate brokers and his sister is a physical therapist. All three returned to their hometown after college and married local residents. Jane was of the opinion that Paul's brothers drank excessively and described his sister as a religious abstainer. Jane also reported that Paul's father was a chronic alcoholic, but that his mother did not drink for religious reasons.

Disagreements between Paul's parents over the morality of drinking occurred frequently during family gatherings and apparently began before Paul was born. Paul's father was persuaded occasionally to admit himself to alcohol abuse units and would stop drinking for a few months. The couple would be reconciled and the family atmosphere would be more pleasant. Interestingly enough, Paul's father's work habits were disrupted only when he was hospitalized. He often presented these facts in his defense and contended that as long as he was able to provide for his family he wasn't a "real" alcoholic.

Paul was very close to his brothers in childhood and made every effort to win their approval. They encouraged Paul to drink as an adolescent and included him in their social functions, which usually included drinking. Paul continued to drink in college and pledged a fraternity known for giving "drunk" parties. Up until this point, Paul's drinking was confined to weekends. During the week he attended classes, worked as a mechanic in the university motor pool, and earned good grades. He met his wife in his sophomore year, when she was a freshman "little sister" with the fraternity. Jane recalls that Paul's drinking habits were similar to those of many students and did not seem out of control at the time.

Paul and his wife generally had few disagreements about his drinking. Jane describes their life style as one that included alcohol at most social functions. Their friends are frequent drinkers, and the family kept a full bar in their home. She remembered several occasions on which her husband's heavy drinking had led to embarrassing accidents in public, yet considered these episodes as rare and atypical for him. Also, until recently, Jane admired her husband's ability to control his drinking when compared with the obvious excesses of his father and brothers. She said that her husband first began to complain about the pressures he felt in his job about three years ago. Yet, he decided to continue as a controller for five years so that he could apply for the less stressful position of controller supervisor. He took on extra assignments to broaden his experience and worked hard to build an exceptional record as a controller. The previous year, the airport opened several new runways, which doubled air traffic, increased the responsibilities of controllers, and intensified competition for supervisor positions. Paul became noticeably more anxious and began to drink during the week.

Throughout the past year, Paul's drinking became more disruptive to his family life and work performance. He was irritable with his children and only sporadically affectionate with his wife (though at the same time dependent on her). Also, his drinking made it difficult for him to get to work on time and to perform well once he arrived. His job requires him to track several planes simultaneously and to make sure that their flight patterns do not cross. He had temporarily "misplaced" several planes in the past few weeks, but there had been no crashes or major crises. These problems had come to the attention of Paul's superiors, who suggested the clinical psychologist. However, at the time Paul was admitted to the hospital, he had attended only one session with the psychologist. During this session, the psychologist had taken Paul's history and arranged for him to be admitted to the alcohol detoxification unit for withdrawal. Paul had agreed to take two weeks of sick leave from work to participate in the detoxification program and to continue supportive psychotherapy later as an outpatient. He then told his wife that he was sure that he could again control his drinking and that he was afraid that entering the hospital for detoxification was admitting that he was an alcoholic. He also feared that such an admission would jeopardize his chances for a supervisory position. Thus, he had abruptly discontinued drinking on the day before his admission, which precipitated the withdrawal reaction that resulted in the emergency admission to the detoxification unit.

Etiology

The symptoms of severe alcohol withdrawal often include sleep disorders; tremors; agitation and depression; sweating; and occasionally auditory, visual, and/or tactile hallucinations. Thus, the reaction may be diagnosed in the emergency room as a psychotic episode. Paul's self-prescribed "cold turkey" program had ironically worsened his pre-existing alcohol problems and ineffective coping style. The symptoms of partial withdrawal and/or supervised detoxification are usually more moderate than abrupt cessation. However, there are some factors in Paul's psychosocial history that probably predisposed him to implement the cold turkey program.

First of all, Paul's father and brothers were models of alcohol abuse (Zucker and Gomberg, 1986). Not only did they set an example for Paul to drink excessively, but they also provided him with an inaccurate decision rule for determining when his drinking was out of control. Paul thought that as long as he could restrict his consumption to nonworking hours, he was not an alcoholic. Such self-deluding decision rules ("I never drink before noon") are common among alcoholics. These rules often follow from the notion that alcoholism is a moral weakness and/or disease of will power. Thus, any restrictions on drinking are incorrectly interpreted by the person as evidence that he or she is not really dependent on alcohol. Paul's drinking had increased during the past year, however, and had generated the social impairments that are part of the DSM diagnoses.

There is evidence that Paul was less prepared than most people for the demanding vigilance and responsibility of a position such as air traffic controller. He was the youngest of three boys and identified more strongly with his brothers' life style than with the religious values of his mother. He was protected (probably overprotected) by his brothers and consequently had minimal experience with stressful situations. Until he began to have difficulties as a controller, Paul had not experienced any significant problems. He handled high school, college, marriage, children, and a career with the aeronautics firm without noticeable frustrations or disappointments. These ostensibly idyllic conditions were, in fact, obstacles to his development of mature and adaptive responses to stress. Negative results from a lack of coping methods generated in response to minor stress are also seen as a factor in the case of "the Postman," discussed in Chapter 3.

When the initial pressures of Paul's job were intensified by the airport expansion, he became even more anxious about obtaining the supervisory position (his planned escape route). Thus, a man with limited experience in coping with stress was exposed to increasingly stressful circumstances from which he could not escape. As Costello (1978) notes, anxiety and ambivalent dependency are common in one type of alcoholic, while more direct aggression and less anxiety mark another type. An attempt to self-medicate depression is also important in many cases (Logue, 1986). Paul turned to the only mechanism he had learned that could relieve him of his anxiety—alcohol. Then, from Paul's point of view, the "cure" for the alcoholism was more unattractive than the problem. Paul felt that entering the detoxification unit would be more threatening to his future than would be his declining work performance, thus the ill-advised cold turkey technique.

Finally, it is possible that Paul was physiologically vulnerable to alcoholism. There is good evidence that individuals can inherit a physiological predisposition to alcoholism, which leads to an unusual craving for alcohol once it has been experienced (Shuckit, 1986). Such a predisposition can also be increased by the body's physiological adaptation to chronic drinking, an adaptation that eventually includes a degree of brain dysfunction (Begleiter, Porjesz, and Chou, 1981). The fact that Paul's father and brothers were excessive drinkers is consistent with the concept of genetic vulnerability. There is evidence that alcohol dependence tends to run in families (Vailliant, 1983). Also, some researchers have found high rates of alcoholism in natural children of alcholics who were adopted by nonalcoholic parents (Goodwin, 1979). However, it is also known that the majority of children with alcoholic parents do not develop a drinking problem. Thus, the role played by genetic factors in alcohol dependence is important, but not compelling, in an individual case (Zucker and Gomberg, 1986; Donovan, 1986; Vailliant, 1983).

In any case, dependence on alcohol typically develops in stages. The sequence of behaviors and symptoms listed below is not necessarily inevitable.

For example, many so-called social drinkers never move into the second stage and become alcoholics. Nonetheless, this progression is fairly common:

1. *Prealcoholic phase:* (a) Social drinking and an occasional weekend drink are the major symptoms. (b) Both tolerance and frequency of drinking increase, usually slowly. (c) Alcohol use serves primarily as an escape from anxiety, mild depression, or boredom.

2. *Initial alcoholism:* (a) Tolerance, frequency, and abuse increase. (b) More is drunk per swallow; often there is a shift to more potent drinks. (c) Depression increases along with loss of self-esteem over drinking patterns. (d) Occasional blackouts occur.

3. *Chronic stage:* (a) True loss-of-control patterns (such as drinking throughout the day and using any source of alcohol) predominate. (b) Inadequate nutrition affects functioning and physical health. (c) Signs of impaired thinking, hallucinations, and tremors emerge.

Treatment

Since alcohol problems are generated and maintained by many causal factors, a treatment approach that employs at least a significant number of the following options is going to be needed in most cases:

1. *Detoxification:* Most alcoholics, such as Paul, need an initial phase in a controlled treatment setting in which to "dry out." This process helps to control the impulse to return to alcohol, especially while the system is physiologically readjusting to the absence of alcohol.

2. *Antabuse:* Antabuse (disulfiram) binds molybdenum, a trace material needed by the liver to detoxify alcohol. Without it, acetaldehyde, a product of that breakdown, is increased, which generates nausea and violent vasomotor spasms. This terribly aversive response only occurs if one drinks alcohol, so Antabuse helps to control that impulse. The only problem is that alcoholics tend to avoid or forget to take it, so it is of limited use unless it is surgically implanted, and even this procedure has not always been successful (Wilson, Blanchard, and Davidson, 1984).

3. *Tranquilizers:* Tranquilizing medication can be used to help lessen the emotional distress of withdrawal. However, there are the dangers of a secondary addiction and untoward side effects, as is discussed in the case of Barbara in this chapter.

4. *Aversion therapy:* Aversion therapy helps to suppress specific habits that facilitate alcoholism; it can be combined with the modeling of more appropriate behaviors. Indications are that the use of nausea-inducing drugs is superior to the use of electric shock (Cannon and Baker, 1981).

5. *Biofeedback:* Alcoholics are surprisingly worse (considering their extensive experience) than normals at accurately assessing their blood levels of

alcohol. Biofeedback can help them more readily recognize differential bodily reactions with different levels of alcohol intake, a critical step if they are ever to return to a moderate drinking pattern (Peele, 1984; Lovibond and Caddy, 1970).

6. *Alcoholics Anonymous:* Although not as effective as proponents of AA (who have a vested interest in favorable results) assert, this organization does provide the alcoholic with a system of support, a place for emotional catharsis, and a source of nondrinking friends (Bratter and Forrest, 1985).

7. *Psychotherapy:* This is helpful, particularly in the early months of treatment, to enable the alcholic to see the many conflicts and unresolved emotions that facilitate and maintain the alcoholism (McInerney, DiGiuseppe, and Ellis, 1986). Dealing with underlying depression is often a critical task (Schuckit, 1986).

8. *Family and/or marital therapy:* Therapy is critical to long-term adjustment, since it helps to heal the wounds in the systems that are so critical in supporting the more positive behaviors being initiated by the alcoholic (Brown, 1985).

Paul's Treatment. Alcohol withdrawal used to be a long and painful process, but tranquilizers do help, albeit introducing a risk of a second drug dependence. Also, vitamins and supplemental intravenous feedings to maintain nutritional balance are included in most modern detoxification programs. These programs have greatly reduced some of the side effects of alcohol detoxification, such as self-injury, distress, convulsions, and hepatitis.

Paul spent three days in the detoxification unit. After detoxification, Paul was retained on the unit for one day of medical observation. When Paul's physical strength was satisfactory, he was transferred to the psychiatry unit for three weeks of inpatient psychotherapy. Paul met with his therapist daily for individual sessions, underwent aversion therapy, and participated in group therapy for two hours each morning. In addition to allowing Paul the opportunity to examine his problems in a comfortable and unpressured milieu, the hospitalization assured his continued abstinence. In the therapy sessions, Paul learned to verbalize the frustrations he experienced with his career and the pressures he felt from his wife in trying to provide for his family. He described his elaborate strategies for appearing sober while continuing to imbibe. As Paul became more open with his therapist and the group members, he was able to devise useful strategies to continue his abstinence after his release from the hospital. He decided to resign his position as air traffic controller and was able to return to the aeronautics firm as a sales manager, with a comparable salary.

After his release from the hospital, Paul continued therapy as an outpatient. In addition to individual psychotherapy, his therapist recommended several sessions with his wife and children. After six months of outpatient therapy, Paul joined Alcoholics Anonymous. In the three years since his release from the hospital, Paul continues to abstain from alcohol. His relationship with his wife and children has greatly improved, and his life style and stress-coping habits have changed. Since he no longer drinks, he and his wife have participated in fewer cocktail parties and have learned interpersonal strategies to avoid pressures to take a drink.

Comment

Alcoholism has been a preeminent disorder since alcohol was first used at least 10,000 years ago. It causes extensive psychological and physiological damage. It is usually generated by multiple causes, and similarly requires a variety of treatments. Unfortunately, most treatment programs for alcoholism have not shown marked success, particularly in the long run.

However, the prognosis for Paul is good. For one thing, he does not show the schizoid aspects that are a negative prognostic sign (Zivich, 1981). He has stopped drinking and has taken on a less stressful occupation. Further, Paul has rearranged his life style so that (1) exposure to alcohol is minimized, (2) overall stress is considerably reduced, and (3) more adaptive strategies for stress relief are available to him. Consistent with the philosophy of AA, Paul and his family still consider him an alcoholic. Paul believes that one drink could trigger the self-destructive cycle that precipitated his hospitalization. It should be noted that there have been several published reports of alcoholics who have learned to drink in moderation (Peele, 1984; Lovibond and Caddy, 1970). However, the total abstinence strategy is efficient, and most therapists recommend total abstinence at least for a substantial period of time for persons who are alcoholic.

Of course, the most efficient way of dealing with alcoholism, as well as with most other disorders, is prevention rather than cure, and this is most effective when many of the following suggested steps occur early in a child's development:

1. If children are to be allowed to drink alcohol at all in later life, introduce it to them relatively early, and, of course in moderation.

2. Associate use of alcohol with food and initially allow its use only on special occasions.

3. Provide a consistent model of low-to-moderate drinking, and use beverages such as beer and wine that have low alcohol content, rather than hard liquor.

4. Never associate drinking behavior with evidence of attainment of adulthood or other identity accomplishments.

5. Label excess drinking behavior as stupid and in bad taste rather than as stylish or "cool."

6. Label help-seeking behaviors in people who have an alcohol problem as evidence of strength rather than weakness.

7. Encourage alcoholism education programs in the community and public health measures such as a restriction on the use of alcohol in certain settings and age groups.

REFERENCES

Abel, E. and Zeidenberg, D. (1985) Alcohol and violent death. *Journal of Studies on Alcoholism, 46,* 228–231.

Begleiter, H., Porjesz, B., and Chou, C. (1981) Auditory brainstem potentials in chronic alcoholics. *Science, 211,* 1064–1066.

Blum, K. (1984) *Handbook of Abusable Drugs.* New York: Gardner.

Bratter, T. and Forrest, G. (1985) *Alcoholism and Substance Abuse: Strategies for Clinical Intervention.* New York: Free Press.

Brown, S. (1985) *Treating the Alcoholic.* New York: John Wiley.

Cannon, D. and Baker, T. (1981) Emetic and electric shock alcohol aversion therapy: Assessment of conditioning. *Journal of Consulting and Clinical Psychology, 49,* 20–33.

Costello, R. (1978) Empirical derivation of a partial personality typology of alcoholics. *Journal of Studies of Alcoholism, 39,* 1258–1266.

Donovan, J. (1986) An etiologic model of alcoholism. *Archives of General Psychiatry, 143,* 1–11.

Goodwin, D. (1979) Alcoholism and heredity. *Archives of General Psychiatry, 36,* 57–64.

Heath, D. (1986) Drinking and drunkenness in transcultural perspective. *Transcultural Psychiatric Research, 23,* 7–42.

Jacob, T. (1986) Alcoholism and family interaction. Nebraska Symposium on Motivation: Alcohol and Addictive Behavior. Lincoln, Neb.

Logue, A. (1986) *The Psychology of Eating and Drinking.* New York: W. H. Freeman.

Lovibond, S. and Caddy, G. (1970) Discriminated aversive control in the modification of alcoholic's drinking behavior. *Behavior Therapy, 1,* 437–444.

McInerney, J., DiGiuseppe, R., and Ellis, A. (1986) *Rational Emotive Approaches to the Treatment of Alcohol and Substance Abuse.* New York: Pergamon.

Peele, S. (1984) The cultural context of psychological approaches to alcoholism. *American Psychologist, 39,* 1337–1351.

Schuckit, M. (1986) Genetic and clinical implications of alcoholism and affective disorder. *The American Journal of Psychiatry, 143,* 140–147.

Vailliant, G. (1983) *The Natural History of Alcoholism: Causes, Patterns, and Paths to Recovery.* Cambridge, Mass.: Harvard University Press.

Wilson, A., Blanchard, R., and Davidson, W. (1984) Disulfiram implantation: A dose response trial. *Journal of Clinical Psychiatry, 45,* 242–247.

Zivich, J. (1981) Alcoholic subtypes and treatment effectiveness. *Journal of Consulting and Clinical Psychology, 42,* 72–80.

Zucker, R. and Gomberg, E. (1986) Etiology of alcoholism reconsidered. *American Psychologist, 41,* 783–793.

/ Prescription Drug Abuse

**The Case of
Barbara**

*One pill makes you larger
And one pill makes you small
But the ones that mother gives
Don't do anything at all.*
— Grace Slick
"White Rabbit"
(Copper Penny Music)

Both illicit and normally prescribed drugs are abused in our society (McKim, 1986; Blum, 1984). Though the DSM does refer to the abuse of specific drugs that are occasionally obtained through prescriptions, such as amphetamines, the specific designation of prescription drug abuse does not exist. This situation is ironic since such a category at least indirectly implicates the people who formulate the DSM categories in the first place—those who do the prescribing. Also, the DSM does not now focus on the concept of addiction as much as earlier DSMs did.

Traditionally, the most commonly abused prescription drug is diazepam (Valium), one of the benzodiazepines (Blackwell, 1979). This drug was abused heavily by Barbara. Blackwell found that during the late 1970s, more than 2 billion Valium tablets a year were prescribed in the United States. This is for only one drug in the benzodiazepine family, which in turn is only one group of the minor tranquilizers. The benzodiazepines primarily act to lessen anxiety and cause muscle relaxation. They are easily habituated to and in severe cases may react with alcohol to cause death by drug overdose (Vogel, 1985).

There is also a danger in triggering a psychotic reaction. Major et al. (1979) assessed thirty-two male alcoholics who were being administered Valium. Seven of these individuals experienced a psychotic reaction as a result of the Valium, and all who reacted had certain blood plasma differences from normal; that is, low levels of monoamine oxidase (MAO). Valium is often administered to alcoholics to help them ease the pain of withdrawal. Major's study suggests that an assessment of MAO blood levels before administering Valium to alcoholics could be very useful.

The Case of Barbara

Barbara is a 42-year-old recently widowed Caucasian female who now lives alone. Her only child, a son, is on active duty in the Navy. Barbara is the second of four children and was born in a small midwestern town. She still lives there and in general feels comfortable in her community. Her family life as she grew up was from her perspective a positive experience. She related well with her siblings and still maintains moderately active relationships with them.

She remembers her father as a generally good provider who seemed to care about his children, though he had difficulty expressing his affection for them openly. He was an assembly line worker at a local factory and had a high school education.

Barbara reports that the major stresses in her early life occurred when her father developed heavy debts, which made him upset and irritable. At such times, he would often come home and vividly curse the bill collectors.

While he drank himself into a stupor, Barbara's mother stayed home as a housewife, took care of the children, and was apparently a good homemaker. She did suffer occasional "spells," during which time she would "have to go under a doctor's care."

Barbara very much enjoyed her high school years, for she was active in several organizations and had many friends. She obtained good grades and graduated in the top third of her class, but did not continue her education. She married during the summer after her high school graduation.

Barbara worked for two years as a clerk in a local department store and then became a full-time homemaker with the birth of her son. Her husband had left high school without graduating but had a good paying job as an ironworker. Her memories of her marriage were quite pleasant. Her husband was killed in a work-related accident when she was 38.

Barbara naturally experienced depression in the period after her husband's death. As she put it, "There was a huge void in my life for a time, and it actually became worse when I realized my son needed to leave home and get out on his own."

Barbara's pattern of involvement in numerous interest groups in high school had subsided during the marriage, and she had little activity to fill her world when her husband died and her son began to assert his independence. She was very depressed for the first couple of months, and even though that moderated, she still experienced insomnia and "nervousness." Barbara first used over-the-counter sedatives and aspirin to combat her upset, and she usually downed these with a "good strong drink." As a result of concern about several cysts, she went into the hospital and had a partial hysterectomy. Her attending physician was apparently unaware of her alcohol use and generously prescribed Valium during and after her stay in the hospital. Valium proved to be more efficient and more pleasant for sleep than was the self-prescribed medication. She asked her physician for a continued prescription after her release from the hospital, and he acquiesced, although he did try to reduce the prescription gradually.

Shortly after her release, her son left home, leaving her without any meaningful interpersonal contacts. Her father died shortly thereafter of a heart attack. Even though they had not been extremely close in the past several years, his death was another stress for her. She began to see another doctor, as well as continuing the contacts with the physician who had performed the hysterectomy. Both doctors were prescribing Valium and in addition she periodically obtained other tranquilizers from neighbors who had prescriptions that they had not used.

Over the four-year period after her husband's death, Barbara gradually increased her intake and tolerance to the Valium to approximately 80 milligrams a day. In addition, she occasionally took other similar-acting prescription drugs and also indulged in alcohol to a mild degree. Finally, she was threatened with losing her job because of the absenteeism and lethargy that were a direct result of the drug abuse.

Her supervisor at the department store at which she was working had become aware of her abuse pattern through the reports of several of her co-workers. He told her he would fire her if she did not immediately seek professional help. Through an acquaintance at work, Barbara became aware of a research program on prescription drug abuse at the medical school in a nearby city and volunteered to participate in the treatment program.

Etiology

Several variables in Barbara's personal history might predict drug abuse of some sort. However, she has few qualities that would push her toward illegal drug abuse. Thus, it is not surprising that she first resorted to alcohol and over-the-counter drugs. Later, she felt more comfortable when using a prescribed drug, both because it had the appearance of legitimacy and also because it did not threaten her self-image by forcing her to label herself as a drug abuser (Zucker, 1986).

Before we proceed to discuss the variables in her personal history, it is important to note some overall cultural factors that contribute to a high level of prescription drug abuse, and, of course, affect an individual such as Barbara.

Prescription drugs serve many purposes beyond effecting physiological changes, which are the alleged primary role (McKim, 1986). Such drugs are the charms and fetishes of our modern society. Some physicians too easily resort to the use of a drug when reassurance and understanding would be sufficient. The change from the bedside manner model of medical care to the office visit model has demanded an efficient cue with which the physician can quickly wrap up the patient contact and at the same time leave the patient satisfied. The prescription does both. When the physician begins to write out a prescription, patients know that the session is over. In fact, many patients feel dissatisfied if no prescription is given; it is as if their problem is not serious enough to warrant the attention they had anticipated. Mellinger and his colleagues (1978) found that when patients with rather ill-defined symptoms (and about 70 percent of medical patients actually fall into this category) saw a family physician, they benefited equally well if they were given reassurance that they were all right and needed no medication. But the important point is that this was only effective when they were given adequate attention and discussion time. Chowka (1979) found that the average consultation time for an office visit with a physician in 1972 was only seventeen minutes, and it may be less than that today.

Another factor contributing to the ease with which mood-altering medication is dispensed is the fact that most such medication is prescribed by nonpsychiatrist physicians, as was the case in the Mellinger study. Unfortunately, these nonpsychiatrist physicians are even more likely to use a prescription in lieu of reassurance and explanation of the psychological issues and also are more unaware than are psychiatrists of the potential for abuse and habituation.

Certainly a share of the blame for the high rate of prescription drug abuse in our society belongs with some drug companies (Orford, 1985). Drug companies constantly and intensively promote their drugs to individual physicians. This intensity can lead them to deemphasize issues such as potential abuse, side effects, and other alternative methods that do not have the inherent problems of drug use.

In Barbara's individual history, several factors made her drug abuse a likely occurrence. The situational factors that led to her depression are important. They left her devoid of social relationships and without a sense of meaning in her world. Her skills at turning this pattern around through new behaviors were minimal; as a result, she needed to dilute the anxiety and apprehension that occurred (Westermeyer, 1985).

Her history manifests clear models for drug abuse. Her father would drink himself into unconsciousness as the stress from his debts mounted. Her mother would use the umbrella concept of "the doctor's care" to avoid demands at various periods when stress became too much for her.

When she went into the hospital for her hysterectomy, her physician routinely prescribed Valium. It is a common practice for such medication to be prescribed well before any signs of anxiety are present. Naturally enough, the fact that a physician has prescribed it attaches a label of legitimacy to it. Barbara found that the Valium calmed her and helped her sleep more effectively than alcohol did, though she still occasionally included alcohol (Vogel, 1985).

After Barbara left the hospital, she continued the medication, which dulled the anxiety she first experienced when she realized her son was going to leave home, and then shortly thereafter, when she had to adjust to the death of her father. By this time, she was habituated to using Valium, not only to counter anxiety and apprehension, but also to go to sleep most nights. She was in the position of fearing to skip the Valium since she did not know if anxiety would occur. It became a magic fetish for her, such that taking it warded off the possibility of anxiety. As with many people, the fear of fear itself, or "discomfort anxiety" (Ellis, 1979), is a prime motivator for such behavior. This negative pattern became routine until situational factors intruded. Fortunately, the threatened loss of her job was enough for Barbara to reflect on her behavior, to the point at which she decided (critical step) that she was willing to proceed into treatment (Bugental, 1980).

Barbara is typical of many individuals who develop prescription drug abuse. The drug is first used to counter real problems that a physician labels as legitimate, and the process of habituation is rather slow, with increasing dosages occurring gradually. The drug then begins to take on other functions in the world of the abuser (such as sedative, anxiety preventer, and so forth), just as it did with Barbara. Also, Barbara's status as a middle age, middle class individual is typical of the prescription drug abuser. She would feel uncomfortable using any illicit drugs, and might verbalize hostility toward people who do use such drugs, without awareness that her drug abuse is similar to theirs (Zucker, 1986; Westermeyer, 1985).

Treatment

Even though there has been some discussion of the etiology of prescription drug abuse in the literature, its treatment has not been researched to any significant degree. Physicians are naturally oriented to prescribe medication, and they occasionally downplay the abuse potential. Also, virtually all psychiatric journals are heavily funded by drug company ads. This circumstance does not lead to a pattern of direct control, but it certainly exerts an omnipresent influence.

Barbara was well motivated to change her pattern of behavior. Such motivation is not atypical since prescription drug abusers generally have middle class values. Once they are directly aware of the fact that they are drug abusers, they are more likely to be willing to change than are people who have abused nonprescription drugs.

Before any significant overall change could be expected, her treatment required a detoxification (Panksepp, 1986), which was done with medical support. She was placed on another drug, hydroxyzine pamoate, which researchers have found reduces the need for benzodiazepines and other tranquilizers and helps to subdue any withdrawal symptoms. (This method is not dissimilar to the use of methadone, which, though it is an addicting drug, is used to help reduce the heroin addict's pattern of substance dependence.)

For the first three weeks, Barbara attended the clinic daily in order to have the drug administered and to allow the clinicians to check on her motivation and progress. The hydroxyzine pamoate was administered in gradually decreasing dosages over the three weeks; at the end of this time, Barbara felt she was able to go without it and also without the Valium (Vogel, 1985).

It was also necessary to deal with the psychological issues that had been primary in promoting her pattern. Her psychotherapist was a clinical psychologist on the staff of the medical center, and together they discussed her various conflicts and coping styles. It quickly became clear that Barbara needed to deal with a sense of meaninglessness in her world (Bugental, 1980) that had resulted from the loss of her husband, her father, and the immediate relationship with her son. She had few social contacts, and though she expressed a desire to increase them, she seemed unaware of how to do so. She was immediately included in group therapy (Sundel and Sundel, 1985). This gave her an arena in which to discuss her problems and also allowed her to meet new people with whom she could develop new social systems. Most importantly, an examination of her vocational situation revealed that she did not feel satisfied with the rewards of her present position. She was tested, found to be bright–normal to superior in intelligence, and was encouraged to enroll in further education. This would increase both her alternatives through mobility and affluence and her self-esteem. She chose to pursue a degree program in business administration and stated that she hoped eventually to obtain her master's degree.

Since one stated purpose of the therapy group was to help the participants increase the effectiveness of their social behaviors, the group was perfect for Barbara. She learned ways of being more assertive in meeting people and began to date, which she had not done since the death of her husband. She also made two close female friends who gave her an outlet for her feelings and facilitated her social contacts.

Barbara was also taught a relaxation technique called progressive relaxation. This technique involves learning to tense and then relax individual muscle groups. She used this to counter upsurges of anxiety, which in the past had been a cue for her to start abusing drugs. She was also counseled in better methods of coping with occasional insomnia, which she felt was an initiating cue for her to abuse both alcohol and Valium.

During the treatment, which lasted nine months, Barbara occasionally slipped into the pattern of using drugs and alcohol. However, by this time she had developed trust in a number of the other group members and could disclose this to them. As a result, she had support so that an individual failure did not signify to her a total failure and did not generate any negative self-labeling. As she progressed in her schoolwork and found she could be successful, her self-esteem markedly increased. This positive cycle led to increased social contacts and then to more effective dating patterns. In that sense, Barbara achieved what could be termed a significant cure that persisted for at least the two years of occasional contact she kept with the center.

Comment

As mentioned, minor tranquilizers (such as Miltown, Librium, and Valium) are the most frequently abused prescription drugs (McKim, 1986; Blackwell, 1979; Chowka, 1979). Unfortunately, some physicians and their patients minimize (or deny) the potential problems associated with the routine prescription and chronic use of these medications. Aside from the physiological side effects (including addiction) of long-term use, the patient is at risk socially, emotionally, and occupationally. Barbara's grief over her husband's death and her distress about her son's leaving home may have run their course without intervention or with only minimal intervention. However, Barbara's increased dependence on Valium delayed resolution of these normal reactions and resulted in further disruption of her social and occupational functioning.

Abuse of prescription drugs is further complicated by social acceptance and implied professional sanction (Brownell, Marlatt, Lichtenstein, and Wilson, 1986). To be sure, there is a small subgroup of people for whom even long-term use of minor tranquilizers and sleeping medications is appropriate. However, the fact that these drugs are legal and prescribed by physicians encourages patients to consider them safe. Consequently, the consideration of dependence occurs only after some dramatic consequence in the environment forces the abusers to seek professional help. In cases such as Barbara's, understandable sympathy on the part of employers, friends, and family members can inhibit the recognition of the problem by protecting and "covering" for the person.

REFERENCES

Blackwell, B. (1979) Benzodiazepines: Drug abuse and data abuse. *Psychiatric Opinion, 16,* 10–37.

Blum, K. (1984) *Handbook of Abusable Drugs.* New York: Gardner.

Brownell, K., Marlatt, A., Lichtenstein, E., and Wilson, T. (1986) Understanding and preventing relapse. *American Psychologist, 41,* 765–782.

Bugental, J. (1980) Someone needs to worry: The existential anxiety of responsibility and decision. In G. Belkin (Ed.), *Contemporary Psychotherapies.* Chicago: Rand McNally.

Chowka, P. (1979) Pushers in white. *East West Journal, 9,* 30–37.

Major, L., Murphy, D., Gersohn, E., and Brown, G. (1979) The role of plasma amine oxidase, platelet monoamine oxidase, and red cell catechol-O-methyl transferase in severe behavioral reactions to disulfiram. *American Journal of Psychiatry, 136,* 717–718.

McKim, W. (1986) *Drugs and Behavior.* Englewood Cliffs, N.J.: Prentice-Hall.

Mellinger, G., Balter, M., Manheimer, I., and Perry, H. (1978) Psychic distress, life crisis, and the use of psychotherapeutic medications. *Archives of General Psychiatry, 35,* 1045–1052.

Orford, J. (1985) *Excessive Appetites: A Psychological View of Addiction.* New York: John Wiley.

Panksepp, J. (1986) The neurochemistry of behavior. In M. Rosenweig and L. Porter (Eds.), *Annual Review of Psychology, 37,* Palo Alto, Calif.: Annual Reviews.

Sundel, M. and Sundel, S. (1985) Behavior modification in groups: A time-limited model for planning, intervention, and evaluation. In D. Upper and S. Ross (Ed.), *Handbook of Behavioral Group Therapy.* New York: Plenum.

Vogel, W. (1985) Interactions of drugs of abuse with prescription drugs. In A. Alterman (Ed.), *Substance Abuse and Psychopathology.* New York: Plenum.

Westermeyer, J. (1985) Substance abuse and psychopathology: Sociocultural factors. In A. Alterman (Ed.), *Substance Abuse and Psychopathology.* New York: Plenum.

Zucker, R. (1986) The development of abusive and addictive behaviors over time: An interactional framework. Nebraska Symposium on Motivation: Alcohol and Addictive Behavior. Lincoln, Neb.

/ A Case of Polydrug Abuse, Primarily Cocaine Abuse

The Case of Colleen

He sniffed the two lines of the four that remained. . . . The way he'd worked it out with Carrie, he was supposed to say to Tina, "I'm not getting high at all, this must have been cut"— but somehow he was having a hard time opening his mouth to speak.

. . . "Good coke," said Sylvia. (p. 87)

— C. Haas and T. Hunter
The Soul Hit

Polydrug (or "mixed drug") abuse patterns have markedly increased in our culture in the last two decades. Such abuse is not likely to decrease in the near future since, (1) our culture has not really taken a strong stand against such abuse, (2) more and higher quality drugs are increasingly available, and (3) there are such enormous profits in illegal drug trafficking.

Often a drug of abuse within a polydrug pattern, cocaine has also in general become a favored drug, especially in recent years. Its abuse by many sports and entertainment idols has received much media attention. Nevertheless, cocaine has been used for centuries. It is an alkaloid derivative of coca leaves, which were chewed by the Aztecs and are still used by at least four million Indians in South American countries such as Peru and Bolivia. Such diverse personages as Arthur Conan Doyle's character Sherlock Holmes, John Phillip Sousa, and even Sigmund Freud have sung the praises of cocaine (Ashley, 1975; Byck, 1974).

A number of people became inadvertently habituated to cocaine in the United States during the late 1800s by drinking Coca-Cola. John Pemberton, an Atlanta druggist, had combined cocaine with sugar and kola nut extract in a brass pot in his backyard to make the original Coca-Cola, which he advertised as a "brain medicine." When the Pure Food and Drug Law of 1906 outlawed the use of cocaine, caffeine was substituted in "the real thing." Today, refined cocaine is usually sniffed in small amounts. Most of what passes for cocaine is not pure ("free base") cocaine but cocaine hydrochloride, a salt that is approximately 85-percent cocaine by weight. Pure cocaine is sometimes smoked, a psychophysiologically more dangerous process than sniffing (Julien, 1985).

Cocaine has become very popular in recent years not only because of the euphoria it produces, but also because it is commonly perceived as neither addictive nor dangerous. Technically, it may not be considered addictive since there are *allegedly* few significant physical withdrawal symptoms upon its discontinuance and because there is no tolerance issue, since, again allegedly, it does not require significantly increasing dosages to produce its usual effect. However, according to Dr. Carlton Gass, a clinical psychologist who has worked with cocaine addicts in Miami, a number of addicts claim they need increasingly higher quantities to get the same high. Indeed, cocaine abuse patterns certainly fulfill several criteria which figure into popular definition of addiction: (1) compulsive use, (2) loss of control over use, and (3) continued use despite destructive consequences (Gass, 1986; Gawin and Kleber, 1986; Blum, 1984). In any case, it is certainly powerfully habituating (Orford, 1985), and it is clearly more dangerous than was originally thought. Research on both animals and humans shows that long-term cocaine use has numerous debilitating side effects, including severe cardiac problems (Julien, 1985; Zucker, 1986). Since the purity of street cocaine varies markedly, a lethal effect may occur when an addict inadvertently takes a very pure dose of cocaine. Any overdose is similarly very dangerous.

An odd testimonial to the dangerous potency of cocaine overdose occurred in the mountains of north Georgia just south of the Tennessee state line in December of 1985. A black bear, weighing more than 150 pounds, came across some packages of cocaine that had apparently been dropped from a smuggler's plane. The bear ripped the packages open, ate with delight, and keeled over dead.

The following case of Colleen demonstrates an unfortunately common pattern in our society: early use of alcohol and/or marijuana, a broadening of this abuse into a true "mixed" or "polydrug" abuse pattern, with increasingly severe abuse of a drug such as cocaine, amphetamines, or heroin.

The Case of Colleen

Colleen was born the second of two children into an upper middle class family in a large midwestern city suburb. Her father was an executive vice-president of a small corporation that manufactured machine tools, and her mother worked part-time as a registered nurse.

Since she was an active, bright child, Colleen was the delight of not only her parents but also her sister, who was already 12 years old when Colleen was born. Colleen was given a lot of attention by all, and had a happy childhood, to the point of being obviously spoiled. This was in part a result of her mother's relatively permissive approach to child-rearing. Her father traveled quite a bit, so he was not a major factor in her day-to-day care, though he did like to play with her and take her on outings when he could get time.

By the time she was 6, Colleen was known as a "tomboy," a marked contrast to her quiet and stereotypically feminine sister. Colleen was always strong and well-coordinated for her age, and quickly excelled in virtually any athletic endeavor. She was also adventuresome and somewhat fearless, and soon became an all-star in youth soccer and basketball. She loved hiking and as she moved into adolescence, her father even took her on a couple of the less dangerous mountain climbing expeditions that he so relished.

Though of above average intelligence, Colleen made only Bs and Cs in grade school and junior high, as she simply refused to discipline herself to study for any length of time. Her parents made sporadic attempts to force her to study but didn't work very hard at this, and Colleen would maneuver around most of their strategies.

It was in junior high that Colleen started to smoke tobacco, primarily to facilitate her friendship with a girl who was to be one of the few close friends she ever had. Throughout her life, Colleen always had many casual friends and acquaintances of both sexes, but only one or two lasting friendships with females and none with males. Colleen really didn't smoke more than a few cigarettes a day until she was in senior high, and at that time she also started smoking marijuana occasionally.

Her parents finally became aware of Colleen's smoking, and when questioned by her father, she also admitted to smoking pot. Her father and mother tried to present the rational reasons for stopping and threatened severe though vaguely described punishments if she continued. The main effect of this confrontation was that Colleen became much more secretive about her activities, but didn't really stop them. Since Colleen had always seemed to resist any dependency on her parents, as well as most other people, there were few lines of communication wherein her parents could know what was going on.

Just after the end of basketball season, in her sophomore year of high school, she began to establish her potential as a future star. Unfortunately, at the same time, Colleen began dabbling with some other drugs, mainly amphetamines, and also started becoming sexually active. It was as if her natural enjoyment of her body combined with a general "greed for experience" to produce a need to try any new and interesting situation or stimulation.

Her drug use increased, and then tapered off when basketball season started in both her junior and senior years. As predicted, she made first team all-state in her senior year and accepted a scholarship to the university in her state that had the strongest tradition as a basketball power.

It was at this time that the drug problem increased to the point that her life was disrupted. In addition to smoking tobacco and marijuana regularly, Colleen's use of amphetamines increased. She also occasionally tried LSD and cocaine and used a variety of "downers" to mute the effects of the stimulants.

She did manage to complete high school, though even her graduation was in jeopardy for a while. But at about that time, her boss at the fast food place where she worked became tired of her unpredictable behavior on the job and fired her. Then, two weeks later, she wrecked her mother's car by bouncing it through a cornfield and into a creek while intoxicated on a variety of substances.

Her parents immediately placed her in an inpatient adolescent drug treatment unit. Colleen stayed there for six weeks and then continued in outpatient therapy. But she showed obvious signs of relapse, became quite depressed, and was placed back in the inpatient program. She stayed for two months, missing the first semester of college. She seemed to decide to change at this time and took a part-time job for the two months she had free before going to the university for the second semester. She was allowed to join the basketball team for practice but was "redshirted" so that she could play for four years. The remainder of her college years were fairly uneventful. Combining her talent with a strong competitive streak, she became a regular on the team in her sophomore year and made third-team All-American in a couple of coaches' polls in her senior year. She had by this time also become a first-rate skier and mountain climber. Her grades never were much above a C level, but she did graduate with a degree in sociology.

She took a job selling insurance for a large national firm. Her high energy level and her ability to meet people combined with her contacts and name recognition to allow her some initial success. However, after two years she became "bored" with the discipline needed to keep her contacts and make new ones, with the routine of the job itself, and especially with the paperwork required. Her performance was now drawing criticism from her superiors.

She was truly in a bind, since these developments conflicted with her natural desire to succeed and her intense competitiveness. Also, her life-long avoidance of deep and supportive friendships and her aversion to dependence on others meant that she was truly alone. Lastly, her outlets for stimulation-seeking (e.g., basketball, skiing, mountain climbing, etc.) were no longer available to her because of her life style.

Though she had been able to break the polydrug abuse pattern of her earlier years, she still smoked tobacco regularly and drank to facilitate the rather frenetic but superficial social life she now used to avoid feelings of loneliness. This social style, plus her upper middle class status, meant that cocaine was readily available, and she began using it again. The habit quickly spiraled and so did her problems with her job. Finally, her boss, who had always suspected that she used drugs, decided to fire her.

In the next few weeks Colleen alternated between looking for a new job and staying high on cocaine to avoid deepening feelings of depression. One night, while high on cocaine, she fell down some stairs at a nightclub, suffering a compound leg fracture and a severe concussion. In the ensuing response by medical personnel and her parents, the extent of her drug problem became obvious. After recovering from her injuries, Colleen again checked into a drug treatment program. After ten weeks she was released, and was helped to find a job as a retail sales clerk.

Though the situation looked somewhat positive, Colleen again became bored and depressed. She impulsively took up with a wealthy older man whose life style centered around gambling and traveling. Colleen left town with him and could not be effectively traced for follow-up data. But it was clear that she had again reverted to a cocaine abuse pattern, and the prognosis is certainly poor.

Etiology

From a psychodynamic perspective, the early spoiling of Colleen developed a high level of narcissism and fixated her at the oral stage of development (Settlage and Brockbank, 1985). Thus, in the face of any lack of success in her narcissistic strivings, or in her consistent inability to satisfy her consciously unacceptable dependency needs, the drugs allowed her to regress to a state of primitive oral satisfaction where a sense of womblike security was artificially induced. In this womblike state, the normal stresses and demands were no longer a source of concern—a short-term world was created in which passivity, noncompetitiveness, and dependency were functional and allowed. This fixation at such a primitive level, consistent with the high level of narcissism, predicts the need for intense, confrontive treatment, followed by long-term psychotherapy to develop eventually more mature character patterns. Thus, from this view, it is not surprising that there was never any long-term success with Colleen.

The humanistic-existential perspective complements rather than directly contradicts the psychodynamic view. Colleen's drug use allowed an avoidance of true "being" (Tillich, 1952) and of authentic life choices. Her early spoiling and her later drug use provided the pleasures of satiation and nonreciprocated dependency without requiring self-defining decisions and the giving of the self. Since few actual limits were set on gratification behaviors, mature self-defining behaviors could never emerge and be affirmed (Spotts and Schontz, 1984).

Colleen thus found herself in the modern dilemma of attempting to find meaning and value amid an abundance of stimulation and pleasure, the polar opposite of the Victorian era conflict of finding pleasure without crippling guilt. Colleen rebelled by refusing the "game of life" presented by parents and society. Instead, she moved to the coping strategies of the withdrawn sensuousness of drug abuse, the uncommitted intimacy of casual friendship and promiscuous sexuality, and, ultimately, the forced nurturance of official caretakers. Thus, drugs are an existential movement away from "being," a participation in a conception of "nonbeing," poignantly expressed by the French poet-humanist Jean Cocteau in his description of the ultimate reason for smoking opium (from which heroin is derived):

> Everything that we do in life, including love, is done on an express train traveling towards death. To smoke opium is to leave the train while in motion; it is to be interested in something other than life and death (Jarvik, 1967, p. 52).

The behavioral and biological perspectives emphasize the direct biological reinforcement value of the drugs; for example, cocaine's ability to almost immediately induce a sense of euphoria that reduces anxiety and alleviates depression (Kendall, 1985). Ironically, after causing a high, which usually lasts about 15 to 30 minutes, cocaine apparently acts on the catecholamine system to produce a biochemical situation often associated with clinical depression — reduced levels of norepinephrine and serotonin. Thus, the effect is self-perpetuating inasmuch as its short-term euphoric effect alleviates its long-term consequences (Julien, 1985; Blum, 1984).

For Colleen, the reinforcement of peer acceptance and the powerful addicting and habituating properties of both alcohol and tobacco quickly established an overall set to use drugs to control mood and emotion, a pattern further reinforced by Colleen's period of "mixed" or "polydrug" abuse (Zucker, 1986). This polydrug habit structure later became focused into a primary pattern of cocaine abuse because that drug was used by her later peer group and because its particular reinforcement properties had a "goodness of fit" with her personality structure. Certainly, there is a definite psychopathic component in Colleen — she was (1) unable to establish close friendships, (2) stimulation-seeking, (3) amoral, and (4) unable to delay gratification and learn from experience (see the case of Andy, the antisocial personality in Chapter 10). There is good evidence that these psychopathic factors facilitate a pattern of drug abuse (Zuckerman, Buchsbaum, and Murphy, 1980; Orford, 1985). The biological response directly engendered by a drug is then complemented by the secondary gain of avoiding environmental demands and providing a structured reinforcement of dependency (her parents and the medical response to her "illness") (Kendall, 1985).

Peer reinforcement, the euphoric response, and the satisfaction of a need for stimulation result in cocaine abuse across all social classes. However, its expense does somewhat limit its abuse in certain subgroups, reflecting the insightful comment of comedian Richard Pryor, who was himself a cocaine addict at one time, "Cocaine is God's way of telling you that you make too much money."

Related to Colleen's pattern, Spotts and Schontz (1984) analyzed middle class and upper middle class male cocaine users, age 21 to 44, using a variety of psychological tests as well as extensive interviews. They found that consistent users in this group, in addition to the peer-acceptance component, were often intense, narcissistic, competitive, and/or achievement-oriented persons who have acquaintanceships and family relationships but who strongly avoid intimacy and vulnerability in relationships. They are often struggling against underlying feelings of depression or anxiety and use cocaine as a "booster" in their competitive or achievement strivings.

Treatment

Colleen received the accepted and most effective treatment modes (Orford, 1985; Sandler, 1985). But, as is not uncommon with severe drug users, who do have high recidivism rates, the treatment is not always successful (Gawin and Kleber, 1986). As it was with Colleen, any inpatient treatment plan should have the goals of (1) detoxifying the person's biological system and (2) directly and strongly confronting the destructive psychological patterns. Confrontation techniques, pioneered with heroin abusers by group treatment centers such as Synanon and Daytop Village, are used with cocaine addicts as well. The goal is to get the addict to assume control of her own decisions, to plan more adaptive behaviors to satisfy vocational, interpersonal, and sexual needs, and then to look at more characterological and existential issues.

In this latter regard, Spotts and Schontz (1984) recommend intensive psychotherapy with a focus on the avoidance of dependency and unresolved spiritual and intimacy-betrayal and intimacy-avoidance crises. Such psychotherapy needs to take into account the often underlying depression and at the same time allow socially acceptable outlets for the commonly higher-than-average level of stimulation-seeking (Zuckerman, Buchsbaum, and Murphy, 1980). As some success is attained here, involvement in a group therapy modeled on AA principles can be effective (Erlich and McGeehan, 1985).

REFERENCES

Ashley, R. (1975) *Cocaine: Its History and Effects*. New York: St. Martin's Press.

Blum, K. (1984) *Handbook of Abusable Drugs*. New York: Gardner.

Byck, R. (Ed.) (1974) *Cocaine Papers: Sigmund Freud*. New York: Stonehill.

Erlich, P. and McGeehan, M. (1985) Cocaine recovery support groups and the language of recovery. *Journal of Psychoactive Drugs, 17*, 11–17.

Gass, C. (1986) Personal communication.

Gawin, F. and Kleber, H. (1986) Abstinence symptomatology and psychiatric diagnosis in cocaine abusers. *Archives of General Psychiatry, 43*, 107–113.

Jarvik, M. (1967) The psychopharmacological revolution. *Psychology Today, 1*, 51–59.

Julien, R. (1985) *A Primer of Drug Action*. New York: W. H. Freeman.

Kendall, P. (Ed.) (1985) *Advances in Cognitive-Behavioral Research and Therapy*. (Vol. 4) Orlando, Fla.: Academic Press.

Orford, J. (1985) *Excessive Appetites: A Psychological View of Addiction*. New York: John Wiley.

Sandler, J. (1985) Aversion methods. In F. Kanfer and A. Goldstein (Eds.) *Helping People Change*. New York: Pergamon.

Settlage, C. and Brockbank, R. (Eds.) (1985) *New Ideas in Psychoanalysis*. **Hillsdale,** N.J.: Analytic Press.

Spotts, J. and Schontz, F. (1984) Drug-induced ego states. I. Cocaine: Phenomenology and implications. *The International Journal of the Addictions*, *19*, 119–151.

Tillich, P. (1952) *The Courage to Be*. New Haven, Conn.: Yale University Press.

Zucker, R. (1986) The development of abusive and addictive behaviors over time: An interactional framework. Nebraska Symposium on Motivation, Alcohol and Addictive Behavior. Lincoln, Neb.

Zuckerman, M., Buchsbaum, M. and Murphy, D. (1980) Sensation seeking and its biological correlates. *Psychological Bulletin*, *88*, 187–214.

10

The Personality Disorders

Common to most definitions of personality is an emphasis on the individual's most enduring traits—that is, on those recurring perceptions and behaviors that are exhibited in a wide range of important social and personal contexts and that are most useful in predicting future behavior. To say that people have a habitual way of dealing with the world is not to say that they are exhibiting pathological behavior. In fact, most people have developed customary and comfortable patterns of interacting with the environment. In the personality disorders, however, these patterns (or personality traits) evidence a rigidity and destructive interpersonal results that make them counteradaptive.

The personality disorders are common patterns. People with a personality disorder are not typically as disturbed or as concerned by their behavior as are friends and relatives. Such people see these particular personality traits as *ego-syntonic*, consistent with their self-perception. Thus, persons with personality disorders are more likely to be brought to the attention of professionals by other people, such as spouses, relatives, or the criminal justice system, than by themselves.

Recognizing that addicted and sexually disordered persons (included as personality disorders in DSM-II) do not necessarily suffer from associated psychopathology, DSM-III and the subsequent revisions and versions excluded these disorders from the category of personality disorders and classified them elsewhere. Also, the hysterical personality was changed to the histrionic personality, and the cyclothymic personality was reclassified as an affective disorder. Explosive, obsessive-compulsive, asthenic, and inadequate personalities were dropped from DSM-II, and six new personality disorders were added. The present personality disorders are listed below in the "appearance clusters" suggested by the DSM:

1. Disorders that appear odd or eccentric
   - Paranoid: hyperalert, suspicious, litigious, and authoritarian

- Schizoid: asocial "loners," not "schizophrenic-like"
- Schizotypal: "schizophrenic-like," but no hallucinations or delusions

2. Disorders that appear dramatic, emotional, or erratic

- Histrionic: emotionally flamboyant and dramatic, though shallow
- Narcissistic: chronically inflated sense of self-worth
- Antisocial: chronic antisocial patterns, does not learn from experience
- Borderline: irritable, anxious, sporadically aggressive and emotionally unstable

3. Disorders that appear anxious or fearful

- Avoidant: shy and inhibited, afraid to "risk" relationships
- Dependent: seeks dependent relationships; naive, yet suspicious
- Obsessive-Compulsive: controlled, formal, perfectionistic; "workaholics without warmth"
- Passive-Aggressive: passively resistant through stubbornness, inefficiency, or threatened aggression

The personality disorders were coded on Axis II in DSM-III, which allowed the unfortunate implication that the personality disorders are not "clinical" syndromes but rather are behavioral and psychosocial conditions and thus are "less important." Though DSM does not always disallow these diagnoses in children, the diagnosis of a personality disorder in a person under 18 is discouraged. In fact, these are critically important disorder patterns and are often generic to more "dramatic" and "severe" psychopathology. By definition, these patterns begin to merge in childhood or adolescence. DSM presents the following relationships between certain personality disorders and certain of the disorders usually first evident in infancy, childhood, or adolescence:

Disorders in Childhood or Adolescence	Personality Disorders
Schizoid	Schizoid
Avoidant	Avoidant
Conduct	Antisocial
Oppositional	Passive-Aggressive
Identity	Borderline

The cases in this chapter were chosen to demonstrate the most important personality disorders and the reader is also referred to the case of Perry, the paranoid personality disorder, in Chapter 6. The histrionic personality disorder, described in the case of Hilde, is a common pattern and often critical to the development of marital and family distress, as well as to eventual personal unhappiness because of negative social feedback. The antisocial personality disorder, the case of Andy, exemplifies the most common personality disorder and certainly the most socially destructive pattern.

/ The Histrionic Personality Disorder

The Case of
Hilde

> *It ain't bragging if you really done it.*
> — Dizzy Dean
> St. Louis Cardinals star pitcher

The specific criteria that mark the histrionic personality disorder include dramatic and intense emotional expressions, efforts to gain the center of attention, and shallow, insincere, and disrupted interpersonal relationships (Kernberg, 1984). Such people are likely to overreact emotionally, even in everyday situations. They have superficial interpersonal relationships, though they easily verbalize the platitudes of intense relationships, and they are inclined toward suicidal gestures to manipulate others. Vanity and self-absorption are common traits, in which sense histrionic individuals parallel the narcissistic personality disorder (Lasch, 1978).

Histrionic personalities appear to be emphatic and socially perceptive, so that they easily elicit new relationships. Since they then turn out to be emotionally insensitive and have little depth of insight into their own role in relationships, they are likely to avoid any blame for the inevitable problems in the relationships. This places them closer to the defense mechanism of paranoid patterns. Histrionic individuals are often flirtatious and seductive, though there is little payoff if one follows these cues (Barrett, 1980). The behavior of the histrionic personality resembles the traditional concept of ultrafemininity, and for that reason it is more common in females than in males. Indeed, the Greek root of the term is *hustera*, meaning "uterus."

Since denial is such a common approach to conflict in this pattern, intellectual accomplishment, relative to potential, is often limited, and analytic thought is deemphasized. As a result, histrionic individuals tend to be gullible and impressionable. Somatic complaints such as "spells of weakness" and headaches are typical. The histrionic individual has commonly been encountered in clinical practice (Gardner, 1965).

The DSM category of histrionic personality disorder was traditionally known as the "hysterical personality." This term has now been discarded since *hysterical* wrongly implies a disorder that parallels the symptom picture of what was previously labeled hysterical neurosis. This latter term has also been changed in the DSM to help eliminate this confusion.

The Case of Hilde

Hilde is a 42-year-old homemaker who sought help from her family physician for a combination of complaints, including headaches, mild depression, and marital difficulties. The family physician had attempted to treat her with quick reassurance and Valium. When these proved ineffective, he referred her to a private psychiatrist. Hilde, still quite attractive, obviously spent a great deal of time on her personal appearance. She was cooperative in the initial interview with the psychiatrist, though at times rambled so much that he had to bring her back to the subject at hand. As she talked, it became apparent that she had not really reflected in any depth on the issues that she discussed and was only pumping out information, much as a computer would. She showed a significant amount of affect during the interview, but it was often exaggerated in response to the content she was discussing at the time. She delighted in giving extensive historical descriptions of her past life, again without much insight into the causal role it had in her present distress.

In fact, many of the descriptions she gave appeared to be more for the purpose of impressing the therapist than in order to come to grips with her problems. When confronted with any irrelevancies in her stories, she first adopted a cute and charming manner, and if this proved ineffective in persuading the psychiatrist to change topics, she then became petulant and irritated.

When she described her present difficulties, she was always inclined to ascribe the responsibility to some person or situation other than herself. She stated that her husband was indifferent to her and added that she suspected he had been seduced by one of the secretaries in his office. This situation, along with a "lot of stress in my life" were given as the reason for the headaches and depression. When pressed for more details, she found it hard to describe interactions with her husband in any meaningful detail.

A parallel interview with her husband revealed that he felt he "had simply become tired of dealing with her." He admitted that his original attraction to Hilde was for her social status, her "liveliness," and her physical attractiveness. Over the years, it became clear that her liveliness was not the exuberance and love of life of an integrated personality, but simply a chronic flamboyance and intensity that was often misplaced. Her physical attractiveness was naturally declining, and she was spending inordinate amounts of time and money attempting to keep it up. Her husband was able to admit that when he had married her he had been reserved and inhibited. He was a competent, hard-working individual but had had little experience with the more enjoyable aspects of life and had viewed Hilde as his ticket to a new life. Now that he had established himself on his own, and had matured and loosened up emotionally, he had simply grown tired of her childish and superficial manner. As he put it, "I still care for her and I don't want to hurt her, but I'm just not interested in putting up with all of this stuff too much longer."

It is interesting that when Hilde was asked about her children, she immediately responded that they were both "wonderful." They were 14 and 16 years old, and Hilde's descriptions of them suggested that they were exceptionally bright and happy children. She was adamant about this, saying, "They are doing fine, and it's my problems that I want to deal with here." Unfortunately, her husband's descriptions of the situation did suggest that both children showed patterns analogous to Hilde's. They were both spoiled, and the older boy in particular had some difficulties keeping up with his schoolwork. He also had become a bit of a loner because of his dramatic and intense behaviors, a pattern that male peers are particularly likely to reject.

Hilde was raised as a prized child of a moderately wealthy family. Her father owned a successful grain and feed operation. Her mother was active socially, joining virtually every socially prominent activity that occurred in the city. She did not have much time for Hilde, yet delighted in showing her off to guests. Hilde was born with many gifts. She had the potential for high intellectual achievement, easily adapted to all the social graces, and was almost stunningly beautiful. The sad part is that the family provided few if any rewards for high intellectual achievements. Hilde was expected to get decent grades, but there was no incentive for high grades, and the family often made fun of others in the town who were "intellectual snobs." Hilde's beauty was obviously prized, and she was taught many ways to maximize her attractiveness.

Her beauty and the response it received from friends in her parents' social circle also provided her with more than simple attention. Her mother delighted in having her stay up and greet guests at their parties, something she never consistently allowed Hilde's sisters to do. Also, Hilde soon discovered that if she misbehaved, a charmingly presented "I'm sorry" to her father usually voided any necessity for punishment.

As Hilde moved into adolescence, she developed a wide circle of friends, though it is interesting that she never maintained any one relationship for long. Her beauty, social grace, and high status in the community made it easy for her to flit about like a princess among her court. Males came to her as bees come to a flower. She had a reputation for being loose sexually, though it is clear this was based on hopes and rumor rather than on actual behavior.

Throughout high school, she was active as a cheerleader and as an organizer of class dances and parties. She was usually elected to be class secretary and once was the class vice-president. No one ever considered her as a candidate for class president, and she herself would not have cared for the position. She had little trouble with her coursework; though she seldom spent much time preparing, she usually obtained Bs and Cs, with an occasional A. Hilde remembers her junior high and high school years as "the happiest time of my life," an assessment that is probably accurate.

Hilde's college years were not unlike her high school years, except that some notes of discord began to creep in. She had to work harder to obtain the moderate grades she had always been pleased with, and she was not always able to carry through with the required effort, particularly since she was wrapped up in sorority activities and cheerleading. She dated many people, though rarely did she allow dating to get to the point of a sexual experience. When she did allow it, it was more to try it out than as a result of any strong desires on her part. She occasionally experienced orgasm during foreplay, though never during intercourse.

After college, she took a job in a woman's clothing store whose clientele were primarily the rich and fashionable. One of her customers subtly introduced Hilde to her son, Steve, a young attorney with one of the most prestigious firms in the region. He courted Hilde in whirlwind fashion. They went out almost every night, usually attending the many parties to which they were both invited. Each was enraptured by the other, and they were married five months after they met. Both families had mild objections to the short courtship, but since each was from "a good family," no strong objections were lodged.

Over the years, Steve's practice developed rapidly. He not only had the advantage of being with an excellent firm, but was also intelligent and hard-working. Hilde meanwhile moved into many social activities, though occasionally abruptly finding that they demanded more than charm and attractiveness. In spite of her best efforts, her beauty is naturally fading, and the bloom has worn off the romance that propelled them into marriage. She and Steve seldom do anything together involving a meaningful interaction. Most of the time he is absorbed in his work, and they go out together only on ritual social occasions. They have sex seldom, usually only after Steve has drunk a bit too much at a party. There is not much conflict in the marrriage, but there is not much of anything else, either.

Etiology

The Greek physician-philosopher Hippocrates provided one of the original explanations for this pattern, holding that the unfruitful womb became angry and wandered about the body, causing hysteria. As is obvious, Hippocrates thought the disorder occurred only in women, a conception that has since proven to be inaccurate. Freud saw conflict over the expression of sexual impulses as critical. Interestingly enough, both Hippocrates and Freud prescribed marriage as the cure. Since marriage would provide a legitimate outlet for sexual desires, in some cases this medicine might be effective (though the side effects might be more than many would wish to risk). Yet, in Hilde's case marriage exaggerated the problem instead of curing it.

Her background has a number of factors that would facilitate the development of a histrionic personality disorder (Kernberg, 1984). Hilde's mother showed little interest in her, except on those rare occasions when she wished to show Hilde off, in essence responding to her as an object. It is common that a lack of consistent maternal attention can produce intense strivings for paternal attention as a replacement, particularly in the female child, and this appears to have been the case with Hilde. Though her father obviously cared for her, he had little time for her. As a result, he, too, responded primarily to her superficial aspects.

In addition, both parents allowed Hilde to use her charm and physical attractiveness as an excuse for not fulfilling the responsibilities that are expected of most children. Hilde never learned to see her personality and decisions as the responsible agents in the problems she naturally encountered. As she grew up, other people would often given her the same allowance, though not to the degree her parents did. The inability to examine and respond effectively to the long-term consequences of her behavior was never reinforced and developed (Rowan, 1983).

As a result, Hilde made a wide range of friendships, but none with any real depth. They were oriented around social activities but involved little self-disclosure or sharing of personal vulnerabilities. Similarly, her parents never openly manifested their own personal vulnerability. They always put forth an optimistic and cheerful facade, even when it was apparent that they were having problems in their own lives.

It is most unfortunate that Hilde's potential for intellectual competence and analytic thinking withered in the face of the type of reinforcement she received from her family. The high level of attention to her physical attractiveness and social skills stood her in good stead during her adolescence. Physical attractiveness naturally decreases with age and does not carry one through the intricacies of any long-term relationship. Analogously, she had long ago learned to see her sexuality as a means of interpersonal manipulation and was never able to focus on the achievement of mutual intimacy and pleasure. It is as if she saw her responsibility ending at the point the male showed initiative behaviors toward her (Eaton, 1985).

Her husband, Steve, came from a family that emphasized status, hard work, and vocational achievement. Hilde appeared to him as a guide to a new world, one in which pleasure, intimacy, and social activity were paramount. It was only when their whirlwind courtship, extravagant wedding, and expensive honeymoon were well behind them that the bloom went off the relationship. He gradually recognized the lack of depth in their relationship, and when he attempted to talk this out with Hilde, she became upset. She accused him of not loving her and even occasionally accused him of having another woman. She also responded by trying to make herself even more attractive, at the same time realizing her physical beauty was declining. She did not age gracefully and Steve even began to think of her as "pathetic" in this regard. Their meager sexual life dissipated even further. He eventually did start to see other women. Since he still cared for Hilde in a platonic way, he attempted to keep these affairs from her, and did so rather successfully.

By this time, Hilde's father had become a kind of patriarch in the area. He was a man of great wealth and still enjoyed indulging his favorite and most beautiful daughter. Hilde emotionally moved back toward her family, though like Steve, she kept up the facade of the marriage. She also became depressed on occasion and periodically drank too much. The cycle spiraled, as if at some level of consciousness she realized her own role in her problems, as well as her inadequacy to deal with them.

Treatment

A number of possible treatments were considered for Hilde. The first and most difficult task was to gain her trust. In that regard, several sessions were held in which the therapist adopted a posture not unlike that employed with the paranoid individual. He listened to Hilde's discussion with empathy, yet at the same time wistfully or bemusingly offered alternative explanations for her behavior. He did not confront her directly, as it had been her life-long pattern, probably both as a result of temperament and parent training (Super and Harkness, 1986), to run away from any confrontation.

As trust developed, other therapeutic modes were tried in order to gradually lessen her defenses. In that regard, bibliotherapy, or the reading of certain prescribed books, was used. She was asked to read various novels and plays that portrayed individuals who had grown up feeling as if they were appreciated for external rather than any essential personality factors. Of course, some of these individuals had developed coping strategies that were not unlike Hilde's. The work of Tennessee Williams, Edward Albee, and Jean Genet convey these concepts quite well. She was then asked to write her own poetry or short stories that focused on characters who developed similar defenses. This led eventually to the use of role-playing. Her therapist would take the role of Hilde's mother, for example, and Hilde would play herself in some typical childhood interaction. It is also effective to play the opposite roles, so Hilde would play her mother and the therapist would play Hilde as a child. This role-playing was expanded to include interactions with her father, her husband, and some of her friends (Yablonsky, 1976).

Unfortunately, at approximately this time Hilde's husband told her that he had fallen in love with another woman and wanted a divorce. He refused to consider marital therapy, said that his decision had been made long ago, and that he had only waited to find a woman with whom he could really become involved. Hilde made a mild suicide gesture, overdosing on a small bottle of aspirin. She obviously did not want to kill herself (Shneidman, 1985), but in line with her dramatic behavior patterns, she had hoped to reverse her husband's decision in this manner. It was unsuccessful, and she and her therapist worked through this situation, again using the role-playing.

At this time, it was recommended to Hilde that she also enter group therapy. Her first reactions were that "those people won't understand me," and "I don't have really bad problems like they do." After the therapist was able to work through her defensiveness, she asked Hilde to commit to at least three sessions. It was agreed that if she felt she could not continue after that, she could leave the group. Hilde made the contract and went for the three sessions. Fortunately, the group was supportive, something she needed at this point, particularly because of the divorce. It is also ironically probable that Hilde enjoyed this forum, in which she could dramatically replay many of the events in her life. She started to attend the group regularly and began to improve her ability to confront her responsibility for the events of her life. She felt she could stop seeing her individual therapist, though at her last contact with her, Hilde was still struggling substantially with the problems of her world. For one thing, her defensive view that her children did not have problems had dissolved. She became aware that they needed much more attention from her and that they also would need professional intervention for some emotional problems. The prognosis for continued improvement in Hilde is good. However, it should be noted that the prognosis for most clients with histrionic personality disorders is not so positive, since their defenses are strong and well-learned and often continue to be at least partially reinforced by some of the people around them (Barrett, 1980).

Comment

The diagnosis of a histrionic personality disorder is associated with behavior that is overly reactive and intensely expressed. Interpersonal relationships are particularly impaired, primarily due to others' perceptions (usually accurate) of the person as shallow, superficial, and insincere. Persons with histrionic personalities are typically attractive and charming; they thus initiate friendships and romantic involvements quickly. However, the rule in these relationships is similar to the course of Hilde's marriage. Once the initial attraction subsides, the histrionic person is unable to develop sustaining intimacy and to participate in a reciprocal relationship. The impression one gets in clinical observations is that such persons have adopted a role (usually ultrafeminine) in relating to others that is compelling in presentation, though eventually disappointing because there is not authenticity (Meissner, 1981).

The higher incidence of histrionic personality disorders among women can be attributed to the close parallel between diagnostic criteria for the disorder and features of the traditional female role. In some ways, however, the personality disorders in general, and the histrionic personality in particular, are social epiphenomena: whether or not a person who meets the diagnostic criteria for a personality disorder will be seen as truly abnormal depends on the context in which the behavior is observed (Eaton, 1985).

Perhaps, then, the earlier prescriptions of marriage for "hysterical patients" were somewhat successful because histrionic features were more consistent with the social expectations of "traditional" married women and mothers. Indeed, excessive emotionality, intense involvements, and superficial (yet manipulative) concern with "serious" endeavors (such as scholastic achievement, political issues, and finances) have until recently been considered desirable traits and were characteristic of a number of popular heroines, including Scarlett O'Hara of *Gone with the Wind* and Meggie of *The Thorn Birds*. However, as is evident with Hilde, marriage is a successful strategy for persons with a histrionic personality disorder only while the expectations of spouses are consistent with the stereotype of an attractive though naive spousal role. Most mates find that the initial glamour of such an individual soon fades and becomes tedious.

REFERENCES

Barrett, C. (1980) Personality (character) disorders. In R. Woody (Ed.), *The Encyclopedia of Clinical Assessment*. San Francisco: Jossey-Bass.

Eaton, W. (1985) *Sociology of Mental Disorders*. New York: Praeger.

Gardner, E. (1965) The role of the classification system in outpatient psychiatry. In M. Katz, J. Cole, and W. Barton (Eds.), *The Role and Methodology in Psychiatry and Psychology*. Washington, D.C.: U.S. Public Health Service.

Kernberg, O. (1984) *Severe Personality Disorders*. New Haven, Conn.: Yale University Press.

Lasch, C. (1978) *The Culture of Narcissism*. New York: W. W. Norton.

Meissner, W. (1981) A note on narcissism. *Psychoanalytic Quarterly, 50*, 77–87.

Rowan, J. (1983) *The Reality Game: A Guide to Humanistic Counseling and Therapy*. London: Routledge & Kegan Paul.

Shneidman, E. (1985) *Definition of Suicide*. New York: John Wiley.

Super, C. and Harkness, S. (1986) Temperament, development and culture. In

R. Plomin and J. Dunn (Eds.) *The Study of Temperament*. Hillsdale, N.J.: Lawrence Erlbaum.

Yablonsky, L. (1976) *Psychodrama: Resolving Emotional Problems Through Role-Playing*. New York: Basic Books.

/ The Antisocial Personality Disorder

The Case of Andy

All universal moral principles are idle fancies.
— Marquis de Sade
The 120 Days of Sodom

The antisocial personality disorder is primarily characterized by the chronic manifestation of antisocial behavior; that is, behavior that in some form violates another's rights. Additionally, antisocial individuals are amoral, impulsive, and narcissistic, are unable to delay gratification or deal effectively with authority figures, and typically abuse alcohol and drugs (Kay, 1985; Cadoret, et al., 1985). They have a heightened need for environmental stimulation, as well as a lack of normal response to standard societal control procedures such as punishment (Nichols and Newman, 1986). The chronicity of the pattern is reflected in their inability to profit from experience. While the disorder is more common in males, the rate is increasing in females (Heidensohn, 1986). Some of the material about this disorder is discussed in Meyer (1980, 1982) and will not be referenced here.

The DSM has specified that the person be over the age of 18 in order to receive this diagnosis, yet it is quite clear that the behavior patterns associated with this disorder are almost always evident before the age of 15. When an individual does display these behaviors prior to age 18, the diagnostic label of *conduct disorder* is given. The DSM requires evidence of the pattern before age 15 (truancy and/or delinquency, for example) and persistent and varied manifestations after 18 in marital, vocational, moral, or criminal disorder patterns.

There has been far more research on the antisocial personality than any other personality disorder, because it is commonly encountered and because the cost to society is high (Kernberg, 1984). There are good data (Gray and Hutchinson, 1964; Hare, 1986), to show that diagnosticians find this concept to be a meaningful one and also that this category is more reliably diagnosed than virtually any other psychiatric diagnostic category (Spitzer et al., 1967).

Evolution of the Term

The term *antisocial personality* has evolved from a number of traditional terms that are still in use, such as *psychopathic* and *sociopathic personalities* (Hare, 1986). Even Pinel began to conceptualize this category with his term *manie sans delire*. However, it was not until late in the nineteenth century that the term *psychopath* first appeared.

The first DSM, published in 1952, clouded the issue by substituting the term *sociopathic personality* to cover those behavior patterns that had been traditionally included in the term *psychopath*. The term *sociopath* was used to emphasize the environmental factors that at that time were felt to generate the disorder. The confusion was heightened by DSM-II (1968), as neither term was included. Instead, the new term used was *antisocial personality*, which has continued until today. One semantic problem with this term is that many people feel it implies specifically criminal behavior. Thus, it may not be clear to some whether or not a formal indictment or conviction is required for the diagnosis. What is required is evidence of a chronic pattern of violating other people's rights, as manifested in particular through the four criteria mentioned earlier.

The Case of Andy

Andy, age 22, was first seen by mental health personnel when he was routinely referred to the psychiatric clinic of a state prison by the screening unit of that institution. He had been incarcerated for auto theft and simple assault. At age 20, he had been convicted of grand larceny but had been given probation.

Andy also had a substantial list of offenses from when he was a juvenile, including auto theft, assault with a deadly weapon, and sexual misconduct. He had been accused of rape, but the girl's prior arrests as a prostitute and the lack of witnesses resulted in the lesser charge. Andy's childhood had been a tumultuous one. He was the second of two children, his brother being a year and a half older than he. His father abandoned the family two years after Andy was born, and though Andy has a general idea where his father lives, he has never had any contact with him. His mother worked as a waitress, though on occasion she accepted "dates" for sexual purposes that she made at the restaurant. In general, she lived on the fringes of society.

She seemed to care about her two boys and gave them as much attention as was possible, given her life style. Yet, on occasion, the frustrations of her world became too much for her, and she would beat them rather brutally. This typically occurred when she became frustrated and confused as to how to cope with the discipline problems that naturally emerge from having two active boys.

She would periodically drown her frustrations in alcohol, and it was at these times that she was especially prone to beat them. As she grew older and they gradually left her care, she developed a sense of being unimportant to anyone, and her alcoholism increased substantially.

Andy was born prematurely during the early part of his mother's eighth month of pregnancy. There were mild complications in the delivery, and Andy experienced a period of anoxia. Though there was no evidence at the time of any resultant gross brain damage, Andy's later performance in school would be consistent with that type of occurrence. Andy was able to walk unaided at 15 months of age, which is average, but he did not speak words adequately until he was two-and-a-half years old, which is later than average. Toilet training was started shortly after Andy was 1 year old and was completed about a year and a half later, though he continued to wet the bed periodically until he was 7.

In addition to the occasional severe spankings he received from his mother, Andy also had been severely beaten by one of his mother's boyfriends. This beating included substantial blows to the head; when they took Andy to the hospital, they told the physician that Andy had fallen down the steps. The issue of child abuse was investigated, but there was no definite proof, and Andy did not implicate the boyfriend.

Andy had been placed in day care since he was two-and-a-half years old, and he made an adequate adjustment there. When he was enrolled in school, he seemed to do well in tasks that involved manual dexterity but could not deal with reading or spelling. He was soon placed in a remedial reading group and never did catch up in this area. When one fails at reading, one naturally has difficulty with many other subjects that depend on it, and this was so with Andy.

In school, Andy exhibited a short attention span and a restlessness that soon crystallized into a classic pattern of hyperactivity. Attentional difficulties resulted in academic problems. Andy's tolerance for frustration was so low that when he was teased by anyone he would lash out aggressively. Disciplinary efforts by his teachers were almost totally ineffective.

He was similarly disruptive in his neighborhood. He would fight with younger children, sometimes brutally kicking them. On one occasion, an older boy in the neighborhood had beaten up both Andy and his brother. The next day, Andy sprayed a can of lighter fluid over his adversary's pet dog and set it afire. He showed no concern in response to the garish scene that ensued.

It is common for someone like Andy to become negative toward school in general. He did so, and began to run away from school. At first, he would just go home and play. Then, when truant officers began to look for him there, he would stay out on the streets of the city finding different things to entertain him. He started to get in trouble as he engaged in mild shoplifting and vandalism.

He also began to run with a gang of boys, and though he had many social contacts, it was clear that he had no deep friendships or loyalties. This gang was constantly in trouble, and it was with the gang that Andy was usually picked up by the police during his juvenile years. Andy's older brother also belonged to this gang.

His mother attempted to set limits for him and explained the ethical issues of stealing. Yet it was clear that in her own life she had few limits, and that she commonly accepted gifts (often of stolen property) from her various lovers and customers. She also was extremely inconsistent in enforcing the rules she laid down, so that neither of the boys paid much attention to them. When Andy was 16 years old, his brother and three other boys robbed a service station. When the attendant resisted, they killed him. Andy's brother was sentenced to prison for murder in the first degree and faces the prospect of a long incarceration.

As Andy moved into middle adolescence, he was constantly in front of juvenile authorities and spent these years going from juvenile detention centers to home and back. Andy's behavior in the juvenile centers was marked by good relations with individuals he could manipulate and indifferent or bad relationships with those he could not. When he was home, he was out in the streets most of the time and would often get into fights with his mother's lover of the moment.

At the age of 18, he was fortunate to get a job as a hospital orderly through the intercession of his juvenile social worker. He seemed to do well there because he liked his fellow workers, was earning some money, and because it was active work.

But after about a year, he was caught stealing drugs from the hospital dispensary and was fired. He had never had a history of prolonged substance abuse. He apparently broke in and took the drugs simply to give them to several of his associates.

Andy had been introduced to masturbation by his older brother when he was about 12 years old. He was having sexual intercourse when he was 15, mostly with girls associated with his gang. Though he eventually had women, each of whom he called "his woman," there was never much evidence of any committed or even particularly affectionate relationships. For a short period of time, Andy pimped for one of his girlfriends, then found the role distasteful and stopped. As he moved into early adulthood, he lived with a series of different women. He showed little evidence of committed behavior while he lived with them and no concern or remorse about breaking off any of the relationships. When he turned 20, he was living with a woman who worked as a maid in the hospital where he had worked. During that time, he was arrested for assault. His girlfriend used most of her savings to pay a lawyer who was able to have Andy acquitted on a technicality. As soon as the incident was over, Andy left her holding the bill for the lawyer's fee.

Like most inmates, Andy claimed innocence of all charges when he was first interviewed at the clinic. He also said that he was interested in treatment. Of course, virtually all inmates quickly learn to show an interest in any self-improvement program and try to get as many of them as possible on their record. There was little evidence that Andy had any real interest in changing himself, but a variety of treatment options were developed nonetheless.

Etiology

Andy's history certainly makes him a prime candidate for developing into an antisocial personality (Patterson, 1986). Even his premature birth probably caused some minimal brain dysfunction that could further inhibit the development of behavioral controls. The mild hyperactivity that he showed throughout his early school years has been linked in some individuals to brain dysfunction from anoxia at birth, and hyperactivity is a major predictor toward later criminal behavior and/or schizophrenic behavior. This is not to say that all hyperactives develop this way, but there is a significant correlation (Hare and McPherson, 1984; Safer, 1976).

In addition to this biological factor, Andy had a number of environmental conditions that would make the probability of antisocial personality disorder quite high (Kernberg, 1984; Wilson and Herrnstein, 1985; Patterson, 1986). First, the absence of any consistent father figure during his childhood and adolescence gave him no real model for appropriate behavior. The only available models were the casual lovers who drifted through his mother's world, and they had few positive qualities to emulate. When he became associated with a gang, it provided further negative role models.

The brutal spankings that he received from his mother, as well as the occasional beatings from one of her boyfriends, certainly reinforced the use of aggression as a coping behavior (Wolfe et al., 1986). Anxiety and upset became discriminative cues for aggression.

In addition to the severe beatings, which primarily reflected his mother's ignorance and frustration over how to cope with her role, her inconsistent discipline and her hypocrisy about verbalized values cemented the development of the antisocial pattern. It was clear to Andy and his brother that she was saying these things because she thought that she should, but that she did not adhere to them herself.

If Andy had been bright, he might have become involved in school activities and received the reinforcement that could have attracted him into more appropriate behavior patterns, thereby opening him up to the influence of teachers as surrogate fathers. Unfortunately, his intellectual abilities were below average, particularly in the verbal areas such as reading. So he received little positive reinforcement and much in the way of punishment, conditions conducive to certain components of both extroversion and psychopathy (Nichols and Newman, 1986). School quickly became aversive for him. He started running away, and easily drifted into delinquent behaviors.

Andy never was able to establish lasting or affectionate relationships with his peers. He seemed to associate with them as a form of status and security and through them found the high environmental stimulation he seemed to need. When he moved into early adulthood, he was not able to establish any committed relationships with women or any pattern of adult responsibility. He maintained contact with these women primarily to have an available sexual outlet. Though it does appear that Andy's mother wanted to care for him and did love him, her manner and life style prohibited this attitude from coming through very clearly, leading to his thoroughgoing egocentricity.

Treatment

A variety of treatment possibilities have been suggested as appropriate for the antisocial personality disorder. Some have advocated psychosurgery, but it has not been markedly successful here (Trotter, 1976). It is unrealistic to assume that specific lesions are going to eradicate the complex and long-standing patterns of behavior that mark this disorder. Drug treatments, such as with the phenothiazines or fluphenazine decanoate, have been of help in some cases. The positive feature of the fluphenazine treatment is that if desired, it can be administered by injection only once every several days. Most antisocial personalities are not particularly likely to follow through with the ritual of taking a prescription drug several times a day. Some antisocial personalities under treatment with these long-acting tranquilizers do become calmer. However, these drugs have significant side effects that must be considered in making the long-term prescriptions that are required, and if the drug offers any potential for abuse, these individuals are likely to do so (Kay, 1985).

In treating the antisocial personality, the major problem is getting the person involved in the treatment (Wilson and Herrnstein, 1985; Yochelson and Samenow, 1976). Most have no interest in changing their behavior and are only in a treatment program because they have been forced by circumstances, as in Andy's case. This kind of motivation can lead to bizarre behavior.

When the senior author was associated with the psychiatric clinic of the Southern Michigan State Prison at Jackson, many inmates used to join the Alcoholics Anonymous program. It later turned out that many of them had never been alcoholics or even had a drinking problem. They just wanted the apparent change in behavior to show up on their record as if they had participated in an additional necessary treatment program. These same individuals were likely to show up at chapel services every Sunday, but spent most of their time reading the paper and playing cards. Their goal was to get their names on the roll to show that they had attended chapel.

Ingenious attempts have been made to get the antisocial personality disorder involved in treatment. Some treatment programs have paid antisocial personalities to come to talk into a tape recorder, allegedly in order for the program to obtain sociological background data on such a population. Several of the individuals who originally participated for the money became so involved in this process that they were willing to continue even after the pay stopped.

Andy's Treatment.   Andy was first confronted with his self-defeating failure patterns. These confronting statements were made in strong language over four different sessions. This technique is not unlike the reality therapy of William Glasser and also incorporates some notions of the work of Yochelson and Samenow (1976). The latter authors have reported success with a therapy in which they confront antisocial personalities with their lies and failure patterns. The effort is to "enhance their self-disgust" and maneuver them into participating in attempts to change their behavior.

After this stage, the treatment consisted of applying various ego-building techniques. In general, these techniques attempt to stimulate new interests and behaviors that could improve confidence. In Andy's case, enrollment in skills that tapped his good visual motor skills were emphasized, rather than continuing to push participation in standard academic subjects that focused so much on reading ability. In addition, there was an attempt to improve his object perception and to improve his ability to evaluate his motivations and feelings. He also received training in empathy, training in developing alternate plans of behavior through mental imagery and symbolism, and efforts to change his beliefs (Weiner, 1986).

One exercise that helped Andy develop some much-needed empathy involved looking at various pictures of individuals who were interacting with each other and then asking him to say what he thought each person was experiencing. At first, Andy was clumsy with this technique. Then he began to develop a wider range of options. His initial descriptions were of physical events; only later could he move into conceptualizing the more complex emotional aspects that people might be experiencing. A variety of exercises were provided in which mental imagery and symbolism were required to plan out later responses to different crisis situations. Andy was given feedback on the validity of his strategies and was also taught some of the self-verbalization techniques of Meichenbaum (1985).

It has been found that individuals such as Andy have a very negative self-image. This image is evident in the way they talk about themselves to themselves, and they are encouraged to state things more positively in these self-vocalizations. Andy was also taught to develop interests in areas that would provide him higher levels of environmental stimulation. This included increased participation in traditional athletic activities, dancing, and any other behavior that required a physically active response to a high-level stimulation. It has been found that antisocial personalities are very stimulation-seeking individuals (Quay, 1965, Zuckerman et al., 1980); if their environment does not provide enough stimulation, they will seek it through deviant behaviors.

Andy was seen in the prison clinic for nine months, during which time he showed a significant improvement. Unfortunately, he still had several years to serve on his sentence, and during that period he did regress from his positive changes, probably as a result of having to live in a prison environment that long. An attempt was made to get him involved in treatment again several months before he was due to be released. However, he continually missed his appointments and clearly no longer had much interest in participating.

Andy left the state shortly after being released from prison, which violated his parole requirements. He was apprehended and convicted two years later in connection with an attempted robbery. Some antisocial personalities are changed as a result of treatment, and some change as a result of aging; the great majority, however, are not changed by their environment or by treatment techniques. It is likely that Andy will continue in this pattern until age robs him of the ability or interest to act out against the environment.

Comment

Considerable effort has been extended toward clarifying the nature of the antisocial personality disorder. To date, attempts to isolate etiological variables and to identify factors related to successful treatment outcomes have yielded generally unclear data (Hare and McPherson, 1984). The symptom pattern of the antisocial personality is one of the more consistently perceived of the personality disorders (Gray and Hutchinson, 1964; Spitzer et al., 1967; Smith, 1978). Descriptions in clinical reports and empirical studies have characterized the antisocial person as selfish, irresponsible, unable to learn from experience, impulsive, and lacking in guilt (Kernberg, 1984; Stewart, 1985).

The essence of the numerous treatment strategies that have been implemented (with varying effectiveness) with the antisocial personality disorder is aimed at developing internal controls over behavior. As evidenced by Andy's case, psychotherapy is difficult because such persons exhibit minimal anxiety, are poorly (or inappropriately) motivated to change, and/or have difficulty perceiving their role in problems with social and occupational adjustment.

However, when a trusting relationship can be established within a setting with strong external controls (such as a correction facility), progress toward socialization can be accomplished. Unfortunately, in Andy's case, the prison environment eventually had a negative effect on his progress because of his extended stay there.

A critical issue in understanding and treating persons with antisocial personality disorders has to do with the prediction of violent and otherwise criminal behavior. Heilbrun (1979) has suggested that violent and impulsive criminal acting-out results from a combination of antisocial traits and lower intelligence. Heilbrun found that evidence of violent crimes was greater for persons with high levels of psychopathy and low levels of intelligence than for other combinations of the two variables. It is unclear at this point whether high intelligence mutes the characteristic impulsivity of the antisocial personality or simply helps the individual avoid discovery by legal authorities.

REFERENCES

Cadoret, R., O'Gorman, T., Troughton, E., and Heywood, E. (1985) Alcoholism and antisocial personality. *Archives of General Psychiatry*, *42*, 161–167.

Gray, H., and Hutchinson, H. (1964) The psychopathic personality: A survey of Canadian psychiatrists' opinion. *Canadian Psychiatric Association Journal*, *9*, 450–461.

Hare, R. (1986) Twenty years of experience with the Cleckley psychopath. In W. Reid, D. Dorr, J. Walker, and J. Bonner (Eds.) *Unmasking the Psychopath*. New York: Norton.

Hare, R. and McPherson, L. (1984) Violent and aggressive behavior by criminal psychopaths. *International Journal of Law and Psychiatry*, *7*, 35–70.

Heidensohn, F. (1986) *Women and Crime*. New York: New York University Press.

Heilbrun, A. (1979) Psychopathy and violent crime. *Journal of Consulting and Clinical Psychology*, *47*, 517–524.

Kay, D. (1985) Substance abuse in psychopathic states and sociopathic individuals. In A. Alterman (Ed.), *Substance Abuse and Psychopathology*. New York: Plenum.

Kernberg, O. (1984) *Severe Personality Disorders*. New Haven, Conn. Yale University Press.

Meichenbaum, D. (1985) Cognitive behavior modification. In F. Kanfer and A. Goldstein (Eds.), *Helping People Change*. New York: Pergamon.

Meyer, R. (1980) The antisocial personality. In R. Woody (Ed.), *The Encyclopedia of Clinical Assessment*. San Francisco: Jossey-Bass.

_____. (1982) *The Clinician's Handbook*. Boston: Allyn and Bacon.

Nichols, S. and Newman, J. (1986) Effects of punishment on response latency in extroverts. *Journal of Personality and Social Psychology*, *50*, 624–630.

Patterson, G. (1986) Performance models for antisocial boys. *American Psychologist*, *41*, 432–444.

Quay, H. (1965) Psychopathic personality as pathological stimulation-seeking. *American Journal of Psychiatry*, *122*, 180–183.

Safer, D. (1976) *Hyperactive Children: Diagnosis and Management*. Baltimore: University Park Press.

Smith, R. (1978) *The Psychopath in Society*. New York: Academic Press.

Spitzer, R., Cohen, J., Fliess, J., and Endicott, J. (1967) Quantification of agreement in psychiatric diagnosis: A new approach. *Archives of General Psychiatry, 17,* 83–87.

Stewart, M. (1985) Aggressive conduct disorder. *Aggressive Behavior, 11,* 323–331.

Trotter, S. (1976) Federal commission ok's psychosurgery. *APA Monitor, 7,* 4–5.

Weiner, M. (1986) *Cognitive-Experiential Therapy*. New York: Brunner/Mazel.

Wilson, J. and Herrnstein, R. (1985) *Crime and Human Nature*. New York: Simon & Schuster.

Wolfe, D., Zak, L., Wilson, S., and Jaffe, P. (1986) Child witnesses to violence between parents. *Journal of Abnormal Child Psychology, 14,* 95–104.

Yochelson, S. and Samenow, S. (1976) *The Criminal Mind*. New York: Jason Aronson.

Zuckerman, M., Buchsbaum, M., and Murphy, D. (1980) Sensation-seeking and its biological correlates. *Psychological Bulletin, 88,* 187–214.

11

Disorders of Impulse Control

The extent to which an individual is in command of and can control fleeting urges to violate social rules is always an important consideration when evaluating emotional development. It is expected that young children will often find behavioral control difficult, but they are expected to achieve increasing mastery as socialization proceeds. Inadequate impulse control is symptomatic of a wide range of disorders, including alcoholism, obsessive-compulsive disorder, exhibitionism, and pyromania. Thus, the category of impulse control disorders could be so extensive and inclusive as to be meaningless. As a result, disorders in which an absence of impulse control is only a component (eating disorders, substance abuse, and paraphilias, for example) are classified in accordance with other symptoms. However, there are at least five disorders for which poor impulse control is the primary feature and that are not elsewhere classified: pathological gambling, kleptomania, pyromania, intermittent explosive disorder, and isolated explosive disorder.

While rape has not been included in the DSM category of disorders of impulse control, it clearly fits in this chapter of this book. Also, since in the particular case discussed here, that of Bret, there is also evidence of a borderline personality disorder pattern, this case allows a ready transition from the preceding chapter on the personality disorders.

Pathological gambling is characterized by chronic and irresistible urges to gamble, with consequent negative effects on the individual's personal, family, and/or vocational endeavors, as is evident in the second case in this chapter, that of Greg. The case of Clare demonstrates the essential feature of kleptomania, a recurring inability to resist impulses to steal things for reasons other than their usefulness or monetary value. In another impulse disorder pattern, pyromania, the individual cannot resist impulses to set fires and is fascinated by burning fires. The explosive disorders are marked by incidents of inability to control aggression, resulting in serious attacks on others or destruction of property. The isolated and intermittent explosive disorders are designated simply as to whether there were one or more aggressive episodes.

In all of the disorders of impulse control, a compelling impulse accompanied by a rising sense of tension is experienced. It may or may not be premeditated and/or consciously resisted. Then, when the act is committed, there is a sense of release, which may be so intense that it can be described as pleasurable or euphoric.

A Case of Rape in a Borderline Personality Disorder

The Case of Bret

She stared at me for a long time. "You think I need a shrink?"

I shrugged. "What you're doing doesn't seem to please you. Maybe a shrink. Maybe a divorce? Maybe a boyfriend on the side? Maybe a job?"

"I think psychology is a lot of crap," she said.

"Okay by me," I said. "All I'm saying is that if you're unhappy, there are other solutions besides balling a bunch of dim-witted college kids." (p. 136)

— Robert B. Parker
The Widening Gyre

The borderline personality disorder (BPD) is a relatively recent addition to the DSM, having been first incorporated into the DSM-III (1980). It does appear to be a meaningful and useful category (Widiger et al., 1986). At the same time, BPD is sometimes a difficult diagnosis to make (George and Soloff, 1986). According to the DSM, BPD is a personality disorder, and thus could logically be discussed in this book's preceding chapter on personality disorders. Also, it can be confused with schizophrenia (Spitzer, Endicott, and Gibbon, 1979), and so could be considered in that section as well. However, since the borderline disorder is often marked by impulsivity, and because the allied behavior pattern in this case, rape, commonly has an impulsive component, BPD will be discussed here.

BPD was a confusing entity in the original DSM-III drafts, but now seems to have been more clearly defined. At first glance, it especially seems to overlap with the schizotypal personality disorder, since both imply an easy transition into a schizophrenic adjustment (George and Soloff, 1986; Widiger et al., 1986). However, individuals in this category are neither as withdrawn socially nor nearly as bizarre in symptomatology as are schizophrenics. Though the DSM does not specifically mention it, this category seems to be a resurrection of an old term at one time much favored by clinicians, the *emotionally unstable personality*. Persons in the BPD category show significant emotional instability, have impulsive and unpredictable behavior, are irritable and anxious, and avoid being alone or experiencing the boredom to which they are prone (Clarkin et al., 1983). There is some evidence that as these individuals improve they show more predictable behavior patterns, yet this is combined with increasing narcissism (Adler, 1981).

To diagnose BPD, at least five of the following are required: (1) unpredictable impulsivity in two areas, such as sex, drug, or alcohol use; (2) physically self-damaging behaviors; (3) uncontrolled anger responses; (4) unstable interpersonal relationships; (5) unstable moods; (6) unstable identity; (7) persistent boredom experiences; (8) avoidance of being alone.

This disorder is thought to be relatively common, yet may be a confusing diagnostic category for clinicians. The category would probably be more commonly used if the older term emotionally unstable personality disorder were reinstituted. If the person is under 18, the diagnosis of identity disorder takes precedence.

Rape

Rape is as much a crime of violence as it is one of sexuality (Malamuth, 1986). The insult and assault to the female victim in a rape carry beyond the actual physical event of the rape itself (Frazier and Borgida, 1985). Potentially demeaning physical examinations and nonsupportive questioning of the rape victim by police officials have abated somewhat in recent years, largely because of pressure from various women's groups and the increasing presence of female officers on police forces and in rape units. Fortunately, Public Law 95-540, passed by Congress in October 1978, limits the circumstances under which evidence of a rape victim's past sexual conduct is admissible in federal court, and most states have now passed similar laws.

The incidence of actual rape is hard to determine, though the incidence of reported rape has continued to rise through the 1980s. Although reported rapes account for 5 percent of all crimes of violence—approximately 1 in every 2,000 women each year—it is estimated that only one-tenth of actual rape victims report assaults to police. Only about 1 rapist in 20 is ever arrested; 1 in 30 is prosecuted; and 1 in 50 is convicted. More than half of reported rapes occur in the victim's home; in almost half the assailant is known to the victim (Webster, 1985; Frazier and Borgida, 1985).

Let us now consider the case of Bret, who combines the BPD syndrome with a pattern of rape.

The Case of Bret

Bret was raised in a pleasant, middle class family. His father was a moderately successful insurance salesman, and his mother had returned to work as an executive secretary when Bret started school.

Bret had a normal birth, and his childhood through grade school was relatively uneventful. His parents did note that he was more moody than his older brother Bob, but felt that this was something they could control. But the moodiness became worse in high school. He was reasonably accepted by his peers in grade school, but aside from an occasional friend, he became a bit of a social outcast during high school. This was a result of rejection by others rather than by his own choice to avoid them. He did make it through with adequate grades, but not without incident.

While a junior, he became very upset when his overtures to a female classmate were rejected; worse yet, she made fun of him. Two days later, his mother found Bret cutting his wrists. He had made only one minor cut when he was detected. She took him to their family doctor who treated him and recommended that they take him for treatment for an emotional problem. Bret's mother, ashamed of the whole situation, never did.

Bret had also been suspended from school for taking a swing at a teacher. The incident was odd in several respects. First, this was a teacher who had always gotten along reasonably well with Bret, and at that specific time, had made only a mildly negative criticism of him. Lastly, the teacher was an ex-college basketball player, stood 6'8" and weighed 265 pounds, and repelled Bret's assault with little effort. Bret also got into occasional fights with classmates, which he usually started and lost. Observers seldom saw any particular stimulus for Bret's outbursts.

After graduating from high school, he attended a local junior college for a year, hoping to major in English literature, and at the same time took a job as a clerk in a local drugstore. However, his work record was unstable, and his unpredictable demeanor often offended customers in one fashion or another. The self-discipline required in college was also too much for him and he withdrew from school in two months, a move obviously designed to avoid failing all his courses.

His parents insisted he go to a local psychiatrist, but Bret went only one time and was generally uncooperative. He had been sent to the school counselor several times during high school, but, in like fashion, had never been cooperative.

At this point, Bret alternated periods of unemployment with a string of jobs that he could not hold. Again, his general impulsivity made him undependable and ineffective, and his moodiness made him obnoxious to customers and co-workers. At the same time, Bret began to show a pattern of promoting himself as having a variety of important-sounding though often nonexistent positions. Similar to Fletch, the hero of Gregory MacDonald's detective novels, which he had read, Bret had several different business cards printed up, with titles like "Consulting Criminal Examiner" and "Insurance Investigator." For the most part, he would use these to facilitate his rather active fantasy life, and he especially enjoyed interacting with people in the part of one of these fantasized characters. For one thing, it relieved the almost overwhelming depression and boredom he felt when he was not working. Yet, he always seemed to retain a degree of control. That is, while he obviously relished playing these roles and at times seemed to live out the roles for a day or two, he seemingly never went over the line and truly believed he was this other personage.

In addition to relieving his almost phobic fear of boredom, this pattern gave him a sense of a positive identity and of power over people that he lacked in his normal life. He would make up hypothetical cases and interact with people on them, delighting in the respect they gave him. One afternoon, he was interviewing an attractive young housewife about an alleged insurance fraud case in the neighborhood. He misread her natural warmth and friendliness as sexual interest in him, and started to make some sexual moves on her.

When she resisted, he became angry and tied her, spread-eagled and nude, to her four-poster bed, had intercourse with her, and then stood over her and masturbated to an ejaculation on her breasts. He found this type of sexual experience to be powerfully arousing, and began to repeat it with other victims. Once, when a victim began to scream, he started to hit her and, losing control of his anger, almost killed her.

Bret was finally apprehended when one of his victims was able to release herself in time to follow him for a few blocks to where he had hidden his car. She managed to get five of the six digits on the license plate. This, and the description of the car, allowed the police to track Bret down and ultimately gain a confession and a conviction.

Etiology

I knew what I would do first after I had been raped.

. . . "Call the Police. Make them take you to the nearest precinct station. Insist on a physical examination within six hours." It reminded me of one of those guides for tourists, each instruction anticipating the next hassle (p. 20).

— M. Brandel
Survivor

As in other violent behavior patterns (murder, assault), it would be a mistake to assume any one cause is operating. Some simplistic theories are tempting, for example, that elevated male hormone levels are the cause. But there is no strong evidence for this theory, even though Rada et al. (1976) did find somewhat higher levels of plasma testosterone in the most violent rapists. Even in these cases, however, there is no proof that higher testosterone levels necessarily cause the behavior; they may merely be coincident with, or even result from, a rape incident.

Cohen, Seghorn, and Calmas (1969) developed a particularly useful classification for rapists that has been widely adopted in the research literature. Their four categories are as follows:

1. *Displaced aggression type.* Sexual excitement in these rapists is absent or only slight. The primary motivation is to physically harm and degrade the victim in the service of an aggressive intent (Malamuth, 1986). They may describe the act as uncontrollable, and the attack often follows an argument with a wife, girlfriend, or mother.

2. *Sex aggression diffusion type.* These people are often sadists, and the violence appears to be necessary for arousal. The rapists see the struggling of the victim as seductive. The rape is a pathological eroticization of aggressive behavior.

3. *Compensatory type.* Most rapists belong to this category, which involves less violence. These individuals use aggression only as a means of acquiring a sexual partner. They are usually in a high state of arousal and are not otherwise antisocial. Although these rapists fantasize about winning the victim's heart with their sexual prowess, they have great feelings of sexual inadequacy and are likely to desist if the victim puts up much of a fight.

4. *Impulsive type.* These rapists appear to be purely opportunistic. The rape occurs unexpectedly, as an extension of predatory behavior after the commission of some other antisocial activity, such as a robbery. The victim just happens to be there. These individuals are narcissistic, and any harm to the victim is incidental but produces no real guilt.

Of course, many rapists may reflect more than one component: Bret would seem to combine elements of both the compensatory and impulsive types.

The earlier chapter on personality disorders detailed a number of general causes for and treatment approaches to personality patterns such as those shown by Bret, and the reader is referred back to that chapter. Also, some components of the personality of John Hinckley, the person who attempted to assassinate President Reagan, and a later case in this book, parallel those of Bret's personality, so that discussion would also be relevant here.

Treatment

Since BPD has a number of different characteristics (Millon, 1981), an equally variable treatment program would be indicated. The impulsivity and fear of boredom (related to the phenomenon of stimulation-seeking) would suggest that treatment approaches useful for the antisocial personality disorder are also useful here. Medication could be indicated for control of Bret's mood disorder, and specifically, some of the MAO antidepressants (see Chapter 7) and anticonvulsant agents can be helpful (Cowdry, 1986). Specific techniques for anger management would also be indicated. Lastly, group therapy would be in order for the substantial interpersonal difficulties Bret has shown. However, clients such as Bret can be difficult to work with, and their behavior may exert such a cost on the group process that it may not be feasible.

Since Bret was convicted of multiple rapes and assault and received a long prison sentence, he did not receive any formal treatment. Any significant personality change, outside of that engineered by aging or the prison experience itself, is improbable.

However, before leaving this case, let us consider, in general, some further cause and treatment issues related to rape patterns.

Prevention of Rape

Three features of our society make the prevention of rape by anyone but the potential victims both difficult and unlikely: (1) the mistaken but common sexist view, even among many police, legal, and judicial authorities, that women "ask for" or enjoy being raped; (2) the related low percentage of prosecutions and convictions of rapists, which poses little or no deterrence and in some cases may even encourage the behavior; and (3) the low incidence of treatment, successful or otherwise, of the few rapists who are convicted (Webster, 1985; Wilson and Herrnstein, 1985). These three factors combine to make wide social measures ineffective in appreciably reducing the incidence of rape. Consequently—and unfairly—the burden of prevention falls on individual women by using such strategies as: (1) avoiding contact with strangers, (2) quickly escaping any situations that appear to be risky, or (3) being prepared to defend oneself (carrying tear gas or a police whistle, learning karate) if confrontation is unavoidable. Unfortunately, almost any effective measure requires either a distrust of males and/or passive or defensive behaviors that women have been trying to escape for many years.

Treatment of the Rape Victim

Rape victims, almost 80 percent of whom are single, divorced, or separated, show a variety of negative after-effects (Heidensohn, 1986). Virtually all suffer bruises or abrasions, and approximately 5 percent suffer severe injuries, such as fractures or concussions. Many suffer injury from being forced to perform fellatio or anal intercourse, and most also suffer emotional trauma. Loss of self-esteem, anxiety, and depression are common reactions, though recently the use of well-trained rape squads has helped. Work adjustment appears particularly negatively affected, and sexual adjustment may be disrupted (LoPiccolo, 1985; see Section 8).

If a woman is raped, she should take the following steps:

1. As soon as she is alone, the victim should call the police or rape hot line, and also a trusted friend or relative who can provide emotional support.

2. The victim should not take off her clothes, douche, or wash until the police have had a chance to gather corroborative evidence. Solid evidence can increase the chance of convicting the rapist, and thus increase conviction rates, which in turn may help to deter future rapes (Frazier and Borgida, 1985).

3. If she lives alone, the victim should consider staying with a friend or relative for a few days.

4. The victim should not deny any of her feelings. If she continues to be anxious or upset, she should get professional help before symptoms crystallize or generalize.

Many of the above issues and problems come from the following mistaken views about rape that are still an integral part of our society.

Mistaken Views About Rape

1. *Rape is an impulsive behavior.* Most rapes are planned, though in some cases no specific woman has been targeted. In many cases, the man develops a strong desire to rape someone, and then systematically seeks out a victim.

2. *Men who rape are assaultists or killers.* Certainly many men pose a real danger to the victim. At the same time, probably not much more than 1 percent of victims are murdered, and less than half are physically injured.

3. *Women are always safer in fighting back; or, women are always safer in using passive techniques (guilt) to resist.* Most experts believe that immediately screaming as loudly as possible, quickly hitting back, and then running away is the best option, especially if the woman is in a situation where such escape is possible, or if other people are nearby. But no technique is the best for all situations. Inducing fear about sexual contact, for example, by saying one has a venereal disease or cervical cancer, may be a good option in some instances.

4. *Only attractive, sexy women are raped; or, only virtuous women are raped.* Women of all ages (including infants and women in their eighties), physical appearances, and personal backgrounds have been rape victims. Appearing vulnerable, and being in situations which suggest vulnerability and/or isolation are more important predictors than level of physical attraction.

5. *Rapists are oversexed and/or "sexual degenerates."* A number of rapists actually have a relatively low sex drive and a sporadic sexual pattern. On the other hand, some are married and have otherwise good marriages. Many rapists appear to be more motivated by power or hostility than by sexuality.

6. *Rapists may avoid prosecution because of an intact hymen in a woman who was a virgin and allegedly penetrated, or because of a lack of semen.* Though either may be a useful piece of evidence, neither is required. Rapists often have a potency problem and some don't even ejaculate during the rape.

7. *Rapes are commonly committed by strangers in dark or hidden places.* Actually, about half of the rape victims know their attackers, and a great many rapes occur on dates.

8. *Exhibitionists and voyeurs will rape if given a chance.* A few voyeurs and exhibitionists do pose a danger, but most are passive and avoid any true interpersonal confrontation or interaction with the victim. Unfortunately, they don't wear signs to let us know which is dangerous and which is not.

9. *White women are often raped by black men.* In the great majority of rapes, the victim and attacker are of the same race.

10. *Certain women enjoy being raped.* Simply untrue. Some women (and some men) enjoy sex play in which there is a veneer of being coerced or forced, but, in fact, both parties retain some control over what goes on.

Treatment of the Rapist

Very few rapists seek treatment. As noted earlier, only a few are successfully prosecuted; fewer still are interested in treatment.

Castration and execution have been society's traditionally preferred ways of dealing with rapists, but there is little evidence that these measures deter other rapists. Aversive techniques help control the rape impulse, in much the same way that they are used to change a homosexual orientation to a heterosexual one. Drugs such as medroxyprogesterone have been used to lower the serum testosterone level in violent rapists, thereby reducing the likelihood of any sexual arousal at all (Walker, 1978; Walker and Meyer, 1981). The major difficulty in this treatment is getting the rapist to cooperate; also, the side effects of these drugs are substantial.

Overall, it is a difficult task to successfully change a rape pattern or eliminate a borderline personality disorder. When they are combined in one individual, as in Bret's case, it is even more difficult.

REFERENCES

Adler, G. (1981) The borderline-narcissistic personality disorder continuum. *American Journal of Psychiatry, 138,* 46–50.

Clarkin, J., Widiger, T., Frances, A., Hurt, S., and Gilmore, M. (1983) Prototypic typology and the borderline personality disorder. *Journal of Abnormal Psychology, 92,* 263–275.

Cohen, M., Seghorn, T., and Calmas, W. (1969) Sociometric study of sex offenders. *Journal of Abnormal Psychology, 74,* 249–255.

Cowdry, R. (1986) Personal communication.

Frazier, P. and Borgida, E. (1985) Rape trauma evidence in court. *American Psychologist, 40,* 984–993.

George, A. and Soloff, P. (1986) Schizotypal symptoms in patients with borderline personality disorders. *The American Journal of Psychiatry, 143,* 212–215.

Heidensohn, F. (1986) *Women and Crime.* New York: New York University Press.

LoPiccolo, J. (1985) Advances in the diagnosis and treatment of sexual dysfunction. Convention workshop. Kentucky Psychological Association. Louisville, 1985.

Malamuth, N. (1986) Predictors of naturalistic sexual aggression. *Journal of Personality and Social Psychology, 50,* 953–962.

Millon, T. (1981) *Disorders of Personality. DSM-III: Axis II.* New York: John Wiley.

Rada, R., Laws, D., and Kellner, R. (1976) Plasma testosterone levels in the rapist. *Psychosomatic Medicine, 38,* 257–268.

Spitzer, R., Endicott, J., and Gibbon, M. (1979) Crossing the border into borderline personality and borderline schizophrenia. *Archives of General Psychiatry*, *36*, 17–24.

Walker, P. (1978) The role of antiandrogens in the treatment of sex offenders. In B. Qualls, J. Wincze, and D. Barlow (Eds.) *The Prevention of Sexual Disorders*. New York: Plenum.

Walker, P. and Meyer, W. (1981) Medroxyprogesterone acetate treatment for paraphiliac sex offenders. In J. Hays, T. Roberts, and K. Solway (Eds.) *Violence and the Violent Offender*. New York: SP Books.

Webster, W. (1985) *FBI Crime Statistics Report — 7/27/85*. Washington, D.C.

Widiger, T., Frances, A., Warner, L., and Bluhm, C. (1986) Diagnostic criteria for the borderline and schizotypal personality disorders. *Journal of Abnormal Psychology*, *95*, 43–51.

Wilson, J. and Herrnstein, R. (1985) *Crime and Human Nature*. New York: Simon & Schuster.

/ **Pathological Gambling**

The Case of Greg

> Money is a vile intermediary.
> — Fidel Castro

Gambling may be one of civilization's oldest recreational activities. Ancient historical documents are replete with examples of man's (or woman's) interest in wagering with friends and others. Although a common-sense view of the gambling phenomenon would easily and quickly lead to recognition of at least its potential for pathological abuse, pathological gambling as a clinical phenomenon was not formally recognized until DSM-III. That edition saw pathological gambling as a disorder of impulse control, with the primary features being (1) failure to resist an impulse, drive, or temptation to perform the act (whether or not there is premeditation or conscious resistance to the impulse); (2) an increasing sense of tension before committing the act; (3) an experience of either pleasure, gratification, or release at the time of the act.

To specifically diagnose pathological gambling, the DSM requires first that persons not meet the criteria for the antisocial personality disorder (Chapter 10), and secondly, that they show progressive preoccupation with gambling, which consequently disrupts their world in at least three of the following ways: (1) breaking the law in order to obtain money for gambling, as by fraud; (2) defaulting on debts; (3) borrowing money illegally; (4) having family or marital problems; (5) losing track of losses or gains; (6) being absent from work due to gambling; (7) having poor judgment in financial issues, perhaps including desperate borrowing from friends.

Estimates of the number of gamblers in the middle 1970s in the United States varied between 1 and 10 million. Since more states have moved toward legalized gambling, thus making it increasingly accessible, it is expected that the rate will continue to rise. Compulsive gamblers, like antisocial personalities, seek stimulation, and both specifically show "disinhibition" or the inability to control impulses (Goldstein et al., 1985; Zuckerman, Buchsbaum, and Murphy, 1980). The initial streak of compulsive gambling is usually set off by one big win.

Many compulsive gamblers report that they feel alive only when they are gambling and may refer to the rest of their life experience as boring. They are generally nonconformists and are narcissistic and aggressive (Dell, Ruzikah, and Polisi, 1981). A number of compulsive gamblers work only to make enough money to gamble heavily when they get to a spot like Las Vegas. Others have a more normal outward appearance, especially those who gamble in more legitimate outlets, such as commodities and stock markets.

Most gamblers are extroverted and competitive individuals who are brighter than average; surprisingly, they often experienced learning difficulties as they grew up. Most had placed their first bets by the age of 15.

The Case of Greg

Greg was born in the early 1940s, and his childhood could be described as generally pleasant and essentially free from extreme pathological influences. He was the only son of an upper middle class family which strove to provide Greg and his sister with every emotional and material advantage. Until approximately the age of 16, Greg attended public school, at which point his parents decided that it would be in Greg's best interest for him to attend a local private school. It was their hope that Greg would receive a better education and consequently be better prepared for college. In addition, some thought was also given to Greg's exposure to a "better class" of people. It was felt that such friendships made in this moderately sized northeastern town would in all likelihood be enduring and hopefully be of value to Greg in later life.

With these and undoubtedly other considerations in mind, Greg began to attend a private college preparatory school. Initially Greg found the increased academic rigors to be challenging but not overwhelming, and a growing sense of self-esteem or pride began to develop. Greg graduated from high school without academic difficulties, but also without any distinction. Generally he was well-liked by both his peers and his teachers. Despite a certain degree of interpersonal or social charm, very few individuals anticipated that Greg would distinguish himself in any fashion in later life. Regrettably, Greg may have also begun to entertain this hypothesis regarding his future.

Aside from the rather obvious academic benefits obtained by attending a private high school, Greg was also exposed to a way of life of which he previously had no knowledge. Atlhough a wide variety of incomes were represented among the families who sent their children to this school, many individuals came from extremely wealthy families. They wore the most expensive clothes, had seemingly inexhaustible allowances to spend on their recreational needs, and frequently drove the most expensive automobiles. Although Greg's family was solidly upper class and he enjoyed all the benefits consistent with that station in American economic life, his family could not compete with many of the other families who sent their children to the same private school. Sadly, it was during this period that Greg had the growing realization that perhaps he could not "compete" with the individuals who were his dearest friends.

Upon graduation Greg entered the state university. His choice of universities was not based on academic reputation but on low tuition. In contrast, many of his friends attended a variety of private colleges with varying reputations for academic excellence; all were very expensive.

Greg's time in college was essentially unremarkable. He received passing grades but failed to live up to any reasonable level of academic ability. He divided his psychic energy between preparation for classes and socializing with his friends, both old and new. Typically all of Greg's friends belonged to the same social circle, and two characteristics could be easily exemplified. First, the vast majority of Greg's friends were extremely wealthy or at least had direct access to large amounts of money. Second, and perhaps most important, a vast majority of them were bored with their lives and depressed over its seeming emptiness and futility. A large number of Greg's friends would receive very large trust funds at designated points in their lives, or upon graduating from college would assume important roles in their families' companies. To some extent his friends saw the passage of high school and college as periods to be endured or even perversely enjoyed instead of periods of intellectual and emotional growth.

As a result of this prevailing group dynamic, a variety of behaviors were practiced in an effort to avoid boredom and simultaneously to instill some semblance of meaning into their lives. Gambling or wagering in a variety of forms was frequently practiced. Greg was first exposed to gambling in the latter years of high school. His interest and personal attraction to wagering was almost immediate and quickly escalated through his college years. He enjoyed gambling in all forms, for example, card playing, betting on a variety of sporting events, and so on, but his greatest joy was extracted from horse racing ("the sport of kings").

After approximately three years of college, Greg decided to drop out and obtain a job. His reasoning for such a move was that he simply needed more income than his parents could provide or that he could supplement with any form of part-time job. Although a variety of excuses were offered, Greg was totally blind to the increasing role that gambling was playing in his life and to the increasing economic toll it was extracting. As Greg was a very likable and engaging individual, his vocational pursuits naturally turned to sales. He began selling jewelry and was an overnight success. His social charm and honesty with his customers were a unique combination which quickly earned him a positive reputation among other dealers and repeat customers.

Unfortunately for Greg, two independent events occurred in his life which were seemingly to have a profound influence. His best and closest friend married an extremely wealthy young woman who was rumored to be one of the wealthiest young women in the United States. Regardless of the economic accuracy of this statement, Greg began to be exposed to a life style that was most enjoyable to him but that he would never have the means to replicate. At about the same time, Greg's sister became engaged to an equally wealthy individual who had generated his own fortune. In both situations Greg had firsthand exposure to the benefits of extreme wealth, including the most expensive personal acquisitions, gifts, homes, boats, airplanes, and so on. Although Greg envied his sister's and best friend's good fortune, he never became jealous. Their good luck only increased his desire to obtain more money in his own life.

As a result of the discontent with his own life, Greg began to significantly increase the frequency and intensity of his gambling behavior. This intensification had a number of rather obvious benefits. In addition to the occasional "big win," Greg was able to associate with his wealthy friends on a somewhat more frequent basis, as they also enjoyed a certain amount of wagering. It also allowed him to maintain a perhaps less-than-conscious dream of one day becoming extremely wealthy as a result of his gambling skills. At a more psychological level the gambling allowed Greg to avoid the emptiness, depression, and futility of his own life. Simultaneously it gave him a unique sense of identity—he was known within his circle of friends as being a gambler. Such an identity allowed Greg to repress his perception of being a faceless man in a world of celebrities.

As might be expected, Greg's compulsive gambling behavior only further escalated his own psychological conflicts, and in addition created a wide variety of problems within his environment. The compulsivity which he effectively utilized in his job was rechanneled over time into his gambling behavior. In short, he worked long hours in order to obtain extra money so that he might gamble more intensely. Unfortunately for Greg, he generally lost more money than he won. The lack of betting savvy frequently necessitated the acquisition of a number of small loans from his friends, which were generally repaid. Over time, as he began to incur larger losses, more sizable loans were acquired from local banks. Finally, a rather large consolidation loan was sought and received as the number of loans became beyond his ability to pay.

As might be anticipated, Greg began to consume increasing amounts of alcohol in order to deal with the growing pressure, anxiety, and depression. As his level of alcohol consumption increased, his level of judgment regarding his everyday life decreased. Finally he began to resort to "borrowing" the down payments for recent jewelry sales without anyone's knowledge or permission. Although the strategy had some temporary value, over time Greg's losses continued. Finally, out of desperation, Greg decided to rob a savings and loan company. His plan was poorly formulated, and his capture was almost immediate. This was the first antisocial behavior in what was to be a very short criminal career. Although Greg had no real belief in the probability of success of this effort, it may be speculated that at less than a fully conscious level he desperately desired for some external force to take control of his life. To this extent Greg's plan was totally successful.

Greg was tried in federal court approximately eighteen months after his arrest. Much of that time had been spent in obtaining a series of lengthy psychological evaluations regarding every aspect of Greg's life. All forensic experts concluded that Greg suffered from an impulse disorder known as pathological gambling. Fortunately, Greg received strong support from a variety of individuals at his trial. As a result, he was sentenced to twenty-five years in prison. With credit being given for the previous one and a half years, the remaining twenty-three and a half years of Greg's sentence were probated. Without question, this was the greatest payoff for any long shot in his life.

As might be anticipated, the presiding judge was extremely adamant in his feeling that Greg receive all appropriate forms of psychological treatment so as to decrease or eliminate the possibility of any recidivist acts. The problem then became one of effective treatment.

Etiology

Little formal research has been done on compulsive gamblers, but it appears that the following factors can predispose a person to pathological gambling (Malkin and Syme, 1985; Dell, Ruzikah, and Polisi, 1981): (1) family values that emphasize material symbols rather than savings and financial planning; (2) an absent parent before age 16; (3) an extroverted and competitive personality; and (4) a gambling model in the family. Tacit cultural acceptance of gambling also increases the number of abusers. For example, Chinese cultural values strongly disapprove of alcoholism but approve of gambling as a channel for seeking stimulation. As a result, the number of pathological gambers is relatively high in Chinese cultures (Marsella, DeVos, and Hsu, 1985).

As Greg's case shows, pathological gambling can be most devastating in an individual's life. Such tendencies, if left unchecked, can easily result in financial insolvency and an inability to support oneself or one's family. As a result, it is quite easy for the pathological gambler to become alienated from his or her family, acquaintances, or self as a unique individual in life. Loss of accomplishments and/or obtainments are frequent sequelae; as a result, suicidal ideation and/or attempts are not uncommon. Other forms of complication may take the form of association with unsavory groups of people who offer quick and easy access to additional money, arrest, or nonviolent crimes, as previously noted, and subsequent imprisonment for such activities.

In utilizing the diagnosis of pathological gambling, careful differentiation must be made between true pathological gambling and social gambling, gambling as a symptom of manic or hypomanic episodes, and gambling as a result of an antisocial personality disorder. In social gambling, economic wagering is limited to special occasions, and a predetermined limit is placed on what will constitute an acceptable loss. In manic and hypomanic episodes, pathological gambling is most likely to follow the onset of the mood disturbance. Gambling prior to the onset of the mood disturbance is much less frequent and/or nonexistent. Finally, it should be noted that gambling behavior is frequently found in the antisocial personality disorder and may be conceptualized as another form of thrill-seeking behavior. In contrast, as seen in the case of Greg, antisocial behavior resulting from the pathological gambling disorder invariably arises from desperation when no other avenues to obtain funds remain open. Finally, in contrast to the antisocial personality disorder, the pathological gambler usually has at least a reasonably stable work history until it becomes disrupted by his or her gambling behavior.

Treatment

A variety of treatment approaches might be used with the pathological or compulsive gambler (Hersen and Breuning, 1986; Walker, 1986). A traditional psychoanalytic approach might be used. Although the length of such treatment would vary greatly, such an approach might easily take three to five years or longer. In the meantime, the gambling behavior may or may not continue at its previous frequency and intensity. Obviously such an approach was not viewed as acceptable in the case of Greg, since any further gambling behavior would have resulted in immediate revocation of his probation and subsequent incarceration for up to twenty-three and a half years.

More specific therapeutic interventions favor the treatment of compulsive gambling similarly to any other type of addictive disorder (Orford, 1985), typically including the following phases of intervention:

1. Elimination of immediate opportunity to gamble by way of inpatient hospitalization. Such hospitalization will often require a variable number of weeks across individuals.

2. Immediate initiation of an educational process about pathological gambling and the insidious role it takes in every individual's life.

3. Individual and group psychotherapy to help the individual explore attitudes and beliefs that have supported his or her gambling behavior over a period of years.

4. Economic counseling for living within a set income.

5. Continued outpatient treatment in the form of weekly sessions that deal specifically with the issue of gambling.

6. Periodic inpatient hospitalization as a preventive measure once every six to eighteen months.

7. Regular attendance at Gamblers Anonymous.

8. Utilization of family and/or couples therapy when indicated.

Comment

Five years after his initial probation, Greg continues to do extremely well in his new life. His motivation for gambling remains under control, and there have been no subsequent regressions of antisocial or criminal behavior. His need for vocational achievement has remained high, and as a result Greg has continued to experience success in this area, but the treatment for his pathological gambling will likely continue in some form for the indefinite future.

REFERENCES

Dell, L., Ruzikah, M., and Polisi, A. (1981) Personality and other factors associated with gambling addiction. *The International Journal of the Addictions*, *16*, 149–156.

Goldstein, L., Mamowitz, P., Novra, R., Swartzburg, M., and Carlton, P. (1985) Differential EEG activation and pathological gambling. *Biological Psychiatry*, *20*, 1232–1234.

Hersen, M. and Breuning, S. (1986) *Pharmacological and Behavioral Treatment*. New York: John Wiley.

Malkin, D. and Syme, G. (1985) Wagering preferences of problem gamblers. *Journal of Abnormal Psychology*, *94*, 86–91.

Marsella, A., DeVos, G., and Tsu, F. (Eds.) (1985) *Culture and Self: Asian and Western Perspectives.* New York: Tavistock.

Orford, J. (1985) *Excessive Appetites: A Psychological View of Addiction.* New York: John Wiley.

Walker, G. (1985) The brief therapy of a compulsive gambler. *Journal of Family Therapy*, 7, 1–8.

Zuckerman, M., Buchsbaum, M., and Murphy, D. (1980) Sensation seeking and its biological correlates. *Psychological Bulletin*, *88*, 187–214.

/ Kleptomania

The Case of Clare

If I make a set of rules, then a guy goes out and steals an airplane. He comes back and says, "It wasn't on the list of rules."

— Abe Lemons
College Basketball Coach

Kleptomania refers to a recurrent inability to resist the impulse to steal. It is important to note that the motivation for the stealing in kleptomania is not the value of or the need for the article. It is to gain the strong feelings of gratification that occur with the release of tension that the act brings. These acts are seldom accompanied by significant preplanning, are primarily impulsive in nature, and are seldom carried out with assistance from others.

Although kleptomaniacs (and the use of the subterm *mania* is unfortunate) may have problems in interpersonal relationships, their general personality functioning is likely to be within the normal range. Kleptomania can begin as early as the first school years, and it is likely to be chronic without some kind of direct intervention. Anxiety and depression, as well as guilt over the fear of being apprehended, may accompany this condition.

Stealing is a common behavior in our society (Farrington and Knight, 1980). Statistics on shoplifting compiled annually by the United States Department of Commerce indicate that about 1 of every 12 shoppers is a shoplifter, but that only about 1 shoplifter in 35 is apprehended. Some 145 million instances of shoplifting occur annually, and shoplifting has been increasing in recent years, especially among women (Heidensohn, 1986). However, only an extremely small proportion of shoplifters suffer from kleptomania. Most shoplifters steal in order to get something they want for free. Also, a substantial proportion of shoplifting occurs in isolated acts, and the person does not repeat the behavior very often. A great many people, particularly adolescents, shoplift in a group to gain peer acceptance, although this condition can act as a catalyst for later kleptomania (Farrington, 1985).

Since this disorder is not necessarily accompanied by significant pathology or by clear-cut childhood syndromes, we will not detail our case history as much as we do with other cases in this book. But it is worthwhile to examine this pattern, particularly as it can be compared to the antisocial personality disorder case.

The Case of Clare

Clare is a bright and attractive young woman of 28 who has an interesting and responsible position in an advertising firm in the large western city in which she grew up. She first talked about her problem with a minister whom she met at a book club she attended monthly, and he referred her to a private psychologist.

Clare reports that she had been compulsively stealing off and on since she was 13 years old. She had never sought treatment before, but several recent events had heightened her fear of being apprehended. On these occasions, Clare was sure that she had been seen stealing by other customers and began to realize that she had been very lucky never to have been caught yet. Also, one day when she was out browsing in a department store on her lunch hour with one of her co-workers, she compulsively stole a pair of stockings, and she is afraid that the co-worker saw her take them. She knows that if she is ever caught and prosecuted it will mean losing her job, and most certainly the blemish on her record would hurt her in many ways.

Clare's description of her emotional responses during the stealing behavior fits the classic kleptomania pattern. She first experiences an intense state of nervousness and general tension, which gradually crystallizes into an irresistible impulse to take some specific object. She tries to resist the impulse, but generally stays within the immediate range of the object, almost as if she enjoys a further tension buildup. Eventually, she steals the object, at which time she experiences a release of tension and a feeling of satisfaction. Her description of these events sounds very much like a description of the buildup and release of tension in orgasm, though on a milder scale.

Though Clare does use some of the items she steals, many others that she takes go unused. For example, she had accumulated a larger supply of women's cosmetics than she could ever hope to use in the next ten years. Also, for some reason, possibly the ease with which she has been able to steal them, she has accumulated a boxful of men's jewelry, such as cuff links. Clare reports that she is not really limited to any subgroup of items in her stealing but responds primarily to her impulses by going into the nearest store and meandering about until the act takes place.

Clare had a basically normal childhood and says that she was happy at this time in her life. She did very well in school and received much attention for this. Her parents loved their children (Clare is the second oldest of four), though at the same time they did not show much physical affection or direct attention to any one child for very long. Many family activities occurred, such as picnics and fishing trips, but seldom did either her mother or father attend for long to any one child, with the possible exception of the older sister. This probably occurred because the older sister did have a period of time when she was the only child, and as a result the parents were used to responding to her individually.

When Clare was approximately 9 years old, she began to steal money on occasion from her mother's purse. She used the money to buy candy and other small items at a small local grocery store. When her parents found out about this, they became very distressed and had a long talk with Clare about the moral issues involved and how people would not trust her any longer. But they did not really punish her, nor did they have her make any meaningful restitution for the acts she committed. As she reflects on this, Clare feels that her parents' concern came mostly from the potential embarrassment that could occur if she began to steal outside the home. She continued to steal occasionally and became more sophisticated about the situation, so her parents rarely caught her. When they did, they only repeated the same moral prohibitions, without forcing any means of restitution on her. When she was 10, Clare attempted to steal candy from the local grocery store but was easily apprehended. The woman who ran the store reported to Clare's parents. This time, they severely spanked her and followed the spanking with a repeat of the discussion of the moral issues involved.

From this point, Clare only stole occasionally until she was approximately 13. She then began associating with four other girls who would occasionally take "stealing trips" to downtown stores. This was not an everyday occurrence, but it was common enough to become a ritual behavior in their social interactions together. They would go downtown, and each of them would try to steal a specific object that was determined before they went into the store. They did this off and on for several years, and amazingly, only one girl was ever caught. She feigned great distress at this time, stating that she had never done anything like this before, and carried off a very emotional scene. The storekeeper responded sympathetically and did not report the event either to the police or the parents.

Clare did exceptionally well academically in high school and enrolled in a premedical program at the university. She did reasonably well during her first year, and the stealing behavior had ceased when she came to college. In her sophomore year, she had trouble with two courses and received low grades. She realized that she was not likely to be accepted into medical school. Coincidentally, she had the first disappointing love affair of her life.

During her high school years, she dated regularly, yet never developed any long-term romantic involvement that had any deep meaning for her. However, she met another student in her first year at the university with whom she fell deeply in love. They dated seriously for the latter part of her first year and into the second year, but then her partner gradually became bored with the relationship and dropped her for another girl. She had had sexual intercourse with him—the first time for her—and she had rationalized it by saying that she thought they would some day get married. When they broke up, she at first had a great deal of guilt that added to her general disappointment.

It was at this point that Clare began stealing again occasionally, and now she was doing it alone. She would experience a buildup of apprehension and then found relief when she would shoplift an item successfully. During this time, she was extremely careful as to how she went about it, usually choosing small stores that had only one proprietor so that the risk was low.

After graduation from the university, she took a glorified secretarial job in an advertising firm. Through her job, she met a man whom she dated for about four months, after which time they somewhat impulsively married. The marriage lasted for two years. It was clear from the start that her choice had been a bad one, for her husband was sexually inadequate most of the time and also had a drug problem. Clare ended up supporting him, and when it became apparent that he was not really going to change his behavior, she left him. She had always believed that "marriage is forever," and so the divorce caused her a great deal of hurt. She threw herself more forcefully into her job, and her intelligence and hard work won her a promotion into a position that was a stepping-stone to executive rank.

Subsequent to divorce, Clare had a series of intense romantic involvements, but she was very fearful of making any new commitments. When she was not involved in a relationship, she was prone to anxiety and depression, and it was at these times that she was drawn to the stealing behavior. As she quipped, "I'm still looking for Mr. Goodbar," but as she also noted later, "At times I'm pretty scared that I'll find him."

Etiology

Clare is reflective of most kleptomaniacs in that there is no remarkable history of pathology in childhood, nor any significant problems of thought disorder, consistent neurotic behavior, or psychopathy. However, like many other antisocial or criminal patterns, the evolution of her kleptomania occurred in several gradual phases (Wilson and Herrnstein, 1985).

Phase one occurred when she was approximately 9 years old. It was marked by behaviors common to many children. She stole money that she found easily available, and like most of these children, she was caught. But in her case, this originally utilitarian pattern was reinforced by the paternal interest and lack of effective punishment. As noted, there was much caring in her family, yet little individualized attention, and the stealing gained her the individual attention. Though it did have negative costs, these were not strong enough to void the reinforcement of her pattern.

She moved into phase two when the stealing not only reflected the reinforcement but, in addition, became a channel for hostility toward her parents. She saw their hypocrisy and was developing clearer anger feelings over not getting any individual attention from them. She stole to lash out at them, and at the same time she again forced them to attend more individually to her.

The next phase in this evolution is a common one in the background of kleptomaniacs. She became involved in a peer group that integrated stealing into their social rituals, and it was a necessary behavior to gain acceptance in this particular subgroup. Clare was happy with these girls, got along well with them, and enjoyed many activities with them, only one of which was stealing. It is interesting that at this point she only stole while she was with her friends.

The fourth and final phase in the evolution of her pattern occurred when she moved from her peer stealing back to individual stealing. The stealing alleviated some of the anxiety and boredom she was experiencing as she went through the trials and tribulations that occur in most people's lives. The disappointment in the failure of her first true romantic attachment came close on the heels of her realization that she would not be able to fulfill her long-sought goal of entering medical school. Thus, she had a lot of self-evaluation to do (Kohut, 1977), which generated anxiety and depression. There is also evidence that these feelings combined with her ambivalent resolution of her sexual needs. Sometimes she would behave rather promiscuously, and at other times she would return to a more restrained pattern. In any case, when she had a buildup of general tension, the stealing behavior would distract her and, in that sense, also give her a thrill and a feeling of satisfaction. Though Clare saw the behavior as ego-alien, she usually could no longer restrain herself.

In this sense, kleptomania is not dissimilar to chronic obesity. In chronic obesity, the buildup of anxiety (or almost any emotion) becomes a discriminative cue for overeating. It is as if the individual cannot sort out the meaning of emotional cues. In the case of Clare's kleptomania, a buildup of any tension was channeled into a cue for stealing behavior. For this reason, she often stole articles that were of no real use to her. It was the act itself that was reinforcing, not the objects that were gained (Wilson and Herrnstein, 1985).

The realization eventually hit her that this behavior put her at risk for enjoying other areas of her life. One could even speculate that she became more careless in her recent stealing behavior from unconscious motivation to shock herself with the realization of the risks she was posing for herself. In the last incident before referral, the presence of her co-worker was a concrete reminder that her job, which was her one positive source of self-esteem, could be lost if she were apprehended. As a result, she sought treatment.

Treatment

As with most of the habit disorders, the treatment must first focus on the specific behavior itself and then later attend to any ancillary issues, such as accompanying anxiety, depression, and/or interpersonal difficulties (Kazdin, 1984). Eliminating the problematic habit behavior is particularly crucial in Clare's case, in which there is a potential legal difficulty if she continues (Farrington, 1985). There has not been much attention in the research to the elimination of kleptomania; the treatment rendered Clare reflects most of the work that has been done.

The first phase of Clare's treatment used an aversive conditioning procedure similar to that used by Kellam (1969) to cure another chronic kleptomaniac. Clare was asked to simulate her entire shoplifting sequence in a room that was made up as much as possible to look like a store. The procedure was videotaped, and Clare was asked to amplify this in her imagination as strongly as she could while the videotape was being replayed. At critical decision points, she was administered a very painful electric shock, which acts to suppress the behavior. To strengthen this effect, Clare was asked occasionally to imagine herself in a shoplifting sequence at various times outside the treatment hour, and she was asked to hold her breath until discomfort occurred. This discomfort, like the electric shock, acts as an aversive cue to help suppress the behavior. A small portable electric shock unit could have been used as an alternative to asking her to hold her breath (Kazdin, 1984).

Once Clare felt she was gaining control over the stealing impulse, she was asked to go to various stores in which she had stolen. She was asked first to respond to any stealing impulses with the "holding the breath" technique. If the impulse could not be suppressed by this approach, she was then slowly and deliberately to pick up a fragile item, such as a vase, and then deliberately drop it on the floor near a number of customers. The idea was to paradoxically generate as much disturbance and embarrassment as possible (Seltzer, 1986). She was to stay around as long as possible while the item was being cleaned up and insist on paying for the item. This action interrupts the compulsive sequence and also pairs the impulse with the unpleasant and embarrassing consequences of an in vivo situation. Over a period of six weeks, the intense application of this three-stage aversive procedure (shock with the simulated videotape, discomfort of breath-holding while imagining the sequence, and embarrassment while in the store) suppressed Clare's desire to go through a shoplifting sequence. She could comfortably go into stores, and though she occasionally felt a twinge of the old impulse, she was able to avoid ruminating about it or feeling compelled to carry it out.

Concomitantly with the aversive approach, she was taught control of a relaxation technique in order to dissipate some of her ongoing anxiety (Kazdin, 1984). It was hypothesized that anxiety and other emotions were channeled into the impulse to steal; hence it was seen as worthwhile not only to suppress the specific problem behavior itself, but also to lessen the anxiety that generated it. She responded well to the relaxation training and did report a gradual lessening of anxiety. She was also seen in weekly psychotherapy for six sessions, during which she clarified some of her interpersonal conflicts.

Clare did shoplift three different times during the first two weeks of this combined treatment approach. But as she gained control of the relaxation response and as the aversive technique took effect, she was able to avoid the stealing behavior altogether. The changes were then solidified by her gaining more awareness of how she mishandled certain areas and also by dissipating some of the feelings that had accumulated around past events in her life. Clare was followed up by her therapist for two years, and there was no recurrence up to that time.

Comment

Clare's case is one in which compulsive stealing became a conditioned emotional response to depression and distress. Her initial stealing from her parents could have remained one of those isolated episodes of misbehavior that characterize the development of most people. The reaction of Clare's parents was only mildly negative, and she was subsequently strongly influenced by the pressures of her peers. Afterward, Clare's period of abstinence from stealing in college was interrupted by her depression when her first romantic relationship ended. At this point, Clare's stealing became part of her standard response to emotional distress.

It seems appropriate to consider Clare's stealing habit a gradually acquired strategy for alleviating anxiety and depression. Buildups in anxiety and/or depression became discriminative cues for stealing. The only negative consequences for stealing were Clare's own mild guilt and self-deprecation. These reactions, ironically, then produced greater anxiety and increased stealing. The initial phase of Clare's treatment involved interrupting the downward spiral characteristic of compulsive behaviors (see the earlier case of Bess). In

Clare's case, aversive conditioning was also helpful (Kellam, 1969). Afterward, Clare learned more adaptive stress responses via relaxation training (Kazdin, 1984), and clarified her interpersonal conflicts through insight therapy (Kohut, 1977).

REFERENCES

Farrington, D. and Knight, B. (1980) Four sides of stealing as a risky decision. In P. Lipsitt and B. Sales (Eds.), *New Directions in Psycholegal Research*. New York: Van Nostrand Reinhold.

Farrington, D. (1985) Delinquency prevention in the 1980's. *Journal of Adolescence, 8*, 3–16.

Heidensohn, F. (1986) *Women and Crime*. New York: New York University Press.

Kazdin, A. (1984) *Behavior Modification in Applied Settings*. Homewood, Ill.: Dorsey.

Kellam, A. (1969) Shoplifting treated by aversion to a film. *Behavior Research and Therapy, 7*, 125–127.

Kohut, H. (1977) *The Restoration of the Self*. New York: International Universities Press.

Seltzer, L. (1986) *Paradoxical Strategies in Psychotherapy*. New York: John Wiley.

Wilson, J. and Herrnstein, R. (1985) *Crime and Human Nature*. New York: Simon & Schuster.

/ Family Violence – Child Abuse and Spouse Abuse

The Cases of Charles and Abby

Throughout history, as well as across cultures, the physical and sexual abuse of children has been clearly documented (Gelles, 1986; Burgess and Garbarino, 1983; Belsky, 1980; Nelson, 1984). Although frequently abhorred, few actual preventive steps were taken, and it is ironic that the first formal legal intervention in a child abuse case, that of Mary Ellen in New York in 1875, had to be prosecuted through animal protection laws and primarily as a result of the efforts of the Society for the Prevention of Cruelty to Animals (Cross, 1984). However, in the spectacularly short time of about five years, child abuse in the United States went from being a virtual non-issue to being a focus of national political concern (Nelson, 1984). All fifty states, partly spurred by the federal Child Abuse Prevention and Treatment Act, have established legal routes to identify and intervene in abusive families. As a result, the number of identified cases has grown enormously, from 7,000 to 8,000 annually in 1967 and 1968 to over 700,000 in 1978, and most believe the number is still increasing.

Because of the private nature of abuse and the reluctance of both perpetrators and victims to reveal it (Dale et al., 1986), clearly identified cases of child abuse are generally believed to represent only a portion of the actual cases. Estimates vary widely and generally do not attempt to report rates according to subtypes. The 1980 National Incidence Study of Child Abuse and Neglect *conservatively* estimated that 652,000 children under 18 are abused or neglected yearly. Severe physical abuse alone may affect 200,000 children annually (National Center on Child Abuse and Neglect, 1981). Using a self-report interview technique with 1,146 parents of two-parent homes, Gelles (1978) estimated that between 1.0 and 1.9 million children are kicked, bitten, or punched by their parents annually. Between 3.1 and 4.0 million receive such treatment at some time while growing up, and an additional 1.4 to 2.3 million will be beaten up sometime by their parents. Such acts of violence decrease with increasing age of the children. Deaths due to abuse reportedly number some 700 to 2,000 per year. Other studies have reported considerably different rates of abuse, ranging from 25,000 to 5 million per year. In the area of sexual abuse, estimates run from 100,000 cases to 40 million cases per year, suggesting no one has any true data here. Retrospective studies of nonclinical populations suggests that between one-fourth and one-third of all children and adolescents have at least one sexual experience with an adult, ranging from exhibitionism to intercourse, and about 75 percent of reported sexual abuse cases involve incest (Finkelhor, 1985; National Center on Child Abuse and Neglect, 1981). The debate over incidence of child abuse will doubtless continue; however, the problem is obviously substantial.

The consequences of abuse to children are usually extensive and debilitating (Browne and Finkelhor, 1986; Fromuth, 1986), and the effect goes beyond consequences to the child to consequences to others with whom the child later interacts, since abused children are prone to grow up to be abusers, as will be seen below in the case of Abby. The figures cited above do indicate that the problem is of massive proportions, far greater than that posed by many DSM syndromes.

When a marriage breaks down, the potential for violence, which may be directed toward the child or toward the spouse, soars (Cross, 1984). There has been increasing attention to marital violence in recent decades (Bornstein and Bornstein, 1986). The type of violence ranges from verbal abuse to physical assault (Gelles, 1986). Also, it is being increasingly recognized that rape can occur within the marriage as a form of spouse abuse. Estimates of the percentage of couples who experience physical violence at some time in the course of a marriage range from 30 to 60 percent, and it is clear that the amount of reported violence is far less than the amount of actual violence (Jouriles and O'Leary, 1985).

In most cases the wife is the victim, though there are a few reports where the husband was abused (Bornstein and Bornstein, 1986). Family therapy can be helpful on occasion, though often by the time the abuse pattern has been made public, the bonding between the two parties has been so violated that reconciliation is highly improbable. As is noted in the subsequent case of Abby, many spouse abusers were themselves abused as a child by one or both of their parents (Jouriles and O'Leary, 1985).

We'll first present a classic pattern of child sexual abuse (the case of Charles), followed by one of physical abuse (the case of Abby).

The Case of Charles

*"A child molester. A real sweetheart. He had
two trained German shepherds. Apparently
he'd enter a housing project, first attract little
kids with his dogs. Then the trained dogs would
herd and hold the little kids in a corner of the
building, or the play yard, and this son of a
bitch would then make free with them."*

. . . "And he got only eleven years?"

*. . . "I'm sure they were eleven hard years,
Fletch. Child molesters are not popular in
prison. They get very few invitations to the
cellblock cocktail parties."*

— Gregory McDonald
Fletch Won

Charles is a 39-year-old civil engineer who lives in a medium-sized city in Kentucky. He works for a large construction business, makes a good salary, and would certainly be characterized as a model citizen by most who know him. He is a long-time member of a church (though he doesn't profess or practice any strong religious beliefs), and belongs to a number of civic organizations. All indications are that he had a normal childhood, and had never sought help for any psychological disorder.

Charles married at age 25. The marriage was certainly a good one at the outset, and both he and his wife were delighted when she had a baby girl, Vicki, when Charles was 30. Unfortunately, the marriage started to deteriorate shortly thereafter. Charles's wife enjoyed the status of being a mother, but not the functions. She returned to her job as a secretary as soon as she could after Vicki's birth, and often hired baby-sitters to escape the routine demands of child care. She had always been a regular social drinker, but now began to drink more secretively and more often, probably to dissolve both guilt and anxiety. Within several years she had developed a true alcoholic pattern. She was just barely able to hold on to her job, but was almost nonfunctional as a wife and mother.

Charles, on the other hand, enjoyed fathering, and developed a strong bond with Vicki, especially since he had few friends or interests away from home. He and his wife now simply tolerated each other, with only rare sexual or emotional encounters. He would satisfy his sexual needs in several ways: an occasional affair, a visit to a prostitute, or by masturbation to stimulation from pornographic magazines and videotapes.

Charles had always allowed Vicki to lie down next to him or put her head in his lap for fifteen minutes or so before she went off to bed. One night, when Vicki was 8, as she lay in front of him on the couch, he let her lay there for almost an hour, enjoying very much the closeness to her, a closeness that was really not available to him elsewhere. Toward the end of this period, he became very aroused sexually, and at that time he sent Vicki off to bed. Several nights later, he was again lying with Vicki and again became aroused. This time, he just lay there. After a while, as Vicki moved around a bit, he suddenly had a strong orgasm. He felt some upset at this time, but allowed a repetition on a couple of subsequent occasions.

Then, a week later, the situation escalated further. When he had become very aroused, he raised the back of her nightgown, and gently rubbed his penis against her buttocks, again having a strong orgasm. He told Vicki everything was all right, and not to be upset, and she wasn't. This, however, was the first time that he had directly engaged in a sexual act with her, and this seemed to break down any remaining inhibitions. He would now on occasion have Vicki reach behind her and rub his penis. Also, he would now touch her occasionally on her genitals and would bring on his orgasm by rubbing his penis between her legs. He eventually asked her to "lick it" at a point of high arousal and would ejaculate on her face, all the time presenting all of this to Vicki as a sort of game, though always emphasizing her need to be secret about it. He did try to penetrate her vagina a couple of times, but quickly backed off when Vicki complained that it hurt.

This pattern went on for about six months. There was some reason to believe that Charles's wife may have been at least vaguely aware of this. But she did nothing; in fact, she had been using alcohol even more heavily over the last year or so. Then, one day while playing with a neighbor girl, the word "penis" came up, and Vicki blurted out, "Well, Daddy lets me lick his." The friend's mother overheard this, asked Vicki what she meant, and Vicki proceeded to describe it all in vivid detail. The neighbor called her husband, who knew where it had to be reported and did so.

When later confronted by a worker with the Child Protective Services Division, Charles broke down and confessed. He was later convicted. But based on his history and the recommendations of a psychologist and social worker, his sentence was probated, with a stipulated requirement for community service and treatment.

Treatment was successful in the sense that Charles never sexually abused Vicki again. But, he and his wife could never reconcile their feelings about this and were divorced within the year. It's not yet clear how much psychological damage Vicki has incurred. However, it was probably quite a bit, and indeed, it's very likely that over time she will be the one to pay the highest price.

The Case of Abby

Then spare the rod and spoil the child.
— Samuel Butler
Hudibras

Abby was born to a poor family in the mountains of West Virginia. When she was four, the family moved to Akron, Ohio, in hopes of getting work in a tire factory, where her uncle already had a job. Unfortunately, this was about the time such jobs were drying up. After struggling for several years, often surviving only on welfare, the family moved to Tennessee in hopes of getting work at a new General Motors plant that was being built there.

There were no dramatic problems or incidents in Abby's childhood. However, child care was minimal and there was little value placed on education or achievement. She seldom had any interaction with her father, who spent his time away from home when he could. When he was home, he spent his time either eating, sleeping, drinking, or beating Abby's mother or one of the five children if they demanded too much of his attention. Abby's mother loved the children, but her emotional, intellectual, and physical resources were overwhelmed to the point that she could do little more than meet her children's basic needs. Abby eventually made it through high school, though with close to failing grades.

She had become pregnant in her junior year of high school, but aborted without letting her parents know. One month after getting out of high school, she discovered she was again pregnant, but this time maneuvered the father into marrying her. They moved to a nearby city and she delivered a healthy girl, and almost immediately became pregnant again. This pregnancy and labor were difficult and the child, a boy, soon showed some signs of brain damage.

Abby's husband soon thereafter had enough of fatherhood, left town, and was seldom heard from again. Abby was not especially attractive, and was neither very bright nor had any marketable skills. With two young children and no money, she did not attract the most eligible of men. She had a string of live-in boyfriends, and several of them would quickly resort to a severe beating of whichever child bothered them in some way, usually the younger child.

Abby herself was confused and overwhelmed by the tasks of child care. Her daughter was quiet and docile, almost to the point of being withdrawn, so she caused Abby few problems. However, as her youngest became more mobile, he became more difficult to control. Abby had few skills or resources to bring to the task, and more and more she resorted to beating this child. A week after yet another boyfriend had abruptly walked out on her, her son broke a small vase that Abby had received years ago from a much-loved grandmother. Abby started shrieking at her son, grabbed him roughly and dragged him by the arm out into the kitchen, and started hitting and beating him. When she finally stopped, he was bleeding and bruised, and it became evident he could hardly move his arm. He was still not moving the arm the next day, and Abby took him to a hospital emergency room, where they quickly recognized the probability of child abuse. Abby at first tried to deny it, but eventually admitted what had happened. She was diverted into a parents' training group and began to make some progress in handling her children. But there were repeat incidents, and then Abby left town with a new boyfriend. No follow-up information is available, but it's probable the abuse occurred again, and would be a legacy her children would carry into their own world as parents.

Etiology

Many factors contribute to the ultimate emergence of an episode of physical and/or sexual child abuse (Belsky, 1980; Cross, 1984; Finkelhor, 1985; Browne and Finkelhor, 1986; Gelles, 1986). These factors are found within three contributing systems: sociocultural, familial, and individual. To the degree these factors are present, the probability of an occurrence of child abuse is increased. At the most basic level are the following *sociocultural* factors which facilitate an increase in child abuse episodes:

1. Lack of affirmation and support of the family unit
2. Lack of emphasis on parent training skills as a prerequisite to parenting

3. Acceptance of and high media visibility of violence
4. Acceptance of corporal punishment as a central child-rearing technique
5. Emphasis on competition rather than cooperation
6. Unequal status for women
7. Low economic support for schools and day-care facilities

These sociocultural factors heighten the probability of abuse in conjunction with the following *familial* factors:

1. Low socioeconomic and educational level
2. Little availability of friends and extended family for support
3. Single parent or merged parent family structure
4. Marital instability
5. Family violence as common and traditionally accepted
6. Low rate of family contact and information exchange
7. Significant periods of mother absence
8. High acceptance of family nudity
9. Low affirmation of family member privacy
10. "Vulnerable" childen (to the degree they are young, sick, disturbed, re-tarded, or emotionally isolated)

The probability of abuse in a specific instance is in turn increased by the following *individual* factors:

1. History of abuse as a child
2. Low emotional stability and/or self-esteem
3. Low ability to tolerate frustration and inhibit anger
4. High impulsivity
5. Lack of parenting skills
6. High emotional and interpersonal isolation
7. Problems in handling dependency needs of self or others
8. Low ability to express physical affection
9. Unrealistic expectations for child's performance
10. Acceptance of corporal punishment as a primary child-rearing technique
11. Presence of drug or alcohol abuse

As with most cases, many though not all of the above factors are found in the cases of Charles and of Abby. Some predict more to physical abuse and some more to sexual abuse, but most factors predict to either type. However, from an overall perspective, the following general factors were evident in the cases of Charles and of Abby:

- *Impulsivity.* The actual incident often occurs in persons in whom either training, temperament, or both, has predisposed him/her to immediately act on impulse, not bring inhibitory belief systems to bear on impulse, and/or to delay gratification. In a similar vein, the demands of child-rearing are too much for an immature personality, who lashes out in retaliation at the cause for these demands. Remorse may follow, but the damage is done.

- *Incompetence.* As with Abby, far too many parents come to this crucial task with little preparation or support (poverty markedly increases the potential for child abuse). When the task overwhelms them, they react with harsh punishments in an attempt to regain control.

- *Disturbance.* Psychological and physical disturbances (not in the child), for example, schizophrenia, drug and alcohol abuse, mental retardation, or as in the case of Charles, a disrupted marriage, generate problems that in turn facilitate child abuse.

- *Modeling.* The child who has been abused, or who has witnessed a pattern of spouse abuse, is much more likely to become an abuser than the average child.

- *Characteristics of the child.* As especially was the case with Abby's younger child, children who have characteristics that make frustration or disappointment more likely (hyperactivity, physical or psychological handicaps) are more likely to be abused. The amount of parental bonding and the vulnerability of the child are also relevant; thus, stepchildren and younger children are more often the victims. Indeed, live-in boyfriends are a common source of child abuse.

Sexual Abuse. The factors that generate physical child abuse are often relevant to cases of sexual child abuse. However, a number of specifically relevant factors are also critical. For example, psychodynamic features here include the interaction of such parental factors as marital discord, personality disorder, loss of an important relationship or fear of disintegration of the family, and emotional deprivation. Finkelhor (1985) related sexual abuse to extreme masculine socialization practices and views, which include equating sexuality and affection, the importance of heterosexual success to self-identity, focusing on sexual acts rather than relationships, and accepting of younger and smaller sexual partners.

The seriousness of consequent disorder in the child resulting from sexual abuse appears to depend on several factors (Browne and Finkelhor, 1986; Fromuth, 1986). More serious problems are likely if (1) the offender is in a close relationship to the child, such as the father; (2) the sexual activity included genital contact, and especially penetration; (3) the child is older (adolescent) at the time of abuse; (4) the abuse is frequent and/or of long duration; (5) the child has strong negative feelings about the abuse and/or is somehow aware of its wrongness; and (6) much upset and/or distress occurs around the event (for instance, via court testimony).

Treatment

The interventions noted in these two classic patterns of Charles and Abby are those typically employed. The emphasis is obviously going to differ depending upon issues of the individual case. However, in addition to individual psychotherapy, there are three core approaches that are potentially useful in almost all such cases:

1. *Family therapy.*   Since the family is virtually always disrupted, family therapy is necessary. Even where the family system eventually changes, as in the case of Charles, family therapy can help to mute the damage to all concerned (Kolevzon and Green, 1985).

2. *Parent training.*   When the abuse comes from a parent, parent training is necessary to deal not only with the problems that led to the abuse, but to those generated by the abuse as well (Goldstein, Keller, and Erne, 1986). Parent training to deal with this latter factor is also important when the source of abuse is external to the family.

3. *Support systems.*   As in the cases of Charles and Abby, abuse often comes where there has been a sense of emotional isolation. In this vein, a community-based counseling and support group is available to abusing parents in Parents Anonymous. This organization works in the same manner as Alcoholics Anonymous (see the case of Paul) or Gamblers Anonymous (see the case of Greg). A similar group is Parents United. Contact with other abusers and the opportunity to share problems with sympathetic and understanding others are helpful for parents for whom abusive behaviors are triggered by psychosocial stressors and a sense of emotional isolation. There are also support groups for the victims of child abuse, which are especially useful with older abuse victims.

The above can also be supplemented by other interventions, for instance, attempts to change the person's employment possibilities or social skills; both would be important for Abby. Where there is a couple involved, marital therapy is likely to be necessary if the marriage is to continue (Bornstein and Bornstein, 1986). Lastly, and from a moral perspective, the most deserving of specific treatment attention is the child victim, or other siblings who may be vicarious victims. In general, the extent of trauma to such victims will depend upon (1) the nature, extent, and duration of abusive incidents; (2) the relationships (and implications thereof) between abusers and victims; (3) the reactions of adults from whom the children seek support; (4) the developmental phase of the children; and (5) the subjective interpretation of these events made by the children.

Many intervention programs specifically designed for sexual abuse have not only focused on crisis intervention but have noted that the consequences of reporting, such as court appearances and foster placement, may be as distressing to a child as were the abusive sexual acts (Browne and Finkelhor, 1986). Techniques such as videotaping the child's testimony may help here, though this would apparently violate the accused's right to confront his or her accuser in court.

One successful long-term program for incest is the Child Sexual Abuse Treatment Program in Santa Clara County, California. The program was developed in large part by Henry Giarretto and is guided by humanistic psychology principles (Helfer and Kempe, 1976). It emphasizes intense and immediate intervention with emphasis on treatment. The result is that about 90 percent of the father-offenders confess and go into treatment, which helps to avoid the negatives of long-term foster care or institutional placement for the children. It is important to note that, contrary to the constant warnings to children about being careful of strangers, about 4 out of 5 sexually abused children are assaulted by people they know, and almost half of the offenders are the natural parents.

The subsequent intervention sequence includes, in order: individual counseling for the child, mother, and father; mother-child counseling; marital counseling; father-child counseling; family counseling; and group counseling. Also, some reconditioning of more appropriate sexual patterns would be important (see the case of Roger). The overall goal is reconstitution of the family and marriage, with growth of individual members. Help in providing for basic needs is also offered, and much time is devoted to expression of feelings related to the incest, with the parents required to admit responsibility and to tell their child that he or she is not to blame. Like other similar programs, this one is family-systems oriented, and though it is certainly not 100 percent successful, it is as good as any other program now available. Unfortunately, even with the development of solid treatment programs such as this one, the problems of physical and sexual child abuse and spouse abuse are likely to continue at significant levels.

Indeed, treatment may help in a specific case (Goldstein, Keller, and Erne, 1986), but the greatest changes will come with efforts at prevention (parent training *before* becoming parents, reduction of the percentage of very young and/or single parents without skills or resources, educational programs in schools) or cultural change (efforts to reduce the acceptance of physical discipline) (Belsky, 1980; Cross, 1984; Finkelhor, 1985; Dale et al., 1986).

REFERENCES

Belsky, J. (1980) Child maltreatment: An ecological integration. *American Psychologist, 35,* 320–335.

Bornstein, P. and Bornstein, M. (1986). *Marital Therapy*. New York: Pergamon.

Browne, A. and Finkelhor, D. (1986) Impact of child sexual abuse: A review of the research. *Psychological Bulletin*, *99*, 66–77.

Burgess, R. L. and Garbarino, J. (1983) Doing what comes naturally? An evolutionary perspective on child abuse. In D. Finkelhor, R. J. Gelles, G. T. Hotaling, and M. A. Straus (Eds.) *The Dark Side of Families: Current Family Violence Research*. Beverly Hills: Sage Publications.

Cross, C. (1984) *Child Abuse and Neglect*. Washington, D.C.: National Education Association.

Dale, P., Waters, J., Davies, M., Roberts, W., and Morrison, T. (1986) The towers of silence. *Journal of Family Therapy*, *8*, 1–26.

Finkelhor, D. (1985) *Child Sexual Abuse*. New York: Free Press.

Fromuth, M. (1986) The relationship of childhood sexual abuse with later psychological and sexual adjustment in a sample of college women. *Child Abuse and Neglect*, *10*, 5–16.

Gelles, R. J. (1986) Family violence. In R. Turner (Ed.) *Annual Review of Sociology*, *11*, Palo Alto, Calif.: Annual Reviews, Inc.

———. (1979) Child abuse as psychopathology. In D. W. Gil (Ed.), *Child Abuse and Violence*. New York: AMS Press.

Goldstein, A., Keller, H., and Erne, D. (1986) *Changing the Abusive Parent*. Champaign, Ill.: Research Press.

Helfer, R. E. and Kempe, C. H. (Eds.) (1976) *Child Abuse and Neglect*. Cambridge, Mass.: Ballinger.

Jouriles, E. and O'Leary, K. (1985) Interspousal reliability of reports of marital violence. *Journal of Consulting and Clinical Psychology*, *53*, 419–421.

Kolevzon, M. and Green, R. (1985) *Family Therapy Models*. New York: Springer.

National Center on Child Abuse and Neglect. (1981) *Child Sexual Abuse: Incest, Assault and Sexual Exploitation*. (DDHS Pub. No. (OHDS) 81-30166). Washington, D.C.: U.S. Government Printing Office.

Nelson, B. (1984) *Making Child Abuse an Issue*. Chicago: University of Chicago Press.

12

Disorders of Childhood and Adolescence

This section documents cases that are characteristic of the earlier years of life. As in all chapters of this book, representative cases have been chosen to sample the relevant range of disorders. We also present here a sampling of cases from different age ranges. Symptoms of the first three cases—developmental language disorder, attention deficit disorder with hyperactivity, and early infantile autism—are usually evident in early childhood. As with many of the childhood disorders, however, they may not cause major disruptions in the child's and/or family's world until the child moves into the structured social demands of day-care and formal schooling. The first case, Delano, a child with a development language disorder, is a particularly good example of this phenomenon. Although the disorder did not emerge until he went to school, there was hard evidence of disorder as early as 18 months of age. Even though all three of these disorders may take a severe toll on the child's later adjustment, Delano's symptomatology is subtle when compared to that seen in the early infantile autism case.

The next two disorders discussed, the oppositional disorder and the separation disorder, are more characteristic of middle childhood, particularly the early school years, though the initial symptoms may appear much earlier. These disorders present contrasting styles of coping with a major developmental task—the establishment of a new and separate sense of identity. In the separation disorder, a too-fearful coping style makes adequate separation very difficult and results in a school phobia, whereas in the oppositional disorder, uncontrolled assertiveness blocks adequate adjustment.

The next disorders discussed, anorexia nervosa and bulimia, listed in the DSM as eating disorders, are most often found in adolescence. Anorexia nervosa, which first focuses on attention to dieting and marked weight loss, may not initially cause parents much concern. However, once the trend progresses to a substantial disorder pattern, the possibility that it will result in death is variously estimated at from 5 to 20 percent. This possibility is of special concern since there is evidence that this condition has been increasing in recent decades.

A number of other childhood disorder patterns also have an analogous pattern in adult syndromes. For example, an unsocialized conduct disorder (either aggressive or nonaggressive) in childhood is likely to reappear in subsequent maladjustment as a personality disorder, particularly the antisocial personality disorder, which is discussed in Chapter 10. Anxiety-based childhood disorders, such as phobias and avoidance patterns, are similar in many respects to the patterns discussed in Chapter 3 on anxiety disorders. The same analogy holds for many of the other adult cases discussed in this book.

/ ## Developmental Language Disorder

The Case of Delano

We spend the first twelve months of our child's lives teaching them to walk and talk, and the next twelve telling them to sit down and shut up.
— Phyllis Diller

Children with language and other skill achievement problems are likely to show signs of such disorder early on (Broman, Bien, and Shaughnessy, 1985; Kegan, 1986). However, it is not until these disorders are manifested in school-related problems that there is a referral for psychological assessment. In such cases, the psychologist's role often focuses on evaluating the child's level of cognitive and intellectual skills and on making recommendations for intervention within the school system. Such intervention often requires the integration of a great deal of history from a variety of sources, with the consequent problem of organizing a small mountain of information into a diagnostic impression of the child.

The term *learning disabled* is often used to describe children who encounter more than the usual degree of difficulty in mastering basic school subjects. Any implication that such children have central nervous system impairment is not accurate. The 1980 Federal Education for All Handicapped Children law (P.L. 94–142) incorporates a definition of the learning-disabled child that is useful here, since it is broad enough to encompass many of the types of school-related problems that clinical psychologists are called on to deal with.

"Specific learning disability" means a disorder in one or more of the basic psychological processes involved in understanding or in using language, spoken or written, which may manifest itself in an imperfect ability to listen, think, speak, read, write, spell, or to do mathematical calculations. The term includes such conditions as perceptual handicaps, brain injury, minimal brain dysfunction, dyslexia, and developmental aphasia. The term does not include children who have learning problems which are primarily the result of visual, hearing, or motor handicaps, or mental retardation, or of environmental, cultural, or economic disadvantage. (P.L. 94-142, sect. 121a. 5(9))

Implicit in such a definition is that a child with a learning disability possesses skills in other areas and is not simply deficient in performance abilities across the board. P.L. 94-142 is one of a series of efforts to characterize adequately a wide range of disorders, all of which appear to have some significance with respect to behavior in educational settings. The long history of efforts to systematize the discussion of these disorders testifies to the perennial interest of specialists from many disciplines in factors that affect a child's performance (Kail and Pellegrino, 1985; Rie and Rie, 1980).

In a general way, the DSM helps identify school-related disorders owing to its expanded treatment of childhood disorders. In particular, a group of disorders termed specific developmental disorders encompasses many of the school-related difficulties encountered by young children. The most commonly identified of these include developmental disorders of reading and language. The former condition is diagnosed when there is a significant discrepancy between a child's IQ score and a standardized assessment of reading proficiency. Developmental reading disorders are generally first identified after a child has been in school long enough for a discrepancy between reading and intellectual skills to develop. In many instances, however, developmental reading disorders may be preceded by the second major category of specific developmental disorders, which involve language.

The DSM classifies language disorders according to whether (1) language is acquired at all; (2) the language deficit is acquired subsequent to normal development; or (3) the onset of language is delayed. The last of these, termed a developmental language disorder, is the most prevalent and is generally thought to reflect the relatively slow maturation of brain structures that mediate linguistic skills. Depending on whether the language deficit predominantly involves problems in understanding or using spoken language, it is termed a receptive or expressive developmental language disorder.

Other specific developmental disorders include a developmental articulation disorder (in which speech has a "babyish" quality), and a relatively rare disorder involving calculation skills, termed a developmental arithmetic disorder. It is not uncommon for children with expressive or receptive developmental language disorders to manifest specific academic disabilities when they enter school; hence, all of these specific developmental disorders bear some relation to each other and frequently occur together. The following case of Delano illustrates a situation in which a receptive developmental language disorder and a developmental reading disorder were concurrently diagnosed.

Specific developmental disorders are covered on Axis II of the DSM multi-axial system, since they are frequently found in conjunction with certain of the mental disorders identified on Axis I (such as anxiety or avoidance reactions). Moreover, in keeping with the other major group of disorders recorded on Axis II (personality disorders), developmental disorders convey a sense of being long-standing chronic conditions, in contrast to the often more dramatic and florid symptom patterns of Axis I disorders.

In Delano's case, a comprehensive psychological evaluation revealed evidence of specific developmental disorders affecting receptive language and reading ability (Chethik, 1986; Rabin, 1986). Although the child's problems became most obvious once he had started school, their origin could be traced to central nervous system impairment evidenced at a very early age by epileptic seizures.

The Case of Delano

Del was referred to a local psychology clinic for a series of tests to determine his overall ability level. Although 7 and a half years old, he was still in first grade, having failed his first time through. Del's parents could not understand his poor school performance and had thought that he possessed at least average intelligence. They described him as a quiet, well-mannered child who was well liked by classmates and teachers.

According to the developmental history supplied by the parents, Del, one of three children, was the product of a planned pregnancy and normal delivery. He was described as a "good baby" but manifested a series of medical problems, including allergies, ear infections, pneumonia, and psychomotor seizures—the last first diagnosed when Del was about 18 months old. At this time, both parents had noticed that Del would occasionally become preoccupied with the movement of his hands, and seem to withdraw from social contact, and take on a glassy-eyed stare. These episodes were reported as occurring before sleep or on first waking, then later began to occur during the day as well. According to the parents, Del's trance-like states could usually be interrupted by calling his name.

Shortly after these episodes began, Del was taken to the family pediatrician, who recommended a neurological examination. As part of the exam, an EEG recording was made. In this technique, small electrodes placed on various parts of the head are used to monitor electrical activity in brain tissue immediately underneath. Because certain characteristic brain-wave patterns emanate from various locations, any abnormalities are readily evident.

In Del's case, the EEG report indicated "mild dysrhythmia," with evidence of a "focal discharge" in the posterior region of the temporal lobe of the left hemisphere. That is, electrical activity in Del's brain was mildly irregular and was comparatively uncontrolled in one specific location. Numerous studies have demonstrated that this region of the brain plays a significant role in understanding speech and language. The presence of irregular electrical activity in this portion of Del's brain suggested that there may have been some disruption of brain structures involved in the ability to understand language. The seizure activity and the underlying irregular brain wave activity were subsequently controlled with a medication (Phenobarbitol), and at the time of the assessment, Del had not had a seizure in years. Nevertheless, it was apparent that the early brain trauma associated with the seizures somewhat curtailed his development of certain skills during the critical early formative years.

Thus, it was not surprising to discover that his speech and language skills developed slowly. He did not speak clearly until nearly age 3, and his parents reported that it was often necessary to repeat instructions endlessly, after which time there was still no guarantee that he would do what he had been told. At the age of 3, he was enrolled in a nursery school, where he displayed a behavior pattern characterized by a short attention span, low frustration tolerance, and social immaturity. This pattern continued into first grade. Despite attending a summer tutoring program before entering school, he did not do well in first grade, which he was repeating when the psychological assessment was made.

One of the most obvious things about Del was that he was a likable child. At the time the psychological testing was carried out, he proved easy to get along with and worked industriously if given clear structure. He was very attentive to task instructions but occasionally misunderstood the examiner, especially when asked to define words. For example, he confused the word *donkey* with *doggie* and repeated the word *diamond* several times, as if trying to form the memory of a word that he had never heard—yet he knew what a diamond was. It seemed that tasks such as word definitions gave Del the most problem; he did best on test items that provided many contextual cues that aided comprehension. It was characteristic of Del to adopt a rather passive—at times almost timid— stance toward testing. He was reluctant to ask that test questions be repeated, even when it was clear that he did not understand them.

In addition, he created the general impression of a somewhat shy child, less talkative than many children of similar age. As it turned out, Del had developed this style because of sensitivity about having to ask people to repeat things that he did not understand the first time; he felt that others thought him stupid. Indeed, several of the kids at school, with their unerring ability to focus on other children's weaknesses, had taken to calling him "Spaceman," because he seemed to be "out of it" a great deal of the time. Nonetheless, despite the reserve apparent in Del's behavior, he was appealing and likable.

The results of the psychological assessment revealed that Del did possess average intellectual skills and the overall mental ability needed to handle normal academic demands. Even this level was felt to be an underestimate of his actual potential, due to the language disturbance that inhibited the expression of intelligent behavior. Not surprisingly, the Wechsler Intelligence Scale for Children (WISC)–Revised, a standardized test of intellectual abilities, revealed that Del's verbal skills were less developed than his abilities that made use of nonverbal activity, such as visual-motor coordination. The examiner had access to Del's scores on the same test when it had been administered about one year earlier; it was significant to note that Del's language skills were not keeping pace with his development in other areas. One of the most significant results of the assessment revealed that Del's performance improved markedly whenever he was able to process test information visually. For example, he performed rather poorly on a vocabulary test in which the examiner read words for Del to define. His performance improved dramatically when vocabulary was assessed by having the examiner show Del pictures of objects or events and ask him to select those that corresponded to words read.

Performance on a number of the tests revealed that Del was quite adept at using contextual cues to obtain meaning from what was going on around him. In this regard, it was fascinating to find that, despite markedly subaverage performance on measures that evaluate basic reading skills (for example, word and letter identification and word comprehension), Del was able to read and comprehend passages in grade-school readers at nearly a second-grade level. It appeared that Del had developed a reading strategy in which he used contextual cues to understand much of what he read. For example, he appeared to search for familiar words in a passage and then to try to fit them together with words whose meaning he was unable to decipher. In the absence of such contextual cues, as when word comprehension was tested, he was at a considerable disadvantage because he was not able to sound words out effectively. (Word sounding is an invaluable skill that helps many readers in triggering acoustic memories that are associated with the visual images of words.) Del, in contrast, relied almost solely on visual cues to make sense out of what he read and was thereby clearly handicapped in his efforts to read all but those materials that were intimately familiar to him.

The overall results of the psychological assessment indicated that, despite possessing visual comprehension skills and reasoning abilities well in excess of his current grade level, Del manifested a significant deficit in auditory processing—specifically, in comprehension. It was found that Del required frequent repetitions of task instructions and items and that his ability to remember orally presented information for immediate recall was markedly below average.

The results of the assessment helped tie together a number of observations that had been made about Del. It became evident that his difficulty in comprehending spoken language went back a long way—to the early stages of his language development—and as a result may have reduced the amount of information about his surroundings that Del was able to assimilate. His difficulty in understanding others led him to become somewhat shy and withdrawn in social situations. He preferred to appear as if he understood what was going on rather than to risk peer censure (comments such as "Earth to Del, Earth to Del . . ."), which inevitably followed his attempts to have people repeat things. The language impairment became a real handicap when he entered school, where he was forced to repeat the first grade despite possessing average intelligence. He appeared to have developed moderately effective compensatory strategies in school-related areas, including the use of visual and other contextual cues. However, the numerous indications that receptive language development had not kept up with relatively normal development in other cognitive skills made this a prime target for remediation recommendations.

By way of summarizing these observations, the following diagnosis, using DSM-III terminology, was made:

Axis I: 313.21. Avoidant Disorder of Childhood
Axis II: 315.31. Developmental Language Disorder, receptive type
Axis III: Mild residual cerebral trauma, dominant temporal lobe seizures
Axis IV: Severity of psychosocial stressors: moderate
Axis V: Highest level of adaptive functioning, past year: Fair

Treatment

A number of specific recommendations were made to help Del overcome the effects of his language disability. First, it was recommended that he receive intensive training in the basic auditory encoding skills necessary for reading. For children who need work in this area, a format such as that provided by the television program *Sesame Street* is often quite effective—sounds are accompanied by visual representations in animated form. This format permitted Del to apply his visualization skills to aid him in such auditory encoding skills as word attack and comprehension. As he became more familiar with the basic sound combinations, the use of visual prompts was gradually phased out (Chethik, 1986; Sternberg and Owens, 1985).

Second, it was felt that Del should participate in second-grade reading classes, since his overall comprehension level was considerably in advance of his first-grade placement. It was felt that since much of the second-grade reading material used extensive pictorial cues, Del would be able to use these in understanding what he read. Moreover, as the additional training in auditory encoding began to have an effect, it was thought that his reading skills would increase even more. Efforts were also made to develop rewards for reading, including giving Del access to appropriate comic books and other texts that employed a lot of visual cues. Del's parents were encouraged to spend time with him going through magazines and other such materials, giving Del additional reading experience, as well as access to the modeling of adult reading behavior. (See Bandura [1978] for a good discussion on the powerful effects of modeling.)

An issue related to developmental language delays concerns Del's difficulty in organizing his approach to various tasks (Kegan, 1986). It is well known that much of our purposeful behavior is shaped and guided by language, and one of the outgrowths of early development is that language comes to play an increasingly significant role in regulating behavior (Broman, Bien, and Shaughnessy, 1985). Del's subaverage language skills had the result not only of cutting down on effective communication with others, but also of making it difficult for him to regulate his own behavior.

Children with this sort of problem profit from several strategies (Dangel and Polster, 1986; Barth, 1986). First, they learn from exposure to role models who provide visual cues regarding task performance and also talk their way through tasks, explaining each step in turn, with frequent repetitions. Second, it is often helpful to sit down with such children before beginning a new task and have them verbally rehearse the steps to be followed, while perhaps jotting them down either in written or pictorial form (Harris, 1986; Meichenbaum, 1977). Many situations existed both at school and at home where it was possible to build such routines into Del's daily activities. For example, his father began to work with Del on building plastic models and adopted an approach in which he would explain, rehearse, and demonstrate the sequences of necessary steps for Del as a means of helping him develop a more organized, less impulsive approach. Model-building soon became a favored activity and provided the basis for more emotional closeness between father and son.

If the list of recommendations seems extensive, it is because deficits in language skills have so many far-reaching implications that must be addressed in planning intervention (Kail and Pellegrino, 1985). In Del's case, every effort was made to keep him in a regular classroom to avoid further stigmatizing him. School officials and parents responded positively to the recommendations and were able to implement most of them without significantly altering Del's daily activities. Within six months, Del had shown marked improvement in basic reading skills and continued to do well in his second-grade reading class. His parents reported that he was becoming socially more responsive around other children and less defensive about his difficulties in understanding. At last report, he was doing well in school, and the administrators were considering a phased promotion plan that would permit Del to move into more advanced classes as his abilities permitted.

Comment

Del's development history was notable for the extensive array of medical symptoms, the most significant of which were the reported seizures. As described by his parents, they fit the description of temporal lobe seizures (also known as psychomotor seizures), which are characterized by (1) bizarre, episodic stereotyped movement patterns; (2) "phasing out" or clouding of consciousness during the seizure; and (3) partial or total inability to remember an event. EEG records of temporal lobe seizure activity commonly show irregularities in the anterior region of the temporal lobes on one or both sides of the cerebral cortex (Salmon and Meyer, 1986). The significance of this in Del's case lay in the site of the seizure activity and in the reported delays in language acquisition, because the area of the brain in which the seizures were triggered mediates much of the language acquisition process. The good prognosis for control and eventual elimination of seizure activity in young children would suggest that Del's language development may continue relatively unhindered from this point on and will eventually permit him to overcome the effects of the mild cerebral impairment, which apparently delayed his development of language skills. Lacking skills in this area, Del may have been at a disadvantage in nursery school, both in terms of verbal regulation of his own behavior and of engaging in interpersonal communication (Reisman, 1986).

Children who manifest early indications of biological vulnerability and developmental delays are often slow to develop socially and interpersonally (Broman, Bien, and Shaughnessy, 1985). They frequently feel somehow different from other children, though are often unable to articulate their concerns effectively (Kegan, 1986). Prompt recognition and treatment of conditions that compromise a child's development and contribute to the child's sense of psychological vulnerability assure the greatest potential for subsequent adequate adjustment. Del appears to have weathered more than his share of developmental problems, and consistent efforts by his parents to seek treatment appear to have helped him greatly in achieving a satisfactory level of adjustment.

REFERENCES

Bandura, A. (1978) *Social Learning Theory*. Englewood Cliffs, N.J.: Prentice-Hall.

Barth, R. (1986) *Social and Cognitive Treatment of Children and Adolescents*. San Francisco: Jossey-Bass.

Broman, S., Bien, E., and Shaughnessy, P. (1985) *Low Achieving Children: The First Seven Years*. Hillsdale, N.J.: Lawrence Erlbaum.

Chethik, M. (1986) Levels of borderline functioning in children: Etiological and treatment considerations. *American Journal of Orthopsychiatry*, *56*, 109–119.

Dangel, R. and Polster, R. (1986) *Teaching Child Management Skills*. New York: Pergamon.

Harris, K. (1986) The effects of cognitive-behavior modification on private speech and task performance during problem-solving among learning disabled and normally achieving children. *Journal of Abnormal Child Psychology*, *14*, 63–76.

Kail, R. and Pellegrino, J. (1985) *Human Intelligence*. New York: W. H. Freeman.

Kegan, R. (1986) The child behind the mask: Sociopathy as developmental delay. In W. Reid, D. Dorr, J. Walker, and J. Bonner (Eds.) *Unmasking the Psychopath*. New York: W. W. Norton.

Meichenbaum, D. (1977) *Cognitive Behavior Modification*. New York: Plenum.

Rabin, A. (1986) *Projective Techniques for Adolescents and Children*. New York: Springer.

Reisman, J. (1986) *Behavior Disorders in Infants, Children and Adolescents*. New York: Random House.

Rie, H. E., and Rie, E. D. (1980) *Handbook of Minimal Brain Dysfunctions: A Critical View*. New York: John Wiley.

Salmon, P. and Meyer, R. (1986) Neuropsychological assessment: Children. In M. Kurke and R. Meyer (Eds.) *Psychology in Product Liability and Personal Injury Law*. New York: Hemisphere.

Sternberg, L. and Owens, A. (1985) Establishing pre-language signaling behavior with profoundly mentally handicapped students. *Journal of Mental Deficiency Research*, *29*, 81–94.

/ *Attention Deficit Disorder and Hyperactivity*

The Case of Matt

> Children nowadays are tyrants. They contradict their parents, gobble their food, and tyrannize their teachers.
> — Socrates

The term *attention deficit disorder* (ADD) is used to describe a condition that involves the persisting inability to keep one's attention focused. Children with ADD are presumed to possess adequate basic cognitive capabilities, but they are typically unable to focus themselves effectively enough to get things done. DSM recognizes two forms of ADD: with or without hyperactivity. ADD with hyperactivity involves behavioral manifestations of attentional problems, including persisting symptoms of restlessness, fidgeting, and constant activity. An association between attentional processes and such motor activity has been suggested by recent work with both normal children (Waber, Mann, and Merola, 1985) and those with diagnosed ADD.

The current recognition of ADD in the DSM reflects the belief of physicians, teachers, and psychologists over the years that persisting problems in regulating both attentional processes and motor behavior comprise a distinct syndrome frequently seen in clinical settings (Rapport, 1983). Originally, terms such as *hyperactivity*, *hyperkinesis*, and *minimal brain dysfunction* were used to characterize the condition, which was believed to involve various forms of mild central nervous system (CNS) impairment. So strong was the association between excessive activity and underlying brain impairment that the corresponding diagnostic terms were used interchangeably for years. In practice, the nature of this deficit was seldom specified, owing to the wide range of disorders and conditions which may have hyperactivity as an associated symptom. This caused endless confusion among professionals, and considerable anxiety on the parts of parents whose children were labeled as having "minimal brain damage" or the "hyperkinetic syndrome."

More recent research, however, strongly suggests that neither attentional problems nor hyperactivity should *necessarily* be assumed to involve CNS damage. Because of these findings, the popularity in particular of the term "hyperactive" has declined. Its inclusion in the DSM as an auxiliary condition used only in conjunction with ADD is consistent with its diminished status from a distinctive diagnostic entity. Current research has amply documented the fact that genetic, physiological dysfunction, nutritional, motivational, social, and environmental factors all may play important roles in the regulation and allocation of attentional capabilities (Kirby and Grimley, 1986; Fogel, Mednick, and Michelsen, 1985; Bloomingdale, 1984).

It is interesting that the DSM has chosen to focus primarily on the attentional component of the disorder, rather than on the motoric aspect. As currently formulated, the diagnosis of hyperactivity would never be made by itself. Instead, it would be listed as an accompaniment to ADD. In practice, both are frequently found together.

Attentional capabilities obviously depend on the integrity of the CNS. In fact, the structures that regulate states of conscious alertness have been extensively studied (Filskov and Boll, 1986). These predominantly involve regions in the brain stem collectively referred to as the Reticular Activating System (RAS). It was hypothesized (Wender, 1973) that impaired attentional processes and/or excessive motor behavior patterns may involve an underactive RAS that does not perform its customary function of helping regulate and focus behavior. Evidence that such problems could successfully be treated in some overactive children through the use of medication which acted on the RAS has provided some support for this viewpoint (Barkley, 1981; Kinsbourne, 1979). Children who responded favorably to this form of treatment showed a paradoxical response: their behavior became more controlled following the administration of drugs that are *stimulants*. These chemical agents, of which Ritalin is perhaps best known, appear to stimulate the RAS to a level where it can exert its normal influence on attention and behavior. However, not all children with attentional problems or patterns of excess activity respond favorably to stimulants. For this reason, it is important to carry out a detailed assessment of any children referred for this problem.

Assessments of children with ADD in school and clinical settings have often been somewhat imprecise, in part because of the difficulty in specifying the criteria for "attention," and in determining just how active a child should be before being considered hyperactive. In recent years, however, a number of advances have been made in diagnostic procedures, resulting in more clearly defined and more stringent criteria for assessing the presence of ADD (Kirby and Grimley, 1986; Barkley, 1981). A number of questionnaires and rating scales have been devised, with the Conners teacher and parent hyperactivity rating scales (Goyette, Conners, and Ulrich, 1978) being among the most popular.

Current assessment practices, however, go beyond simple behavioral ratings. A thorough assessment (Salmon and Meyer, 1986; Wallander and Conger, 1981) includes an evaluation of the following factors: (1) the child's overall behavioral repertoire and patterns of interactions with the environment; (2) patterns of motor activity: and (3) how the child typically approaches and works through tasks. Frequently, by the time an evaluation has been completed, a child with attentional problems may have been assessed by pediatricians, teachers, psychologists, and parents. Each of these individuals has a specific perspective on the child's behavior that must be taken into account in designing appropriate intervention strategies (Rapport, 1983).

The Case of Matt

It was not until Matt was nearing the end of first grade that his inattention and poor concentration became apparent. He was a bright child, according to the results of school-readiness testing, and began the year with predictions of great accomplishments. At first, he seemed to live up to his promise, but as the months passed he seemed to have persistent difficulty absorbing new information and finishing his daily lessons. His teacher felt that, from the outset, he had been considerably more active than his classmates, but attributed this to a high level of curiosity that constantly led him into new undertakings.

At home, Matt had never really been considered a problem child. The second of five children, he had grown up in a family that encouraged independence and imposed minimal constraints on the children's behavior. As a result, he was not watched especially closely by his parents, but was instead encouraged to develop his own interests and keep himself occupied. With four other children, the level of ongoing activity was rather high, and Matt's behavior did not seem markedly atypical by his parents' standards.

The problem at school involved the fact that Matt found it extremely difficult to focus his attention on his work. Moreover, he seemed to be restless and physically agitated a good deal of the time. Accustomed as he was to working on things that interested him, and at a pace that suited his somewhat high-strung temperament, Matt found it quite difficult to work under the constraints imposed by his teacher at school. He seemed to fidget constantly in his seat, was easily distracted by things going on around him, and seldom completed his assignments on time. Because his behavior was not especially disruptive to others, it initially received little attention. But after the first few months of school, his teacher had become aware that the quality of his work consistently failed to measure up to the standards she felt were reasonable, based on his aptitude test scores.

By the end of the first grading period after Christmas, Matt was passing all his academic subjects, but received several "unsatisfactory" ratings in such areas as "Paying Attention," "Completing Work on Time," "General Work Habits," and "Ability to Work Independently." His parents were surprised and puzzled by these comments, since they had always seen Matt as someone who could occupy himself for hours at a time. A meeting with Matt's teacher achieved no particular resolution, mostly because it was difficult to specify precisely just what Matt needed to do in order to work more effectively. His teacher did suggest that Matt have a physical examination, however, since she felt that his restlessness might have a physical basis.

Matt's physical health had been generally good throughout his early development. His mother's pregnancy was free of major complications, and though the labor had been difficult, he was born without incident. He was sometimes colicky as an infant and seemed more demanding than her other children had been. She viewed him as more active than the other children right from the start and recalled that his attention was constantly being diverted from one thing to another. This did not create any particular problems at home, because the children were given considerable freedom to do as they pleased. Moreover, routine physical examinations had uncovered no major health problems. Thus, the first real suggestion that anything might be amiss did not occur until after Matt had started school.

Matt's pediatrician once again found him to be in basically good health, though on the basis of the teacher's report and his own observations he felt that the boy's behavior might warrant a consideration of "hyperactivity." He explained to Matt's parents that hyperactivity was a condition that could develop from any number of causes, and was difficult to definitively diagnose. He explained further that some children who are excessively active respond well to certain stimulant medications that have a paradoxical calming effect. Until Matt's behavior was evaluated more precisely, however, the pediatrician was reluctant to prescribe the medication. He recommended that Matt be evaluated by a clinical psychologist in private practice and that a decision regarding medication be postponed until the assessment was completed.

Matt's parents were perplexed and somewhat upset by the unclear definition of Matt's problems. They were also distressed by the apparent insinuation that Matt's problems might have a psychological basis. Despite these reservations, they proceeded with the recommendation and had the evaluation. Matt and his parents were seen by the clinical psychologist, who saw the entire family together as a unit after an initial interview with the parents. She also carried out basic psychological testing on Matt, using tests designed to assess general mental abilities, school achievement levels, work habits, and basic personality dimensions. Finally, she visited Matt's school to observe his reported problems firsthand.

The results of the assessment suggested that Matt had greater difficulty than most children in sustaining concentration and attention. In addition, his typical activity level at school appeared markedly in excess of the other children.

Evidence came from several sources. First, Matt's performance on a standard IQ test (the Wechsler Intelligence Scale for Children–Revised) showed an overall above-average level of performance, but relatively poor performance on a group of component measures that collectively form a "Freedom from Distractibility" factor. Each of these tests demands sustained, careful attention to a fairly complex task, an undertaking that was beyond Matt's powers of concentration. On the remaining portions of the Wechsler IQ scale, Matt's performance was at a level indicating above average general abilities. Further testing revealed that, though he possessed sufficient basic academic skills to master the demands of his schoolwork, Matt seemed at a loss in controlling the process of analyzing the various parts of any complex task and working systematically toward a solution.

Classroom observations by the psychologist tended to corroborate the test data. Matt's work habits were observed during a number of different classes throughout one morning. It soon became apparent that when left by himself, he seemed unable to work out and stick to a plan for getting his work done. He dawdled, played with objects in his desk, looked around the room, and accomplished very little during the study time allotted him. Some part of his body seemed to be perpetually in motion, even during rest periods when many of the other children were napping.

The available information suggested that Matt's inattentive behavior fit the DSM criterion for an ADD with hyperactivity. It was stressed to Matt's parents that he was a child of above average abilities, whose problems involved chiefly his manner of approaching tasks and an excessively high level of activity. The psychologist developed a program for Matt's teacher and parents designed to help him focus his attention on tasks more effectively. She also referred the parents to the pediatrician for a trial use of Ritalin, which was to be used in conjunction with an activity rating form completed daily by the teacher.

Treatment

The intervention program for Matt involved elements of both behavioral and cognitive approaches. Relaxation training was helpful for the hyperactivity (Raymer and Poppen, 1985). However, basic to the treatment was a technique of teaching Matt to "talk to himself" as a means of keeping his attention focused on a particular task (Fisher and Wollersheim, 1986; Santostefano, 1985). This involved active demonstrations of on-task behavior in which the therapist performed an activity while describing exactly what she needed to do each step of the way. The goal was to provide Matt with a model of effective verbal problem-solving strategies. At first, his tendency was to ignore the instructions and to work inconsistently as he had habitually done. But gradually, through a combination of judiciously selected activities and an animated, often humorous style of verbal modeling, the therapist succeeded in capturing Matt's attention and engaging his participation.

One activity that he particularly enjoyed was assembling model autos and trucks. Normally he worked so quickly and haphazardly that the finished product bore little resemblance to its namesake. With the therapist's assistance, Matt learned to slow his pace, plan each step in advance, gather the necessary materials before starting, and work at a slow, steady pace. At the outset, the therapist had him talk himself through each step before actually doing anything. There were many occasions at first when she either had to prompt him directly or else remind him to prompt himself. Gradually, the use of language as a task mediator became more habitual, to the point that Matt was able to work systematically without having to say anything at all.

This procedure was combined with a behavioral program at school in which Matt was issued periodic rewards for staying in his seat and working on his assignments (Dangel and Polster, 1986). The combination of these techniques achieved the basic goal of engaging Matt's attention more consistently than before. More importantly, his added powers of concentration contributed to a demonstrable improvement in his work quality. As this occurred, the satisfaction derived from good schoolwork provided a source of intrinsic motivation which further engaged his interest.

In a matter of weeks he had made considerable gains in three important areas: First, he became much more effective at planning and monitoring his work. Second, his ability to work both productively and independently improved markedly. Third, his overall grades improved to the point where his performance was beginning to approach the potential his parents and teachers knew he possessed. In addition to these gains, Matt's motor activity diminished somewhat as a result of the Ritalin. He was described by his teacher as somewhat calmer, but fortunately seemed to have lost none of the curiosity and alertness that characterized his behavior.

Comment

Matt's situation is one that is commonly experienced by young schoolchildren. "Paying attention" is a skill that is generally taken for granted, but one which is much too important to go unevaluated (Dangel and Polster, 1986). Matt did not lack basic intelligence; rather, he was unable to harness it effectively to get things done at school. Having been raised without many rules and regulations, he had perhaps never really learned effective work habits. He was adept at entertaining himself while alone, but had never cultivated the sorts of verbal skills that have such a powerful influence on learning.

In terms of the underlying etiology, no single specific factor came to light, though in many similar cases genetic or birth defects appear to be causal (Fogel, Mednick, and Michelsen, 1985; Bloomingdale, 1984). It did appear that, in their effort to let their children be independent of adult authority, Matt's parents may have erred somewhat by not providing effective role models. At school, observation confirmed that off-task behavior earned Matt considerable attention from the teacher, who left him alone at other times. This undoubtedly served to reinforce subtly his distractible tendencies. Underlying these factors appears to have been a temperament characterized by high levels of energy and activity, which can sometimes get in the way of effective channeling of concentration. Temperament factors, reflecting inborn metabolic and physiological characteristics, may at least create a vulnerability for disorders such as ADD (Kirby and Grimley, 1986; Kinsbourne, 1979). In Matt's case, the hyperactive behavior may have stemmed from biologically based temperament factors; his medical examination turned up no indications of an underlying neurological disorder.

One problem that did crop up involved the difficulty of getting the treatment effect to generalize from school to other daily activities. Generalization of treatment effects are sometimes difficult to achieve, and require consistent follow-through by those engaged in the therapeutic program (Hobbs, Moguin, Tyroler, and Lahey, 1980). In Matt's case, careful coordination by the psychologist with the parents, teacher, and pediatrician helped ensure that everyone involved was fully aware of the stated goals and the techniques being used. This provides a good example of effective treatment planning (Rapport, 1983).

This case illustrates the effective application of a "multi-modal" intervention program. (See also the case of Roger). A combination of psychological and medical procedures was employed to treat a problem that, years ago, probably would have been diagnosed and treated exclusively from a medical standpoint. Viewing problems such as ADD from a broader perspective that encompasses both psychological and physical factors makes it feasible to consider a wide range of intervention techniques, each of which makes a unique contribution to the problem's solution.

REFERENCES

Barkley, R. (1981) *Hyperactive Children: A Handbook for Diagnosis and Treatment*. New York: Guilford.

Bloomingdale, L. (Ed.) (1984) *Attention Deficit Disorder*. Jamaica, N.Y.: SP Medical and Scientific Books.

Dangel, R. and Polster, R. (1986) *Teaching Child Management Skills*. New York: Pergamon.

Filskov, S. and Boll, T. (1986) *Handbook of Clinical Neuropsychology* (Vol. 2). New York: John Wiley.

Fisher, D. and Wollersheim, J. (1986) Social reinforcement: A treatment component in verbal self-instructional training. *Journal of Abnormal Child Psychology, 14,* 41–48.

Fogel, C., Mednick, S., and Michelsen, N. (1985) Hyperactive behavior and minor physical abnormalities. *Acta Psychiatrica Scandinavica, 72,* 551–556.

Goyette, C., Conners, C., and Ulrich, R. (1978) Normative data on revised Conners parent and teacher rating scales. *Journal of Abnormal Child Psychology, 6,* 221–238.

Hobbs, S., Moguin, L., Tyroler, M., and Lahey, B. (1980) Cognitive behavior therapy with children: Has clinical utility been demonstrated? *Psychological Bulletin, 87,* 147–165.

Kinsbourne, M. (1979) Models of hyperactivity: Implications for diagnosis and treatment. In R. L. Trites (Ed.) *Hyperactivity in Children: Etiology, Measurement, and Treatment Implications*. Baltimore: University Park Press.

Kirby, E. and Grimley, L. (1986) *Understanding and Treating Attention Deficit Disorder*. New York: Pergamon.

Rapport, M. (1983) Attention deficit disorder with hyperactivity: Critical treatment parameters and their application in applied outcome research. In M. Hersen, R. M. Eisler, and P. M. Miller (Eds.) *Progress in Behavior Modification* (Vol. 14). New York: Academic Press.

Raymer, R. and Poppen, R. (1985) Behavioral relaxation training with hyperactive children. *Journal of Behavior Therapy and Experimental Psychiatry, 16*, 309–316.

Salmon, P. and Meyer, R. (1986) Neuropsychological assessment: Adults. In M. Kurke and R. Meyer (Eds.), *Psychology in Product Liability and Personal Injury Law*. New York: Hemisphere.

Santostefano, S. (1985) *Cognitive Control Therapy with Children and Adolescents*. New York: Pergamon.

Waber, D., Mann, M., and Merola, J. (1985) Motor overflow and attentional processes in normal school-age children. *Developmental Medicine and Child Neurology, 27(4)*, 491–497.

Wallander, J. and Conger, J. (1981) Assessment of hyperactive children: Psychometric, methodological, and practical considerations. In M. Hersen, R. M. Eisler, and P. M. Miller (Eds.) *Progress in Behavior Modification* (Vol. 11), pp. 250–291. New York: Academic Press.

Wender, P. (1973) *The Hyperactive Child: A Handbook for Parents*. New York: Crown.

Early Infantile Autism

The Case of Audrey

> We are all born mad. Some of us remain so.
> — Samuel Beckett
> *Waiting for Godot*

Infantile autism is a pervasive, debilitating disorder having its onset prior to 30 months of age. The term *autistic* connotes a failure to relate effectively to one's environment. People described as autistic are viewed as being absorbed in a private world of their own that is inaccessible to others. Historically, the term was used by Bleuler to describe one of the cardinal symptoms of schizophrenia. However, it has since been associated with other forms of psychopathology, most notably with the pattern of disturbed behavior in childhood first described by Leo Kanner in the 1940s and named "early infantile autism" (Kanner, 1943). The children studied by Kanner manifested a pattern of detachment that made effective communication all but impossible.

Detailed studies of these children have revealed a number of additional symptoms as well, including emotional withdrawal, cognitive impairments, and unusual behavioral mannerisms. Among the latter, echolalia and self-stimulation are especially notable. Children with echolalia continuously repeat words and phrases uttered by another person, making effective communication all but impossible. Self-stimulation, another common characteristic of children with autism, may take several forms. A child may sit for hours waving a hand in front of his or her face, transfixed by the movement. Other children engage in more destructive behaviors, such as head-banging, pinching, or biting themselves. Observations of such behaviors has led to the suggestion that autistic children are especially sensitive to what is termed *proximal* stimulation, which is very tangible and immediate. They are less responsive to *distal* stimulation, which emanate from sources that are more remote (such as the sound of someone speaking from a distance of several feet).

In terms of cognitive functioning, autistic children are frequently found to possess isolated "splinter skills" within a broader context of impaired mental functioning. Splinter skills refer to isolated capabilities possessed by autistic children which in some instances are developed to exceptionally high levels. Mathematical, artistic, and various other skills have all been found in autistic children whose behavior is otherwise globally impaired.

Kanner's work with autism led him to believe that the disorder was essentially the result of severe emotional deprivation. He noted that the parents of these children seemed in general to be intellectually and analytically oriented, while lacking in emotional warmth. The term "icebox parent" resulted from characterizations such as this and fostered the impression that autism was essentially an acquired condition. According to this theory, the unremitting exposure to non-nurturing parents brought about progressive withdrawal from the world and increasing self-absorption.

In retrospect, it is unclear whether this conclusion was erroneous, being the result of biased sampling procedures (Schopler and Mesibov, 1985; Schopler, 1983). In actuality, there is a great deal of diversity among parents of children with autism with respect to intellectual capabilities and emotional qualities. The most telling criticism of this theory comes from increasing evidence that symptoms of autism are in fact present *at birth* in the form of neurological and related abnormalities (Fisch et al., 1986; Colman and Gilberg, 1985; Ornitz and Ritvo, 1976). This in turn suggests that parental aloofness, when present, reflects essentially a defensive reaction to a child whose behavior is atypical and frequently characterized by unresponsiveness.

Autism is treated within the DSM system as one of the disorders of infancy, childhood, or adolescence. It is categorized as a pervasive developmental disorder, and is identified by the diagnostic term infantile autism. The onset must be prior to 30 months, which in part distinguishes infantile autism from another DSM category, childhood onset pervasive developmental disorder. The major characteristics of infantile autism include (1) unresponsiveness to others, (2) grossly impaired language development, and (3) bizarre responses to the environment.

Differential Diagnosis. Autism has often been confused with schizophrenia (see Chapter 6) and especially with mental retardation. The term *schizophrenia* in reference to young children is not used in the DSM classification system. Instead, a diagnosis of childhood onset pervasive developmental disorder is made based on evidence of profoundly disturbed social relationships, multiple manifestations of odd behavior, and onset after 30 months but before 12 years of age. Unlike autism, this condition is presumed to develop in early childhood and may result from extreme psychosocial trauma. Typically, a period of relatively normal development is followed by either a gradual or sudden deterioration in adaptive behavior.

Mental Retardation

A comparison of infantile autism and mental retardation reveals several points of contrast. A fundamental difference concerns the scope of the two terms. Whereas autism involves a very specific behavioral syndrome, the term *mental retardation* encompasses a descriptive classification system with many variations. Mental retardation (MR), characterized by impaired intellectual and social skills, is a condition that may be associated with a variety of psychological disorders, and may stem from a wide range of psychological, physiological (Kail and Pellegrino, 1985; Plomin, 1986; Barrett, 1986), and genetic causes (Colman and Gilberg, 1985).

A diagnosis of MR is based on evidence of impaired intellectual and social functioning, with an onset before age 18. Unlike autism, MR is classified according to severity, based on the following groups:

Mild MR, the largest subgroup, is associated with IQ scores between 50 and 70. Individuals in this category are referred to as "educably mentally handicapped," and comprise approximately 80 percent of all retarded persons. Many acquire sixth- or seventh-grade academic skills by the time they reach middle adolescence.

Moderate MR encompasses IQ scores from 35 to 49, and represents approximately 12 percent of the MR population. People in this group require at least moderate supervision, and seldom progress beyond a third-grade achievement level.

Severe MR (IQ range 21–23) comprises about 7 percent of the total population. People in this group generally do not benefit from vocational training, though they usually learn elementary self-care skills.

Profound MR (IQ below 20) designates a small subgroup of individuals who invariably show accompanying signs of significant physical and/or neurological impairment.

Persons whose intellectual functioning falls above these levels but below the normal range (that is, from 71 to 84) are given a diagnosis of "borderline intellectual functioning," provided there is evidence of impaired social adjustment.

The Case of Audrey

Audrey was born a full-term infant, her parent's third child. She was a beautiful baby, whose exquisitely delicate features were cause for endless comment by her family, relatives, and the hospital staff. However, shortly after Audrey's birth, her mother began to worry that her daughter was not as responsive as her previous children. Audrey did not respond to being held like most children; rather than "molding" herself when cradled in her mother's arms, she was stiff and rigid. This made nursing a significant problem, and it was not long before she was weaned to a bottle because of the tension and inconvenience involved in feeding her.

Audrey's physical development appeared to advance at a somewhat accelerated pace, at least in terms of basic motor skills. However, she did not seem to vocalize as consistently as most children, and it was difficult to engage her in the sort of make-believe baby talk that is so much a part of early parent/child interactions. Despite reassurances from the pediatrician that Audrey's language was merely delayed, her parents felt that the problem went deeper.

As the months passed, their concerns increased. It proved extremely difficult to toilet train Audrey, largely because she seemed unwilling or unable to follow even simple instructions. Frequently, she would parrot instructions or phrases verbatim, repeating them continuously in a sing-song rhythm. Even getting her attention proved difficult, since she tended to either avoid eye contact or else direct her gaze in such a way that anyone holding her would feel that she was looking through them.

One afternoon, her mother found Audrey sitting on the nursery floor staring at her left hand, which she dangled before her eyes and shook at a rapid pace. When she tried to intervene, Audrey resisted her attempts and began to cry loudly. Nothing her mother could do appeased the child, who eventually returned to her place on the floor and continued to play with her hands.

Audrey made no friends during this time. She seemed frightened by nearly any changes in her customary routine, including the presence of strange people. She tended either to shrink from contact with other children or avoid them altogether, seemingly content to play by herself for hours at a time. Efforts to introduce her to other children in the presence of an emotionally supportive adult were unsuccessful, and she showed no inclination whatsoever to seek out contact with either children or adults.

She scrupulously maintained her toys and other possessions in precise arrangements. She initially shared a room with an older sister, but was so particular about the placement of various objects that it was not long before she was given a small room of her own right next to her parents. Here she spent hours each day arranging and rearranging things, staring at her hand, gesturing and making incoherent sounds, and occasionally running around the room, whirling herself in circles.

Realizing that Audrey's behavior was becoming increasingly unmanageable, her parents had a thorough physical and psychological evaluation conducted at the local medical school. Their experiences with Audrey during the preceding two years prepared them somewhat for the results of the evaluations, but it still came as a shock when they were told that Audrey's condition was diagnosed as infantile autism.

They were put in touch with a nearby school for children with serious psychological handicaps, administered by the local board of education. During their initial visit, they were surprised to see a number of other children very much like Audrey. Virtually all of the children manifested significant communication difficulties, and there was little if any contact between them. The staff members worked both individually and in small groups with the children, using techniques reflecting a behavioral approach. Token reinforcers were everywhere. They were used as rewards to painstakingly shape verbal responses to questions, to reward socially appropriate behavior, and to acknowledge the childrens' efforts in doing seat work. To Audrey's parents, the school appeared to tolerate a great deal of noise, confusion, and disorder. But as they became more familiar with the setting, they began to realize that the needs of each child were so diversified that highly individualized treatment plans were needed, and that, at least for part of the day, children worked at a great many activities either singly or in small groups.

Audrey was enrolled in the school, which prepared a detailed treatment plan. Initially, emphasis was placed on helping her develop some basic self-care skills and to learn rudimentary communication skills. Her parents were instructed in the techniques employed by the staff, and were invited to participate in a parenting group run by the staff for parents of severely disabled children. Great care was taken to make them feel as though they were an integral part of the treatment program, and a staff psychologist spoke with them on occasion to help alleviate their unfounded fears that they were directly responsible for their daughter's condition.

Audrey made slow but perceptible progress in the program. Language development was targeted as a primary treatment goal, and she was immediately assigned to a staff member who held several daily sessions with her, working on basic skills like naming and identifying people and common objects. At first, a great deal of effort was required simply to capture her attention for a few seconds. Eventually, a combination of simple directives (such as "Audrey, look at me now") and both primary and verbal reinforcers achieved the desired effect. Once this was achieved, it was possible to draw Audrey's attention to other features of the environment and help her begin to identify them.

Audrey's treatment involved other activities as well. Toilet training and personal hygiene were stressed from the beginning, and Audrey's parents were enlisted to help with a behaviorally based program that was employed both at school and at home to train these skills. Social skills training comprised yet another aspect of the program, as it did for most other children at Audrey's level of development. Once she had begun to establish something of a relationship with the staff member who was teaching her language skills, another child was introduced into their interactions for a brief period each day. Initially, the children ignored each other, or became irritated if one was deprived of attention in favor of the other. Gradually, however, transactions began to take place between the two, initially in response to highly specific prompting by the staff worker.

Audrey's stay in the program was characterized by periods of significant progress and regression. By the end of the first year, she had a working vocabulary of between eighty and one hundred words, largely nouns, that she was beginning to use spontaneously. She did not speak in sentences, but gestured and used individual words on occasion to make her intentions known. Her use of language was characteristically that of a younger child, who basically uses single words to name things and telegraphs his or her intentions using gestures and simple vocal expressions.

In other areas, Audrey made more limited progress. Toilet training proceeded quite slowly, in part because of minor neuromuscular abnormalities that were detected on a neuropediatric examination. Social skills training eventually made it possible for Audrey to greet and attend to several very familiar members of the staff and her family. However, her lack of effective communication skills coupled with an ability to entertain herself alone for hours at a time made it difficult to engage her in interactions with others in any but a highly routinized manner.

Audrey was at her best when making drawings. Quite by accident, she was discovered to have notable artistic talent, and a number of her scribbled drawings suggested a maturation level several years in advance of her age. Her favorite subject was cats, which she drew in a variety of shapes, sizes, and poses. She seemed fascinated with small animals, and would attempt to keep the family cat captive during her long periods of solitary play. She did not really play with the animal, but would hold and pet it in a rote, mechanical manner while it tried to escape. It was after one of these exchanges that she had picked up a pencil and drawn the head of a cat in a surprisingly detailed manner.

By the time she was 5, Audrey had made a significant number of advances, although she was never able to enter into a regular school program. Her working vocabulary continued to increase somewhat, though she retained the telegraphic style of communication that had been characteristic of her earlier.

Comment

Audrey's case is not unusual as far as the syndrome of autism is concerned (Schopler and Mesibov, 1985; Schopler, 1983; Ornitz and Ritvo, 1976). Despite making reasonable progress, she was left permanently with problematic language and social skills that made it impossible for her to participate in regular classroom settings. The treatment she received is characteristic of many current programs, which blend features of milieu and behavioral therapies in their activity programs (Barrett, 1986; Schopler and Mesibov, 1986; Lovaas and Koegel, 1973). The procedure for shaping basic language skills has been extensively developed with a behavioral paradigm in which the work of Ivar Lovaas is best known (Lovaas and Koegel, 1973). More recent work in this area has begun to bridge the gap between simple linguistic skills like naming and more complex communication skills (Schopler and Mesibov, 1985).

A significant shift in attitudes toward the causes of autism has occurred in recent years. No longer are parents made to feel as though they are responsible for their children's aberrant behavior. The preponderance of recent research data points to either prenatal or genetic factors as likely explanations for the condition (Colman and Gilberg, 1985; Fisch et al., 1986; Plomin, 1986). As early as 1964, specific types of brain damage were being hypothesized as being the cause of autism (Rimland, 1964). Because of this, parents with autistic children are nowadays much more likely to become involved in collaborative treatment efforts with professional staff members (Schopler and Reichler, 1971).

Despite advances in these and related areas, both the precise nature and definitive treatment of infantile autism remain elusive. It remains a debilitating disorder, afflicting children at so early an age that the usual forms of stimulation that shape normal development seem to have little impact. Audrey's parents took great pride in her progress at school, but were all too aware that their child was markedly different from most others and would probably never be truly free of her impairments.

REFERENCES

Barrett, R. (Ed.) (1986) *Severe Behavior Disorders in the Mentally Retarded*. New York: Plenum.

Colman, M. and Gilberg, C. (1985) *Development, Genetics, and Psychology*. New York: Praeger.

Fisch, G., Cohen, I., Wolf, E., Brown, W., et al. (1986) Autism and the fragile X syndrome. *American Journal of Psychiatry, 143*, 71–73.

Kail, R. and Pellegrino, J. (1985) *Human Intelligence*. New York: W. H. Freeman.

Kanner, L. (1943) Autistic disturbances of affective content. *Nervous Child, 2*, 217–240.

Lovaas, O. I. and Koegel, R. (1973) Behavior therapy with autistic children. In C. Thorenson (Ed.), *Behavior Modification and Education*. Chicago: University of Chicago Press.

Ornitz, E. M. and Ritvo, E. R. (1976) The syndrome of autism: A critical review. *American Journal of Psychiatry, 133(6)*, 609–621.

Plomin, R. (1986) *Development, Genetics, and Psychology*. Hillsdale, N.J.: Lawrence Erlbaum.

Rimland, B. (1964) *Infantile Autism*. New York: Appleton-Century-Crofts.

Schopler, E. (1983) New developments in the diagnosis and definition of autism. In B. B. Lahey and A. E. Kazdin (Eds.), *Advances in Clinical Child Psychology* (Vol. 6), pp. 93–127. New York: Plenum.

Schopler, E. and Mesibov, G. (Eds.) (1985) *Communication Problems in Autism*. New York: Plenum.

Schopler, E. and Reichler, R. J. (1971) Parents as co-therapists in the treatment of psychotic children. *Journal of Autism and Childhood Schizophrenia, 1*, 87–102.

Separation Anxiety Associated with School Refusal

The Case of Julie

To be adult is to be alone.
— Jean Rostand
Thoughts of a Biologist

The term *separation anxiety* was first coined by Johnson and his associates in 1941 to describe the acute distress and attachment behavior exhibited by some children when separating from their mothers to go to school. In more current use, the term refers to a more general disorder of childhood in which excessive anxiety occurs when a child is separated from major attachment figures or from home and other familiar surroundings. Anxiety reactions may range from displays of anger and protest to symptoms of panic. Discussions in the clinical literature suggest that the disorder is fairly common, with approximately equal prevalence among boys and girls, and that children are initially seen in treatment for a variety of problems, including somatic complaints, sleep disorder, disrupted peer relationships, excessive fears, low school achievement, and school refusal (Broman, Bien, and Shaughnessy, 1985; Breit, 1982).

The DSM outlines the range of symptoms generally associated with separation anxiety, many of which directly reflect fears of separation and loss. These children frequently experience discomfort when they travel away from home and may display "clinging" behaviors around their parents, following them closely about the house and holding onto them excessively when in public. When separated from parents or other attachment figures, the children often become obsessed with fears of accidents or illnesses befalling themselves or significant others. These fears may be expressed openly and verbally or may be apparent in nightmares and fantasies. Sometimes fears are displaced onto animals, strangers, or surroundings (Bowlby, 1982; Breit, 1982).

Sleep disorders, including nightmares and sleep terror, are frequently associated with separation anxiety, and children may experience great difficulty falling asleep alone and require that someone, usually a parent, be with them when they fall asleep. Somatic complaints are also common in this disorder and may range from headaches to dizziness to stomachaches and nausea. Typically, these symptoms arise in response to separation or the threat of separation, and may be associated with other symptoms of anxiety.

The relationship between separation anxiety and school first described by Johnson et al. (1941) remains an important one, and symptoms of "school phobia" are often associated with separation anxiety and in some cases may precipitate referral for treatment. Refusal or reluctance to go to school often accompanies separation anxiety, though the use of the term "school phobia" to describe these children is frequently misapplied. Whereas simple phobias refer to anxiety responses associated with specific stimuli, such as school, and typically involve otherwise stable personalities, disorders such as separation anxiety and agoraphobia generally suggest more deep-seated personality disorders and are characterized by an overlay of symptoms, which may include generalized anxiety, depression, and somatic complaints. For the child experiencing separation anxiety, it is usually not the stimulus of school from which she retreats that is of clinical significance, but the attachment to parents or others that she seeks. Thus, "school phobia" is a misnomer when applied to children experiencing separation anxiety associated with refusal or reluctance to attend school, and "school refusal" is generally more appropriate.

The clinical literature is in substantial agreement regarding the personalities and behaviors of children with separation anxiety and their parents (Bowlby, 1982; Breit, 1982; Eisenberg, 1958). With the exception of the symptoms associated with the disorder, these children are generally well-behaved, though they often appear shy, overly anxious, and socially inhibited (Ziller and Rorer, 1985). Families are usually intact, with close relationships between parent(s) and children, and family members have often not experienced long or frequent separations from home. A clear distinction can be drawn between these children and conduct disorder children who may also refuse to attend school or other activities, but typically come from highly unstable families with a long history of separations. Whereas conduct disorder children characteristically do not stay home when truant and engage in a variety of antisocial behaviors, the school refuser is generally quiet and cooperative once in school and may not exhibit emotional or behavioral symptoms when separated from parents.

The problem of school refusal may appear to be clear and straightforward when first addressed in treatment. Yet, the dynamics of separation anxiety are often deeply enmeshed in a larger family context and may involve a variety of issues of clinical significance, as is the case of Julie, described here.

The Case of Julie

Julie P., an 8-year-old second-grader, was court-referred for outpatient treatment because of school truancy. During her first year in school, Julie had refused to enter her classroom without her mother and would scream and throw herself on the floor if her mother tried to leave her at school. As a result, Mrs. P. accompanied Julie to her classroom each day and would stay with her for the remainder of the morning. If Mrs. P. tried to leave the classroom, Julie would again throw her "mad fits," and only Mrs. P. was able to calm her. Because Mrs. P. held a job during the afternoon, she devised a plan in which she would accompany Julie to the lunchroom, and leave her when she was eating her lunch. Although Julie resisted this with screams and anger at first, she gradually became accustomed to it, and this pattern was maintained for the remainder of the school year. In her mother's absence during the afternoons, Julie was generally well-behaved, though she was extremely shy and interacted little with the other children. She also consistently refused to complete any schoolwork without her mother.

In second grade, Julie's teacher would not allow Mrs. P. to remain with Julie in the classroom, and when Mrs. P. protested to the school principal, she supported the teacher's decision. Following this, Julie began to miss an excessive number of days in school for a variety of somatic complaints, including headaches, nausea, and stomachaches. When the school insisted that the child be seen by a doctor, the doctor reported no apparent physical basis for her problems and the school insisted that she take the school bus each day and maintain regular attendance. Although Mrs. P. reported that she tried to force Julie to take the school bus, Julie refused to do so for fear that it would crash, and her attendance did not improve.

After numerous attempts were unsuccessful to encourage Mrs. P. to force Julie to go to school, the school filed a truancy petition with the court. In accordance with an Alternative to Court Program, a caseworker was assigned to the family to assess the situation and to monitor Julie's attendance. When her attendance did not improve, the case was brought to court and on the recommendation of the caseworker, Julie was ordered to attend school and Mrs. P. was ordered to seek treatment for her.

During intake, a number of clinical symptoms were reported, along with school refusal, to suggest a diagnosis of separation anxiety. Julie was plagued with obsessive ruminations of catastrophe befalling her mother, her grandmother, or herself, and she frequently personalized news stories, fearing that whatever disaster or tragedy was reported on the television news would soon befall the P. family. She also reported ongoing fears of begin kidnapped or killed in a motor vehicle accident, such as a school bus crash.

In addition to these conscious fears, Julie experienced terrifying nightmares on a regular basis in which she or another family member would mysteriously disappear, become lost, or be killed. Typically, she would awake from these dreams in a panic state, and as a consequence she reported a great fear of sleeping and insisted that sleep was not very important anyway. Because of her fears, Julie refused to sleep alone, and as a result she slept occasionally with her 11-year-old brother, Gary, though more often with Mrs. P. accompanying her to bed.

As noted earlier, Julie also experienced a variety of somatic complaints which became exacerbated at the threat of separation from her mother or her home and were generally most severe on school mornings. Samples of Julie's somatic complaints, as well as her "mad fits," in which she would shriek, cry, and bang her hands on the floor and table, were observed on several occasions at the clinic when her mother was encouraged to leave her for brief periods of time. Once separated, Julie would regain her composure, sometimes dramatically, though she would generally remain withdrawn and unable to concentrate on tasks for more than a few moments.

A series of family interviews revealed a number of significant events in the history of the P. family, though only Gary was willing to discuss these in any detail, with Julie and Mrs. P. more likely to argue about issues such as Julie's clothes or Mrs. P.'s mother, who had been living with the P. family for the past three years.

Mr. and Mrs. P. were divorced when Julie was 4 and Gary 7, with Mrs. P. retaining custody of both children. Shortly after the divorce, when Julie was in the care of her father one weekend, she was allegedly sexually abused by a friend of her cousin's, who had reportedly taken her clothes off and had her "play games with him." Mrs. P. reported that Julie had told her of this the following week while she was taking a bath. Mrs. P. would not discuss this in the presence of the children and reported that it had never been mentioned since the bath. Following this incident, which Mr. P.'s family insisted could not have happened, Mrs. P. refused to allow Julie's father or anyone else in his family to see the children.

While a heated family argument was carried on regarding Mrs. P.'s decision, Mr. P. was killed in a motor vehicle accident some three weeks later. Mrs. P. reported that she did not bring the children to the funeral or cemetery because she believed they would not understand, and she stated that they seemed to cope with their father's death very well, particularly Julie. Gary, on the other hand, did begin to steal things for no apparent reason, and Mrs. P. brought him to a mental health clinic on one occasion for this problem. At this time, Mrs. P. reported that she was told that there was nothing wrong with Gary but that she was "crazy," and she terminated treatment. Not long after, Gary's stealing behavior stopped of its own accord, and he did not exhibit any behavior problems in school or at home thereafter. Julie, like her brother, rarely mentioned her father during the year following his death, but more recently had begun to insist that she be taken to visit him at the cemetery.

When Julie was 5 years old, her maternal grandmother moved in with the family. Mrs. P. described her mother as a demanding, helpless woman who always complained of her health and rarely got out of bed. She also reported that her mother was an extremely anxious and fearful woman who had not left her apartment for fifteen years following her husband's death, suggesting the possibility of an agoraphobic condition. Prior to moving in with the P. family, the grandmother had lived in a nearby apartment where Mrs. P. could cook her meals, clean the apartment, and run her errands. After the move, Mrs. P. continued to provide these functions for her mother with Julie's help.

As Julie reached school age, Mrs. P. became involved in a protracted dispute with the local board of education over the correct school district for Julie, and as a result Julie's entrance into first grade was delayed for one year. Once Julie started school, the problems described above began to surface, and when Mrs. P. brought Julie to the outpatient clinic for an intake, she described herself as a nervous wreck, fearing on the one hand that the court might take Julie away from her, and on the other that Julie "might be crazy." Mrs. P. reported that she had had a "nervous breakdown" herself when Julie was 2 years old and Mr. P. had started a new job that required extensive travel away from home. She was hospitalized at this time for two weeks with symptoms of acute anxiety and depression and discharged with a prescription for a minor tranquilizer, which she took for one month. Following this, Mr. P. quit his new job and returned to his previous position where he was not required to travel.

Etiology

The history and symptoms of this case suggest several issues of etiological significance. First, as Bowlby (1973, 1982) has suggested, fears of separation and loss are generally traceable to real loss events in the individual's history. Thus, in the case of Julie, it is certainly important to note the significance of the loss of her father, the alleged sexual abuse, and the subsequent cutoff of her father's family in the development of her presenting symptoms, including her nightmares, her fears of catastrophe befalling her mother, and her fears that she herself would be kidnapped or killed in an automobile accident. All of these symptoms involved themes of separation and loss of attachment figures, which reflected unresolved issues of grief and an underlying feeling of insecurity regarding the stability of the world around her. The development of anxious attachment behaviors, such as a reluctance to sleep alone, school refusal, and agitation at times of separation reflected Julie's fear that she might suddenly be left alone. In this sense they represented adaptive responses in that they served to promote attachment to significant others and to prevent further loss.

Second, it is generally believed that a child's model of self is a function of stable parent-child or other attachment bonds (Ziller and Rorer, 1985; Bowlby, 1982). Thus, a child who experiences severe instability in her relationships with major attachment figures is likely to develop feelings of personal inadequacy and interpersonal insecurity which will be reflected in her relationships with peers and her ability to engage in age-appropriate games and work habits. Thus, Julie's difficulties in establishing peer relationships, participating in play, and concentrating on purposive behaviors such as schoolwork likely reflected a poor self-image that was based in the losses and family instability she had experienced.

Third, it is clear that Julie's refusal to attend school was as much a function of her mother's unwillingness to let her go as it was a function of her own fears (Kennedy, 1965). Despite her insistence that she had tried to force Julie to attend school, Mrs. P. had implicitly condoned and reinforced Julie's "problem" behaviors from the start. On a typical day, Julie would wake up, complain of feeling ill, and then refuse to meet the school bus for fear that it might crash. If her mother tried to insist, Julie would become extremely agitated, scream, and throw things about the house. Once the school bus had come and gone, she would quiet down, Mrs. P. would fix her a nice breakfast, and they would watch the soap operas and game shows on television for the rest of the day while taking care of Julie's grandmother.

In one sense, both Julie and her grandmother provided a means for Mrs. P. to meet her own needs for adequacy and self-worth by playing the roles of underadequate persons who required her attention. Thus, despite Mrs. P.'s verbal protests regarding Julie's school refusal, it is clear that Julie's symptoms resulted in secondary gain for both parties and that Julie's behaviors reflected a well established family pattern of separation and dependency issues, as well as her own fears and anxieties.

Finally, the history of anxiety-related problems in Julie's mother and grandmother suggest both a role model for her symptomatology as well as a possible biochemical or neurological predisposition for an anxiety disorder (Eysenck, 1985). Certainly the overall level of anxiety and overt tension was high among all members of the P. family, supporting the possibility that genetically weighted variables such as emotional reactivity may have increased the overall risk of individual family members developing anxiety-related disorders.

Treatment

Cases of separation anxiety such as Julie's provide an opportunity for treatment from a variety of theoretical perspectives, due largely to the range of clinical symptoms that arise and the nature of etiological factors. From a behavioral perspective, treatments involving contingency management programs and systematic desensitization (SDT) have been successful in reducing symptoms of anxiety and improving school attendance (Cattell, 1986; Dangel and Polster, 1986). In these treatments, emphasis is placed on developing a relaxation response in association with a feared stimulus (school, separation from mother, riding a school bus, and so on), in an attempt to reduce and eventually eliminate fear responses, while at the same time assessing the system of overt and covert reinforcers that is maintaining the target behaviors. In Julie's case, school refusal was clearly being reinforced by her mother when she would fix Julie a nice breakfast and allow her to watch television following her school refusal. In a contingency management program, reinforcers such as these would be used to reward school approach behaviors rather than school avoidance behaviors, and school refusal would result in punishments such as time out, loss of privileges, or extra household chores.

From a psychodynamic or developmental perspective, symptoms of separation anxiety may be seen as defense mechanisms which function to reduce the anxiety generated from intrapsychic conflict (Bowlby, 1982). In Julie's case, unconscious conflicts involving object loss and individuation would need to be worked through using the therapeutic relationship as a change mechanism, and perhaps involving techniques such as psychodynamic play therapy, fantasy storytelling, and art therapy to express unconscious material indirectly.

Using a family systems model, the structure of family relationships might be emphasized, with one goal of treatment being to restructure family boundaries and communication patterns (Kolevzon and Green, 1985). In Julie's case, attempts might be made to strengthen the parental boundary between Mrs. P. and Julie and to more clearly establish family roles for all family members, including the grandmother.

Julie's Treatment.   In the case of Julie, family treatment was recommended and accepted by Mrs. P. The P. family was subsequently seen for approximately two months on a weekly basis. Despite the therapist's early efforts, the grandmother never joined the family for sessions, which thus consisted of Julie, Gary, and Mrs. P.

During the first sessions great effort was expended by the therapist to side with Mrs. P. on all issues in an effort to support her role as executive of the family. To this end, seating was arranged so as to place the children together on one side of the room, Mrs. P. on the other, and the therapist in the middle. The therapist frequently moved physically to side with Mrs. P.

Interventions initially included encouraging Mrs. P. to view Julie's school refusal and other behaviors as misbehaviors rather than problems or signs that she was "crazy." In keeping with this, a system of punishments was devised to make staying at home less favorable for Julie. While this met with early success in improving Julie's attendance, she soon began to fear the school bus again and Mrs. P. did not enforce the punishment system out of sympathy for Julie's fears.

At this point, Julie was praised for not going to school and, in so doing, keeping the family together. Mrs. P. was praised at the same time for recognizing Julie's authority to do this out of respect for Julie's role as the holder of all family problems. Paradoxical approaches of this nature (Seltzer, 1986) were designed to generate sufficient anger in Mrs. P. so that she would begin to more forcefully govern the family. This began to have a dramatic effect on family dynamics when Mrs. P. refused to feed her mother one evening, insisting that she feed herself. Not long after this, Julie's attendance began to improve significantly.

As family boundaries began to change (Kolevzon and Green, 1985), however, and Julie's school attendance continued to improve, Mrs. P. began to cancel sessions. While Mrs. P.'s resistance to changing the family system was predictable and could have potentially provided valuable material for future sessions, the school and court again intervened at this time, when the school year was drawing to a close and Julie would not have completed the requisite number of days to be passed on to third grade. Though Julie's attendance had shown improvement, this improvement was not great enough to keep the P. family out of court, where removal from the home was threatened before Mrs. P. agreed to voluntarily sign Julie into an inpatient treatment facility.

After two weeks of inpatient treatment and near-perfect school attendance, however, Julie convinced her mother to sign her out of the treatment facility against the strong recommendations of the treatment staff by promising her that she would never miss school again. When she returned home, Julie again refused to go to school and, sobbing and frightened, begged her mother never to let anyone take her away again.

At this time, the P. family's caseworker became so angry with Mrs. P. that she dropped the case; it was returned to court, where removal from the home was to be considered.

Comment

Along with the diagnostic and treatment issues that are raised here, this case also highlights the need for carefully planned, well-organized intervention programs when several social systems are involved. In the case of Julie, commendable clinical progress was being made in both an outpatient and an inpatient treatment program, only to have this progress undermined by legal proceedings that threatened to permanently remove Julie from her home, which in the context of her previous traumas of separation and loss, would likely be devastating.

The need for coordinated effort from all systems is further seen in the fact that the P. family might likely have never sought treatment had it not been for the insistence of the school system and the courts. Thus, while it would appear on the one hand that the courts, the school system, and the mental health system were working at cross purposes, the goals of each were reasonably equivalent. The observation that similar goals can at times result in conflicting intervention attempts is an important factor to remember when dealing with cases that involve a number of social systems in a community mental health setting.

REFERENCES

Bowlby, J. (1973) *Attachment and Loss. Vol. 2: Separation Anxiety and Anger.* New York: Basic Books.

_____. (1982) Attachment and loss: retrospect and prospect. *American Journal of Orthopsychiatry, 52,* 664–678.

Breit, M. (1982) Separation anxiety in mothers of latency-age fearful children. *Journal of Abnormal Psychology, 10,* 135–144.

Broman, S., Bien, E., and Shaughnessy, P. (1985) *Low Achieving Children: The First Seven Years.* Hillsdale, N.J.: Lawrence Erlbaum.

Cattell, R. (1986) *Psychotherapy by Structural Learning.* New York: Springer.

Dangel, R. and Polster, R. (1986) *Teaching Child Management Skills*. New York: Pergamon.

Eisenberg, L. (1958) School phobia: A study in the communication of anxiety. *American Journal of Psychiatry, 114*, 712–718.

Eysenck, H. (1985) Incubation theory of fear/anxiety. In S. Riess and R. Bootzin (Eds.), *Theoretical Issues in Behavior Therapy*. Orlando, Fla.: Academic Press.

Johnson, A., Falstein, E., Szurek, S., and Svendsen, M. (1941) School phobia. *American Journal of Orthopsychiatry, 11*, 702–711.

Kennedy, W. (1965) School phobia: Rapid treatment of fifty cases. *Journal of Abnormal Psychology, 70*, 285–289.

Kolevzon, M. and Green, R. (1985) *Family Therapy Models*. New York: Springer.

Seltzer, L. (1986) *Paradoxical Strategies in Psychotherapy*. New York: John Wiley.

Ziller, R. and Rorer, B. (1985) Shyness-environment interaction. *Journal of Personality, 53*, 626–639.

/ The Oppositional Disorder

**The Case of
Phyllis**

Give to a pig when it grunts and a child when it cries, and you will have a fine pig and a bad child.

— Old Danish proverb

The oppositional disorder is characterized by intensely negative responses to attempts by parents or other authority figures to control the behavior of the child or adolescent. Stubborn and/or hostile resistance is manifested in a variety of behavior patterns, including consistent violation of minor rules and pouting with an occasional temper flare-up. Oppositional disorder can be diagnosed as early as 3 years of age, and receives a lay diagnosis even before then—the "terrible twos" (Provost, 1985). When it emerges most strongly in adolescence, as it often does (and as it does in the case of Phyllis), similar behaviors usually had been evident in the child's earlier history (Attili, 1985).

Adolescence is commonly a stressful period for teenagers, their families, and school officials. Pubertal changes, the task of identity formation, the renegotiation of relationships with parents, and rapid changes in the social environment can precipitate a variety of problematic behaviors for teenagers (Reisman, 1986). Certain adolescents are unable to effect a logical or objective break from their earlier emotional bonds with parents, and thus teenagers' struggle for an autonomous relationship with parents may be a significant source of problems. As a result, teenagers may become rebellious, emotional, or hypercritical in order to convince parents that they are no longer "children," that they must be accorded greater independence.

Though a degree of rebellion in adolescence is considered normal, some teenagers believe that true autonomy can be attained only by making a complete break with their parents. These youngsters are openly and consistently defiant of parental authority and may solve their problems by moving out of the home. Other teenagers remain in the home yet resist parental and school authority as being excessive and unreasonable. In extreme cases, these teenagers may take such exception to rules and regulations that their behavior is intensely hostile and antisocial. The usual diagnosis in these cases is one of the conduct disorders (Stewart, 1985).

Another group of adolescents, who perceive the expectations of parents, teachers, and peers as overwhelming, respond with the growth-inhibiting symptoms of adolescent anxiety disorders. A third group of teenagers evidence continued disruption of emotional development resulting from pervasive developmental disorders, mental retardation, or other disorders with childhood onset. A final group of rebellious adolescents respond to age-appropriate developmental tasks with a confused self-definition that manifests itself in temper tantrums, disobedience, negativism, and provocative violations of minor rules, resulting in a diagnosis of oppositional disorder. These strategies, however, remain within the boundaries of age-appropriate social norms and do not violate others' rights to the extent evidenced in adolescent conduct disorders.

Oppositional teenagers, though emotionally unpredictable and argumentative, may elicit a generally positive response from others and may evidence stubbornness and emotionality rather than an antisocial value system or deliberate disregard for others' feelings. Also, oppositional behavior has a compulsive component, which maintains the problematic behavior despite detrimental (and undesired) consequences (Rachman, 1980). Oppositional behavior is consistent with the traditional concept of the neurotic paradox; that is, the behavior is goal-directed (aimed toward emotional autonomy and independent thinking), but not goal-attaining (usually resulting in descriptors such as "immature" or "irresponsible"). As in the case of Phyllis, compulsive violations and seemingly reflexive negative responses merely elicit mistrust and anxiety from authority figures, resulting in criticism and further restrictions of freedom, to which the oppositional person responds with intensified negativism. Consequently, relationships with authority figures deteriorate and become increasingly conflict-ridden and frustrating.

The Case of Phyllis

Throughout Phyllis's childhood, her parents were United States embassy officials in several South American countries. When Phyllis entered high school, her parents moved back to the United States and joined the political science department of a small private college. Phyllis attended public high school for two years and was suspended four times. Her parents enrolled her in a private girls' academy, hoping the structured atmosphere would "settle her down." However, Phyllis was suspended from the academy twice in the first semester, and the principal threatened permanent expulsion if her school behavior did not improve. The school had a weekly "detention hall" for students who broke rules. Phyllis's suspensions resulted primarily from noncompliance with detention hall and the sheer number of outstanding detentions. The infractions for which she received detention were generally minor, such as talking during class, violations of dress code, and tardiness for detention hall.

Phyllis, the youngest of five girls, was the only daughter who still lived with her parents at the time she was referred by her school's guidance counselor to a clinical psychologist. Phyllis's married sisters lived in other states and were employed as a nurse, kindergarten teacher, medical technologist, and engineer, respectively. There were four years separating Phyllis and the next youngest sister (the medical technologist). Phyllis's parents described the family as close and loving. They said that the older girls had gone through brief periods of rebellion during adolescence but that they had all grown out of it. The family was very achievement-oriented, and everyone except Phyllis had distinguished academic records.

Phyllis had been behaviorally normal through childhood, though she had been very stubborn and difficult when 3 years old and had often been prone to temper tantrums, causing her father to semi-affectionately dub her as "the little witch." Phyllis had always produced an inconsistent academic performance. Throughout grammar school, she often earned above-average grades, yet her teachers consistently concluded that Phyllis's potential was higher than her grades indicated. Junior high school was characterized by a particularly erratic performance. Phyllis received her first failing grade in the seventh grade, and from then on would fail one or two subjects each grading period. Her parents would restrict her privileges and closely supervise Phyllis's homework in the failed subject(s). In subsequent grading periods, Phyllis would earn high marks in the previously failed subject(s), only to fail a different subject. After transferring to the academy, Phyllis's overall performance level improved, though it remained inconsistent.

Similar inconsistencies were observed in Phyllis's social relationships. She had several "personality conflicts" with teachers, on whom she blamed her low grades, and her parents described her as "moody and difficult to get along with" as she neared adolescence. At home, frequent arguments erupted over Phyllis's grades and her failure to complete household chores. When the tension in the home became intolerable, Phyllis would visit one of her sisters. However, these visits were often prematurely terminated by some disagreement with her sister or brother-in-law concerning Phyllis's curfew.

In grade school, Phyllis apparently got along fairly well with her classmates. The family moved every two or three years, however, and Phyllis had not continued any of her childhood friendships. In high school, she moved from one close girlfriend to another, often within a few weeks. These friendships seemed to die from lack of interest from the other girls and seldom because of any argument. Phyllis dated frequently but did not have a steady boyfriend. This was an additional source of conflict in the family, since her mother suspected, without any hard evidence, that Phyllis was sexually active.

Etiology

Adolescence has been described by Erikson (1959) as a period in which one must resolve the crisis of self-definition by committing oneself to a role and adopting an ideology (attitudes, beliefs, moral values). The apparent ideology and role adopted by Phyllis is one of counter-dependence. That is, although her behavior is directed toward demonstrating autonomy, she remains defined by the external environment because her coping strategy is generally limited to acting in the opposite direction of perceived external forces. These dynamics are generally frustrating for everyone involved—including Phyllis. In addition to the predictable negative reactions of parents, peers, and teachers, the oppositional adolescent's behavior does not result in feelings of autonomy or independence. Rather, Phyllis is likely to feel that emotionally charged situations escalate too quickly and that she is unable to control her behavior. Phyllis said, "Sometimes I just get mad because someone's ordering me around. So I just don't do it, and then I get in trouble I'm sorry for later."

How adolescents arrive at maladaptive ideologies and roles is a phenomenon about which there is considerable speculation and scant empirical data. Generally, adolescent behavior problems are attributed to predisposing family dynamics and/or deficient coping skills on the part of the teenager (Broman, Bien, and Shaughnessy, 1985; Reisman, 1986). In Phyllis's case both groups of variables contributed to her poor adjustment. She was the youngest in her family and was no doubt accustomed to relatively unconditional affection, despite implicit expectations of high achievement. In addition to the typical problems experienced by adolescents with successful older siblings, Phyllis's process of self-definition was hampered by her family's indulgence and overprotection, which resulted in her lack of problem-solving experience. Phyllis was able to meet the social and educational demands of grammar school with minimal effort. However, the level of Phyllis's effort and coping ability remained rather constant despite the increased demands of adolescence.

Moreover, because of the family's many moves, and her age difference from her sisters, Phyllis's only stable relationships were with her parents (who had become part of the problem). Harry Stack Sullivan (1953) found that an important predictor of problematic interpersonal relationships is the absence of an intimate same-sex relationship in preadolescence. Sullivan thought these friendships could correct egocentrism, childishness, yearning for everyone's approval, and other maladaptive behavior patterns acquired in childhood. These friendships provide experiences with intimacy, essential reality testing, and a broader perspective from the combined experiences. Phyllis had missed this significant experience in childhood, and the constantly changing environments and associated behavioral norms (complicated by cultural differences among her numerous schools) had interfered with her development of a consistent set of attitudes and behaviors. It is not surprising that she adopted a rigid approach to the environment, which was defined by being against the expectations of her parents and teachers.

Treatment

The many approaches to treatment for adolescents often correspond with theoretical orientations of therapists, such as behavior therapy, psychoanalysis, client-centered therapy, Gestalt therapy, adolescent group therapy, and community mental health. In addition, some professionals are skeptical about the effectiveness of any treatment program for adolescents that does not include parents and other family members (Dangel and Polster, 1986). These professionals conceive of adolescent behavior problems as overt manifestations of larger problems with the interpersonal dynamics of the family. At the same time, it is important to remember that the oppositional disorder is functionally similar in some respects to the aggressive personality disorders (Attili, 1985; Stewart, 1985). Thus, the treatment principles useful for those syndromes are relevant here (Feindler and Ecton, 1986).

Since persons with an oppositional disorder often avoid accepting responsibility for the difficulties they encounter, the reality therapy techniques that William Glasser (1980) developed while working with delinquent adolescent girls, who are especially inclined to avoid responsibility, can be appropriate here. Adlerian therapy (Garfinkle, Massey, and Mendel, 1980), which melds some analogous approaches into a traditional psychodynamic therapy, is also successfully applied here.

Once some of the oppositional tendencies can be muted, either client-centered or nondirective therapies (variations of the original explorations by Carl Rogers, 1951) can be used to explore the conflicts over defining identity while adjusting to parental constraints. Similarly, Gestalt therapy techniques (Perls, Hefferline, and Goodman, 1958; Nichols and Fine, 1980) can help the adolescent with oppositional disorder confront the underlying feelings toward parental figures, often in the "empty chair technique." Here, the adolescent pretends the parent is in a chair and holds a dialogue by taking both parts, which helps him or her get in touch with the parent's perspective.

Phyllis's Treatment. Phyllis's treatment took place over ten individual therapy sessions, which included Adlerian and Gestalt techniques, followed by weekly adolescent group therapy for three months. Her parents were given advice on reactions to Phyllis's behavior and list of books and magazine articles written especially for parents of teenagers. Phyllis was slow to disclose spontaneously with the therapist, though she was willing to answer questions and negotiate contracts for more appropriate behaviors. She was motivated by the threat of expulsion of school and by her desire to effect more harmonious relationships with her parents, teachers, and peers. As is often the case with adolescents, a major portion of Phyllis's problems stemmed from inadequate social skills and an inability to communicate feelings in socially appropriate ways. Consequently, individual sessions concentrated on more appropriate assertive behaviors for Phyllis, including contracts for in vivo trials with parents and peers (Feindler and Ecton, 1986). These strategies dramatically reduced the intense tension between Phyllis and her parents.

The therapy group in which Phyllis participated consisted of eight to ten teenagers who had similar problems in relationships with authority figures, school achievement, and maintaining stable peer relationships. This group functioned in a manner similar to the intimate preadolescent friendships described by Sullivan (1953). Group members assisted one another in problem-solving and reality-testing within an accepting atmosphere. The group was open-ended—members could "graduate" as their individual needs were met. Some of the group members became close friends and continued their relationships even after they left the group. Phyllis was more disclosing in the group setting and was relieved to discover that other group members had similar experiences. Behavioral contracting and behavior rehearsal were used extensively in these group meetings (Barth, 1986). These techniques were particularly successful for Phyllis, and she gradually abandoned her oppositional position.

After three months, Phyllis's improvement was evidenced by more pleasant interactions with her parents, significant decreases in school detentions, and better grades. She has maintained the friendships formed in the group, enjoys more stable relationships with schoolmates, and the school has removed the threat of expulsion. Also, Phyllis now reports that she is happier and more confident.

Comment

As the oppositional coping strategy generalizes and behavioral controls increase with maturation, the individual may refine this strategy instead of acquiring more adaptive ones (Broman, Bien, and Shaughnessy, 1985). However, Phyllis has acquired an adaptive repertoire of coping behaviors that will probably preclude recurrent episodes of oppositional disorder and the subsequent development of a passive-aggressive personality disorder.

Behavioral contracting and group therapy are treatments of choice with adolescents in general for several reasons (Barth, 1986; Decker and Nathan, 1985). First, both therapeutic strategies are consistent with normal developmental tasks. Contracting provides adolescents with opportunities to exhibit responsible and independent behavior without parental "nagging" (which irritates adolescents and often provokes even more oppositional behavior). Also, behavioral contracts structure situations, particularly parent-child relationships, in such a way that everyone's expectations are clear and thus provide consistent feedback about the appropriateness of behaviors. This consistency serves to reduce the emotional nature of relationships and thus to increase opportunities for positive reinforcement and enhanced self-esteem.

Phyllis's case is an example of how singularly unremarkable life circumstances can combine to predispose adjustment problems in adolescence. The developmental tasks of adolescence are such that teenagers must draw on the experiences of childhood and/or social resources for adequate resolution of the identity crisis (Erikson, 1959). Phyllis's childhood experiences, though superior in many ways, did not include adequate practice in frustration tolerance or in the maintenance of long-term peer relationships. Also, her status as the family's youngest and later as the only child in the home combined with deficits in social skills restricted her socially. Phyllis did not know how to rely on the support of peers or siblings for credible feedback about her behavior, and she was forced to use the expectations of her parents and teachers as guidelines for judgments. Many teenagers in this position abandon efforts to attain autonomy and consequently conform without protest to the expectations of adults. Such conformity may simply delay rebellion until early adulthood (or even much later), when the social consequences are more serious and the environment considerably less tolerant of oppositional behavior. Phyllis had chosen to rebel early (within limits) and, fortunately, was eventually directed into more positive patterns.

REFERENCES

Attili, G. (1985) Concomitants and factors influencing children's aggression. *Aggressive Behavior, 11*, 291–302.

Barth, R. (1986) *Social and Cognitive Treatment of Children and Adolescents*. San Francisco: Jossey-Bass.

Broman, S., Bien, E., and Shaughnessy, P. (1985) *Low Achieving Children: The First Several Years*. Hillsdale, N.J.: Lawrence Erlbaum.

Dangel, R. and Polster, R. (1986) *Teaching Child Management Skills*. New York: Pergamon.

Decker, P. and Nathan, B. (1985) *Behavior Modeling Training: Principles and Applications*. New York: Praeger.

Erikson, E. (1959) Identity and the life cycle. *Psychological Issues, 1*, 18–164.

Feindler, E. and Ecton, R. (1986) *Adolescent Anger Control*. New York: Pergamon.

Garfinkle, M., Massey, R., and Mendel, E. (1980) Two cases in Adlerian child therapy. In G. Belkin (Ed.), *Contemporary Psychotherapies*. Chicago: Rand McNally.

Glasser, W. (1980) Two cases in reality therapy. In G. Belkin (Ed.), *Contemporary Psychotherapies*. Chicago: Rand McNally.

Nichols, F. and Fine, H. (1980) Gestalt therapy: Some aspects of independence and responsibility. *Psychotherapy: Theory, Research and Practice, 17*, 124–135.

Perls, F., Hefferline, R., and Goodman, P. (1958) *Gestalt Therapy*. New York: Julian.

Provost, M. (1985) Social and cognitive aspects of the development of aggression in infancy. *Aggressive Behavior, 11*, 283–290.

Rachman, S. (1980) *Obsessions and Compulsions*. Englewood Cliffs, N.J.: Prentice-Hall.

Reisman, J. (1986) *Behavior Disorders in Infants, Children and Adolescents*. New York: Random House.

Rogers, C. (1951) *Client-Centered Therapy*. Boston: Houghton Mifflin.

Stewart, M. (1985) Aggressive conduct disorder. *Aggressive Behavior, 11*, 323–331.

Sullivan, H. (1953) *The Interpersonal Theory of Psychiatry*. New York: W. W. Norton.

/ *The Eating Disorders: Anorexia Nervosa and Bulimia*

The Case of Anna

Ask your child what he wants for dinner only if he's buying.

— Fran Lebowitz
Social Studies

Anorexia nervosa (which, literally translated, means "not eating because of nervous causes") refers to a strong and persistent concern about becoming too fat, usually accompanied by a feeling that one is fat even when there has been some weight loss. The DSM also requires evidence of an eventual loss of approximately 25 percent of original body weight, depending on age and previous weight. Even though anorexia nervosa and bulimia are listed simply as eating disorders in DSM, we include them here as disorders of childhood and adolescence since they so commonly originate in middle and late adolescence.

Anorexia nervosa most often occurs in middle class and upper middle class female adolescents, though older people can suffer from it, as was seen in 1986 when actress Joey Heatherton developed the disorder. Approximately 1 in 250 females between ages 12 and 18 suffers from it at some point in life. There is usually a manifest disinterest in sex, and, as the disorder progresses, there is also a disruption if not a complete cessation of menstrual flow (amenorrhea). Other indications of associated physiological disorder appear as the disorder continues. Estimates of eventual death from this disorder range from 5 to 20 percent (Bruch, 1978, 1981).

Anorectics are usually shy and inhibited, but at the same time are passively controlling and stubborn. The parents of anorectics are characteristically loving and devoted. At the same time, the parents are also controlling, show high expectancies for academic and moral performance, and usually punish a child by expressing disappointment and inculcating guilt. Anorectics focus on food to regain a sense of control in their psychological world. Significant others are often enmeshed in frustrating attempts to prepare foods that the anorectic will eat, and the whole issue often becomes the family focus for a long period of time (Kagan and Squires, 1984; Logue, 1985; Ruderman, 1986; Agras, 1987). Most of these characteristics are evident in Anna's case, which we will consider below.

A number of anorectics also show episodes of bulimia, another DSM eating disorder. The term *bulimia*, which derives from the Greek words for ox and hunger, refers to a pattern of binge eating. Overall, those anorectics who also associate bulimia are more disturbed than anorectics who do not (Casper et al., 1980).

Bulimia has as its essential feature, according to the DSM, recurrent eating binges that are often followed by depression and remorse and that are attended by an awareness that the pattern is disordered and cannot be stopped. It is associated with attempts to control weight by diet or vomiting, and also by eating high-calorie foods in an inconspicuous manner.

While anorectics are typically shy but passively controlling and stubborn, bulimorectics (even those who are also anorectic) are more likely to be extroverted perfectionists who attempt to control their peers in direct ways and are prone to depression (Walsh et al., 1985). Some bulimorectics are obese, though many weigh in at normal levels, whereas anorectics are usually almost cadaverously thin. Both disorder groups commonly come from families in which food is a focus, as in socialization or recognition. Anorectics will often cook exotic meals for others, although they may eat only a small portion themselves. Bulimorectics do not usually like to cook because they are afraid they will eat all the food before the guests show up (Agras, 1987; Striegel-Moore, Silberstein, and Rodin, 1986; Walsh et al., 1985).

The Case of Anna

Anna had a rather quiet though pleasant childhood. She was unusually resistant of attempts to toilet train her, yet otherwise showed no real problems in development. As a shy but bright child, she quickly became "the apple of her father's eye," and he would occasionally use the example of Anna's good behavior to chastise her older brother, who more often violated his parents' rules.

Anna's father owned a large and successful insurance agency. Her mother was an industrious and even compulsive housewife and was deeply involved in a number of church and community activities. Neither parent felt comfortable using physical punishment with Anna, though on rare occasions her father would lose his temper and give her a hard spanking. Their more usual mode of punishment was to sit Anna down and talk to her about how she had been "bad" and had disappointed them. Her parents would tell friends that they never tried to pressure Anna or her brother to achieve academically beyond their ability. This was true regarding overt statements, but in many subtle ways they made it clear that they had high expectations for both children, and they would show hurt rather than anger when either child did not "measure up," as if this would bring criticism upon the parents.

Anna's brother was able to escape the brunt of the guilt that can easily develop as a result of such a parenting style. Anna's father expressed a common double standard of behavior; while Anna was expected to be quiet and conforming, her brother was allowed exuberance and occasional rule infractions under the rubric, "that's just the way boys are."

As Anna entered adolescence, several situations were disturbing her apparently calm adjustment to life. Sexual impulses were emerging, and she had little in the way of instruction about this area except for a single almost formal lecture from her mother that focused only on anatomy. In addition, there were both overt and implied messages from her parents that sex was "bad" and "dirty." Anna had also just received her first C in school, and she was beginning to tire of the piano lessons she had been taking regularly since she was 5. Yet when her initial complaints about the piano lessons were ignored by her parents, she did not persist in any direct attempt to stop practicing.

At this time, three months after her 15th birthday, Anna had on occasion gone on eating binges, putting on a lot of weight very quickly. Now, she announced to her family that she wanted to diet and lose some weight. She then weighed 110 and stood 5'3" tall. Of course, that weight and height meant she was not really significantly overweight. Her brother had occasionally called her "fatty," as had a boy at school in whom Anna had some romantic interest.

Shortly after beginning her diet, she announced that she was going to be a vegetarian. When her family tried to talk her out of this, she would show them studies in health magazines lauding the vegetarian life style, and she adamantly refused to eat meat. Her parents became concerned about her evident weight loss and began devising special diets for her, especially in order to make up for the protein she was missing in not eating meat or seafood. Anna became more and more finicky with her food. She would only eat at certain specific times and only after she went through several preparatory rituals, which were analogous to the obsessive-compulsive patterns noted in the case of Bess in Chapter 3.

Anna's parents had taken her to their family doctor just after the start of her diet. She told them it was "just a phase" and not to be concerned unless Anna started getting sick. However, it soon became apparent that Anna was losing more than just a little weight. They returned to their physician, who referred them to a clinical psychologist specializing in child and adolescent disorders. He immediately suggested that she start in individual therapy, but just as importantly, that the family as a whole also enter therapy. This angered Anna's father, as he could not see it as other than a physical problem and/or "Anna's damned stubbornness."

Unfortunately, by this point Anna had lost about thirty pounds. Her mother discovered that Anna was often going to the bathroom and purposely vomiting up some of the small amounts of food she was eating. Her schoolwork was progressively worsening, and she was gradually withdrawing from her friends. Anna, who had always been healthy, now seemed to have a constant cold and was obviously very weak. An internist who was called in to consult advised hospitalization and Anna's parents agreed.

Etiology

Some early theorists pointed to the disturbed menstrual flow (amenorrhea) that is commonly associated with anorexia nervosa to support the hypothesis that an underlying physiological disorder is the causal agent. However, there has been little other data to support this. Also, there is good evidence that any condition that leads to significant starvation is also likely to cause a menstrual disorder (Bruch, 1978, 1981).

Psychoanalysts have also taken note of the amenorrhea but have related it to conflicts around sexual impulses. Specifically, anorexia has been seen as reflecting symbolic conflict and denial of fantasies of oral impregnation by the father (Waller, Kaufman, and Deutsch, 1964). There has been little empirical validation of this theory, and there was no evidence to suggest that it was meaningful in Anna's case.

Bruch (1978, 1981) hypothesizes that arbitrary mothering produces in the child an inability to accurately perceive internal cues such as hunger and satiation. Affective states may be similarly mislabeled. As a result, the child cannot act on the basis of her internal states and cannot develop a feeling of control over her life. She remains dependent on her family, and develops neither a sense of autonomy and competence nor a clear concept of body image. In adolescence, turmoil develops as pubertal changes and social pressures demand increasing autonomy and maturity. The symptoms of anorexia nervosa are the attempt to gain control over the body and, thereby, over identity.

White (1983) sees a rigid, transgenerational belief system as a hallmark of anorectic families. Belief in loyalty to the family results in tenuous peer relationships, and opposition to this rule builds a "currency of guilt." Family members also believe in their ability to know other family members' intentions, and attempt to exert consequent control, often in a subtle fashion. This belief blinds them to the nature and consequences of family patterns. In addition, a specific role of sensitivity, devotion, and self-sacrifice (in a context of seeking perfection) is prescribed for the anorectic member of the family. Together, these conditions result in self-denial, repression of emotions, vulnerability, and anorectic symptoms.

One clue as to why the disorder is more common in females comes from a rather clever research approach by Fallon and Rozin (1985). They showed a set of nine figure drawings (arranged from somewhat underweight to somewhat overweight) to 248 male and 227 female undergraduates, and asked them to indicate their current body figure, their ideal figure, the figure they felt would be most attractive to the opposite sex, and the opposite figure to which they would be most attracted. For men, the current, ideal, and most attractive male figure were almost identical. But for women, their perception of their own current figure was significantly heavier than the most attractive figure, which in turn was heavier than the ideal female figure. Both sexes err in estimating what the opposite sex would find attractive, but in opposite directions. Men think women like a male figure of a heavier stature than the women reported they really like, and women think that men like women to be thinner than the men actually reported they like. So, overall, Fallon and Rozin find that men's perceptions tend to keep them satisfied with their figures, while women's perceptions place pressure on themselves to lose weight. Thus, the greater incidence of dieting, anorexia, and bulimia among women is not surprising.

The findings of Fallon and Rozin (1985) are also relevant to the etiology of bulimia. Striegel-Moore and her associates (1986) find that although about 20 percent of bulimic women don't show any specific personality pattern, the other 80 percent are divided between those who show an obsessive-compulsive pattern (see the case of Bess) and those who show a more classic addictive pattern (see Chapter 9). In addition, they note a number of other specific factors that increase the tendency to develop a bulimic pattern: (1) acceptance of a traditional feminine role, (2) middle to upper class social status, (3) attendance away from home at college or a boarding school, (4) early physical maturation, (5) lower metabolic rate, (6) higher stress, (7) tendencies toward depression, (8) prolonged history of dieting attempts, (9) family isolation along with high value on appearance and thinness, and (10) high belief in the ability to use one's will to control self and the world.

Treatment

Behaviorists have not spent much effort trying to formulate the etiology of anorexia or bulimia. Rather, they have focused on devising token economy, aversion therapy, and contracting programs that have been useful in the overall treatment package (Leitenberg et all., 1984; Garfinkel and Garner, 1982).

In addition to these behavioral approaches, psychotherapy designed to give clients a better awareness of their denial of both dependence and stubborn manipulativeness is also usually critical. Family therapy, which is an acknowledgment that this disorder at least in part reflects a disturbed family system, is usually necessary if either the anorectic or bulimorectic is to make and maintain a full recovery.

The hospital treatment for Anna centered around a sociobehavioral modification program (Barth, 1986; Garfinkel and Garner, 1982), wherein medication may also be of help (Halmi, Eckert, LaDu, and Cohen, 1986). This treatment was instituted only after a long session with Anna and her parents, during which time the program was fully described and permission to proceed was obtained. Naturally enough, the first goal was weight gain. If Anna avoided eating, she was subjected to intravenous and/or forced feeding, which she found very aversive. Eating at least a minimal amount of food gained her a minimum though sparse level of privileges (such as amount of television time, things she was allowed to have in her room, amount of time allowed for visits, participation in desired activities, amount of time for visits to home). As she ate and gained more weight, a correspondingly greater number of privileges were allowed.

As Anna improved, the focus of treatment shifted to how she ate rather than how much she ate, and then to the accompanying patterns of emotional disorder that would be equally applicable to bulimia (Weiss, Katzman, and Wolchik, 1985). Anna was now rewarded for eating a greater variety of foods, in diverse settings, and for doing so without resorting to the rituals that she had needed in the past. One technique that was useful in counteracting the rituals was a form of paradoxical intention (Seltzer, 1986). She was first asked if she could increase the ritual patterns. She clearly saw this request as stupid, but complied. She was then asked to vary the rituals in all sorts of ways. As she did this, the message that she did have some control became apparent, and she was gradually able to reduce the rituals.

At the same time, she was seen in individual psychotherapy three times a week. Through these sessions, Anna finally became aware of how she had been using her anorectic patterns to regain a sense of control in her interaction with her parents. She also came in touch with a great deal of hostility toward them, as well as with how difficult their "hurt and disappointment" parenting patterns had made it for her to express criticism or anger. Whenever she had begun to show anger, they had quickly made her feel guilty for hurting such loving parents. The logical next step for Anna was a regimen of assertiveness training. She was enabled to begin to express her anger more openly and to make demands appropriate to her reasonable needs for privacy and in line with the need to make more of her own decisions (Barth, 1986).

Anna's parents easily agreed in principle to support these changes. However, after nine weeks, when Anna returned from the hospital, having made a number of moderate changes, all did not go smoothly. Her parents did not so easily accept her more assertive behaviors and tried to mold her back to the quiet and docile child they had known. As a result, family therapy was necessary. The particularly difficult task here was to get the family members to see that they were not doing this "for Anna"; rather, that her disorder was in large part the natural evolutionary result of a specific system of family expectations, values, and controls (Agras, 1987). It was only when Anna stopped being "the patient" and the family became "the client" that real improvement was noted.

It is also very interesting that as Anna improved, particularly in the ability to make her own decisions, her father began to show a number of psychophysiological complaints (especially headaches) and also occasionally erupted into tantrums of rage. He attempted, without much success, to control the headaches with medication and was quite resistant toward accepting the idea that they were psychologically generated. The focus in the family sessions had now swung from Anna to him. Finally, during one session he lost his temper, and began accusing the family of not loving him. He said he felt that they only loved him because he made the money they needed. He then gradually came to realize how he had needed his sense of sacrifice as a means of self-affirmation and whenever his children and wife made moves away from needing him in that mode, he felt very threatened. The other family members gradually began to realize how they had taken his role for granted. More importantly, he began to move more into activities that he had always expressed a desire for ("I've always wanted to get a houseboat, and really get into that") yet had put off because "we need to save money." This is not a bad goal at all, but the family had already saved more than they would need for most contingencies. He eventually was able to ask his wife to go back to work and was pleasantly surprised that she seemed happy that he asked.

Anna's improvement continued and was generally complete. She did become less rigid in her behavior patterns, though she later went into accounting, where success requires at least a degree of compulsivity. It is interesting that later in life she became a well-informed gourmet and periodically taught cooking classes. These examples suggest how residual behavioral patterns can be channeled into more adaptive behaviors.

In addition to many of the above techniques, an adolescent group therapy experience is also especially helpful for bulimia. This provides a sense of control as well as a source of feedback. The adolescent group can be useful for anorectics as well, but only after they have made substantial improvement through other techniques. The bulimorectic also especially needs counseling for simple control of eating behaviors, such as is used with the more standard problem of obesity and persistent eating disorders (Johnson, Connors, and Stuckey, 1983; Ruderman, 1986).

There are other treatments specifically useful for bulimia (Tsu and Holder, 1986; Root, Fallon, and Friedrich, 1986). Patients are taught to eat foods they like (exposure phase), without being allowed to vomit afterward (response prevention phase), thus teaching them they have some control in this area (Leitenberg et al., 1984). Clients are instructed to eat in a regular pattern in a specific place, and are also given training in relaxation, assertiveness, and methods of controlling the development of depressive responses (Tsu and Holder, 1986; Weiss et al., 1985; Johnson, Connors and Stuckey, 1983).

Treatment Difficulties. Anorexia nervosa and bulimia are difficult to treat effectively. One reason is the dropout rate. For example, the dropout rate for anorectics during inpatient treatment was determined by Vander Eycken and Pierloot (1983) to be 50 percent of the 145 female patients investigated. The highest number of dropouts during intensive care and weight-gain programs was for older patients and patients with less education and lower SES than non-dropout groups. Even in those who do recover, perhaps one-third to one-half never do so fully; from 13 to 59 percent of patients in several studies remained amenorrheic at follow-up, 50 percent purposefully avoid any high-calorie food, bulimia is present in 14 to 50 percent, vomiting in 10 to 28 percent, and laxative abuse and anxiety about eating are common.

Attempts have been made to determine characteristics of anorectics and bulimorectics that may predict successful outcome. As is often the case, later age of onset and lack of prior hospitalization are the most reliable indicators of good outcome, as are shorter duration of illness, an acute disorder, less weight loss, the presence of social stressors, and the presence of a good social or work history (Vander Eycken and Pierloot, 1983; Kagan and Squires, 1984; Logue, 1985; Agras, 1987).

Comment

Since anorexia nervosa is often a life-threatening pattern, it is important to be aware of how a focus on dieting, physical attractiveness, and conflict over self-expression can juxtapose into this disorder, particularly in middle to upper class adolescent females. In addition to examining the intrapsychic issues and the specific behavioral reinforcements that may perpetuate either bulimia or anorexia, intervention in the family system may be required (Root, Fallon and Friedrich, 1986). At least one of the parents is usually highly invested in passively controlling the children and/or spouse. Also, just as in other systems in which disorder emerges at one point, control of that point is likely to result in disorder elsewhere (in this case, Anna's father's headaches and rage reactions), until some change in the overall system occurs.

REFERENCES

Agras, W. (1987) *Eating Disorders.* New York: Pergamon.

Barth, R. (1986) *Social and Cognitive Treatment of Children and Adolescents*, San Francisco: Jossey-Bass.

Bruch, H. (1978) *The Golden Cage: The Enigma of Anorexia Nervosa.* Cambridge, Mass.: Harvard University Press.

———. (1981) Developmental considerations of anorexia nervosa. *Canadian Journal of Psychiatry, 27,* 212–216.

Casper, R., Eckert, E., Halmi, K., Goldberg, S., and Davis, J. (1980) Bulimia. *Archives of General Psychiatry, 37,* 1030–1035.

Fallon, A. and Rozin, P. (1985) Sex differences in perceptions of desirable body shape. *Journal of Abnormal Psychology, 94,* 102–105.

Garfinkel, P. and Garner, D. (1982) *Anorexia Nervosa: A Multidimensional Perspective*, New York: Brunner/Mazel.

Halmi, K., Eckert, E., LaDu, T., and Cohen, J. (1986) Anorexia nervosa: Treatment efficacy of cyproheptadine and amitriptyline. *Archives of General Psychiatry, 43,* 177–181.

Johnson, C., Connors, M., and Stuckey, M. (1983) Short-term group treatment of bulimia. *International Journal of Eating Disorders, 2,* 199–208.

Kagan, D. and Squires, R. (1984) Eating disorders among adolescents: Patterns and prevalence. *Adolescence, 19,* 15–29.

Leitenberg, H., Gross, J., Peterson, J., and Rosen, J. (1984) Analysis of an anxiety model and the process of change during exposure plus response prevention treatment of bulimia nervosa. *Behavior Therapy, 15,* 3–20.

Logue, A. (1986) *The Psychology of Eating and Drinking.* New York: W. H. Freeman.

Root, M., Fallon, P., and Friedrich, W. (1986) *Bulimia: A Systems Approach to Treatment.* New York: W. W. Norton.

Ruderman, A. (1986) Dietary restraint: A theoretical and empirical review. *Psychological Bulletin, 99,* 247–262.

Seltzer, L. (1986) *Paradoxical Strategies in Psychotherapy.* New York: John Wiley.

Striegel-Moore, R., Silberstein, L., and Rodin, J. (1986) Toward an understanding of risk factors for bulimia. *American Psychologist, 43,* 246–263.

Tsu, L. and Holder, D. (1986) Bulimia nervosa: Treatment and short-term outcome. *Psychological Medicine, 16,* 65–70.

Vander Eycken, W. and Pierloot, R. (1983) Drop-out during inpatient treatment of anorexia nervosa: A clinical study of 145 patients. *British Journal of Medical Psychology, 56,* 145–156.

Waller, J., Kaufman, M., and Deutsch, F. (1964) Anorexia nervosa: A psychosomatic entity. In M. Kaufman and M. Heiman (Eds.), *Evolution of Psychosomatic Concepts.* New York: International Universities Press.

Walsh, T., Roose, S., Glassman, A., Gladis, M., and Sadik, C. (1985) Bulimia & depression. *Psychosomatic Medicine, 47,* 123–131.

Weiss, L., Katzman, M., and Wolchik, S. (1985) *Treating Bulimia.* New York: Pergamon.

White, M. (1983) Anorexia nervosa: A transgenerational system perspective. *Family Process, 22,* 255–273.

13

Organic Mental Disorders

Those consistent behavioral, affective, and intellectual patterns of disturbance that result when there has been damage to the normal brain are referred to as the organic mental disorders. Brain cells can be functionally impaired or destroyed by a wide variety of injuries, diseases, and toxic chemicals. Damage to these brain structures, which are involved in cognition, affect, and/or impulse control, can lead to inadequate psychological functioning. The extent to which a person's psychological functioning is impaired depends on the location and extent of neural damage, the person's prior psychological adjustment, and the quality of the person's life style. The effects of an organic mental disorder can range from mild memory disturbances to severe psychotic reactions.

The DSM-III distinguishes between "organic mental disorders" and "organic brain syndrome"; so the former label is now applied when there is a known or easily inferred etiology. Thus, organic brain syndrome would apply to disorders in which no real reference is made to etiology, which is usually only the first stage of diagnosis.

This chapter presents a case of Alzheimer's disease, as well as a case (Bjorn) in which an organic brain condition strongly affects emotional functioning. But, first we will turn to a rather incredible case in which a person (Harry) had an entire hemisphere (one half of the brain) surgically removed in his youth. Not only did he survive to live a somewhat normal life, but he actually achieved an overall adjustment at well above the average level.

/ *Recovery of Functions Following Removal of Dominant Brain Hemisphere*

The Case of
Harry

I experience this vacuum just a few inches above my head. This empty space of unknowing.

— Jakov Lind
Travels to the Enu

While the human brain is fragile, it is at the same time remarkably adaptable. People have been known to sustain massive brain damage due to motor vehicle accidents, tumors, and other lesions, yet show remarkable degrees of recovery (Kertesz, 1979). Of course, the eventual level of recovery depends on a number of factors, including age at the time of injury, severity of damage, and the particular region (or regions) of the brain that sustained damage (Smith, 1962). The psychological assessment of people who have sustained brain injuries should therefore consider changes in performance that are likely to occur for some time after the original insult. For this reason, many clinical neuropsychologists make it a habit to follow-up on their clients and to retest them periodically in order to document changes that occur over time.

The processes by which the brain recovers from injury are currently being studied by a number of investigators, most of whom emphasize the capacity of nondamaged brain areas to compensate for injury to other areas by assuming new functional roles. This line of reasoning implies that there is not a strict one-to-one correspondence between brain structures and behavioral or mental activity, even though under ordinary circumstances certain regions of the brain appear to exert dominant influence over specific functions (Kail and Pellegrino, 1985).

Many years ago, it was believed that there existed a strict correspondence between brain regions and behavior (Harrington, 1985). According to this model, popularly called phrenology, discrete regions of the brain controlled very specific behaviors or mental processes. Thus, specific brain regions allegedly were responsible for such states as euphoria, anger, and intellectual superiority. An implication of this view of brain functions is that damage to a given region would be expected to affect only certain psychological functions, leaving others relatively intact. Indeed, early anatomical studies tended to lend some support to this theory. For example, in the late nineteenth century, French neurologist Paul Broca discovered that impairment of expressive speech followed damage to a relatively circumscribed region to the left (or dominant) cerebral hemisphere (Lezak, 1983).

Subsequent attempts to localize brain centers that control particular functions have met with varying degrees of success. It is evident that even though there is certainly a general relationship between brain structures and psychological functions, the correlation is by no means exact (Walsh, 1978; Harrington, 1985). It is well known, for example, that the two cerebral hemispheres each control some relatively distinct functions (Kail and Pellegrino, 1985). In healthy and mature right-handed persons, the left cerebral hemisphere plays the dominant role in mediating language skills, and the right hemisphere exerts correspondingly more control over what are known as visuospatial abilities. Visuospatial abilities are manifested in activities such as drawing, finding directions, and being able to visualize spatial arrangements such as one might encounter in geometry problems. At a more general level, a distinction regarding the two hemispheres emphasizes the capacity of the left hemisphere for rational, logical, and analytic thought processes, in contrast to the right hemisphere's role in more holistic, intuitive processes (Gass and Russell, 1985; Lezak, 1983).

The axis of the brain extending from front to back is referred to as the anterior-posterior dimension. Luria (1973) has suggested that the frontmost regions play a significant role in planning and executing behavior patterns. Structures in the posterior regions appear to be more involved in processing information taken in by the various sensory systems.

A third part of the brain extends inward from the surface. Surface regions — collectively called the cortical mantle — appear to mediate most of what are called higther mental processes, such as language, abstract thought, and reasoning abilities. Areas of the brain beneath the cortical mantle, by contrast, control a wide range of activities, including vegetative (life support), reflexive, appetite, and emotive functions. From an evolutionary standpoint, these are the oldest, most primitive regions of the brain, collectively referred to as the allocortex, in contrast to the outermost cortical regions, known as the neocortex.

Regarding the functional localization and implications for recovery processes, it is evident that regions, or zones, of the brain are usually responsible for mediating certain psychological functions. We have grouped these functions according to three dimensions — left/right, anterior/posterior, and brain surface/inner regions. Although these dimensions do imply a degree of functional specificity, there is by no means a precise one-to-one correspondence between regions of brain tissue and specific behavior patterns or thought processes (Walsh, 1978; Gass and Russell, 1985).

It is interesting to note that this absence of a strict correspondence holds true to a greater degree for the so-called higher functions than for the lower functions (Harrington, 1985). For example, lesions in regions of the visual system concerned with basic perceptual processes may have very pronounced and permanent effects, such as blind spots or reductions in the visual fields (the area of sight from one visual periphery to the other). By contrast, brain lesions in areas controlling cognitive activities such as language may disrupt certain linguistic processes, but without such clear-cut effects. There are several possible explanations for this. One is that language, because it is such a complex process, is mediated by a greater proportion of brain tissue than are relatively less complex functions. As a result, focal damage is less likely to affect adversely all of the regions involved in this skill. A second possibility is that higher-level functions such as language may be reduplicated in adjacent or even more distant brain regions. Thus, damage to a zone that ordinarily controls or mediates may be compensated for by other structures, which provide a sort of back-up coverage (Reitan and Wolfson, 1986).

Along these lines, it has been suggested by several researchers (for example, Kinbourne, 1971) that both the right and the left cerebral hemispheres manifest language capabilities, though to different degrees; ordinarily, the left hemisphere is considered dominant. Until recently, the role of the right hemisphere in language activity was not well understood. However, the results of studies of patients who have undergone certain surgical procedures have made it clear that the right (or nondominant) hemisphere has a capacity for language-related activity. In one such procedure (a hemispherectomy), an entire cerebral hemisphere is removed, leaving the individual with essentially half a brain. Understandably, these operations are rarely performed. Those that are have been carried out either to arrest malignant tumors that have infiltrated one hemisphere, or as a means of controlling severe seizure activity that has not responded to less dramatic therapy.

The case of Harry is one of the most dramatic instances reported in the literature. Early in childhood, the left hemisphere of Harry's brain was removed. The removal was followed by a remarkable recovery of speech and language functions, as assessed by follow-up evaluations years later. Originally described in an article by Smith and Sugar (1975), Harry was briefly seen by the author some three years later, at which time a follow-up evaluation was being performed.

The Case of Harry

The product of a full-term, cesarean birth, Harry soon afterwards began to manifest signs of significant brain impairment in the form of seizures. These seizures increased to nearly a dozen per day by the time he was 5 years old. A left hemispherectomy was performed shortly thereafter, and within a few months, the seizure activity had abated. Testing prior to surgery had revealed distorted speech, doubtless due to the disruptive effects of damage in the left hemisphere.

Remarkably, Harry's performance on tests of language and other abilities improved significantly in the months and years following surgery, despite nearly complete removal of the cerebral hemisphere that normally mediates language skills. Follow-up testing of Harry fifteen and a half and twenty-one years after surgery revealed that he was performing in the high average range of intelligence, with a verbal IQ score in the superior range.

Subsequent contact with Harry suggested that these high performance levels had been sustained and that he was adjusting extremely well. He successfully graduated from college and at last report was working in an executive-level position for an industrial company and contemplating attending graduate school. He had compensated remarkably well for the aftereffects of surgery, which included loss of sight in the right visual field and motor-control problems on the right side (it is characteristic of damage to either hemisphere that control of the contralateral side of the body is affected). Harry was a talkative, quick-witted person who was undoubtedly functioning very effectively with half of an intact brain.

Comment

The case of Harry contains several important implications concerning the long-term effects of brain injury on behavior. First, the development of above-average language capabilities following removal of the cerebral hemisphere that normally mediates these functions suggests that the nondominant hemisphere may possess greater linguistic capabilities than previously realized. More generally, it is at least evident that brain-behavior relationships do not correspond to a strict one-to-one functional relationship. Instead, compensation for or reduplication of control mechanisms appear to exist for certain cognitive processes.

In Harry's case, it may be concluded that right hemisphere structures were responsible for subsequent development of language skills, despite the fact that the right hemisphere's role in language skills is normally thought to be comparatively minor. Finally, the radical changes and improvements in Harry's mental functions underscore the importance of assessing the effects of brain injury over time and emphasize the central nervous system's recuperative powers in certain situations. As noted in the introduction, the brain and related nervous-system structures comprise an incredibly complex yet flexible and adaptive system (Reitan and Wolfson, 1986).

As far as Harry is concerned, it is likely that the early age at which surgery occurred enhanced his recovery potential, since brain structures do become more rigid with age. Furthermore, the degree of recovery may indicate that Harry possessed exceptional potential to begin with, and for this reason does not provide a truly representative picture of recovery potential. Nonetheless, a discussion of this case is important to counteract tendencies either to view various functions as being strictly localized in the brain, or to assume that any brain damage results in a corresponding permanent loss in psychological abilities.

REFERENCES

Gass, C. and Russell, E. (1985) MMPI correlates of verbal intellectual deficits in patients with left central lesions. *Journal of Clinical Psychology, 41*, 664–670.

Harrington, A. (1985) Nineteenth-century ideas on hemisphere differences and "duality of mind." *The Behavioral and Brain Sciences, 8*, 617–660.

Kail, R. and Pellegrino, J. (1985) *Human Intelligence.* New York: W. H. Freeman.

Kertesz, A. (1979) Recovery and treatment. In K. Heilman and E. Valenstein (Eds.), *Clinical Neuropsychology.* New York: Oxford University Press.

Kinbourne, M. (1971) The minor cerebral hemisphere as a source of aphasic speech. *Archives of Neurology, 25*, 302–306.

Lezak, M. (1983) *Neuropsychological Assessment.* New York: Oxford University Press.

Luria, A. (1973) *A Working Brain*. New York: Basic Books.

Reitan, R. and Wolfson, D. (1986) *Traumatic Brain Injury: Recovery and Rehabilitation*. Tucson, Ariz.: Neuropsychology Press.

Smith, A. (1962) Ambiguities in concepts and studies of "brain damage" and "organicity." *Journal of Nervous and Mental Diseases, 135*, 311–326.

Smith, A., and Sugar, O. (1975) Development of above normal language and intelligence 21 years after left hemispherectomy. *Neurology, 25*, 813–818.

Walsh, K. (1978) *Neuropsychology*. New York: Churchill Livingstone.

/ Organic Affective Syndrome

The Case of Bjorn

Sickness is better than sadness.
— Thomas Fuller
Gnomologia

An advantage of the DSM-III and IV classification systems over their predecessors lies in their expanded treatment of mental disorders based on central nervous system (CNS) impairments. The multi-axial system permits the diagnostician to address a number of issues crucial to an assessment of the psychological impact of CNS damage. These issues include (1) specific mental disorders associated with CNS trauma (Axis I); (2) specification of the underlying structural damage (Axis III); (3) associated psychological stressors that frequently accompany brain damage in an individual (Axis IV); and (4) an estimate of the client's previous level of functioning (Axis V). Axis II—personality disorders and pervasive developmental disorders—is somewhat less frequently used; although in certain instances, characteristics of a long-standing personality disorder are either exacerbated by the effects of CNS trauma or else result in maladaptive recovery patterns.

The following case illustrates some of the psychological correlates of CNS trauma that resulted in a diagnosis of organic affective syndrome. In this condition, the most prominent psychological sequel to CNS impairment is a distinct change in mood or emotion. The case involves Bjorn, a 21-year-old student who, prior to a motor vehicle accident, was reportedly well adjusted and an active participant in school activities.

Changes in mood or emotion are quite common in cases of CNS trauma (Reitan and Wolfson, 1986; Walsh, 1978). Perhaps the most commonly reported reaction is depression, which probably reflects both an overall slowing of responsiveness due to the impact of trauma on the brain and a personal reaction as the individual becomes aware of loss of abilities and of newly imposed limitations on behavior (Gass and Russell, 1986). Generally, depression is succeeded by a more optimistic outlook as recovery proceeds and by the gradual return of cognitive and behavioral capabilities. Of course, not everyone recovers from the effects of CNS trauma. Factors such as severity, region or regions of the brain affected, and the age of the individual all play a role in determining the likelihood of subsequent recovery. To the extent that depression continues unabated despite evidence of recovery of other functions, it is likely that it reflects a functional disorder rather than a direct result of CNS trauma. Pervasive depression and passivity can be a real impediment to recovery (Salmon and Meyer, 1986), as the following case illustrates.

The Case of Bjorn

Bjorn and Tom were working on a construction crew during the summer to help earn money for school tuition. They had been good friends ever since childhood and were constant companions throughout high school and in college. They had scanned the work ads earlier that summer in search of jobs and were sufficiently enterprising to convince the foreman of a local construction crew to hire them despite their lack of experience.

One afternoon, while en route at a high speed to deliver some supplies from the warehouse, their pick-up truck lurched off the unpaved access road to the construction site and overturned. Tom, the passenger, escaped uninjured. Bjorn, who was driving, was thrown forward against the windshield pillar with considerable force. He apparently turned his head at the last instant as if to avert direct impact, and was struck on the left side of his head. The blow fractured his skull and caused contusions in the underlying brain tissue. Bjorn lost consciousness, and awakened some time later in the local hospital's emergency room.

Subsequent physical and neurological examinations revealed him to be groggy and lethargic. Within the first week of recovery, two grand mal seizures were recorded. An EEG made at this time revealed a focal electrical discharge in the left posterior region of the brain, corresponding to an area known as the angular gyrus. Bjorn was subsequently placed on a low dosage of Dilantin, a medication effective in controlling seizure activity. His condition improved markedly from this point on, and no further seizure activity was noted. Bjorn was subsequently discharged from the hospital and appeared to be on the way to a good recovery. The skull fracture healed, and subsequent EEGs revealed a decrease in abnormal brain wave activity. A subsequent neurological examination revealed that the degree of residual cerebral trauma was comparatively mild. By this time, the fall semester was about to begin, and Bjorn made plans to return to college and resume his studies.

During this period, both Tom and members of Bjorn's family noted that his behavior had undergone a definite change despite medical evidence of only minimal residual cerebral impairment. Before the accident, he had been a studious, hard-working chemistry major who was also highly sociable and quite active in campus activities. He now spent all his time either studying or sleeping. He had become increasingly irritable and complained about many physical maladies for which he blamed the accident. Although his grades did not decline significantly, Bjorn spent a great deal more time than before on class and laboratory preparation. He complained that he found it difficult to concentrate and that his attention frequently wandered. In addition, despite no real difficulties in understanding either lectures or demonstrations, he now found it more difficult to take notes and integrate the material into a form that he could readily understand. Somewhat surprisingly, his memory appeared to be relatively intact, which he attributed to the use of memorization strategies he had learned and practiced early in college.

The complaints of persisting, recurrent physical pains became more frequent, and Bjorn appeared to be quite depressed and lethargic. He stopped dating at one point and became involved in a conservative religious sect that advocated the cultivation of spirituality through personal meditation while discouraging physical expressiveness. Somewhat alarmed at these developments, Bjorn's parents decided to have him hospitalized for observation some eighteen months following the accident. At the time of admission, he was quiet and somewhat withdrawn, complaining only of pain in his lower back. He proved to be a willing patient, cooperating fully with the hospital staff, and actually appeared to enjoy all of the attention that he received.

Etiology

A full battery of medical and psychological tests were carried out during the five days that Bjorn was hospitalized. A thorough neuropsychological evaluation revealed a pattern of cognitive deficits compatible with mild residual cerebral trauma, though not of sufficient magnitude to interfere markedly with day-to-day functioning. Indeed, his intelligence quotient (Kail and Pellegrino, 1985) fell in the high average range (an IQ of 108) of intellectual achievement, which compared favorably with estimates of prior levels.

It did appear that the locus of the cerebral injury that Bjorn had incurred had some specific effects on his behavior (Gass and Russell, 1986). The region of the brain in which damage had occurred—the angular gyrus of the dominant hemisphere—appears to integrate information processed by the various systems. Many brain specialists believe that this region is one of the cornerstones of distinctly human thought processes (Walsh, 1978). The impact of the damage in this region was rather subtle in Bjorn's case, being manifested primarily in his very slow responses to questions, plus evident difficulty in making new associations between stimulus materials, despite evidence that his sensory abilities were basically intact (Reitan and Wolfson, 1986). This finding was compatible with Bjorn's reported difficulty in integrating his class material, for which he had partially compensated by making extensive tape recordings that he played again and again. Additional evidence of residual cerebral impairment rested chiefly on indications of impaired attention and concentration, mild slowing of the right (dominant) hand on manual dexterity tests, and a mild form of speech dysfluency known as dysarthria, in which the pronunciation of long words is slurred.

The predominant impression conveyed by Bjorn was one of depression, motor slowness, and emotional flatness. As part of the evaluation, he completed the Minnesota Multiphasic Personality Inventory (MMPI) so that these observations could be validated. Not surprisingly, clinical scales on the MMPI that are sensitive to depression, withdrawal, and alienation were significantly elevated (Newmark, 1985). These results were consistent with both the observations of Bjorn's behavior and background information obtained during an interview and history taking. Since the indications of depression appeared to comprise the chief manifestation of the residual effects of cerebral trauma, a diagnosis of organic affective syndrome was made. According to DSM criteria, this disorder is diagnosed when a mood disturbance without significant loss of intellectual abilities accompanies diagnosed CNS impairment.

As the assessment of Bjorn continued, it became evident that there was no apparent physical basis for his numerous physical complaints. What became strikingly clear instead was a pattern of behaviors, which had evolved within Bjorn's family, that tended to reinforce his passivity and unresponsiveness. These behaviors included overly solicitous responses to Bjorn's reports of pain, such as suggestions that he immediately lie down and not exert himself. Moreover, family members frequently made unsolicited comments such as, "Gee, you sure don't look well — is something wrong?" or "We hope you'll get back to being the same person you used to be pretty soon!" Bjorn's response to comments like the last was to withdraw in confusion and ruminate on just what it was that made him so different.

Another factor that evidently played a role in the dynamics of Bjorn's behavior was the frequency with which medical advice was sought. By becoming increasingly reclusive, Bjorn had a great deal more time to focus on and monitor his internal state, with the result that he became highly sensitive to even minor fluctuations of his various bodily systems (Meister, 1980). It turned out that in the months since the accident, Bjorn had had more than three dozen appointments with the family physician beyond those required for routine checkups. Despite this, the results of the comprehensive assessment carried out eighteen months after the accident found no evidence of significant physical or central nervous system trauma. Based on these findings, a diagnosis based on DSM criteria was made as follows:

Case Studies in Abnormal Behavior

Axis I: (293.83) Organic affective syndrome
Axis II: Deferred
Axis III: Mild residual cerebral trauma, left posterior cerebral hemisphere
Axis IV: Severity of psychosocial stressors: moderate
Axis V: Highest level of adaptive functioning, past year: fair

Treatment

An initial recommendation stemming from this assessment was for family therapy (Kolevzon and Green, 1985). The intent of this recommendation was to help both Bjorn and his family deemphasize reactions to complaints of pain, as well as to discourage excessive medical consultation beyond normal checkups. In a series of therapy sessions, family members were coached in ways to encourage Bjorn's skills and competencies, without comparing present and past behavior. It became evident that family members experienced considerable frustration in dealing with the prominent shift in Bjorn's moods following the accident, yet were afraid to confront him for fear of disrupting his "delicate" condition. At the same time, Bjorn was encouraged to become more responsive to others to counteract his introspective tendencies. Privileges that had been denied him out of well-intentioned but misplaced concern were reinstated, including driving and staying out at night. As a result, Bjorn began to feel less like a prisoner at home and began acting more spontaneously toward family members and friends. A follow-up interview with Bjorn six months later revealed that he was making a satisfactory adjustment both at home and in school and that he had not sought medical consultation in the interim, aside from a routine checkup.

Comment

Bjorn's case is interesting for several reasons. First, it illustrates the broad scope of issues relating to behavior that psychologists may be called on to evaluate. In Bjorn's case, these issues ranged from assessing the behavioral effects of localized brain injury to evaluating the social context of his behavior.

Second, it demonstrates that the presence of documented cerebral impairment does not rule out the possibility of effective psychological intervention (Smith et al., 1972; Reitan and Wolfson, 1986). In this case, the psychologist working with Bjorn and his family focused on aspects of the social environment that acted to exaggerate and maintain physical symptomatology beyond a time when there was any obvious physiological basis for these complaints. Psychologists have long recognized that change in the status of a family member can disrupt accustomed relationship patterns, the outcome of which can be either a gradual return to health and familial equilibrium, or, in some cases, a reorganization of communication patterns in a way that promotes dependence and passivity in the affected member (Haley, 1971).

In Bjorn's case, there is no question that the accident had resulted in actual brain damage: this was documented by neurological examinations, EEGs, and other measures at the time of the accident. Moreover, subtle signs of residual cerebral impairment were evident nearly two years after the accident, as documented by the neuropsychological assessment (Salmon and Meyer, 1986). However, the fact that at this later time Bjorn was functioning in a high average range of intelligence and was doing reasonably well in school suggested that the residual effects of brain trauma per se were relatively slight and could not by themselves account for the chronic depressed state into which Bjorn had lapsed. Thus, the family system appeared the logical place on which to focus psychological intervention and ultimately proved effective in altering these problems.

Also, a clear implication of the assessment results is that the diagnosis of a mental disorder in an individual—even when based on verified cerebral impairment—should not exclude consideration of the role of social networks in maintaining symptomatology (Bornstein and Bornstein, 1986). Perhaps in Bjorn's case it would have been equally appropriate to characterize his entire family as in a depressive state, rather than singling out any individual.

Finally, the reports of significant changes in behavior and eventual recovery attest to the marvelous recuperative powers of the central nervous system (Smith and Sugar, 1975; Reitan and Wolfson, 1986). Bjorn's age undoubtedly was a factor in his recovery; had he sustained the injury when he was older, recovery might not have been as complete. Nonetheless, it is evident that recuperation from even serious CNS traumas occur routinely, although the exact mechanisms through which this takes place are not completely understood.

REFERENCES

Bornstein, P. and Bornstein, M. (1986) *Marital Therapy*. New York: Pergamon.

Gass, C. and Russell, E. (1986) Differential impact of brain damage and depression in memory test performance. *Journal of Consulting and Clinical Psychology*, *54*, 261–263.

Haley, J. (Ed.) (1971) *Changing Families. A Family Therapy Reader*. New York: Grune & Stratton.

Kail, R. and Pellegrino, J. (1985) *Human Intelligence*. New York: W. H. Freeman.

Kolevzon, M. and Green, R. (1985) *Family Therapy Models*. New York: Springer.

Meister, R. (1980) *Hypochondria*. New York: Taplinger.

Newmark, C. (1985) The MMPI. In C. Newmark (Ed.) *Major Psychological Assessment Instruments*. Boston: Allyn and Bacon.

Reitan, R. and Wolfson, D. (1986) *Traumatic Brain Injury: Recovery and Rehabilitation*. Tucson, Ariz.: Neuropsychology Press.

Salmon, P. and Meyer, R. (1986) Neuropsychological assessment: Adults. In M. Kurke and R. Meyer (Eds.), *Psychology in Product Liability and Personal Injury Law*. New York: Hemisphere.

Smith, A. and Sugar, O. (1975) Development of above normal language and intelligence 21 years after left hemispherectomy. *Neurology*, *25*, 813–818.

Smith, A., Chamoux, R., Leri, J., London, R., and Muraski, A. (1972) *Diagnosis, Intelligence, and Rehabilitation of Chronic Aphasics*. Ann Arbor: University of Michigan Department of Physical Medicine and Rehabilitation.

Walsh, K. W. (1978) *Neuropsychology*. New York: Churchill Livingstone.

/ Alzheimer's Disease

The Case of Al

> Eric thought how much he didn't want to be where he was, watching the remains of what once was probably a wonderful human. Some people hated cancer more than any other disease; Eric hated senility. (p. 248)
>
> — William Goldman
> *Control*

Alzheimer's disease is a form of dementia caused by the progressive deterioration of brain cells. It is referred to as a "presenile dementia" because the age of onset can be as early as 50. This distinguishes Alzheimer's disease from other forms of neural deterioration associated with the latter phases of the lifespan, which are collectively referred to as the "senile dementias." In actual practice, the distinction between "presenile" and "senile" dementias is a problematic one, because there is some disagreement regarding the age at which "senile" should be first used (Dubler and Melnick, 1985). Also it is now generally believed that the forms of neural degeneration in both types are essentially the same (Katzman, 1976; Salmon and Meyer, 1986; Ridley, Baker, and Crow, 1986).

Unlike certain forms of CNS impairment, Alzheimer's disease involves widespread deterioration of brain tissue so that a broad range of cognitive, behavioral, and physical capabilities eventually become affected. Nerve tissues are invaded by pathogenic structures, known as neuritic plaques and neurofibrillary tangles (Mace and Rabins, 1981), which interfere with nerve conduction impulses. The course of the disease is fairly rapid, with death generally occurring within four to five years from the time of onset.

Diagnostic Signs

At the beginning, manifestations of Alzheimer's disease are typically rather subtle (Nott and Fleminger, 1975). Often the first indications take the form of slight but persistent memory difficulties or of a perceptible loss of efficiency in going about one's daily activities (Strub and Black, 1980). Gradually, a more severe and generalized impairment of intellectual capabilities becomes evident. Cognitive skills such as reading, writing, and reasoning begin to show impairment as an increasing number of brain centers are affected. Signs of neurological impairment become evident, with abnormalities in EEG and visual-evoked potentials being reliably reported (Harding, Wright, and Orwin, 1985). Changes in emotional status are evident as well, as bouts of depression, lability (fluctuating mood states), and heightened irritability become increasingly frequent. Eventually, the disease progresses to where the patient is persistently confused, incoherent, and disoriented. At this stage, there is usually a failure to recognize even spouses and children. Self-care and basic hygiene skills deteriorate, and there ensues an almost total dependence on others (Association, 1985; Kelly, 1984).

Alzheimer's disease is one of several conditions that are classified as forms of dementia in the DSM. For the diagnosis to be made, it is typically required there be evidence of (1) memory loss; (2) impaired generalized intellectual functioning; and (3) evident impairment in one or more specific cognitive capabilities, such as speech, reasoning, drawing, or writing. There must also be accompanying evidence that these impairments are related to an underlying neurologically based condition. This is somewhat difficult to determine in the case of Alzheimer's disease because the neural changes involved in the disease are not easily detected by standard neurodiagnostic techniques such as CT scans or EEGs, particularly during the early stages.

Researchers Iyer and Surwillo (1986) of the University of Louisville

School of Medicine are working on a painless test for Alzheimer's that would resemble an average hearing test. While the test would not immediately replace current ones, it would complement them and someday could be a primary tool for diagnosing the disease.

The test is relatively quick and measures how quickly the brain reacts to sound. A suspected Alzheimer's sufferer listens to a series of tones through a headset while electrodes placed on the head and ears measure brain waves. As a person grows older, the brain usually takes longer to react to the tones— within a specific range. If the reaction time exceeds this range, clinicians know the person suffers from dementia—a progressive deterioration of mental functions. Then they can eliminate other causes of dementia to determine if the patient suffers specifically from Alzheimer's.

In some instances, therefore, a confirming diagnosis can now only be made via post-mortem examination (Price, 1986). However, the *functional* behavioral and neurological manifestations of Alzheimer's disease become increasingly pronounced as the disease progresses, leaving little doubt as to the presence of underlying CNS impairment.

Psychological Assessment

Psychological assessments of patients with Alzheimer's disease are of greatest help during the early stages of the disorder. There are three major ways in which these evaluations contribute to the diagnosis and management of the disease. First, early manifestations of Alzheimer's disease often include subtle changes in memory, mood, and cognition that can frequently be detected or validated via psychological testing (Newmark, 1985). In conjunction with a neurological evaluation, this information may provide some of the earliest indications of the impending changes in mental status that result from the disease. Second, a thorough assessment of psychological capabilities can help both patient and family develop realistic strategies for coping with the disease. Significant issues such as employment status and disability determination must be confronted, and psychological assessments can provide useful information to help make informed decisions in these areas. Finally, periodic psychological assessments can help evaluate the patient's ongoing status, in much the same way that repeated physical and neurological examinations do (Salmon and Meyer, 1986; Kelly, 1984).

Plainly, victims of Alzheimer's disease, as well as their families, must confront a variety of psychological stressors. The patient must deal with the progressive deterioration of mental capabilities whereby routine activities can eventually turn into confusing ordeals. A particularly stressful period comes when a tentative diagnosis has been made while the patient continues to be basically alert and oriented. At this phase, the prospect of facing an ultimately fatal illness following the gradual loss of behavioral and mental control is highly stressful and frequently triggers secondary disorders such as depression (Association, 1985).

Family members face several key stressors and often need help at this point (Hoopes, Fisher, and Barlow, 1984). Many report that the increasing inability of a parent or spouse to recognize them as the disease progresses is especially disturbing. Related to this is the distress of adapting to the inevitable changes that transform a previously healthy, vital individual into someone who is debilitated, frequently depressed, irritable, and eventually totally dependent on others (Levinson, 1986). Many families encounter significant problems in locating health care services for the patient, particularly as home management becomes less and less feasible. Finally, families of patients with Alzheimer's disease frequently must endure extraordinary financial hardships as well. This is most evident in situations where the patient has been the chief economic provider and is afflicted with the disease at a point in his or her career when maximal earning power is nearing its peak.

Many of these issues are relevant to a discussion of Al, a physician who was first diagnosed as having Alzheimer's disease when he was 55.

The Case of Al

Al was a physician with a successful private practice in his midwestern home town. Married and the father of four children, he was highly respected for his work as a pediatrician and seen as a vital member of his community. The children whom he saw and their parents alike had a great deal of confidence in his clinical skills. Moreover, they found him to be a warm, caring person who devoted a great deal of time and attention to everyone he saw.

He had been in practice for twenty years, after graduating from medical school near the top of his class. He had received a prestigious research fellowship in pediatrics following graduation and was able to study with a world-renowned specialist in his area of interest. He retained an active interest in research, occasionally writing articles of clinical interest based on data collected over years of work with his patients. He attempted to keep himself aware of current developments in the field by reading professional journals and attending various workshops. He had even recently purchased a computer system to help organize his clinical work and research.

Al had reached an age where most professionals of comparable stature are leading highly productive lives, are economically well-off, and may be starting to contemplate either retirement or at least a gradual reduction in workload in the coming years. Although he met all these criteria, Al was worried.

Beginning shortly after he turned 53 he began to notice some things that bothered him. He occasionally found it difficult to remember the names of patients he'd seen since they had been infants. He found it increasingly necessary to check and recheck patient files for basic information he'd previously prided himself on knowing from memory. While reading medical journals, he found himself occasionally perplexed by terminology and concepts that had long been familiar to him. The installation of his computer system, which he hoped would ease record-keeping and other routine tasks, provoked added worries. On occasion he found himself reading procedural manuals again and again, yet remembering or understanding little of what he read, though at other times, he seemed to grasp the information with no difficulty. Finally, he noticed that his moods seemed to fluctuate a bit more. He was well-known for his even, gentle disposition, yet found himself from time to time feeling unaccountably depressed or irritable.

Al had done some basic psychiatric coursework while a resident and knew that people in his age range are sometimes prone to bouts of depression and a generalized loss of efficiency. This condition was traditionally referred to as *involutional melancholia* and viewed as essentially a functional disorder. Al reviewed the features of involutional melancholia in his old textbook on psychiatric disorders and initially felt satisfied that this was the best way of explaining his symptoms. He believed, moreover, that the condition was a temporary one and that things would improve with time.

Unfortunately, things became worse. Al experienced more extensive periods of irritability and depression, to the point where family members and patients noticed the change. He continued to have trouble with his memory, and a few weeks later he forgot to administer a key medication to one of his patients, who subsequently became quite ill. Although it was never proven that his error was responsible for the illness, he felt that he could no longer ignore the symptoms. He consulted a psychiatrist for assistance.

Initially, depression was suspected, because of the periods of dysphoria and unhappiness which Al reported. However, a mental status examination turned up some surprising findings, including the fact that Al found it difficult to remember number sequences shorter than a phone number. Moreover, his conversational speech occasionally revealed errors such as unintentional word substitutions, mispronunciations, and lack of clarity in self-expression. Most surprising was Al's inability to recall easily either the medical school he had graduated from or his year of graduation. Despite these problems, Al remained well oriented to his surroundings and proved quite conversant with the technical aspects of his profession.

It was decided at this point that further neurological and psychological workups were necessary. Al voluntarily agreed to suspend practice pending the outcome of these tests and turned his patients over to another member of his group practice. The results of subsequent evaluations were in some conflict. Although the CT scan did not show any clear indications of major pathological changes in the brain, there were suggestions of very mild atrophy (degeneration) that was considered somewhat atypical for someone of Al's age. An EEG detected some generalized, mild arrhythmic patterns, but overall appeared to be within normal limits.

A neuropsychological assessment, on the other hand, turned up evidence suggesting that cerebral efficiency was notably impaired. At the most general level, a test of basic intellectual skills, the Wechsler Adult Intelligence Scale-R (Newmark, 1985), revealed current functioning to be barely in the "high average" range. Available information suggested that this represented a decline from prior capabilities, estimated to have been in the "superior" range.

Additional measures in the neuropsychological battery suggested somewhat impaired performance. Evidence for this was of four types. First, Al showed marked slowing on tests of motor speed and dexterity. Second, he was severely taxed by tests requiring new learning of any sort. For example, when asked to form and remember associations between pairs of unrelated words, Al recalled only a few, even after numerous learning trials. Third, Al struggled considerably with problem-solving tasks, such as arithmetic calculations with multiple steps. Even when using paper and pencil, the effortful quality of his performance was noticeable and seemed uncharacteristic for someone with such a high level of achievement. Finally, there were once again indications of occasional errors in speech and language of the sort initially uncovered in the psychiatrist's mental status examination.

Any one of these symptoms might reasonably be attributed to anxiety or other purely functional causes, engendered by the prospect of the examination itself. However, that there were several indications of impaired cognition in selected areas made the attribution to anxiety alone questionable. Moreover, Al actually denied feeling much anxiety during testing. Instead, he conveyed a sense of mild impatience, as if to suggest that the testing was somewhat beneath his capabilities. Beyond this, the fact that Al's intellectual capabilities appeared to have undergone a decline suggested the presence of a more debilitating underlying condition.

Although the results of these evaluations were not unambiguously conclusive, there were enough indications of functional impairment that Al was advised to give up his medical practice. Although he initially protested this decision somewhat, he subsequently expressed some feelings of relief that he no longer had to make decisions regarding the diagnosis and treatment of his patients. For a few weeks, his condition appeared to improve somewhat, no doubt caused by alleviation of some of the pressures under which he had labored.

Unfortunately, the improvement was short-lived, and Al's condition began to decline more obviously in the succeeding months. He began to experience periods of confusion and disorientation that both he and his family found frightening. His ability to make decisions concerning even simple family matters became increasingly impaired, to the point that his wife quietly took over all the administrative aspects of running the household.

Occasionally, he became depressed and tearful over his inability to practice medicine, and at one point he accused his family of conspiring to keep him from returning to work. Although a few of his colleagues had attempted to maintain contact with him after he stopped work, his bouts of increasing irritability and depression became so frequent that it was difficult for people to communicate effectively with him. As his condition worsened, he began experiencing flashbacks to his days as a medical researcher, often mistaking those around him for former colleagues and assistants who he ordered to carry out various tasks.

Repeated medical, neurological, and psychological evaluations documented his declining status, and within four years of the onset of his symptoms, Al had to be placed in a comprehensive care setting because his family was no longer able to meet his caretaking needs. Eight months later he died, and the subsequent autopsy revealed the neural degeneration uniquely characteristic of Alzheimer's disease.

Comment

At present, Alzheimer's disease, perhaps the best known of the presenile dementias, is a condition for which there is no known cure (Price, 1986). As far as the cause is concerned, it is known that victims of Alzheimer's disease are deficient in the chemical choline acetyltransferase (Mace and Rabins, 1981), which is needed to produce the neurotransmitter acetylcholine. Neurotransmitter insufficiency has led researchers to explore treatment based on replacing the missing substances, and short-term improvements in memory and cognitive skills have been reported (Davis and Mohs, 1982). The immediate cause of Alzheimer's disease involves degeneration of brain cells in the region where acetylcholine is produced. Why this occurs is less clear. Explanations ranging from viral infections to immunological deficiencies and even metal toxicity have been advanced. So far, the most compelling explanation is one based on hereditary vulnerability (Mace and Rabins, 1981; Ridley, Baker, and Crow, 1986).

Al's situation illustrates a number of characteristics of the disease. First is the time of onset, which is earlier than would be the case for CNS deterioration due primarily to the natural effects of those conditions associated with the aging process. Second, the ambiguity surrounding the diagnosis of Al's condition is not uncommon in clinical practice. Often multiple diagnostic assessments will reveal somewhat conflicting data, leaving the patient and physician uncertain at the outset. It is only as the disease progresses that unmistakable signs of CNS impairment become more evident (Dubler and Melnick, 1985).

Finally, note must be taken of the impact of Al's illness on both himself and his family (Association, 1985). Afflicted at a point when his professional career was at its peak, and at a time when his family was totally dependent upon him financially, Al found it very difficult to accept either the inevitability of his condition or the fact that he had been afflicted to begin with. His family experienced chronic, unremitting stress during the years of his illness, and his wife found it necessary to seek outside employment for the first time in her life. Her distress at seeing the gradual erosion of her husband's many capabilities and qualities led her to seek supportive therapy both with an individual therapist and with a local support group for victims of Alzheimer's disease and their families (Hoopes, Fisher, and Barlow, 1984; Patterson, 1986).

REFERENCES

Association for the Understanding of Alzheimer's Disease. (1985) *Alzheimer's Disease and Related Disorders*. New York: Scribner's.

Davis, K., and Mohs, R. (1982). Enhancement of memory processes in Alzheimer's disease with multiple-dose intravenous phyostigmine. *American Journal of Psychiatry*, *139*, 1421–1423.

Dubler, N. and Melnick, V. (Eds.) (1985) *Alzheimer's Disease: Dilemmas in Clinical Research*. Clifton, N.J.: Humana.

Harding, G., Wright, C., and Orwin, A. (1985) Primary presenile dementia: The use of the visual evoked potential as a diagnostic indicator. *British Journal of Psychiatry*, *147*, 532–539.

Hoopes, M., Fisher, B. and Barlow, S. (1984) *Structured Family Facilitation Programs*. Rockville, Md.: Aspen Systems.

Iyer, V. and Surwillo, W. (1986) Personal communication.

Katzman, R. (1976) The prevalence and malignancy of Alzheimer disease. *Archives of Neurology, 33,* 217.

Kelly, W. (1984) *Alzheimer's Disease and Related Disorders.* Springfield, Ill.: Charles C. Thomas.

Levinson, D. (1986) A conception of adult development. *American Psychologist, 41,* 3–13.

Mace, N., and Rabins, P. (1981) *The 36-Hour Day.* Baltimore: Johns Hopkins University Press.

Newmark, C. (1985) *Major Psychological Assessment Instruments.* Boston: Allyn and Bacon.

Nott, P. and Fleminger, J. (1975) Presenile dementia: The difficulties of early diagnosis. *Acta Psychiatrica Scandinavica, 52,* 210–217.

Patterson, C. (1986) *Theories of Counseling and Psychotherapy.* New York: Harper & Row.

Price, D. (1986) New perspectives on Alzheimer's disease. In W. Cowan (Ed.) Annual Review of Neuroscience, *9,* Palo Alto, Calif.: Annual Reviews, Inc.

Ridley, R., Baker, H., and Crow, T. (1986) Transmissible and non-transmissible neurodegenerative disease. *Psychological Medicine, 16,* 199–207.

Salmon, P. and Meyer, R. (1986) Neuropsychological assessment. Adults. In M. Kurke and R. Meyer (Eds.), *Psychology in Product Liability and Personal Injury Law.* New York: Hemisphere.

Strub, R., and Black, F. (1980) *The Mental Status Examination in Neurology.* Philadelphia: F. A. Davis.

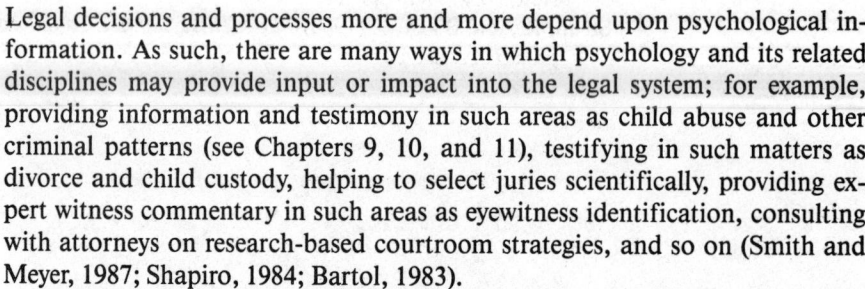

14

Legal Issues and Psychological Practice

Legal decisions and processes more and more depend upon psychological information. As such, there are many ways in which psychology and its related disciplines may provide input or impact into the legal system; for example, providing information and testimony in such areas as child abuse and other criminal patterns (see Chapters 9, 10, and 11), testifying in such matters as divorce and child custody, helping to select juries scientifically, providing expert witness commentary in such areas as eyewitness identification, consulting with attorneys on research-based courtroom strategies, and so on (Smith and Meyer, 1987; Shapiro, 1984; Bartol, 1983).

However, some of the most common and important input comes in the areas of evaluating criminal responsibility, competence to stand trial or to handle one's affairs, gauging potential dangerousness and its relationship to involuntary civil commitment, and the appraisal of honesty or truth-telling by participants in the criminal justice system as well as in other areas. The first case in this chapter, of Ingrid, provides a ready transition from the prior chapter (Organic Mental Disorders), as it deals with the significant and widespread issue of deciding when the psychological and physical ravages of aging require a decision that a person is no longer competent to handle his or her personal affairs. The second case, of Frank, is concerned with the assessment of truth-telling, in this instance as it relates to either possible malingering or to the unique and interesting factitious disorder. The last case focuses on the issues of deciding a person's competence to stand trial, the level of criminal responsibility, and the potential for dangerousness through the well-publicized but not always well-understood case of John Hinckley, who attempted to assassinate President Reagan.

REFERENCES

Bartol, C. (1983) *Psychology and American Law*. Belmont, Calif.: Wadsworth.
Shapiro, D. (1984) *Psychological Evaluation and Expert Testimony*. New York: Van Nostrand Reinhold.
Smith, S. and Meyer, R. (1987) *Law, Behavior, and Mental Health: Policy and Practice*. New York: New York University Press.

Central Nervous System Dysfunction and Legal Incompetence from Aging and/or Alcohol

The Case of Ingrid

> *"Nothing doing," Appleby said. "Although, mark you, it's astonishing what the forensic chaps can conjure up out of what seems to be empty air."*
>
> *"You mean, the idea that I'm of a disordered mind. . . ?" (p. 25)*
>
> — Michael Innes
> *Appleby and Honeybath*

As the other cases in this chapter will show, there are a variety of areas in which psychologists are frequently called on to address the issue of an individual's mental competence (Grisso, 1986; Reissner, 1985). "Competence" in the legal arena can refer to competence to manage one's daily affairs, to make a will, or to stand trial (defined in *Dusky* v. *United States*, 362 U.S. 402 [1960], as the ability to consult rationally with an attorney and to understand the relevant legal proceedings). For the purpose of this case, competence refers to the extent to which individuals are presumed capable of managing their daily affairs. This concept is especially important when applied to older persons. Although the majority of people will remain mentally alert (and presumably competent) throughout most of their lives, aging processes are accompanied by increasing changes that may compromise a person's mental status for any of several reasons, most commonly due to deterioration of the central nervous system (CNS) (Salmon and Meyer, 1986).

The term *dementia* is often used to signify the presence of CNS-based mental deterioration sufficient to interfere with a person's functioning, and is more commonly though inaccurately termed *senility*. As discussed in the DSM, dementia is diagnosed when there is evidence of significant intellectual decline, plus evidence of more specific cognitive deficits, one of which involves memory loss. Dementia need not have a specific cause; rather, it can result from a wide range of conditions that adversely affect the brain and other CNS structures (Reitan and Wolfson, 1986).

Dementia is often thought of as an essentially irreversible condition, particularly when evident in older persons; yet this is not always the case. For example, in many older persons, the arteries that supply blood to the brain gradually become occluded due to accumulated deposits of fatty substances (arteriosclerosis). This process curtails blood flow to the brain, reduces metabolic efficiency, and thereby lowers the activation of increasing forgetfulness, absentmindedness, and a general lowering of behavioral efficiency—in short, every indication of dementia, particularly when the condition has progressed to the point at which brain blood supply is markedly reduced. A significant effect of surgery to help restore brain blood supply (called an endarterectomy) is the often abrupt reversal of symptoms of dementia and the restoration of mental alertness.

Signs of evident dementia may diminish or reverse themselves in other instances, also. For example, unremitting alcohol consumption may cause a deterioration of mental functioning; this process can be reversed when the person gains control over the drinking (Vailliant, 1983). Whether or not dementia is actually present in such cases depends on whether it can be established that the contributory condition has had a demonstrable effect on CNS functioning.

The assessment of mental competence thus often involves a determination of whether dementia is present to a significant degree (Grisso, 1986). This task may be complicated somewhat by the fact that other mental disorders—particularly depression—can easily be confused with dementia (Lobel, 1984). This distinction is a very important one to make when assessing older persons, who in addition to being more biologically vulnerable to factors underlying true dementia are quite likely to experience events that trigger depressive reactions. For example, the death of a spouse or other loved one typically results in a depressive reaction characterized by brooding, preoccupation, and withdrawal. To outsiders, these reactions may appear as a condition indicative of dementia (or its more popularized cousin, senility).

An evaluation of mental competence in older persons thus requires a careful evaluation of events surrounding the reported onset of symptoms (Grisso, 1986). In addition to carrying out formal psychological testing, the psychologist must obtain a detailed history of the client's problems. It is of crucial importance to be able to distinguish true dementia from a depressive reaction, since the latter condition is by definition transient, with a correspondingly good prognosis. Furthermore, it is important to evaluate symptoms of dementia to see if the underlying process is progressive or in remission.

The following case highlights some of the issues involved in the determination of mental competence. It is a description of Ingrid, a 77-year-old woman who was referred for an extensive psychological assessment to aid the court in determining her mental competence.

The Case of Ingrid

Ingrid's husband Charlie had died three years earlier, following a long series of illnesses. They had been a devoted couple, and his death sent Ingrid into a deep depression. For the first time in her life, Ingrid began to drink heavily as a means of washing away the emotional pain that accompanied Charlie's death. She appeared to others to become absentminded and forgetful, as if lost in a dream-like reverie. On several occasions, Ingrid's neighbors noticed her doing strange things, such as working in her garden in midwinter and taking out the trash when only partially dressed. Charlie had left her a sizable estate – ample to meet her needs plus an inheritance for the children. On one or two occasions, she talked about giving all the money to a charity, as if any reminder of Charlie's former presence was too much to bear.

Alarmed at these developments – particularly at the prospect of having his inheritance jeopardized – Ingrid's son (age 53) petitioned to have his mother declared legally incompetent to manage her affairs. The petition was upheld in a court hearing, and Ingrid's financial holdings were turned over to a court-appointed trustee, who provided her with ample funds to live on in a local nursing home. At the hearing, the attorney retained by Ingrid's son argued that her advanced age made it reasonable to assume that the depression following Charlie's death was only part of a broader picture of mental deterioration indicative of encroaching senility. By way of contrast, expert testimony included the report of a clinical psychologist who, although agreeing that Ingrid showed signs of significant mental impairment, felt that the condition was only temporary and should not be presumed to be accompanied by dementia (senility) merely because of the client's advanced age. He recommended that Ingrid's condition be reevaluated several months hence, should it appear that she showed signs of remission.

Eighteen months later, Ingrid herself wrote a meticulously worded, impeccably reasoned letter to the judge requesting that her case be reopened, and at the same time she hired a new attorney. She was in much better spirits and seemed optimistic that they would succeed in overturning the earlier ruling. As part of the proceedings, a thorough neuropsychological assessment was carried out. In addition to evaluating global intellectual performance, it assessed five groups of cognitive skills that are sensitive to CNS impairments: speech and language skills, visuospatial abilities, attention and concentration, memory, and sensory-motor areas.

The results of this assessment suggested that Ingrid appeared mentally competent, and that whatever condition(s) had been responsible for her earlier mental relapses were no longer apparent. There was no indication of dementia – Ingrid manifested an intelligence quotient in the upper portion of the average range, possessed adequate memory skills, and showed no significant indication of other specific thinking disorders. She appeared to have compensated well for some sensory and motor impairments (poor eyesight, slight hearing loss, plus an obvious motor tremor), and appeared for the assessment as a socially alert, cooperative, well-groomed woman, fully aware of the purpose of the evaluation and related events. As stated in the evaluation (reproduced here in summary form):

> On the Wechsler Adult Intelligence Scale (WAIS), Mrs. A [Ingrid] achieved a Full Scale IQ score which places her at a level slightly above average for individuals of similar age. Her performance was highly consistent, notable for the absence of diagnostic indicators on the WAIS associated with signs of cerebral impairment. These results were obtained despite evidence of sensory and motor deficits including pronounced motor tremor, bilateral cataracts, and possibly transient hearing difficulty. Mrs. A appears to have developed compensatory strategies

which included guiding the right hand with the left to minimize tremor, use of a magnifying glass, plus slow visual scanning patterns; and postural adjustments to maximize auditory volume, along with requests for repetition of test items on occasion. Overall, results of the WAIS were compatible with the client's educational and job history and reveal normal age-related slowing of response speed and information processing efficiency, without evidence of additional intrusive factors which would interfere with intellectual performance.

Overall, the assessment of this 78-year-old woman reveals intellectual and cognitive capabilities in an above-average range, above-average memory abilities, and a well-focused, organized approach to the tests. Verbal and linguistic fluency appears developed to a higher degree than corresponding skills in visuoperceptual areas—a discrepancy which may be enhanced by the visual and motor problems apparent to casual observation.

A court verdict in Ingrid's favor was returned, legally restoring her rights and privileges to manage her own affairs.

The results of formal testing give only a hint of the range of observations needed to provide a clear picture of Ingrid's mental status. These observations contributed to a three-dimensional image of a competent, well-adjusted individual. We will now discuss some of these factors in more detail.

The evaluation was conducted in two different locations—first in the examiner's office and then at the nursing home where Ingrid lived. By carrying out the assessment at two different times and in two different locations, it was possible to evaluate the consistency of Ingrid's behavior. On both occasions, she was neatly groomed and dressed and acted in a most cordial fashion. When seen in her own room at the nursing home, it was immediately apparent that Ingrid's living environment reflected active interests. A desk, set up near the bed, contained neatly organized materials—pencils, pens, a work lamp, stationery, plus a vase of freshly cut flowers. She had organized her business papers in one section of the desk; and on one occasion, after stating that she wished to show the examiner some pertinent material, unerringly located them without hesitation or confusion. The material turned out to be a handwritten copy of the letter she had recently sent to the judge requesting a new competency hearing.

Ingrid proved well aware of the purpose of the evaluation and was able to explain clearly the events leading up to the current situation. She was quite frank in discussing the particulars of her history, readily admitting that the grief, fear, and even anger engendered by her husband's death had caused her to do some unfortunate things. Neither her manner and affect, nor the details of her account of these events varied appreciably between the two assessment sessions.

Her response to the testing was characteristic of many older persons faced with taking tests—she was anxious (DeRivera, 1984). She expressed some trepidation regarding the nature of the tests and was concerned that her lack of recent experience with similar sorts of activities would markedly compromise her performance. In addition, she was dismayed at the prospect of having to analyze problems without the aid of paper and pencil (or her new calculator, which she had recently learned to use as an aid in analyzing her investments). It is important to consider a client's reaction to the tests themselves, as extreme anxiety can have a markedly adverse effect on performance. Ingrid was well aware that the results of the assessment would be used in the determination of her legal competency, yet she managed to master whatever anxiety she felt and performed well on the tests.

During the initial assessment session, Ingrid failed to solve an arithmetic problem involving the computation of a percentage. As a former bookkeeper, she was quite upset at her performance on this particular test item.

She remembered the details of the problem, however, and at the beginning of the following session five days later, produced the correct solution, along with the results of several similar problems that she had made up. This gave evidence of a number of things, including excellent memory skills, persistence in problem-solving, a desire to improve on performance, and perhaps a degree of overcompensation and compulsiveness. It was evident that well into her advanced years Ingrid had retained a strong desire to both please and impress people. The only difference was that she now found herself trying to please subordinates both in age and experience and to prove to them that she could perform up to standards that people far younger than she had set.

Additional indications of mental competency accrue from other sources. A sense of humor, for example, is frequently treated as a sign of mental alertness. Ingrid possessed a mildly self-deprecatory sense of humor, and more generally, an overall attitude that appeared uplifting and optimistic. A number of test responses indicated interpersonal sensitivity and awareness of social conventions. Thus, her behavior in this regard was much in keeping with social norms. Finally, a chance question asked during a mental status examination — "Who is President of the United States?" — revealed additional evidence of considerable mental alertness: Ingrid replied that Jimmy Carter had been President up until that very morning but had been replaced by Ronald Reagan!

These and other indications of behavioral consistency, alertness, and socially apt behavior, apparent during the course of two test sessions, provided evidence of mental competency that amplified and individualized the rather bland assertion that Ingrid possessed "average intellectual functioning." A comprehensive description of Ingrid based on these observations took on additional significance in light of the opinion that people were prone to form of her based on first impressions. For example, at the onset of the evaluation, she stated that the examiner would have to speak somewhat loudly, and she closed in to a distance that violated usual though unspoken standards regarding how close two people normally get. Unless able to use a magnifying glass, she resorted to scanning visual materials with her face very close to the page. When writing, she had to steady her right hand with the left in order to lessen the effects of a pronounced motor tremor. Such behavior, from a distance, could easily create a stereotyped image of an incompetent individual. And yet it was precisely this sort of behavior that attested to Ingrid's awareness of her limitations and to her successful efforts to adapt to them. It is not uncommon to find individuals of any age who appear superficially incompetent simply because they are not active and do not behave in ways that might betray their limitations, or to find still others whose behavior is maladaptive because they are not aware of their limitations. By comparison, Ingrid really was quite competent and well-adjusted.

Treatment

While certain drug combinations have shown some success in improving memory in persons with problems similar to Ingrid's, it was not deemed necessary here, nor was any formal psychological intervention undertaken. When she learned of the favorable decision, she promptly reinvested a portion of her estate in money market funds, sold the family homestead, and purchased a condominium in a progressive retirement community that provided increasing levels of health care as needed by the members. Having quickly dispatched these tasks, she took her first vacation in years—a long cruise. She commented that the outcome of the hearing had given her a new lease on life—at age 78!

Comment

The results of the extensive neuropsychological assessment carried out on this woman corroborated other diagnostic tests. All of the tests concluded that Ingrid's mental status was unimpaired and that there were no indications of any underlying CNS impairment which would seriously compromise her ability to think and reason effectively. The assessment did turn up evidence of normal age-related changes in test performance—chiefly a slowing of reaction time and somewhat lower flexibility when confronted with new information. Nevertheless, it was concluded that these factors would not impede Ingrid from competently carrying out her daily affairs—a conclusion amply confirmed by her subsequent behavior.

Beyond merely ruling out the presence of dementia, the thorough assessment of cognitive, intellectual, and social skills tended to highlight Ingrid's patterns of strengths and weaknesses and served to individualize her as a person. Thoroughness is important because a comprehensive assessment can help to counteract a tendency to view older persons (or any other nominal group) as homogeneous with respect to almost any characteristic (DeRivera, 1984). Although events associated with aging may predispose individuals to deterioration of mental capabilities, it is inappropriate to assume that such decline is inevitable, as demonstrated in Ingrid's case.

The most significant aspect of Ingrid's situation concerns the somewhat unusual reversal of a competency ruling in a person of relatively advanced age (Grisso, 1986). The outcome of her case further counteracts the popular tendency to view mental abilities in older persons as suspect (at best) and, if compromised, not readily recovered.

REFERENCES

DeRivera, J. (1984) Development and the full range of emotional experience. In C. Malatesta and C. Izard (Eds.), *Emotion in Adult Development*. Beverly Hills, Calif.: Sage.

Grisso, T. (1986) *Evaluating Competencies: Forensic Assessments and Instruments*. New York: Plenum.

Lobel, B. (1984) *Depression*. Rockville, Md.: Dept. of Health and Human Services (DHHS publication # (ADM) 84-1318).

Reissner, R. (1985) *Law and the Mental Health System*. St. Paul, Minn.: West.

Reitan, R. and Wolfson, D. (1986) *Traumatic Brain Injury: Recovery and Rehabilitation*. Tucson, Ariz.: Neuropsychology Press.

Salmon, P. and Meyer, R. (1986) Neuropsychological assessment: Adults. In M. Kurke and R. Meyer (Eds.), *Psychology in Product Liability and Personal Injury Law.* New York: Hemisphere.

Vailliant, G. (1983) *The Natural History of Alcoholism: Causes, Patterns, and Paths to Recovery.* Cambridge, Mass.: Harvard University Press.

/ Malingering, Factitious Disorder, or True Disorder

The Case of Frank

Listen . . . I don't know how accurate they are,
but I know they scare the hell out of people.
— Ex-President Richard M. Nixon
on lie detectors

Whenever the factitious disorder is considered as a possible diagnosis, the possibility of malingering must also be considered. Each label refers to a voluntary production of symptoms on the part of the client in an attempt to be labeled physically sick or psychologically disturbed. The primary differences arise from the motivations for this presentation. The malingerer tries to appear ill to gain some logical goal, such as exemption from criminal responsibility or financial compensation for alleged injuries (or skipping a test?) (Kurke and Meyer, 1986; Schachter, 1986). While malingerers may qualify for some DSM diagnosis, malingering itself is a description, not a diagnostic category.

In the case of factitious disorder, also known as Munchausen's syndrome, the motivation to appear to need treatment stems from the client's own peculiar psychology, rather than from an easily shared goal, which is malingering. Thus, although there is conscious deception, it is not technically malingering. The Munchausen syndrome was named after Baron Von Munchausen, an eighteenth-century German equivalent of America's Paul Bunyan, both of whom are associated with tall tales (Jones et al., 1986). The range of symptomatology is limited only by the imagination and the degree of sophistication about medical information. Some experience with hospitals or medical situations, either through previous hospitalizations or knowledge from family members who were involved in the medical profession, can contribute to this disorder. These persons rely on ill behaviors to elicit care from others, including physicians, nurses, and psychologists. Not surprisingly, most persons with Munchausen's syndrome lack close personal relationships that might provide alternative supports. At least one skilled patient, a Mr. McIlroy, was able to obtain over 200 separate hospital admissions, during which he was subjected to thousands of diagnostic procedures and hundreds of treatments, many of them quite painful (Pallis and Bamji, 1979). The willingness of these persons to submit to such rigors reveals the strength of their compulsion to be seen in the patient role. Though the disorder is relatively rare, it has been reported consistently since the first published systematic description in 1951 (Asher, 1951).

Bursten (1965) presented the following as major characteristics of Munchausen's syndrome:

1. The patient makes a dramatic presentation of one or more complaints, usually physical.

2. "Pseudologia Fantastica"—contrived, exaggerated, and intriguing accounts of the supposed illness.

3. The patient uses hospitals, clinics, and physicians in different geographical areas, so as to minimize communication among them.

As noted, Munchausen's syndrome has generally been identified in medical settings. Some authors (Sussman and Hyler, 1980; Hyler and Spitzer, 1978) have suggested that factitious psychological symptoms are less frequently detected if other legitimate symptoms are also present. Since most persons with the disorder qualify for some other diagnosis, this possibility bodes ill for improved detection.

In either malingering or the factitious disorder, the clinician's acumen in detecting deception is crucial (Ekman, 1985; Beaber et al., 1985). Both types of individuals are highly motivated and may have had considerable "training" in presenting their symptoms convincingly, depending on their prior experiences.

The Case of Frank

Frank presented himself at the university hospital emergency room complaining of severe abdominal pains, nausea, weakness, and recent weight loss. More dramatic was his assertion that he had dark blood clots in his stools and feared that he might have bleeding ulcerations somewhere in his digestive tract. An initial physical exam and laboratory work indicated the presence of coagulated blood, as he had suggested. Frank was admitted to the hospital and scheduled for a variety of diagnostic procedures, including barium enemas and swallows, blood tests, and endoscopy. None of these procedures yielded positive results, though Frank continued to report the above symptoms. Internists were puzzled by the finding that Frank's blood tests gave no indication of anemia, though this should have been a logical finding if he were losing blood internally and his symptoms were consistent with such a condition. After forty-eight hours in the hospital his stools no longer contained blood and his physicians, encouraged by the lack of significant findings, began to consider discharging him with outpatient follow-up.

Frank responded with hostility to this suggestion, claiming that only incompetent doctors could fail to identify the cause of his symptoms. He gave a history of prior admission for similar complaints and suggested that his bleeding was likely to recur. By the fourth day of hospitalization Frank's prediction was realized, as he again showed signs of modest internal bleeding along with extreme abdominal pains. His reports of pain seemed exaggerated, but he received large doses of narcotic drugs to ease his discomfort. He also demanded a considerable amount of attention from the nursing staff. Diagnostic studies continued to yield no conclusive evidence on the cause of his complaint.

On the sixth day in the hospital Frank was scheduled to be interviewed by a psychologist with the hospital's consultation/liaison service. A variety of staff members sought recommendations on how to deal with this difficult and demanding patient. Frank was initially resistant to any contact with the psychologist, claiming that his physicians were trying to divert attention from their failures by making him out to be "crazy." After three visits by the psychologist he established some rapport and became more open to talking about his illness. However, he gave little information about his personal history, family, or current life style. The psychologist found a number of reasons to disbelieve Frank's presentation of his illness and requested closer monitoring by the nursing staff. After it was discovered that Frank was tampering with his intravenous (IV) tubing in some way, his physicians became more confrontive in doubting his illness.

Following one such confrontation, Frank began to act strangely. He was assaultive toward staff members, often making paranoid statements indicating that he believed they were plotting against him. He also began to hallucinate, hearing voices which demanded that he throw objects across the room, and the like. He was transferred to the psychiatry ward, where he was observed to hallucinate continuously for several hours. Neuroleptic medications did not suppress these symptoms, until he became so sedated that he fell asleep. Upon awakening, Frank's behavior was still strange, but not overtly psychotic. He continued to verbalize paranoid delusions and seemed intent on provoking confrontations with other staff and patients. He was given a complete battery of psychological tests and subsequently identified as having factitious disorder with both physical and psychological symptom presentation.

The staff on the psychiatry ward refused to accept Frank's pathological presentation and established clear limits on the behavior they would tolerate. Over the course of several days his behavior became increasingly normal, and he was started in psychotherapy. He was then discharged and seen through the outpatient psychiatry service. Eventually, his physical symptoms subsided as a result of a rather long and thorough therapy process.

Etiology

Like many who manifest Munchausen's syndrome, Frank had a variety of experiences which seemed to predispose him for the disorder. He came from a small family which he described as cool and undemonstrative. His father worked for a television production company and was often quite busy and uninvolved with his family. His mother enjoyed tennis and bridge and spent the majority of her time at a country club. He only received attention from his parents when he suffered from the flu and other childhood illnesses. On these occasions his mother would spend the entire day with him, and his father would arrive home early bearing some gift to cheer him up. This pattern established Frank's expectation that he would only be cared for by others if he were ill. Not surprisingly, Frank experienced more frequent illnesses than most young people.

Frank had difficulty relating to peers and spent most of his time watching television rather than playing actively with other children. The maid, who looked after him during the day, enjoyed the dramatic hospital soap operas shown each afternoon, and Frank watched these with her. These shows often depicted mysterious illnesses and exaggerated, almost histrionic responses to these conditions by other characters. Viewing these shows may have heightened Frank's expectation that suffering from some malady would elicit tremendous caring from others.

Frank was perceived as an anxious, emotionally constricted boy. He continued to be isolated from others his age and so became increasingly dependent on adult figures such as his parents and teachers. His parents continued their reticence toward him, and teachers were pleased by his academic talents but resisted giving him more attention than the other students. The more Frank seemed to demand attention from others, the more they resisted him. Consequently, he learned to use very indirect, passive ways of interacting with others. Despite his social awkwardness, he did well academically and by high school was encouraged to think about college and a career. He became interested in medicine, which pleased his parents, who felt that he could succeed in this field.

As a pre-med major in college, Frank did well in his studies, but his social life was poor. He was often lonely and depressed and received little comfort from his parents. On the one occasion that he earned a poor grade he was informed that they "were very disappointed" in him. Frank applied himself to his studies. However, he experienced intermittent illnesses that kept him from class, and he subsequently began to develop stomach problems, in part due to his chronic anxiety. Whenever he felt poorly, he would go to the student health service, which was staffed primarily by youthful medical residents. Frank enjoyed interacting with these young people, and his identification with medicine and the patient role were strengthened by the care he received there, particularly because he had no other source of support. Rather than spending time with other students, Frank attended lectures and presentations at the university hospital, often wearing a white lab coat; around the campus he wore the aqua slipover shirts typically seen on hospital personnel. His enthusiasm impressed the medical school faculty, and he was admitted upon graduation from college.

The stress of medical school eventually proved too great for Frank. He developed a peptic ulcer and had to be admitted to the hospital for treatment. Compared to the harried and stressful life of a medical student, being a patient was a pleasant change, despite the painful symptoms he experienced. Classmates and medical school faculty took time to visit, though normally none of these persons took any interest in him. Much like his experiences as a child, this episode served to demonstrate that life was more pleasant when he was perceived as sick, because others became interested and caring. His convalescence required that he drop out of medical school for that term, but he did not return home, feeling that his parents would not welcome him.

When he resumed classes the following term, Frank found it difficult to manage the renewed stress. People who had seemed concerned for him during his illness once again perceived him as boring, insecure, and overly dependent. He subsequently dropped out of the program and obtained an unsatisfying job as an orderly at a local nursing home. He had no friends and spent all of his free time reading or watching television. Kohut (1977) has noted that the self-examination that follows such a change in career goals can lead to increased depression and anxiety.

After several months Frank felt compelled to gain readmission to the hospital and, drawing on his knowledge of medicine, chose to present new gastrointestinal symptoms. He obtained a large quantity of beef blood from a butcher shop, which he drank for several days prior to his appearance at the emergency room. Because he lost no blood of his own, he did not appear anemic. The reappearance of blood in his stool was managed by disconnecting the lower part of his IV tubing and using it to suck small quantities of blood from his arm. Faced with exposure following his discussions with the psychologist, Frank decided to present himself as "crazy," feeling that this might deflect attention from his previous deception while being more difficult to detect as dissimulation.

Detection. The psychologist who consulted in Frank's case was instrumental in identifying his internal bleeding as factitious. The referral request from Frank's internists reported that he seemed particularly anxious and possessed an unusual knowledge of medical terminology and methods. It was initially thought that his anxiety might be exacerbating some underlying medical condition, such as colitis. The nursing staff reported that Frank was extremely demanding of staff time and that he seemed to relish any opportunity to regale them with accounts of his illness. When he was told to limit his demands on the nurses, he became quite angry and insulting. Finally, while many patients respond with ambivalence when they are scheduled for a psychology or psychiatry consult, few respond as Frank did, becoming very secretive about everything but his illness. As a result, the psychologist gave special attention to the possibility that Frank was being deceptive.

Three approaches to detecting deception were employed in this case, with the first centering on the interviews with Frank. The consultant was careful to gather as much information about the case as possible prior to interviewing Frank for the first time, thus ensuring that any changes in his presentation would be detected. Frank's behavior during these interviews was analyzed as well. Ekman (1985) and others (Schachter, 1986) have described several behavioral changes that accompany the stress that deceivers experience, and the psychologist was careful to attend to these indicators. Finally, the psychologist worked with the internists to formulate several direct questions designed to circumvent any preparation on Frank's part. These included: "Why do you think your blood tests don't indicate anemia, when this should be the case?" These questions were asked in rapid succession with careful attention to potentially conflicting answers.

Following the discovery that Frank had tampered with his IV tubing, he chose to present a psychotic front to the staff. Of course, his credibility was now in doubt, and he was transferred to the psychiatry ward primarily for observation. While it is possible to fake a serious psychological disorder for a short time, it is very difficult to maintain this facade. In fact, Frank's behavior was an ineffective simulation of hallucinations. Typically, though certainly not always, hallucinations involve more than one sensory modality and are linked to some delusional system, but Frank reported only hearing voices, and their commands had nothing to do with his alleged delusions. He was observed to "hallucinate" continuously for several hours, although hallucinations are generally intermittent. Also, they seemed to decrease when he did not think he was observed. Finally, persons who hallucinate usually experience reduced symptoms on fairly large doses of neuroleptic medications, but are not totally tranquilized. Frank's hallucinations were not suppressed by medication because he tried to maintain his dissimulation right up to the point of unconsciousness. Observation thus indicated that Frank was feigning a severe disturbance.

A final approach to detecting deception involved the psychological test battery given to Frank. This battery included the Minnesota Multiphasic Personality Inventory (MMPI), the Rorschach inkblot technique, and a short test, the M test, devised by Beaber and his associates (1985) to discriminate between individuals who are psychotic and showing bizarre symptoms and those who are faking such symptoms. On the Rorschach, Frank was able to fake the content but not the processes of psychotic thinking, and he also showed a malingering pattern on the M test. On the MMPI Frank gave answers that elevated nearly all of the clinical scales, but his responses also indicated a blatant attempt to endorse all kinds of psychopathology. The psychologist found that Frank had endorsed obviously pathological items, while answering only a few of the more subtle pathology items in the scored direction (Posey and Hess, 1985). This pattern is typical of persons attempting to "fake bad," but who lack knowledge of the details of the disorder(s) they are attempting to imitate. Examining a number of special derived MMPI scores also indicated that Frank was faking. Grow, McVaugh, and Eno (1980) have reported on a number of techniques for detecting deception on the MMPI, and other standardized tests such as the Cattell 16PF and Millon Clinical Multiaxial Inventory allow for similar methods.

Physiological Measures of Deception. While inappropriate in the case of Frank, a number of approaches to detecting deception through physiological measurements have been popularized. The most widely used method is the polygraph, or lie detector. In fact, the polygraph measures physiological arousal, which can arise from a variety of emotional experiences including the distress of lying, but also including fear, anger, and even sexual arousal (Alpher and Blanton, 1985). The polygraph is so named because it actually measures several bodily functions, usually including at least respiration, heart rate, and blood pressure. The results obtained through a polygraph examination are strongly influenced by the questioning techniques employed, the skill of the examiner in getting the client to believe deception wil be detected, and the client's willingness to accept this belief.

Because the polygraph may "detect" such a variety of sources of arousal, it is often quite difficult to infer that a subject is being dishonest on the basis of polygraph records. While professional polygraphers claim extraordinarily high rates of accuracy in making such judgments, methodologically sound research indicates only modest validity. A key problem is the tendency of the polygraph to depict most subjects as lying. While 77 to 98 percent of deceptive subjects may be correctly identified, as many as half of all truthful subjects may be wrongly identified as liars (Landis and Meyer, 1987). In this regard, the Office of Technology Assessment, which provides data on important technological matters to the U.S. Congress, reviewed all of the available research on the polygraph (U.S. Congress-OTA, 1983). This review concluded that the polygraph may be useful in isolated cases where the information in question is very narrow and specific, but that these techniques are far less useful if the examiner is fishing for information, if the subject is not convinced of the polygraph's efficacy, or if the examiner is not well qualified, a finding corroborated by other reviews (Alpher and Blanton, 1985; Lykken, 1980; Landis and Meyer, 1987).

Other physiologically based methods of detecting deception produce even less satisfactory results. These methods include analysis of microtremors in the voice, monitoring of respiration with a radar-like device, and the study of capillary dilation in the inner eye. None of these approaches has yet shown any significant validity in controlled, independent studies (Landis and Meyer, 1987).

Treatment

Treatment for the factitious disorder must logically proceed on two fronts. First, the client's false presentation must be confronted, but in a way that does not completely alienate the client from staff who might help. Techniques derived from reality therapy (Glasser, 1969), or paradoxical therapy responses to the factitious symptoms (Seltzer, 1986), may be helpful in the initial stages, but flight from treatment is often a problem. Persons with this disorder are extremely resistant to psychotherapy, but they rarely qualify for involuntary commitment. Hence it is easy for them to leave one institution and gain admission at a hospital or clinic elsewhere. Because these people have tremendous unmet dependency needs, they may be well-motivated for therapy if this initial resistance can be overcome.

If the client is enlisted in an ongoing therapy effort, the bulk of the work centers on the dearth of social and coping skills that is usually evident (Goldstein and Myers, 1985). This lack of resources has led the client to resort to sick role behaviors to gain support and caring from others. Initially, the therapist may work toward developing insight into the role of early experiences in shaping the client's behavior, including the role of parents or other caretakers who were ineffective in nurturing the client. More adaptive behaviors are then cultivated. Social skills and assertiveness training may be undertaken to help the client acquire more direct and mature ways of interacting with others. Typically, the social skills efforts would focus on developing new, age-appropriate relationships in an effort to combat the loneliness and depression that the client experiences.

Relaxation training may also be useful for two reasons. It can be used in conjunction with social skills exercises if these new behaviors cause some anxiety. It may also have a more direct effect on the continuing high levels of anxiety experienced by those manifesting the factitious disorder.

Frank's Treatment.   Following Frank's evaluation on the psychiatry ward, the staff confronted him with their suspicion that his physical complaints and the majority of his psychological symptoms were false. They were careful to do this so as to reflect concern for his welfare, emphasizing to him the potential complications that could arise if he were to succeed with his maneuvers and receive unnecessary medical treatments. Frank was surprised both by their concern and the fact that they did not reject him for being deceptive. He agreed to continue contact with the hospital through the outpatient mental health service.

Frank's therapist spent a number of weeks asking about his life style and family background and was able to point out the variety of ways that he had been "trained" to present himself as ill in order to gain support and caring from others. Frank was able to recognize and understand these factors. At the same time, relaxation training was undertaken to help Frank alleviate his chronic anxiety.

Following this initial phase of treatment, Frank was given extensive social skills training by his therapist and by a volunteer working toward a graduate degree in counseling. This work included field exercises with the volunteer, who would accompany Frank to restaurants, shopping malls, and parks while he practiced meeting new people and interacting with them appropriately. He was initially very shy and became anxious during these exercises but was able to draw upon his relaxation training to combat this discomfort. As he became more at ease Frank acquired some ongoing acquaintances that provided appropriate social supports and emotional outlets. He was also coached through the process of getting a job more suitable for him. Following these gains his depression lifted considerably.

Frank subsequently joined a mixed outpatient therapy group. He had previously interacted with others on a superficial level, particularly women. The group required him to present himself honestly, and to respond appropriately to the emotional needs and difficulties of others. Frank found this experience very rewarding and came to regard himself as a good listener and empathizer. This realization helped him regard himself as worthy of attention and caring from others, and gave him confidence to enter into a serious romantic relationship.

Frank was seen for a total of eighteen months, though only the first six entailed intensive individual psychotherapy. His prognosis is good, largely because his pattern of factitious complaints was poorly developed when he was detected. Had he been more entrenched in these habits he would have been likely to travel to another setting where he could have presented a more convincing illness. The clinical acumen of the hospital staff in identifying his problems as factitious and recognizing that Frank needed understanding and therapy were crucial in producing this positive outcome.

Comment

As is evident in the case of Frank, detection of persons with factitious disorder early in their pattern is important (Jones et al., 1986). At this stage they are less convincing and less committed to a life as a "professional patient." Unfortunately, many health professionals are hostile and rejecting toward those with factitious disorders, complaining that they "have better things to do than work with fake diseases." These professionals ignore the obvious; for while the complaint initially presented is false, those with factitious disorders have real problems that need to be dealt with, both for their own good and to prevent needless waste of medical or psychological services. These persons need to be enlisted in treatment that firmly denies their factitious symptoms, but recognizes their legitimate needs for intervention.

Because there was no identifiable external motive for Frank to develop his problems, he was not labeled a malingerer. Still, the question of deception was crucial in making an accurate determination of the services he needed. The psychology consultant used by the hospital employed the same sorts of techniques that would have been relevant in forensic and military settings where malingering is more common. If Frank had been eligible for worker's compensation or other benefits, malingering could have seemed a more likely explanation (Kurke and Meyer, 1986). As noted at the outset, it is the motivation for the false presentation of symptoms that is crucial in differentiating between factitious disorder and malingering. While it is important that clinicians be able to accept what clients tell them, it is also inappropriate to ignore the possibility of deception, especially in settings where it is most common.

Greater attention to the factitious disorders and malingering could help to reduce the rising costs of health care by reducing unnecessary services while providing appropriate interventions for those who need them.

REFERENCES

Alpher, V. and Blanton, R. (1985) The accuracy of lie detection. *Law and Psychology Review*, *9*, 67–75.

Asher, R. (1951). Munchausen's syndrome. *Lancet*, *1*, 339–341.

Beaber, R., Marston, A., Michelli, J., and Mills, M. (1985) A brief test for measuring malingering in schizophrenic individuals. *The American Journal of Psychiatry*, *142*, 1478–1481.

Bursten, B. (1965) On Munchausen's syndrome. *Archives of General Psychiatry, 13,* 261–268.

Ekman, P. (1985) *Telling Lies.* New York: W. W. Norton.

Glasser, W. (1965) *Reality Therapy.* New York: Harper and Row.

Goldstein, A. and Myers, C. (1985) Relationship-enhancement methods. In F. Kanfer and A. Goldstein (Eds.), *Helping People Change.* New York: Pergamon.

Grow, R., McVaugh, W., and Eno, T. (1980) Faking and the MMPI. *Journal of Clinical Psychology, 36,* 910–917.

Hyler, S., and Spitzer, R. (1978) Hysteria Split Asunder. *American Journal of Psychiatry, 135,* 1500–1504.

Jones, J., Butler, H., Hamilton, B., Perdue, J., et al. (1986) Munchausen syndrome by proxy. *Child Abuse & Neglect, 10,* 33–40.

Kohut, H. (1977) *The Restoration of the Self.* New York: International Universities Press.

Kurke, M. and Meyer, R. (Eds.) (1986) *Psychology in Product Liability and Personal Injury Law.* New York: Hemisphere.

Landis, E. and Meyer, R. (1987) The detection of deception. In S. Smith and R. Meyer, *Laws, Behavior, and Mental Health: Policy and Practice.* New York: New York University Press.

Lykken, D. (1980) *A Tremor in the Blood.* New York: McGraw-Hill.

Pallis, C. and Bamji, A. (1979) McIlroy was here or was he? *British Medical Journal, 1,* 973–975.

Posey, C. and Hess, A. (1985) Aggressive response sets and subtle-obvious MMPI scale distinctions in male offenders. *Journal of Personality Assessment, 49,* 235–239.

Schachter, D. (1986) Amnesia and crime: How much do we really know? *American Psychologist, 43,* 286–295.

Seltzer, L. (1986) *Paradoxical Strategies in Psychotherapy.* New York: John Wiley.

Sussman, N. and Hyler, S. (1980) Factitious disorders. In H. Kaplan and B. Saddock, *Comprehensive Textbook of Psychiatry* (3rd edition). Baltimore: Williams and Wilkins.

U.S. Congress, Office of Technology Assessment (1983) *Scientific Validity of Polygraph Testing* (OTA-TM-H-15). Washington, D.C.: U.S. Government Printing Office.

/ Criminal Responsibility, Competency to Stand Trial, and Dangerousness

**The Case of
John Hinckley**

> I feel the insanity defense should be retained. I bear no grudge against John Hinckley, but I sure don't hope he wins the Irish Sweepstakes.
>
> — James Brady
> Victim of John Hinckley

As violent crime plagues American society, citizens strive to accept judicial decisions while living in a world in which they fear for the welfare of their friends and families. Perhaps no other legal concept raises as many moral ambiguities as the concept of "criminal responsibility," popularly known as the insanity defense. Rightly or wrongly, the insanity defense is often portrayed as a choice between liberty and security for both the accused and society (Van Todd, Dodd, and Billing, 1985). Despite the behavioral sciences' strongest efforts to draw a firm line of distinction between "madness and badness," this boundary continues to shift under interwoven social, political, economic, and other pressures of our society.

When an individual is charged with a crime and an insanity defense is raised, each juror (or in some cases solely the judge) must determine the moral responsibility within the contexts of mental health testimony and legal culpability. Such determinations are never easy, not only because of the real ramifications on the defendant(s), victim(s), family members, and so on, but also because the legal concept of criminal responsibility raises the broadest of ethical questions about the limits of one individual's responsibility to another.

Although the issue of criminal responsibility may be reviewed as a singular concept, in judicial application it is nearly always interwoven with the defendant's competency to stand trial. Indeed, as Bartol (1983) points out, the issues of criminal responsibility and competency to stand trial are often confused by mental health experts involved in the judicial process. Criminal responsibility refers to the state of the defendant's mind at the time of the alleged crime, while competency to stand trial refers to the defendant's psychological state at the time of his or her trial (Schwitzgebel and Schwitzgebel, 1980). Such a temporal distinction is crucial in the assessment of these issues.

For a punishable criminal act to occur, two related but independent factors must be present. First, an act or behavior legally defined as illegal must occur (the "actus rea"). Second, the individual committing the act must have the general intent to do so (the "mens rea"). Both an illegal act and guilty mind must be present before a punishable crime has occurred.

Consideration of both the act and the intent has occurred for at least the last 2,000 years of recorded history (Howell, 1982). The American judicial process has historically encompassed a variety of criminal responsibility standards. The McNaughten Rule was borrowed from English case law (Daniel McNaughten's Case, 1843) and states the following (Blau, 1984):

If as a result of mental disease or defect, the defendant did not understand what he did or that it was wrong, or if he was under a delusion (but not otherwise insane), which, if true, would have provided a good defense. Thus, if one does not understand what he was doing at all or did not know that it was wrong, he is excused. He is also excused if due to an insane delusion he thought he was acting in self defense or carrying out the will of God. Often called the right/wrong test.

In England, a man named Daniel M'Nagheten, who is said to have the paranoid delusion that a conspiracy of persons headed by Sir Robert Peel, the Prime Minister, were out to do him harm, shot and killed Peel's secretary—apparently by mistake, his intended victim being Sir Robert. M'Nagheten entered a plea of insanity. He was tried and acquitted on that ground.

Detweiler said: "He sounds crazy, to get the wrong man that way." (p. 286)— Thomas Berger *Killing Time*

The criminal responsibility standard continued in this form until the irresistible impulse or volition test was added (*Davis* v. *United States*, 1895). The question became whether the individual had been robbed of his free will to control his behavior due to mental disease or defect, despite knowing such behavior was wrong (Shapiro, 1984).

In 1954 the Durham Rule was set forth (*Durham* v. *United States*, 1954), within which Judge David Bazelon greatly widened the standard. The Durham Rule states that "an accused is not criminally responsible if his unlawful act was the product of a mental disease or defect" (Brooks, 1974). In the face of much criticism, in 1972 Judge Bazelon rejected the Durham Rule (*United States* v. *Brawner*, 1972) and adopted the Model Penal Code as submitted by the American Law Institute (ALI, 1962). In general, the ALI standard asserted that an individual is not criminally responsible if, by reason of mental disease or defect, he lacked substantial capacity to appreciate the wrongfulness of his conduct or lacked the substantial capacity to conform his behavior to the requirements of law (Shapiro, 1984). The ALI standard thus narrowed the Durham Rule, but was not as restrictive as the older McNaughten Rule.

In the United States, use of the various criminal responsibility standards is about equally divided. The McNaughten Rule is used in almost half of the states, while the ALI standard is incorporated into the statutes of 26 states, the District of Columbia, and all federal jurisdictions (Blau, 1984).

In a similar fashion, wide diversity also exists regarding the issues of burden and level of proof. In approximately one-half of the state jurisdictions, the burden of proof lies with the defense by a "preponderance of the evidence." In the remaining states, the burden of proof lies with the prosecution at a level of proof which is "beyond a reasonable doubt." In the states where the defense bears the burden, the defense must prove their client's insanity by approximately 51 percent of the evidence, while in the other states, the state must disprove the defendant's insanity by a significant preponderance of the evidence. "Beyond a reasonable doubt" has never been defined in the law, though 90 to 95 percent might be a reasonable estimate. (Interestingly enough, a judge will refuse to define the term if asked to do so by a juror.) Recently, federal statutes have been reversed, and the burden of proof now lies with the defendant in the federal courts.

As previously noted, the issue of competency to stand trial deals with the defendant's current state of psychological functioning as related to the judicial process. While the concept of criminal responsibility may trace its roots to English case law and beyond, the principle of competency to stand trial is based firmly in the Sixth Amendment to the United States Constitution, as follows:

> In all criminal prosecutions, the accused shall enjoy the right to a speedy and public trial, by an impartial jury of the state and district wherein the crime shall have been committed, which district shall have been ascertained by law, and to be informed of the nature and cause of the accusation; to be confronted with the witnesses against him, etc.

Case law provides specific guidelines for the determination of competency to stand trial. *Dusky* v. *United States* (1960), which provided the standards used in most jurisdictions after 1960, states that the accused must generally fulfill three broad criteria. First, he or she must have some factual understanding of the judicial proceedings. Second, he or she must have a rational understanding of the proceedings. Third, he or she must also be able to consult with an attorney with a reasonable degree of rational understanding. It should be noted that forensic opinions regarding competency to stand trial are only clinical opinions and the final determination is a judicial decision (Lipsitt, Lelos, and McGarry, 1971). This point has been judicially underscored in case law (*United States* v. *Zooluck*, 1977; *United States* v. *Horowitz*, 1973).

Other cases have also clarified the court's position regarding related issues of competency to stand trial (Grisso, 1986). In *Pate* v. *Robinson* (1966) the court determined that the competency issue may be raised at any point during the judicial process. Should a defendant be found not competent to stand trial, then he or she may not be confined for further treatment for an indeterminate period of time, as set forth in *Jackson* v. *Indiana* (1972).

Forensic Evaluation

The clinical evaluation of the forensic patient is often an imposing task. Because great weight may be given to its conclusions and they will consequently have strong impact on the individual's life, every effort should be made to enhance an evaluation's reliability and validity. This can be best achieved by taking an organized and comprehensive approach as endorsed by Ruzicka (1979), Shapiro (1984), and Blau (1984).

Among many factors, the psychologist must have an absolutely clear understanding as to the purposes of the forensic evaluation. Once this goal has been identified, the evaluation should include a comprehensive clinical interview with the patient. Such an interview may require a number of hours, depending on the referral questions raised, the patient's intellectual and personality style, physical limitations imposed, the interview setting, and so on. Special attention should be given to gathering a complete social history including previous legal problems, sexual abuse, alcohol/drug usage, mental health history of family members, and so on.

Psychological testing often may clarify an otherwise confusing clinical picture. A battery of tests should always be tailored to the individual, and yet may frequently include both objective and projective personality measures and tests of intellectual and neuropsychological functioning. Specific tests which are commonly used include the following: Minnesota Multiphasic Personality Inventory (MMPI); Millon Clinical Multiaxial Inventory (MCMI); Sixteen Personality Factors Test (16PF); Clinical Analysis Questionnaire (CAQ); Meyer Sentence Completion Test; Thematic Apperception Test (TAT); Rorschach Inkblot Test; Wechsler Adult Intelligence Scale–Revised (WAIS-R); and possibly a neuropsychological battery.

Special forensic devices have been developed to assist in answering specific referral questions (Grisso, 1986). The Competency to Stand Trial Test (CST) and Competency Assessment Instrument (CAI) developed by Lipsitt, Lelos, and McGarry (1971), and the Lawrence Present Mental Competency Test (Law Comp) attempt to address the issue of competency to stand trial.

In a similar fashion the Rogers Criminal Responsibility Assessment Scales (Rogers, 1986) presents a decision tree model in which the psychologist may carefully and comprehensively review his or her data. Such an externally imposed framework forces the psychologist to look at all important factors of potential importance and understand the importance of those factors within the insanity model as defined by state or federal law.

Finally, collateral data should be reviewed. Such data may be obtained from a variety of sources including the following: family; friends; co-workers; neighbors; spouse, girlfriend, or boyfriend; witnesses; arresting and investigating officers; victims. Such data provide an additional perspective of the patient, and help to consensually validate clinical hypotheses drawn from other data sources. Reviews of investigation reports, evidence reports, defendant transcripts, and audio- or videotapes can be helpful for similar reasons.

In summary, criminal responsibility and competency to stand trial are complex legal issues. Typically, forensic mental health professionals are brought into the legal arena in an effort to simplify psychological concepts as they relate to the forensic questions. Regardless of the clinical factors involved, such a task is never easily accomplished.

The Case of John Hinckley

On March 30, 1981, shortly before 2:30 P.M., John Hinckley aimed and fired six shots from a .22-caliber revolver. Four of the six Devastator bullets found human targets with tragic results. The first shot struck presidential Press Secretary James Brady. Although the exploding bullet did extensive neurological damage, Mr. Brady lived and has begun the long rehabilitation process. The second shot struck District of Columbia police officer Thomas Delahanty; he survived his back wound. The third bullet hit a building across the street from the Washington Hilton. The fourth bullet struck Secret Service agent Timothy McCarthy. His chest wound was serious, but he survived. The fifth bullet struck the glass in the presidential limousine but did no other damage. The sixth and final bullet ricocheted off the rear panel of the limousine and entered the chest of President Ronald Reagan, who also survived.

The entire attack lasted only a few seconds. A Secret Service agent later testified to his feeling of desperation as he attempted to stop the gunfire. He continued, "I came down on top of the assailant, with my right arm around his head. . . . He was still clicking the weapon as we went down." Understandably, such violent and senseless brutality raised many questions regarding Hinckley's psychological motivation, history, stability, and so on. Subsequent testimony in the defendant's seven-week trial indicated his ultimate goal was to capture the love and respect of Yale University student and movie star, Jodie Foster. Although unsuccessful in this goal, Mr. Hinckley's behavior did lay the foundation for major revisions in legal culpability statutes at federal and state levels (Low, Jeffries, and Bonnie, 1986).

Background

John Hinckley was born in Oklahoma in 1955. His childhood was not unlike many other people's. At the age of 4 he moved to Dallas, Texas. Recreational activities included quarterbacking his elementary school football team and playing basketball in high school. At the age of 9 Hinckley became a fan of the Beatles. His interest in music and possible identification with John Lennon continued into his adulthood. At the age of 12 Hinckley moved with his family to a prominent Dallas neighborhood and almost immediately lost social status. In short, he was no longer the "kingpin."

Graduation from high school in 1973 prompted a move to Evergreen, Colorado. Shortly thereafter, he decided to attend Texas Tech University in Lubbock. Although Hinckley's future dreams frequently included pursuit of a college degree in Lubbock, repeated efforts over the next five to six years were generally unproductive. In approximately 1974 Hinckley quit school at Texas Tech and moved to Dallas. He wanted to be on his own and "dreamed of future glory in some undefined field, perhaps music or politics" (Caplan, 1984, p. 34). A move to Hollywood in 1976 to sell his music was unsuccessful, but did result in his viewing the move *Taxi Driver* about fifteen times that summer. In the spring of 1977, Hinckley returned to Lubbock.

Roesch (1979) reports that it would appear that his overall adaptation and emotional adjustment were beginning to decline at this point. In the next year he began to experience a number of minor health problems and received treatment. In October 1978 he became interested in the American Nazi movement via the National Socialist Party. In August 1979 he purchased his first firearm, and in September of that year began to publish the *American Front Newsletter*. Hinckley appointed himself national director and fabricated membership lists from thirty-seven states. By this point he had moved seventeen times since high school.

In 1980 Hinckley experienced his first anxiety attack. At this time he had gained some sixty pounds since high school, and he had also bought a second gun. In May 1980, *People* magazine announced that Jodie Foster, an actress in the movie *Taxi Driver*, would be attending Yale University. Such a circumstance was most important to Hinckley and appears to have fueled his belief that he could win Foster's attention and love. A disappointing telephone conversation with Foster on September 20, 1980, resulted in the following diary entry by Hinckley:

> My mind was at the breaking point. A relationship I had dreamed about went absolutely nowhere. My disillusionment with everything was complete (Caplan, 1984, p. 38).

Between the September 20 phone call and the death of John Lennon on December 8, a retrospective review of Hinckley's behavior indicates that unknown psychological forces were tragically shaping his destiny. During this period he bought the Devastator exploding bullets and six more guns. He took numerous flights to distant places, including Colorado; Washington, D.C.; Columbus, Nebraska; Nashville; and others. Perhaps most serious was Hinckley's decision to begin following and perhaps stalking ex-President Carter and President Reagan.

Despite psychiatric treatment by John Hooper, M.D., between October 1980 and February 1981, Hinckley failed to divulge his thoughts, fantasies, or planned activities. Without this information, Dr. Hooper and Hinckley's family formulated a plan to encourage his independence and emotional stability. Despite these efforts, Hinckley took a bus from Los Angeles to Washington, D.C., arriving on March 29, 1981. After breakfast on March 30, Hinckley learned of President Reagan's schedule, and having written a final love letter to Foster, he loaded his gun and began his vigil outside the Washington Hilton. In seconds, his plan to obtain glory and thereby the love of actress Foster was enacted.

The Trial
The trial of John Hinckley was well publicized. The thirteen criminal charges included the attempted assassination of the president. Lawyers for the prosecution and defense differed little on the events, but considerable disagreement existed over the defendant's true psychological condition. The raising of the insanity defense resulted in a trial which lasted slightly over seven weeks. Mental health experts testifying or assisting the prosecution received over $300,000 in fees. Defense experts received fees in excess of $150,000. Such bills did not include salaries for court officials, ancillary staff, media coverage, etc. Defense attorneys may have received between $500,000 and $1 million. (Caplan, 1984).

After two to three days of deliberation by the jury, Hinckley was found not guilty by reason of insanity on all thirteen counts. He was automatically committed to Saint Elizabeth's Hospital in Washington, D.C., for treatment, to stay there until he is viewed by the hospital as no longer dangerous as a result of his mental illness (Low, Jeffries, and Bonnie, 1986).

Effects of the Trial
In the following weeks, twenty-six different bills were introduced to modify the federal statute covering the insanity defense. As a result of these efforts, two important changes occurred in federal law pertaining to the issue of criminal responsibility. First, the volitional component (the irresistible impulse concept), was removed from the original McNaughten model. At present, a successful insanity defense is based solely on the defendant's inability as a result of mental disease or defect to appreciate the criminality of the alleged conduct. Second, the burden of proof (whose responsibility it is to demonstrate the viability of the defendant's psychological state) was shifted from the prosecution in the Hinckley case to the defense. The level of proof required for the prosecution was also reduced when applied to the defense. Thus the level of certainty required of the jury when viewing the evidence was reduced from 90 to 95 percent (an estimate) to 51 percent or greater. Although these changes were significant in federal law, they only serve as models to state courts, which hear by far the greater number of insanity defenses each year.

In summary it should be noted that fate played an interesting hand in the outcome of the Hinckley case. In May and November 1981, the defense attorneys offered to have their client plead guilty to all counts if the prosecution would agree to recommend to the court that penalties on all counts run concurrently, rather than consecutively. Under this arrangement their client would be eligible for parole in fifteen years.

The prosecution declined this plea offer because, among other reasons, it was viewed as improper and unseemly to plea-bargain a case involving the attempted assassination of the President. Also, such an offer, in the perception of the prosecution, hinted at a weakness in the defense's reliance on an insanity defense.

Today John Hinckley is still undergoing treatment at Saint Elizabeth's Hospital. He may be released at the recommendation of the hospital and with approval of the presiding judge. Such a recommendation will occur only when the hospital feels that Hinckley no longer poses a threat to society or to himself. Such predictions of violent potential are of critical interest to the courts in court-ordered hospitalizations and pose great difficulty for the mental health practitioner whose job it frequently becomes to participate critically in that judgment.

Prediction of Violent Behavior

> *You couldn't even prove the White House staff*
> *sane beyond a reasonable doubt.*
>
> — Edwin Meese
> Counselor to Ronald Reagan

The prediction of violent behavior is perhaps one of the most formidable tasks required of the forensic psychologist. At a personal level it may be viewed as an unpleasant, anxiety-producing situation that brings the psychologist too close to the darkest side of the human condition (Van Todd, Dodd, and Billing, 1985). On a professional level, Monahan (1981) thoroughly describes many of the problems inherent in making such judgments. These include (1) arriving at a working definition as to what constitutes violent behavior, (2) determining how accurate such judgments must be, (3) deciding how predictions of future violent behavior violate the individual's civil liberties (impingements are placed on a person's life for a behavior he or she may not enact), and (4) reconciling the fact that efforts at prediction are at odds with the mental health professional's traditional role of "helping."

Monahan's (1981) review of this topic suggests that a wide variety of factors be taken into consideration prior to a final judgment. Such considerations may be divided into two groups: personality factors and situational factors. Megargee's (1976) model identifies three types of personality factors which must be assessed: (1) a judgment regarding the nature of the person's motivation for violent behavior; (2) a quantified judgment regarding the presence or absence of an inhibition system that would prevent the individual from acting on his or her motivation; and (3) the strength of the individual's habit for violent behavior (how much reinforcement the violent behavior has received in the past).

Situational factors are the degree to which the family and/or peer environment or attitude system is important to the individual and supports or discourages violent behavior; the individual's ability to obtain and maintain steady vocational employment; availability of preferred victims; availability of alcohol and/or drugs; availability of weapons; and other such factors.

Finally, the psychologist must assess the interaction effect of personality and situational variables. As the interaction effect becomes statistically larger, the probability of future violent behavior increases. Caution must be exercised in such judgments as personality variables and situational variables are frequently correlated; for example, alcohol (a situational variable) is likely to be present if an individual possesses an addictive personality (personality variable). Thus an individual is not potentially more dangerous because he or she possesses both factors, as these factors are not statistically independent from each other. A second factor must contain new information about the individual that is not conveyed by the first.

Judgments regarding personality and situational variables and interaction effects take on greater predictive power when viewed within the framework of major actuarial correlates of violent behavior. Actuarial correlates are those factors that have statistically demonstrated their predictive value. Monahan (1981) identifies six such factors: (1) past crime, particularly violent crime; (2) age; (3) sex; (4) race; (5) socioeconomic status and employment stability; and (6) drug and alcohol abuse. Note that each factor does not have equal weight or equivalent predictive power.

Thus it can be seen that predictions of future violent behavior are in all cases complicated and can be highly imprecise. Judgments made about individuals who have been hospitalized for long periods have the opportunity for in-depth analysis of personality factors, but accurate assessment of situational factors is then more difficult as the psychologist must artificially extrapolate from the hospital environment to the non-hospital environment regarding the likelihood of inappropriate behavior. However, the public is naturally less concerned about an individual's in-hospital behavior and more concerned about the potential degree of danger to which society is exposed.

REFERENCES

American Law Institute Model Penal Code, Section 4.01 (1962).

Bartol, C. (1983) *Psychology and American Law*. Belmont, Calif.: Wadsworth.

Blau, T. H. (1984) *The Psychologist as Expert Witness*. New York: John Wiley.

Brooks, A. (1974) *Law, Psychiatry, and the Mental Health System*. Boston: Little, Brown.

Caplan, L. (1984) *The Insanity Defense*. Boston: Godine.

Daniel McNaughten's Case, 10 Cl. and Fin. 200, 8 Eng. Rep. 718 (1843).

Davis v. *United States*, 160 U.S. 469 (1895).

Durham v. *United States*, 214 F. 2d. 962, 874–875 (D.C. Circuit, 1954).

Dusky v. *United States*, 362 U.S. 402 (1960).

Grisso, T. (1986) *Evaluating Competencies: Forensic Assessments and Instruments*. New York: Plenum.

Howell, R. J. (1982) In defense of the insanity plea. *Bulletin of the American Academy of Forensic Psychologists, 3(1)*, 1–2.

Jackson v. *Indiana*, 406 U.S. 715 (1972).

Lipsitt, P. D., Lelos, E., and McGarry, A. L. (1971) Competency to stand trial: A screening instrument. *American Journal of Psychiatry, 128(1)*, 137–141.

Low, P., Jeffries, J., and Bonnie, R. (1986) *The Trial of John Hinckley, Jr.* Mineola, N.Y.: The Foundation Press.

Megargee, E. (1976) The prediction of dangerous behavior. *Criminal Justice and Behavior, 3*, 3–21.

Monahan, J. (1981) *Predicting Violent Behavior.* Beverly Hills, Calif.: Sage.

Pate v. *Robinson*, 383 U.S. 375, 86 S. Ct., 83C, 15 L. Ed. 2d 815 (1966).

Roesch, R. (1979) Determining competency to stand trial: An examination of evaluation procedures in an institutional setting. *Journal of Consulting and Clinical Psychology, 47(3)*, 542–550.

Rogers, R. (1986) The R-CRAS and criminal responsibility evaluations: An update. *Bulletin of the American Academy of Forensic Psychology, 7*, 6–7.

Ruzicka, W. (1979) *Psychodiagnostic Assessment Procedures in the Criminal Justice System.* Palo Alto, Calif.: Psychological Health Services.

Schwitzgebel, R. L. and Schwitzgebel, R. K. (1980) *Law and Psychological Practice.* New York: John Wiley.

Shapiro, D. L. (1984) *Psychological Evaluation and Expert Testimony.* New York: Van Nostrand Reinhold.

United States v. *Brawner*, 471 F. 2d. 969 (D.C. Circuit, 1972).

United States v. *Horowitz*, 360, F. Supp. 722 (D.C. P.A., 1973).

United States v. *Zooluck*, 425, F. Supp. 719 (D.C. N.Y. 1977).

Van Todd, C., Dodd, G., and Billing, A. (1985) *Attacks on the Insanity Defense.* Springfield, Ill.: Charles C. Thomas.

AUTHOR INDEX

SUBJECT INDEX